FROM WILLIAM MORRIS TO SERGEANT PEPPER

Studies in the Radical Domestic

Peter Stansky

The Society for the Promotion of Science and Scholarship
Palo Alto, California

The Society for the Promotion of Science and Scholarship, Inc.
Palo Alto, California
© 1999 The Society for the Promotion of Science and Scholarship
Printed in the United States of America

The Society for the Promotion of Science and Scholarship is a nonprofit corporation established for the purposes of scholarly publishing. It has special interests in European and British Studies.

The author of this volume would like to thank the following for their kindness in granting permission to reprint material, with some modifications: *The Atlantic Monthly*, *The Boston Globe*, *English Literature in Transition*, *Jewish Social Studies*, *Journal of British Studies*, *The Los Angeles Times* (copyright © 1999, reprinted by permission), *The New Republic*, *The New York Times* (copyright © 1999 by the New York Times Co., reprinted by permission), *The Pacific Historical Review* (copyright © 1990 by the American Historical Review, Pacific Coast Branch; reprinted by permission), *Studies in Zionism*, University of Texas Press, *The Threepenny Review*, *Victorian Studies*, and Cecil Woolf Publishers. (The relevant works are cited in full in the Bibliography.)

CIP data appear at the end of the book.

For Billy, 1919-1998

PREFACE

In the pages that follow I've made a selection of essays and reviews that I've written over the years, some of which have not been previously published. The phrase that I believe best sums up my understanding of that aspect of England that interests me most is the "radical domestic," a term I have borrowed from the work of the brilliant young art historian Christopher Reed. I believe those perhaps slightly contradictory two words suggest an extremely important aspect of English society, a major source of both its strengths and weaknesses. Reed uses the phrase in his discussion of Bloomsbury, and it is particularly appropriate in his tracings of the connections between it and the Arts and Crafts Movement. Change does take place in England, but it is rarely the sort of sharp break that one might find in other societies. Violence is hardly unknown in England, but one suspects that it is rarer and might well manifest itself in what Christopher Isherwood has called "tea tabling": that the most appalling events are taking place while others are quietly having tea, the sort of juxtaposition found in the famous first sentence of a chaper in E. M. Forster's *The Longest Journey*: "Gerald died that afternoon."

One of my favorite illustrations of this contrast was an experience that I had years ago when emerging from the Roundhouse Theatre, in Camden. There was some political protest going on against the theatre's management, and a mimeographed sheet was thrust at me as I emerged from the theatre by an extremely fierce young woman. As she handed the sheet to me, she said, with great vehemence and a face twisted with anger, "Fascist Pig." I looked at the sheet and saw that it was blank. I pointed this out, and the woman then said to me in quite a cultivated tone, "Oh, I'm terribly sorry." Perhaps wrongly,

I felt that this was a society in which a revolution was extremely unlikely. But change there is, and it is likely to take place on a domestic
scale. It may be less exciting, and it runs the risk of being smug, but
it is change all the same. Radicals are co-opted and become Life
Peers. Is this a failure or an accomplishment? Many of the pieces that
follow are, in their various ways, discussions of this theme, of the
nature of change, and of the interplay of radicalism and domesticity.
I can only hope that the reader may find that they shed some illumination on the English world, the study of which I have devoted myself to for almost fifty years.

Doing such a collection as this has been in my mind for some
time. I am deeply grateful to the Society for the Promotion of Science
and Scholarship for being willing to publish it (and the University of
Washington Press for distributing it), and most particularly to
SPOSS's Executive Officer, Janet Gardiner, and the advice of one of
its Trustees, that wise publisher Norris Pope. Great help in the selection of what pieces to include was given with great effectiveness
some years ago by John Dean and Stewart Weaver, and most significantly over the past year by Rodney Koeneke, who also did much to
prepare the manuscript for publication. Philippe Tapon has given
excellent advice. My greatest debt, as always, is expressed in my
dedication. What little I know of writing, life, and love has largely
been learned from my companion and collaborator, Billy Abrahams.
Before he died, he knew that this collection was forthcoming, and I
hope that this gave him some pleasure. I fear that I was a poor recipient of his bounty and fell sadly short in my ability to equal his
extraordinary generosity of spirit. He cast a severe and I think loving
eye on all the words that follow.

Peter Stansky
April 1999

CONTENTS

PART ONE

BIOGRAPHY AS HISTORY

1

The Crumbling Frontiers of History

Years ago William Langer, in his famous American Historical Association presidential address, "The Next Assignment," was a somewhat improbable conveyor of a message that we should all be psychoanalyzed. An interesting group of historians—the most prominent being Peter Gay—have fallen or risen to this category. But their work demonstrates not so much the importance of the psychoanalytical approach as that historians who are of the highest quality will write good history, in most cases, whatever their system may be. Those who aren't, won't.

More recently, but still quite a few years ago, we were told that we should all be quantifiers. That fashion seems to have passed, to the relief of the more innumerate of us. The most distinguished representative of quantification in my own field of modern British history is William Aydelotte. In his pioneering work, he was likely to tell us what was wrong about the old generalizations, but he was less successful in giving us new generalizations in their place. His students, John Phillips and W. C. Lubenow, are demonstrating how quantification can enrich our understanding of nineteenth-century Britain. (I try to repress, not too successfully, the temptation to skip whenever I see a chart. I admire those studies that provide their material both in charts and in prose.)

Now it seems to me that the "best and the brightest" are urging us to be theoreticians. One advantage (or disadvantage) of being a historian is that it makes one rather cynical: one feels that this vogue too will pass. Even so, I am convinced that the present interest in theory will enrich our study of history. This is almost always true of new approaches, forcing us to think about the past in new ways. So the frontiers will be penetrated and redrawn, but certain characteristics of the heartland may remain.

It is to a somewhat different frontier that I wish to turn now: the frontier, if such it be, between history and biography. I think that it has long been crumbling, but the relationship between remains a matter of concern, and quite a few recent collections of essays from America and from England have focused on questions of biography. Collections that come from England tend to emphasize an empirical approach and resolutely refuse to work out a theory of biography. As an American who is a historian of Britain, I shall remain in the British empirical tradition here, and try to use myself as a case study of how one crosses back and forth across the frontier between history and biography, a "common market" that is so free that one certainly does not need a visa, and perhaps not even a passport. (This reminds me of a panel on biography some years ago at an Anglo-American Conference of Historians at the Institute of Historical Research in London. Lady Antonia Fraser spoke first and gave as her opinion that she was first because on the panel she was the only one who would put on her passport "biographer" rather than "historian." I suspect she knew that she spoke first because she was both a lower and upper case Lady.)

I would maintain that some historical training is useful for the biographer. Bernard Crick attacked William Abrahams's and my first study of Orwell (1972) in his later biography of that writer (1980) because one of our mutual informants had told him that we had got some particular points wrong. Crick seemed to be quite unaware that a biographer's and historian's function is to take all the available "facts," which are often contradictory, and judge which interpretation of them may seem the most "truthful." Such a decision obviously may not agree with a particular person's memory of what he or she may have said, or left unsaid, or remembers later. In short, testimony must be treated by the biographer much as the historian evaluates a compilation of documents—the raw material, so to speak.

This issue of testimony underlines the significance of the debate that arose around the pieces by Janet Malcolm in *The New Yorker* on the relationship between biographer and subject and between biographers and those who provide testimony about a subject. Malcolm seems to believe that journalists and, by extension, most seekers for information, frequently need to mislead their informants, if not downright lie to them. Or they will, conducting an interview, indicate more agreement than they may feel. It can, at times, be something of a fine line, and someone who is being interviewed may well misinterpret silence or politeness for agreement.

One gathers historical documents, whatever their form, and then comes to the best judgment one can make as to their degree of validity, which in any case is a relative and definitely not an absolute term. Perhaps the only reality is what the observer thinks it is, as the "truth," whatever that may be, is unknowable. But even the created reality must have a convincing logic. One hopes that one's instincts about this become honed; and it is clear that in arriving at these decisions, the procedures of a historian and of a biographer are very similar.

Yet history and biography are different areas of endeavor—in a few, some, or many senses. But how? A biography is the telling of one life. History is a study of a group—or an individual—or of certain events—or an institution, or of one, or innumerable problems. It may be a vast panorama covering centuries, or a monograph that may concentrate on one seemingly minute topic that still, one hopes, has great significance. The distinctions are often quite blurred. It is perfectly possible to imagine a fine work of history in which there is no sense of an individual life at all. Ironically, this may be more apparent in quantitative history, which deals with individuals in the mass than it is in many other forms. And there can be fine, if possibly rather dull, institutional or thematic histories that have little sense of the individuals who may nevertheless be part of the landscape of the work. It is possible for biographies to have similar problems; drawing a portrait so shorn of historical context that it's all foreground and no background. Or a biography will give too much of the life and times.

A biography is a collection of events in a particular life that is held together by the arbitrary fact that they are all experiences of one person. But as with the historian, so it is, I believe, with the biographer. The obligation is to impose a greater significance upon the story and try to persuade the reader that such a picture makes sense. If that is not done, then the biographer is primarily a chronicler, selective or comprehensive as the case may be. Such an approach can bring forth very important achievements, such as Martin Gilbert's multivolume study of Winston Churchill (1971-1988). There is obviously some shaping done in the act of deciding what to include, even in a study as monumental as Gilbert's. Yet in some sense such a biography passes the buck to the reader: here is the material, you make the judgment. Biographers should certainly present as much as they can of the material they consider important. But as critical reviews and later biographies make fully evident, other interpretations are possible using as a base the same material put forward in an earlier study. Thus, as in any intellectual endeavor, the creator of the work has the obligation to say what he or she thinks the story told might mean. I hasten to add, this need not be done in a sledgehammer way: after all, one is writing a biography not a polemic.

I think of myself professionally as a historian, and yet my interests, researches, and publications seem frequently to elide into the biographical. My hope, as a historian, is to attempt to enter into the texture of English society. For that purpose a life can serve as well if not better than a more straightforward historical subject, a life as it is lived by a particular person in a particular society in a particular period. To use the sort of language that is in vogue nowadays, both historical events and individuals are "texts" that can be attended to. I've noticed this pattern in my work ever since my undergraduate days. Without a special intention to be a biographer, I tend to become one. Perhaps it is an incorrigible interest in other people, what some might cruelly call a love of gossip, and a tendency to avoid a more abstract approach. And I find myself particularly fascinated by my subjects' younger days, when their personality was being fashioned.

I have constructed a pattern for the shaping of my interests, but who knows how accurately it corresponds to what actually happened. According to my schematized memory, one of my favorite records when I was growing up in the long-gone days of phonograph records that went at the 78 speed was the recording of the songs of the International Brigade of the Spanish Civil War sung by Ernst Busch. I particularly remember the heavily accented English in that verse by Brecht: "Zo left, two, three! zo left, two, three! . . . for you are a vorker too" and how moved I was by his rendition of "Freiheit." In the first few years after the Second World War, before the Cold War hit its stride, it seemed to me, in my naïveté, that political activism was no longer necessary. Even if it had been, I suspect that was not the way I operated. Many historians, it is true, are both interested observers of the past and observer-participants of the present as well. I suspect that for me the past is a sublimated present, and one reason for my interest in particular figures of the past is that they have taken actions I might have been very interested in taking myself.

A decade after the event the question I put to myself about the Spanish Civil War—would I have been tempted to go to Spain to fight for the Loyalists had I been of an age to do so?—may have been arbitrary and misleading. But that question, and the songs of the International Brigade, are what I remember leading me to an interest in the war, when I was an undergraduate at Yale in the early 1950s. Perhaps I was also responding to the so-called quietism of that period. I became a history major, and although I never took a course in British history, I found myself increasingly drawn to it. Perhaps it was the Anglophilia of Yale and teas at the Elizabethan Club that led this way; certainly it was the two weeks spent in England the summer after my sophomore year, which included a trip to Cambridge guided by a graduate of King's College—not surprisingly he made me feel that that college was where I would like to study next. I was also deeply influenced by a Yale classmate whose family knew T. S. Eliot and who himself seemed to know and relish the ins and outs of the English literary world.

Back in New Haven, I became increasingly fascinated by the effort of trying to understand another world, both past and foreign—with which I had no connection of any sort. I took growing pleasure in the joys of research, the serendipity of wandering the stacks of the library and finding appropriate books. My original intention was to study in some sort of general way the English who had fought in the International Brigade, the volunteers on the Loyalist side. But I found myself quite quickly gravitating to the literary figures who were involved in the struggle. A study more in keeping with today's thinking and in many ways a more "culturally correct" way of proceeding would be to try to find out more about the working-class members of the Battalion, who made up most of it. But those were not my interests and I found my greatest absorption where social, cultural, literary, political life met. As W. H. Auden wrote in *Spain*, the poem he later disowned, it was the world, falsely romantic, of "poets exploding like bombs" that captivated me. I decided that I would write about four young Englishmen of the 1930s who went to Spain, and quite rapidly I settled on John Cornford, Julian Bell, Stephen Spender, and George Orwell. Naturally I fell into a desire to find out as much about their lives as I could, given the resources of the Yale and the New York Public Library. I felt that I should say something about Spain as well, about which I had little background. As one of the faculty readers of the essay pointed out, that was the least successful part of the enterprise.

I discovered that not only was I interested in lives, but the early days were what tended to interest me most: the parents and childhood, adolescence, and youth—I wonder if that was part of the appeal, tragic as it was, in the very short lives of two of the figures I had chosen to study: John Cornford, who had been killed in Spain on his twenty-first birthday or the day after, and Julian Bell, killed there when he was only twenty-nine. Certainly their backgrounds were impressive and led me directly into what Noel Annan has called the "intellectual aristocracy."

Julian Bell was Virginia Woolf's nephew. She was already a figure of literary prominence, but this was years before Bloomsbury became a cottage industry. When, during my senior year, I applied to study at King's College, Cambridge, that outpost of Bloomsbury was bemused that Virginia Woolf and her friends should be of much interest to anyone outside the charmed circle (although J. K. Johnstone was just about to publish in 1954 what may have been the first study of the group). John Cornford was Charles Darwin's great-grandson, and his parents, Francis and Frances Cornford, were at the center of the intellectual life of Cambridge. (I remember I. A. Richards, himself no slouch as an eminent figure, telling me how flattered he was to be taken up by the Cornfords, whom he regarded as the Dukes of Cambridge.) The two better-known literary figures came from less distinguished backgrounds. Stephen Spender was the son and nephew of well-known journalists, Harold and J. A. Spender. The most famous figure of the four, George Orwell, was the son of a minor civil servant and had memorably defined himself as a member of the "lower-upper-middle class."

As I began my work before the Bloomsbury boom, so too it was before the Orwell boom, despite the success of *Animal Farm* and *Nineteen Eighty-Four*. One of my great joys was tracking down Orwell essays, some of which have now become canonical, available then only in their first periodical publication. *Homage to Catalonia* had just been issued for the first time in America in a Beacon Press edition, the Spanish Republican flag proudly on its cover, with its highly regarded but in my view misleading introduction by Lionel Trilling, a powerful document in the Cold War. My work was deeply satisfying to me, and quite unsophisticated. But even in those early days, I had the feeling that the historian, like the anthropologist, could find out about a society through its growing-up rituals— "Coming of Age in Britain"—and in any case I felt compelled to find out as much as I could about the early years of the men I had perhaps rather arbitrarily chosen.

My object was not simply a biographical recital but rather an attempt to discover why they had come to Spain—not, as it turned out, in the way I had originally intended, as members of the International Brigade, although Cornford was affiliated with it at the end of his life. Bell was an ambulance driver, in homage to his family's pacificism. Orwell fought with the POUM in Catalonia although he had intended to join the International Brigade. When he was caught up in the May Days in Barcelona, he had no choice, given his character, but to stay with the underdog. Spender went to lend his support to the cause and to follow a lover.

The importance of the early days of my figures was made particularly vivid when Orwell's memoir of his childhood, the now famous "Such, Such Were the Joys" was just being published posthumously in the *Partisan Review*. (There was even some question whether Orwell had written the essay for publication, although it is hard to imagine that as a professional writer he did not intend it to be read at some point.) In fact, the formidable headmistress of Orwell's prep school, whom I would meet years later, felt that it libeled her and prevented it from being published in England until after her death. There, in 1968, it made a belated appearance in the four volumes of Orwell's letters and essays and immediately it became the classic version of his childhood.

Crick worries unduly, in an excessively literalist way, about the exact truth of Orwell's memories. Such questions are important, but more important is the way in which the memoir was psychologically true. And what a splendidly scary picture it is of the rituals of childhood in the middle and upper classes. Although I was attempting to pursue a subject that was not purely biographical—why did some English young go to Spain to support the Republic?—the dynamic for me became the biographical. From the beginning I was caught in a delightful position of trying to ply my way between the general and the individual. As I understand it, the anthropologist finds out about the life of a tribe through the stories of many individual members. As I'm sure is true for all societies but vividly and fascinatingly true for Britain, ways of behavior tell one about a society. In the years I happen to be interested in, from the latter part of the 19th century to the mid-20th century, the rituals of behavior and their class significance were, I believe, at their most intense in Britain.

It would be excessively egotistical to go through my own work in similar detail looking for a pattern, but it seems to me that self-history, autobiography, is again parallel to biography, and to history itself. The pattern I now discern was not, as far as I can tell, deliberate. Frequently the precipitating event was fortuitous and serendipitous. As a graduate student, I was not tempted to write biography, but I was drawn to the interplay of personality and principles among the leaders of the Liberal party in Britain in the last two decades of the nineteenth century. Some years later, by chance, I was asked to write a short political biography of Disraeli. Disraeli is a fascinating figure usually set in opposition to his political opponent, Gladstone. Contrary to a common view, I do not feel that it is necessary to choose between them. Rather, one may admire and see defects in both, and in some ways they do have their similarities. Like all the greatest politicians and statesmen they had an uneasy but nevertheless mutually reinforcing mixture of opportunism and principle. I suggested substituting Gladstone for Disraeli as I had come to know him better through my earlier research. I found it particularly interesting to dwell on the shaping of the future prime minister in his earliest days in Liverpool, Eton, and Oxford. A similar pattern asserted itself when I was at work on William Morris and his influence in both design and politics. Again, history and biography were intermingled.

However fascinating the individual life may be as a subject, to have its greatest interest for me it needs to be placed in the context of its society. So I see myself as a historian first, but one who has an abiding interest in whomever I study, and not just as these figures are playing out the roles for which they became well known, but in their earlier days when they were being shaped by their parents, their schooling, and the beginnings of their careers.

Gladstone as prime minister, William Morris as artist and political activist: these roles tell us about the influence of the two figures on their worlds. But Gladstone and Morris in youth—their early days tell us about the shaping of the great figure, when the great men were still in the process of *becoming*, when they were in some respects more "typical" of their country, their age, and their class than the "eminent Victorians" they later became.

At one point in my life, I was intrigued by deathbed remarks. Perhaps my favorite was Gertrude Stein's. "What is the answer?" she asked as she lay dying. Then, after a pause, "What is the question?" As often happened with Stein, the order may seem startling but the logic is irreproachable. I won't insist upon the remark's relevance to historians and biographers; enough to say that in history and biography questions and answers are gloriously intertwined.

2

THINKING ABOUT BIOGRAPHY

As a part-time biographer, I every once in a while wonder a little about biography as a discipline, and indulge in those high-flying, vaporous generalizations so beloved of critics and academics. Most frequently, however, I am content to proceed in the traditions of English empiricism, writing the biography in hand and not worrying too much about theory. I have, as it were by instinct, a notion of my own as to what biography is, or should be, and do my best to conform to it—which is not to say that when the book is done, it bears an ironclad resemblance to the idea of it I had in mind before I started writing.

Some years ago, in 1975, as one of the three judges in the biography category of the National Book Awards—I wondered about the nature of biography—of autobiography too, as such books are also eligible—more often and more seriously than usual. No doubt this had come about as a defense against the cascade of books I received threatening to inundate both myself and the local postman—it would seem that the old cliché that "everyone has a novel in him" will have to be revised to take into account the nonstop activities of the biographers, ranging from the excellent heights to the unspeakable depths, with oh so many earnest souls coming to rest on a plateau of unblemished mediocrity. There are few things I enjoy more than receiving free books, but with privilege comes responsibility, and I desperately tried to sample and examine, read and digest, hoping I had not been swayed by the reputation of an author, or the attractiveness of a subject, or the fame of certain books which arrived loaded down with praise.

I should note some conspicuous trends in biographical subjects that year. For example, the outpouring of bicentennially inspired

lives. Perhaps, though, it is not so surprising that authors and publishers should have been keenly aware of the approaching event, and
they can only pray that the public—particularly now that the government no longer was showing its previous generosity in supporting
library purchases—will share their interest in figures out of our historic past. One of the most distinguished such books is the story of
an American loyalist, Thomas Hutchinson. But most of the Bicen-
tennial biographies are of figures on the winning side of the Revolution. Two of Thomas Paine. Two of Jefferson, one speculating at
length on his love life. Biographies of John Marshall, of Patrick
Henry, of George Washington. Going back a bit in time—two of
William Penn. And biographers go forward also, up to the present
day, coping with other aspects of the American dream—at times
verging on the nightmare. A fat celebration of Henry Kissinger. The
inevitable presidential lives: not only, as mentioned, Washington and
Jefferson, but also a vast Eisenhower; Truman in his own words as
taped by an interviewer—one does wonder, by the way, who is the
author of such a book, the subject, or the author with the recording
apparatus? We have even had, prompt upon his inauguration, a biography of our president-by-appointment, Gerald Ford, by his former press secretary, who resigned from the job immediately after his
boss pardoned his former boss and benefactor Richard Nixon.
Speaking of Nixon, the question of bias in biography is peculiarly
apt. It is hard for me to imagine an unbiased biography of our only
president to resign from office when threatened with impeachment.
Or to put it another way, it is very hard for me to believe that a biography of Nixon that did not show him in an unfavorable light—
necessarily so, given the wealth of documentation, taped and otherwise, to draw on—could be an accurate, that is, an unbiased one.

My own belief is that a biographer should aim for a combination
of truth, dispassion, and sympathy—a combination that is not, I
would argue, unattainable. When it is attained, one passes from bias
to point of view, without which a biography, unless it is printed out
by a computer, can hardly be said to exist. Let me admit candidly
that I would find it very hard to write a biography of someone I totally disliked. This is not to say that one can't be critical of one's
subject, or recognize faults, even as one puts the emphasis on virtues.
And yet, obviously, biographies of villains are needed—from the
Hitlers and Stalins down to the Neroes and Caligulas. I would just
leave them to other authors, with different temperaments and principles. Such books, to the degree that they are truthful—and I am not

thinking now of the ludicrous efforts to paint black white, and present, say, a delicious picture of the home life of the Stalins, or of Adolf Hitler, the misunderstood water-colorist and music-lover—must be exceptionally painful to write.

Even when they are truthful, I find muckraking biographies tedious to read unless they are done with great sophistication, subtlety, and above all, a sense of proportion—there is, let us agree, a scale of villainy—in which case one would be less aware of the bias of the author, and more sympathetic to his point of view. I read one such biased work on an American philanthropist and businessman, and found its endless, one-note vilification, had a contrary effect to the one intended—surely he couldn't be as unmitigatedly wicked as the author maintains?

The biographer generally needs some degree of sympathy, some degree of identification, with his subject—all the while attempting to maintain objectivity. For this reason, as I have suggested, it would seem to me peculiarly difficult to write a biography of an unsympathetic subject. True, if one were a stylish enough writer, one might have a delightful time and delight one's readers, doing in a hateful subject. But that is something else again, leaving one to consider the difference between a biographer and an entertainer.

Entertainers vary of course, but it's my observation that when they are not hating too much, they tend to be loving too much; and this is especially true when they are writing of figures from the world of entertainment. So, at least, I concluded from that year's meager crop. The underlying assumption of such books is that the readership—by which I mean the fans who can read—likes stories and jokes. Some are very well told, and sometimes they are even funny. But the authors generally seem to feel that the telling of "jokes" and "inside stories" is enough. Their books tend to be shapeless, offering in a clip-clop superficial way the "life story." The plain unavoidable fact is that a biography, or autobiography, must be shaped—it cannot simply be one damned thing after another. Otherwise, the computer to which I have already alluded might be set busily to work, fed a raw pile of data and offer us a depersonalized printout, from a birth to a death, with all the "life" mysteriously absent. One thinks, at times, in reading show-business biographies, that their authors have successfully avoided thinking.

But autobiography—whether by theatrical or literary or historical somebodies, or by mere nobodies—is, I suspect, even more difficult to write than biography. It is not that sympathy is wanting. With your typical autobiography, there is a generous supply of that for the beloved object under scrutiny, but dispassion and objectivity are all too often in short supply. No man may be a hero to his valet, as they used to say, but he is, with pen in hand and mirror discreetly lighted, a hero to himself.

Reticence plays no part at all in a new group, or genre, of biographies that seem to be coming to the fore—chronicles of pain, suffering, and personal loss. Such books are a little hard to cope with, or to get an appropriate fix on, whether of the bias of the author, or one's own bias as a reader. These books tend to be powerful, but seemingly artless—so candid in their revelations, rather like the photographs of Diane Arbus—and however unimpeachable in their truthfulness, I fear that they appeal to the soap opera instinct in us all, and to our pleasure in voyeurism. These books deal with death and disease—the husband dying of cancer, the son dying of leukemia—and are written by survivors. It is hard to sort out one's reactions—there is a certain fascination, but also distaste, for the exposure. With their transparent sincerity and clinical exactitude these authors do "get at one," but is this a sign of their individual merit; or does it reflect something larger, more free-floating and pervasive: that we are all believers, and disbelievers in death? I do think there may be a certain correlation between the sense of malaise that many of us feel in and about American society, and the marked increase in the number of books about death—in most cases, unfair death. The death of children, as in Doris Lund's *Eric* which was interesting to read, but which one put down with a saccharine taste in one's mouth. Or the early death of a husband, as in Lynn Caine's powerful *Widow*. Or the death which is a blessed relief, as in Madeleine L'Engle's *Death of a Great-Grandmother*. These books bring forth, I feel, ambiguous reactions, a compound of approval and disapproval, fascination and fear. What is the extent of the value of sharing such experiences? Strangely enough, the ancient exemplary purpose of biography is perhaps most vividly presented in such lives and deaths— these are examples. But aren't our emotions—no doubt unintentionally—being played with? *Widow* may well bring tears to the eyes, and there is no question of the author's courage and suffering; but what one looks for and doesn't find in such works, perhaps it is unreasonable to expect to find it, is dispassion or objectivity: one can't escape from the bias that has occasioned their writing.

Of course, twentieth-century biography was transformed by one of the most prejudiced of writers, Lytton Strachey, who felt that the nineteenth-century monuments, those multivolumed quasi-official biographies of the illustrious dead, were travesties of the truth. Full of indignation against the immediate English past—the past of his parents and grandparents—he was determined to cut it down to its proper size with his malicious, but extremely witty and perceptive sketches of Thomas Arnold, Florence Nightingale, General Gordon, and Cardinal Manning. But even Lytton Strachey mellowed, became sympathetic as well as dispassionate, and wrote a generally affectionate biography of Queen Victoria, not to speak of an adulatory biography of Queen Elizabeth, with whom, in the oddest sort of way, he seems to have identified. Ironically Strachey himself, not long ago, became the subject of a biography of Victorian proportions, and certainly the mammoth biography has come back into style. But Strachey seems to have permanently disposed of biography as hagiography. And perhaps the modern dominant approach to biography is a combination of pre- and post-Stracheyan attitudes: that is, a skeptical sympathy.

At least, that is the attitude which I try to follow myself. Of course I am in a special position to compensate for, or perhaps to double, the problem of bias—I write in collaboration, with an editor and novelist, William Abrahams. He tends to react to the figures we are dealing with—both the central figures themselves and those surrounding them—more vehemently, both favorably and unfavorably, which may be a contrast between the historian's and the novelist's temperaments, or simply a contrast in temperament. We try to aim at one tone in our writings—generally achieved by rewriting each other's manuscript—but obviously, that there are two points of view means, I believe, that the problem of bias is somewhat lessened. We write about English subjects—John Cornford, Julian Bell, and George Orwell—and that has the disadvantages of distance, of not knowing a society from the inside—but it has the advantage of being able to look at it more dispassionately and without bias, perhaps seeing English society with somewhat more clarity and less prejudice than a native might experience. One hopes that my experience as an historian and William Abrahams's insight as a novelist are of assistance in getting, to the degree to which we do, into a society, and to an understanding of our characters, as they respond to the society in which they lived, and rebelled against, and adapted to—the latter, especially, in Orwell's case. None can be thought of as "typical"; all three had much in common, not least their having fought for the Republic in the Spanish Civil War, in which Cornford and Bell were killed and Orwell was wounded, returning to England a changed man, his personality as a political writer and critic of society fully formed.

What is the experience of a biographer? Drawing upon my own adventures and difficulties, and what I would gather from that of the biographies of writers I read that year, it tends to be a rather long-drawn-out business, not to say ordeal. An attempt to master whatever there may be in print about the subject; and then an examination for sources, whether documents and manuscripts for those who are long dead, or documents and manuscripts and survivors for those of this century. As is probably true of any subject one writes about, it does seem to acquire a life of its own, demanding that more and more be done. As one discovers more about something, it suggests further avenues that could be explored—the possibilities are frequently almost infinite, and eventually one has to call, almost arbitrarily, a halt. In my own experience the manuscript resources were comparatively limited—Bell and Cornford had died quite young, and Orwell left surprisingly little in the way of manuscripts and letters. There was, in the case of John Cornford, a most memorable moment when we were meeting for the first time his brother Christopher, who was then living in his parents' house in Cambridge. He mentioned in passing that there might be some papers in the room behind the boiler. But he was doubtful, and his wife was extremely skeptical that anything might be found. But I knew that I would not rest easy unless I looked and we found quite extraordinary material—not in quantity, but some very important letters between John Cornford and his mother, the poet Frances Cornford, some unpublished literary material, and most exciting of all, his diary—with very sparse entries, it is true—which he had with him in Spain, and which contained the manuscript of his most famous poem, "The Last Mile to Huesca."

Interviewing, as one might expect, provides a veritable field day for bias, on the part of the witness, who has his or her version of events to put forth. And then there are one's own reactions to the witness, and to what degree that colors one's faith in what one is being told. One must be polite; yet it is necessary also to be somewhat skeptical, to allow for the changes that time has made in memory, and of course, the prejudices and point of view of the person to whom one is talking, as they are evident or surmised.

One experience I've had with bias in connection with biography has been with the study which William Abrahams and I have done of the first 30 years of the life of George Orwell. To begin with, we have had the rather interesting problem, and one that has to a degree complicated the project, of the bias or prejudice of the subject himself against the idea of biography. In his will, Orwell, who died in 1950, requested that no biography of him be written. And you may say, that should have been the end of it. But can a public figure forbid that a biography be written, particularly a writer as important as Orwell—and I pass over the irony of Orwell, of all people, exercising a kind of posthumous thought control, the kind of tyranny he devoted his life to opposing. One of his literary executors assured us that it was not a very profoundly held wish. Mentioned very casually in the will, it reflected no more than a fear on Orwell's part that he might be written up extravagantly or luridly immediately after his death. His widow, the other literary executor, seems to have agreed it was a temporary proviso, for in the early 1950s she asked Malcolm Muggeridge to write the biography, which he began, but then abandoned. But the wish does make one somewhat uneasy. Why did he express such a wish? He was, or appears to be, an intensely autobiographical writer, and he felt, I believe, that he had used his own experience as he wished it to be used—to point a particular moral. He was not interested in other people poking around in his life and using the material in a different, perhaps contradictory way. There is, after all, more than one way of looking at the truth—not, I hasten to add, that there appear to be any skeletons knocking around in his closet. But one thing that makes Orwell fascinating as a writer was his use and transformation of his own experience. It is that relation between his art and his life which we, as biographers, found particularly challenging, not only as a life story, but for its insight into the artistic process. This very distancing—the psychology which made it necessary for him to write under a pseudonym—makes it more imperative that a biography of him exist than it might for most other writers.

In the case of Orwell we have also experienced another form of bias which we did not find with our first book, *Journey to the Frontier*, the study of Cornford and Bell. They were comparatively unknown figures, and we were restoring more or less forgotten lives. But Orwell is a much more famous figure, and he is a man whom many have their own ideas about, ideas which they do not like to have challenged. The dominant legendary picture of Orwell—and we can only hope that it has now been somewhat modified—is of a sort of Lawrentian figure, in cloth cap and riding a bike, who came from

the lower classes of England and preached a form of honest egalitarianism. For some, especially those who pick and choose among
his writings and wish not to know anything of his life as it actually
was, he was a kind of plaster saint. In fact, he was a good deal more
complex than this, a good deal more admirable because more human, faults and all, more logical too in his development from one
sort of man to another.

We believe that we depicted an Orwell—in his own terminology,
a member of the lower-upper-middle class—an old Etonian, who as
he evolved into the author of *Homage to Catalonia*, is a far more
fascinating figure than the Orwell of simpleminded legend, a man
who was an artist, determined to shape his own reality, and not
merely a reporter of what he saw. To what degree we succeeded—
both in *The Unknown Orwell* and *Orwell: The Transformation*—we
must, like any biographers, leave to our readers to decide and we can
only hope that they will read us without bias.

3

SOCIAL HISTORY

Three volumes of *The Cambridge Social History of Britain, 1750-1950* (1990), edited by F. M. L. Thompson, provide an opportunity to assess the present state of social history, granting that so much has been and is being written in the area that even these three volumes are a comparatively small sample. Possible definitions of social history are numerous, and this vast compendium by many hands demonstrates the point to an almost bewildering degree. I believe that the classic traditional definition of social history might be that area where economic concerns and individuals meet. It is certainly the message conveyed in the photographs of poor urban children reproduced on the dust jackets of these volumes.

In many ways social history is a flourishing, indeed one might have said, triumphant, field. To paraphrase Sir William Harcourt, a stalwart Liberal if there ever was one, "We are all social historians now." For the last thirty years or so, social history has been in the ascendant, with scads of publications, and many articles that would appropriately be called social history appearing in many journals. The ascendant status of social history has been a matter of a generation.

Of course the tilt began quite a few years ago. One cannot underestimate the continuing importance for social history in general and for British social history in particular, richly deserved, of E. P. Thompson's *The Making of the English Working Class*, published more than thirty years ago—and now subjected to many criticisms, as any great work should be, a sign of its continuing vitality. The lack of explicitly feminist concerns in the book itself and the recent general flight from Marxism, even in the non-doctrinaire version to be found in Thompson, may have made the work, unjustly, less respected than it once was. Now we appear to be entering upon the less known, if not totally unrelated fields, of gender, cultural studies, and theory. Certainly the political agendas in the new approaches are different from that put forward by E. P. Thompson. Yet in much of social history, particularly for those who are interested in Britain, he has been and remains the powerful formative figure. The more dominant figure at present appears to be the philosopher referred to by the history graduate students at Stanford as the "F word," Michel Foucault.

But this is to anticipate. Social history has been around for a long time, at first as a rather poor relation to the rest of history, sitting below the salt. It had a popular middle- to lower-middle-brow existence as rather antiquarian history, accounts of customs, organizations, "everyday life," with a fair amount of color but little or no analysis. Politics, diplomacy, and the growth of nationalism were undoubtedly the dominant interests in the study of history through the 1950s. There was a brief interregnum dominated by quantitative history. But by the late 1960s, with the postwar glow diminishing, and the experience of Vietnam, the triumph of the Western nation-state appeared less valuable and less assured. It was time for alternative histories, or, better, alternative ways of doing history. It is always fascinating for the historian to watch the playing out of these trends, although at the price of making one rather cynical about cycles. Contrary to what some may think, the only certainty is change and flux. The current debate on university campuses about diversity and multiculturalism, and the revolt against a hierarchy of values in literary and cultural studies, although in some aspects part of what I see as the next wave, is also reflective of some of the same causes that led to the ascendancy of social history. In any case, social history has become much more varied and sophisticated over the years. And it is certainly true that its scope has become extremely broad. It may have become so broad, perhaps lacking in controlling ideas, that it is now increasingly difficult to venture any generalizations about what is social history. Nevertheless, the publication of these three volumes might, one would have thought, provide an opportunity to make such an assessment.

Is it possible to derive any sort of conclusion from twenty-two long essays written over an extraordinarily wide range of material, particularly when, attractively, there is clearly no party line being imposed upon the authors? (One can appreciate why essays by various hands are in fact so rarely reviewed.) Most of the pieces cover, as the title states, fifty years on each side of the nineteenth century. The essays are impressive, based on wide reading, although mostly of secondary material. But one wishes there were more ideas. British pragmatism has its charms, but also its limitations. How much more interesting it generally is to have a controversial controlling idea to provide shape, rather than general discussions, however intelligent. Surveys do need to be provided, but reading these volumes does make one rather yearn for the rich particularity of archival history. An understandable editorial decision has been taken, but one that downplays the areas of dispute that might have made the collection more exciting. As Thompson writes in his preface, reprinted in each volume: "questions of class, social relationships, gender differences and roles, and social conflict are discussed in the context of a series of particular themes which constitute the main elements in that framework" (1: xiii; 2: xiii; 3: xi).

Volume One is concerned with regions and communities. Thompson leads off with the first essay, "Town and City." A preeminent historian of land, he sees a conflict and a confluence of urban and rural values—social seasons taking place in provincial towns, but London itself as the greatest town of all, the great city a conglomeration of towns. Urban values have triumphed in Britain; yet it is hard to imagine a society in which a conception of rurality, the country, has continued to have such power, falsely romantic as it so frequently is. Thompson tends to portray a rather peaceful society where there is little conflict and not much urban despair. W. A. Armstrong, who follows him, deals with the countryside, and in his version the story is not very dramatic: stability over class conflict. These bland, rather approving, approaches are characteristic of most of the essays. There tends to be a flattening out; less weight given to the significance of those old revolutions: Industrial, Agricultural, French. Perhaps the more interesting side of the coin is to see the continuance of preindustrial customs and relationships despite the "ever-increasing infiltration of urban values into the remotest corners of English rural life" (Armstrong 1: 123). What has received attention of late, as in Patrick Joyce's work, is the intriguing paradox of the persistence of older values within the very locus of change, the factory itself. But continuities, significant and intriguing as they may be, are rarely as interesting as change.

Scotland is covered in two essays of a century each, the first one by Rosalind Mitchison and the second by T. C. Smout. The one essay on Wales is by two authors, D. W. Howell and C. Baber, and

presents, not surprisingly given Wales's history, a view that is powerfully done, but is more consistent with one's ordinary understanding.
"The transformation of a nation of poverty-stricken, politically subservient peasants into a modem and democratic society, it will be
apparent, was engineered by industrialisation, by the rapid expansion of mining and manufacturing activities throughout the later
eighteenth and nineteenth centuries" (1: 300). Actually there has
been a renaissance in Welsh studies, an emphasis on the differences
in that nation, the first of the constituent kingdoms that was made
subservient by England, a history frequently not given its due. "It is
their separate history, instinctive radicalism in religion and politics,
contempt for social pretentiousness, personal warmth and exuberance, sociability, love of music and near-obsession with rugby that
mark them out as Welshmen" (1: 354). An emphasis connecting social history with economic concerns continues to dominate the re-
gional chapters: a highly intelligent but traditional picture of the relationship of economic developments to the people of the area. This
is particularly true in J. K. Walton's chapter on the northwest, familiar from so many accounts of the industrial revolution. D. J.
Rowe on the northeast is dealing with an area that is less well known.
F. L. Garside on London and the Home Counties concludes the volume, continuing its useful way. It would be nice if there were a little
more spark and eccentricity, bold hypothesis and dramatic insight.

Volume Two has as its topic "People and Their Environment." It
begins with M. A. Anderson on demographic change, then Leonore
Davidoff on the family in Britain. Her study does not have the
splendid richness and particularity of her and Catherine Hall's recent
and mammoth *Family Fortunes: Men and Women of the English
Middle Class, 1750-1850* (1987). The essay is intriguing if impres-
sionistic in the way it marks the growth of the private idea of the
family, the decreasing playing out of its life in public. The family
moves from "The World is but one great family" to "Our family is a
little world" (2: 128-29). Another important idea Davidoff puts forward is the change in the conception of women's sexuality in the
middle class. Before the mid-eighteenth century women had been
seen as "insatiable sexual beings dominated by their desires, who
would drain men's vitality with their carnal demands." But in the
nineteenth century "it was now men whose nature embodies the sexual drive" except for those women who had "fallen" (2: 84). But one
does wish that Davidoff had ventured an explanation of why and
how this change had taken place.

The Patrick Joyce chapter on work is one of the most intriguing in the three volumes, and is written in clearer prose than his *Work, Society and Politics: The Culture of the Factory in Later Victorian England* (1980). Nowadays, in labor history some of the most intense controversies touching on social history are in process. If Marxist history should deal with anything it should be what is happening with work, particularly in the factory. The workplace, that most real of locations, is now being explored in new, and at times Foucauldian, ways. Marxist analysis tended to be somewhat teleological, leading to a growth of consciousness, of a reality of which language was primarily the indication. Now language in itself is taken more seriously, as in Gareth Stedman Jones's work on the Chartists, with an increased emphasis on the meaning of what is actually said; its apparent political nature should be taken more at face value. Self-consciousness should not be underrated. As Joyce writes: "There has recently been a welcome turn to the study of language and the constitution of ideology and consciousness, owing much to post-structuralist influences, especially that of Foucault" (2: 170). Joyce wishes to put much more emphasis on multiplicity, uneven developments, and the preservation of older forms. Ideologies and institutions are seen as semi-independent, connected in complicated ways with politics and economics. There is the continual challenge of attempting to explain the conservatism of the British working class. While not denying the importance of class, Joyce's emphasis on diversity and lack of consistency, on the continuance of older traditions of paternalism, the ambiguities, the lack of regularity, the slowness of change, all present a new varied social history that can provide insights into what actually happened in Britain. The remaining essays in the volume on housing by M. J. Daunton, on food, drink, and nutrition by F. J. Oddy, and on leisure and culture by H. Cunningham are all useful and suggestive. The essay on leisure in particular, while recognizing the older theme of the growth of respectability in sport, in keeping with so much else in these volumes, puts more weight on continuities and comparative stability, and suggests that the industrial revolution was not such a severe break. Cunningham argues that it is easy to exaggerate the degree of commercialization of sport and leisure activities, and the decline of participation. The study of brass bands, choirs, village cricket—there could be numerous examples—would provide many examples of rich social history that if done with historical sophistication could be revealing about the modern British world.

Perhaps the concerns of the second volume are the "purer" forms of social history; the state is a factor, a crucial part of the story, but without it there would be work, leisure, housing, no matter to what degree they are shaped by the state and politics. Volume Three, "Social Agencies and Institutions," has the state as a central concern. This is social history with the politics put back in. Pat Thane discusses government and society up to 1914, while José Harris writes about the twentieth century. Harris's is a brilliant essay on "the social history of the state" (3: 65), which charts the growth of an expectation that the state would be more interventionist. It reinforces the generally optimistic tone of the essays, that even despite the depression real wages were increasing and that "even for people out of work average unemployment benefit in the 1930s was higher than unskilled real wages twenty-five years before" (3: 83). Perhaps a depiction of the social composition of the state emphasizes its continuities and strengths. A study of changing politics on the surface of the state or the shifts of class at its base would present a picture more devoted to change. Harris endorses Harold Perkin's view in *The Rise of Professional Society: England Since 1880* (1989) that the crucial decisions are made by private and public professionals, "a horizontal context between different sectors of the professional middle class rather than a vertical struggle between two different social classes" (3: 112). The essay is particularly important in its awareness that economic changes during the nineteenth century, and the debates on the role of the state, did so much to shape the procedures and activities of the British state today.

Most of the essays in these three volumes are status reports, most of them well done, such as Gillian Sutherland on education and Virginia Berridge on health and medicine. In the latter we see the domestication of the Foucauldian insight, and a marking of the abandonment of the older Whiggish view that social services improve as time passes. "The treatment of the mad was no longer seen within a progressive framework, but in terms of the strategies of professionalisation, the labelling of social deviance, the elaboration of social control through medicalisation. Overtly penal and punitive approaches were replaced, in the modern capitalist state, by the social policing function of institutions and asylums" (3: 210).

But it seems to me that the two most imaginative essays—those that are more willing to take risks, those that are less "responsible"—are the Joyce essay I have already discussed and V. A. C. Gatrell on "Crime, Authority and the Policeman-State." Gatrell's is the most radical in the volume, taking the view that the cost of the state crime establishment is greater than the cost of crime that it combats. Gatrell does not quite suggest that we might be better off if we eliminated the forces of "law and order" although, as he states, the cost of crime "even today is relatively trivial" (3: 249). "The history of crime, accordingly, is largely the history of how better-off people disciplined their inferiors" (3: 245) even though most working-class criminals committed crimes against their social equals rather than against their superiors. He also argues that it is a myth that as society became more "modern," crime increased. The essay is a brilliant combination of descriptions of the specifics of crime itself and a discussion of the state purposes served by fighting it.

The three remaining essays in the volume are by James Obelkevich on religion, F. K. Prochaska on philanthropy (particularly interesting in pointing out how active the poor themselves were as philanthropists), and R. J. Morris on clubs, societies, and associations. By this time, the reader feels social historied out. Thompson's assemblage is a formidable undertaking and useful for any student of Britain, particularly with the bibliographies provided for each chapter. The discipline is in a stage of high maturity, and perhaps betrays a certain complacency. With few exceptions, only the chapters on work and crime suggest ferment and controversy. The overwhelming impression is of comparative stability and lack of conflict. Essays could probably be written that would present a far more turbulent conception of British social history, but this collection, I suspect, may be representative of the dominant consensus at the moment, come to by a group of serious scholars.

Is there a new approach that might challenge the dominance of social history or might move it into the next stage in the understanding of modern Britain? The use of the Foucauldian "tag word" "discourse" in Joyce's essay may be suggestive about the future. Although the language is new, the emphasis on discourse may have been around for some time. G. M. Young could hardly be further from the French philosopher. Yet he stated as his historical aim an attempt to hear the figures of the past talking, as the way of truly understanding the past. Penetrating "discourse" may be this generation's way of accomplishing the same object. As Foucault was, so G. M. Young too was interested in questions of power and how new values asserted themselves. One need not move away from archival work, which is after all the recovery of language, of statements that were made in the past.

Various recent monographs, such as Susan Kingsley Kent's *Sex and Suffrage in Britain 1860-1914* (1987), Alex Owen's *The Darkened Room* (1990), Patrick Brantlinger's *Rule of Darkness* (1988), and Martin J. Wiener's *Reconstructing the Criminal* (1990), to name but a few, have demonstrated the variety of uses to which the Foucauldian approach can be put. As the cycle of historical analysis continues, this approach may prove to be particularly appropriate as it encourages a social reconstruction of the past—reality then being what contemporaries said it was. The impressive Thompson collection tells us where much of the social history of Britain has been and where it is now, but is also suggestive about its future.

4

Lytton Strachey's *Eminent Victorians*

I wish to discuss the contribution of Lytton Strachey to the art of biography, particularly his *Eminent Victorians,* and his present relevance to that flourishing genre. Biography exists in a somewhat uneasy relationship with its sister arts. It is impressive that it should be one of the themes for the congress of historians in Madrid in August 1990, for in the view of some historians, quite wrongly in my opinion, it is not a proper field of history but quite a different discipline—and a lowly one at that—of its own. I think that there is a feeling that biography is less rigorous, less professional than the pursuit of history itself, that all the writer has to do is tell the story, put one thing after another. But what could be more interesting and frequently more complex than an individual's life story, and potentially more subject to the use of elaborate theory—although such has not happened, with few exceptions, in the field of biography. (Of course it is undoubtedly true that Freud has been a great influence upon biography: in Strachey's case, in his third major book, *Elizabeth and Essex* [1928]. But it is rare that Freud's theory is used in a rigorously scientific way even by those who think very highly of it.)

Ideas about biography, at least in the English case, may have become intertwined with the English class system, the cult of the amateur and the gentleman: that it does not do to be too professional about one's activities. Unlike other forms of writing, it would appear to be a genre that any person of the right class might undertake. Strachey built on a double tradition of biography. That of the short, frequently ironic essay, goes back a long way in England (and perhaps elsewhere), as in, for instance, the famous sketches by John Aubrey in the seventeenth century. This genre of brief biography is a strong one and perhaps has not received its due in the making of the modern biography and its influence upon Strachey. As is well known, his *Eminent Victorians* of 1918 was reacting against the pietistic life and letters of the nineteenth century. In the eighteenth century, as in Boswell's life of Johnson, and Johnson's own writings, and in the seventeenth century, English writing had not always been thus. Even the Victorian age had exceptions to the reverent tradition, such as in Mrs. Gaskell's biography of Charlotte Brontë (1857) and J. A. Froude's biography of Thomas Carlyle (1892-94). But the stereotype of the Victorian biography was a multivolume tome or tomb that did not contain an ill word about its subject and would not bring a blush to the cheek of a young lady. Such books can be useful for the primary material within them, although frequently documents were modified when printed and the originals lost or destroyed thereafter.

Although mammoth biographies—"good reads"—appeared throughout the nineteenth century, and presumably were a mainstay of the lending libraries that charged for their services (particularly at a time when books were comparatively expensive) and were much patronized by the middle class, there also flourished during the century in England and into the present, the shorter sketch. Written by journalists and published in the numerous serious and not so serious journals of the times, these sketches were frequently collected in book form, and are still available at very low prices at many used book dealers. One ever-popular form of such brief biographical efforts were the paragraphs written to accompany the famous caricatures of *Vanity Fair*. Although at times these essays were characterized by rather heavy-handed attempts at wit, derived in part from the Clubland where so many Victorian journalists spent so much of their time, they tended to be far less respectful of their subject than the posthumous biographies of far greater length. Yet there was generally, but not always, an underlying assumption even in the short sketch of a certain affection for the figure being depicted.

Strachey would make that attitude far less common. The two contrasting traditions in England came in their turn to influence biography. One is that of the outward show to be made, as in the pious posthumous biography. There everything is perfect and imperfections are not to be revealed—"not before the servants" and the lower classes. But also there is the tradition of chaffing and often extremely mean teasing (see any account of the growing up of the Mitford sisters). This takes place both within the family, and then in the schooling of the young, particularly the male, of the upper and middle classes: the prep school entered at eight, the "public" boarding schools, and then possibly even at university, in the "rags" and pranks frequently inflicted by "the hearties" upon aesthetes. Irony might serve as a defense against this cruel world and ironic writing skill was an aim of the shorter sketches. Through family connections—Strachey's cousin, Joe St. Loe Strachey, was the editor of the Spectator, for which Lytton would occasionally write—and as a member of those classes who read the serious press, Strachey would have been deeply familiar with both traditions. Indeed, so much of English upper class education is based on being trained to write the short elegant essay. In the latter half of the nineteenth century, an increasing number of well-educated young men were turning to serious journalism, as was Strachey himself. They wished to turn their writing skills to profit, while maintaining their gentlemanly status.

Strachey's public life was quite conventional up until the First World War: a young man of good family of a literary bent writing for the *Spectator*, at work on a dissertation on Warren Hastings, the controversial British leader in India. It was a topic consistent with Strachey's family background—his father had been a famous general and civil servant in India. Strachey wished, unsuccessfully as it turned out, to win a fellowship at Trinity, his Cambridge college. While an undergraduate, he had achieved the distinction of being a member of the Apostles, the informal Cambridge discussion society, which in the late nineteenth and early twentieth century had its most distinguished period since its founding earlier in the nineteenth century. Strachey was unconventional in his private life, being uncloseted to his friends as a homosexual, corresponding on such questions as the attractiveness of certain undergraduates, with his great friend and contemporary Maynard Keynes. Through another great friend (who was not an Apostle), Thoby Stephen, Lytton met Thoby's sisters Vanessa and Virginia, a crucial event in the early history of Bloomsbury.

In the private sphere, Bloomsbury was resolutely against Victorian hypocrisy. Its members believed in being frank and honest, and being able freely to discuss sexual questions. This is best captured in a famous episode related by Virginia Woolf—with perhaps some exaggeration—in a private memoir. The incident was first recounted by her nephew, Quentin Bell, in his biography of 1972, and then published in *Moments of Being* in 1976. "Another scene has always lived in my memory—I do not know if I invented it or not—as the best illustration of Bloomsbury Chapter Two. It was a Spring evening. Vanessa and I were sitting in the drawing room. The drawing room had greatly changed its character since 1904. The Sargent-Furse age was over. The age of Augustus John was dawning. . . . Suddenly the door opened and the long and sinister figure of Mr. Lytton Strachey stood on the threshold. He pointed his finger at a stain on Vanessa's white dress. 'Semen?' he said. Can one really say it? I thought and we burst out laughing. With that one word all barriers of reticence and reserve went down. A flood of the sacred fluid seemed to overwhelm us. Sex permeated our conversation. The word bugger was never far from our lips. We discussed copulation with the same excitement and openness that we had discussed the nature of good."

Private life was dedicated to what Strachey and his friends in Bloomsbury saw as the truth, not only in the philosophical questions that they had discussed at the meeting of the Apostles, but in terms of their personal lives. As Woolf noted in the same quotation: "The Watts' portraits of my father and my mother were hung downstairs if they were hung at all." The Victorians were banished and despised, as Strachey indicated in a letter to Woolf in 1912 about George Meredith. "Is it prejudice, do you think, that makes us hate the Victorians, or is it the truth of the case? They seem to me a set of mouthing bungling hypocrites; but perhaps really there is a baroque charm about them which will be discovered by our great-great-grandchildren, as we have discovered the charm of Donne, who seemed intolerable to the 18th century. Only I don't believe it."

But in his writing career Strachey had hardly been concerned with the Victorians. His dissertation had been on Warren Hastings, a figure from the history of British India in the late eighteenth century. His one book before the war, *Landmarks in French Literature*, was published in 1912 and had nothing to do with England. Of the one hundred and twenty-five reviews and a few essays he published before the war, very few dealt with the nineteenth century. It might, however, be worth noting that in the *New Statesman* on August 1, 1914, two days before the outbreak of the war, he published a review of Matthew Arnold. There he made apparent his disdain for the Victorians and for Arnold in particular. But he did not yet have the venom to be found in *Eminent Victorians* that would go so far to mark a major change in biography. As he wrote. "Reputations, in the case of ages no less than of individuals, depend in the long run upon the judgments of artists; and artists will never be fair to the Victorian Age. To them its incoherence, its pretentiousness, and its

incurable lack of detachment will always outweigh its genuine qualities of solidity and force. . . . The Age of Victoria was, somehow or
other, unaesthetic to its marrow-bones. . . . If we look at its criticism
of literature alone, was there ever a time when the critic's functions
were more grievously and shamelessly mishandled?"

Although he maintained his urbane and mandarin style, his hatred
of the First World War transformed his disdain for the Victorians
into a much more powerful emotion. He had, it is true, been thinking about writing about the Victorians for some time, but now his
desire to strip them of their pretensions became much more intense.
In 1912 he wrote to Lady Ottoline Morrell: "I am . . . beginning a
new experiment in the way of a short condensed biography of Cardinal Manning—written from a slightly cynical standpoint." He
wrote the four essays—Cardinal Manning, Florence Nightingale,
Thomas Arnold, General Gordon—as the war was going on. *Eminent Victorians* was published in May 1918 and was an instant success.

He wrote at the end of the first paragraph of his essay on Florence
Nightingale: "And so it happened that in the real Miss Nightingale
there was more that was interesting than in the legendary one; there
was also less that was agreeable." She emerges as a megalomaniac
monster. But his more permanent legacy to the art of biography is
not his growing hatred of the Victorian Age. (And even he could
change quite quickly: he presented a surprisingly somewhat sentimental picture of Queen Victoria in his biographical study of her in
1921.) Rather, he pointed out in good Bloomsbury fashion, that appearances and reality are not the same. Delving below the surface,
the biographer's obligation is to explain and have a point of view.
Such an approach also makes for a better biography than one that
simply presents a life in an unreflective way.

Eminent Victorians has been continuously reprinted ever since,
including an illustrated edition by Weidenfeld and Nicolson with a
foreword by Frances Partridge. Her introduction is slight, and she
believes that Strachey put forward a rather benign Florence Nightingale. Partridge knew Strachey well, being a younger figure associated
with Bloomsbury, and a participant in its complicated personal affairs. She was the sister of Ray Marshall, who married David Garnett, and she herself became, in 1926, the lover of Ralph Partridge,
who was part of the ménage à trois with Strachey and Dora Carrington at Ham Spray House.

After Strachey's death in 1932 and Carrington's subsequent suicide, Frances and Ralph Partridge were married. Despite knowing Strachey well, but presumably with some mixed feelings, she has not made a significant contribution. Rather it is the editors of the Albion Press who have added pleasant and interesting illustrations with quite extensive captions. They have, however, intentionally or not, done their best to subvert the view of the Victorian Age Strachey himself put forward. The illustrations emphasize a positive and rather sentimental picture of the age, even including, for instance, praise—with which Strachey himself would have disagreed, as we've seen—for Matthew Arnold under an heroic portrait of his father, Thomas. An unillustrated text would have done more justice to the work.

Strachey's famous preface is faithfully reprinted and tells us a great deal about his biographical approach. It is clear that he is a man of ideas, and that he never put himself forward in these comparatively brief sketches as a thorough historian. "The history of the Victorian Age will never be written: we know too much about it. For ignorance is the first requisite of the historian—ignorance, which simplifies and clarifies, which selects and omits, with a placid perfection unattainable by the highest art." In the most famous line in the preface he reveals what sort of biographer he aimed to be: "He will row out over the great ocean of material, and lower down into it, here and there, a little bucket, which will bring up to the light of day some characteristic specimen, from those far depths, to be examined with a careful curiosity. Guided by these considerations, I have written the ensuing studies." Rather disingenuously, Strachey suggests that he has "no desire to construct a system or to prove a theory. . . . It has been my purpose to illustrate rather than to explain."

On the contrary, Strachey's book launched a tradition that if handled too parodistically by his imitators might become reductionist, explanatory biographies. But if well done, it resulted in a biography written with attention to language and with a point of view rather than a mere mindless laudation. As Strachey argued in his preface, the art of biography "seems to have fallen on evil times in England. We have had, it is true, a few masterpieces, but we have never had, like the French, a great biographical tradition. . . . With us, the most delicate and humane of all the branches of the art of writing has been relegated to the journeymen of letters; we do not reflect that it is perhaps as difficult to write a good life as to live one. Those two fat volumes, with which it is our custom to commemorate the dead—who does not know them, with their ill-digested masses of material, their slipshod style, their tone of tedious panegyric, their lamentable lack of selection, of detachment, of design?" As he says, he used the older biographies both as sources of information and as examples of what was to be avoided. He ends his preface with a quotation from Voltaire, and he was equally passionate, while maintaining a front of not being so—except with the power of the very last word. "To preserve, for instance, a becoming brevity—a brevity which excludes everything that is redundant and nothing that is significant—that, surely, is the first duty of the biographer. The second, no less surely, is to maintain his own freedom of spirit. It is not his business to be complimentary; it is his business to lay bare the facts of the case, as he understands them. That is what I have aimed at in this book—to lay bare the fact of some cases, as I understand them, dispassionately, impartially, and without ulterior intentions. To quote the words of a Master—'Je n'impose rien; je ne propose rien; j'expose.'"

Strachey was being a little disingenuous, but he is nevertheless making the argument for the biography as a constructed work of art that will aim at the psychological truth of the matter. He has rightly been faulted as a historian and in his research, and those criticisms are valid, but they miss the main point: the role of a biographer as a writer, indeed as an artist, but also committed to creating one form of the truth.

As a coda to Strachey's contribution to biography the significance should be noted of Michael Holroyd's two-volume biography of him that appeared in 1967 and 1968. It was ironic that an author who considered himself something of a miniaturist should be celebrated in that monumental fashion, as if he were a Victorian worthy. But the work was done by an author with literary skill who brought forward sixty years later the further implications of the meeting of Lytton Strachey and the Stephen sisters in their Bloomsbury drawing room. Holroyd was as frank about Strachey's private life as his sources permitted; nothing was held back. It is not clear how much Bloomsbury would have approved. Much as they pursued such honesty among themselves, they were in many ways respectful of public conventions and did not necessarily approve of coming "out of the closet" unless, in their view, it was really necessary. During the war Strachey, whose frail health exempted him in any case from conscription, nevertheless issued a passionate statement against the war. He died in 1932 long before the days of gay liberation. But as he himself advanced the art of biography in *Eminent Victorians*, he might well have approved of the step forward represented by his own biography. He was not a plain writer and a good biography need not be as cleverly written as Strachey's had to be, given the nature of his talent. But *Eminent Victorians* survives and so do its contributions to the art of biography and to the history of intellectual attitudes in postwar England.

5

THE FIRST WORLD WAR

One doesn't know quite where to begin to praise Paul Fussell's *The Great War and Modern Memory*, a book in which literary and historical materials, in themselves not unfamiliar, are brought together in a probing, sympathetic and finally illuminating fashion. It is difficult to think of a scholarly work in recent years that has more deeply engaged the reader at both the intellectual and emotional level. Reading Fussell one is moved and instructed. His subject is "the British experience on the Western Front from 1914 to 1918 and some of the literary means by which it has been remembered, conventionalized and mythologized." If, as he argues persuasively, "the war was relying on inherited myth," he is equally persuasive when he claims that the war "was generating new myth, and that myth is part of the fiber of our own lives."

Almost all of Fussell's previous work had been on English literature of the eighteenth century, and one would like to think that his study of Swift was of use to him as he approached the most Swiftian image of our century: the great line of trenches, extending from the top of Belgium to the border of France and Switzerland, infested with rats and reeking with shit, where a generation of young men were senselessly slaughtered. Fussell's reading and collection of material has been prodigious: this is clearly a labor of love, and hate, which has gone a long way past both the descriptive and analytic aspects of its foreground subject to an interpretation of our contemporary sensibility, the continuing legacy of the Great War. The brilliant manipulation of language combined with a desperation about the human condition that distinguishes the work of Heller, Mailer, and Pynchon has its roots, Fussell contends, in the gallant, grotesque, absurd, and ultimately meaningless "trench experience."

He leads one inexorably to this conclusion. Almost at the start of the book we hear the voice of Henry James in a letter to a friend the day after Britain entered the war in August 1914: "The plunge of civilization into this abyss of blood and darkness . . . is a thing that so gives away the whole long age during which we have supposed the world to be, with whatever abatement, gradually bettering, that to have to take it all now for what the treacherous years were all the while really making for and meaning is too tragic for any words." Approaching the book's end, we hear the interior musing of Brigadier Pudding in *Gravity's Rainbow*, as he thinks of Passchendaele— "The mud of Flanders gathered into the curd-crumped, mildly jellied textures of human shit, piled, duck-boarded trenches and shell-pocked leagues of shit in all directions, not even the poor blackened stump of a tree . . . "—and goes on to the coprophagous ritual with the Mistress of the Night that will ultimately kill him. There, freed of the inhibitions that had kept the filthy secret a "secret" for decades, the uncensored contemporary novelist is free to find an imaginative equivalent to the realities of what men were put through by their Yahoo generals on the Western Front: the plunge into the abyss.

I fear I may be doing Fussell a disservice by speaking of his conclusions as though they were the substance of his book. In fact, while he does very powerfully, persuasively, and properly explain how we have come to regard our world as absurd, teetering from one irony (a favorite, even an overworked word of Fussell's) to the next, he offers a meticulous discussion of British literature of the First World War and its extraordinary emblematic importance. Siegfried Sassoon, Robert Graves, Wilfred Owen, Isaac Rosenberg, Rupert Brooke, Edmund Blunden, David Jones—all the expected "classic" names are to be encountered, some in shrewdly judged formal studies, as well as other literary names, little known or virtually forgotten. And attention is paid too to the merely "ordinary" men, whose amateur memoirs, scores of them, Fussell has examined in the Imperial War Museum. Throughout he is himself very much the professional literary critic, aware when necessary of the artistic limitations of the work under discussion, but by the same token aware of how much of the best of it represents a deliberate esthetic achievement— how false it is, for example, to regard Sassoon's fictional trilogy as a random memoir rather than a conscious selection and arrangement of material as in a novel; or to take Graves's *Goodbye to All That* too literally, rather than as the quasi-farcical tale it was intended to be. The book is full of sustained literary arguments, as when a convincing claim is entered for Isaac Rosenberg's "Break of Day in the Trenches" as the greatest poem of the war. At times, if anything, Fussell is a shade too much the "critic," and he seems to me unduly intent to make his analysis consistent with the critical categories of Northrop Frye.

It is, of course, an abundantly "literary" war he is concerned with, far more so than any other war of this century—in part, I suspect, because of the extraordinary numbers of potential "writers" who went off to the front to fight; in part because of the altogether traumatic effect of the trench experience—so different, so unlike anything anyone had expected, so painfully at odds with the myths that a generation of golden-haired young men had been nurtured on. And then there was all that free-floating literary sensibility, an accumulation of centuries.

Fussell evokes the desperation and filth of the trenches with an agonizing fidelity, but he does not overlook the degree to which, ironically, certain niceties of British life were imported to the trenches: so close to London were they that the amenities of a London club, at least where periodicals were concerned, could be found in the officers' quarters; and the trenches were flooded not only with water but with books being sent out to the troops, most particularly *The Oxford Book of English Verse*. Echoes of Shakespeare, Milton, Wordsworth, and others of the pantheon are to be heard in the prose, poetry, and letters of the soldier-writers, and even in those unpublished amateur memoirs in the Imperial War Museum. Conventional flower symbols were much used, gay at first; later, however, they gloomed over, as the war went interminably, bloodily on, and the roses and poppies significantly darkened.

Fussell locates in the Great War a crucial transformation of vocabulary: the change from older words of heroism romantically familiar to many through such works as William Morris's *The Well at the World's End* and the language of quest shaped by Bunyan's *Pilgrim's Progress*. The more fanciful use of language begins to fall away under the influence of the war—then as the horror intensified, romantic diction yields to euphemism. But, of course, the transformation Fussell has in mind goes far deeper than styles of rhetoric.

In his sophisticated and complex fashion he is returning to an older view of the Great War as the "knife-edge," marking off one kind of world and style (prewar) from what came afterward (postwar); or as he puts it in one of his less felicitous moments, "the passage of modern writing from one mode to another, from the low mimetic of the plausible and the social to the ironic of the outrageous, the ridiculous, and the murderous." Actually, we know that the " modern" movement, as such, was not a postwar phenomenon, and had its beginnings long before the outbreak of the war. But it is hard not to agree with him that the Great War marked the end of innocence and encouraged the growth of the ironic mode. British "coping," indigenous as it was to the national character, was never without its ironic aspects, certainly in its traditions of understatement and phlegm. But the defensive, mocking way of regarding the world—the cynicism that by now is inherent in our own lives in all circumstances—is directly a consequence of the slaughters of 1914-1918, and nothing that has happened since has altered that strategy. "I am saying," Fussell tells us, "that there seems to be one dominating form of modern understanding; that it is essentially ironic; and that it originates largely in the application of mind and memory to the events of the Great War."

Historically, he is on solid ground: his detailed knowledge, his range, his humanity—all these make for a book of exciting connections which help one better to understand both the past and the present. Perhaps he does not sufficiently emphasize the greatest irony of all—that the war itself was so ludicrously unnecessary—nor does he make enough of the pleasure with which the outbreak of war was greeted, by the crowds in London and elsewhere. Graves's sense of being rescued by the war from the dull routine of his life was not unusual; Rupert Brooke, that Edwardian Apollo, thanked God in a sonnet for having matched him with the glamorous hour. Those were the realities of 1914.

And yet society was already changing in Britain before the war began; after 1918 it was a changed world to which the survivors returned from the trenches, or rather, it was a world attempting to come to terms with the consequences of the war. Fussell himself does not deal with the social changes, many of them for the better, which the war helped to bring about—an irony he might have savored. But his concern is with the essence of the war, its myth and its memory and how they were transmitted to us, shaping our vision of them, and of ourselves. We try to keep up a brave, if self-deprecating front, but our basic view of the world reflects an ironic melancholy, and this exciting book—looking both backwards and forwards—locates the impelling force of that sad, skeptical vision in the British trenches on the Western Front.

6

THE BRITISH WAY WITH CULTURE

This is a formidable group of books dealing with the shaping of culture in Great Britain—Paul Fussell's study less so than any of the others—reaching back into the beginning of the century and continuing up until 1970 with the end of the Third Programme on the BBC.* The peculiarly British aspect of the discussion is suggested by the title *A Culture for Democracy*. In the British context there is something highly positive and, one might almost say, yearning in that very phrase—democracy should have culture, and culture of a higher sort. Yet there also might be something almost contradictory in the concept. One is not sure that many British, in their heart of hearts, believe that culture of the higher and desirable sort can, or perhaps even should, be a matter for the masses.

D. L. LeMahieu has written a deeply impressive study about the connections between commercial and elite cultures and their special relationship this century, characterized by collusion, collision, cooperation, mendaciousness, recriminations, mutual profit, and continuing tension. In order to support culture for all in society, the question of how it is to be paid for cannot be neglected. Then one asks, of course, about the role of the paymaster—and who indeed is the paymaster? Is it the government, which has become increasingly active in matters of culture in this century? Is it the commercial

---

*The following works are discussed in this essay: D. L. LeMahieu, *A Culture for Democracy: Mass Communication and the Cultivated Mind in Britain Between the Wars* (1988); Paul Swann, *The British Documentary Film Movement, 1926-1946* (1989); Clive Coultass, *Images for Battles: British Film and the Second World War, 1939-1945* (1989); Paul Fussell, *Wartime: Understanding and Behavior in the Second World War* (1989); and Kate Whitehead, *The Third Programme: A Literary History* (1989).

firms, most notably newspapers but also commercial filmmakers and producers, as well as firms who make advertising films? (Nowadays, of course, the emphasis is on corporate sponsorship.) Is it the public, the ultimate source of the funds—so frequently low down in the list of considerations except when some special interest wishes to evoke the vagaries of public opinion on its side—ultimately hard to assess in either qualitative or quantitative senses? (Recent events in Chicago—over the question of the portrait of Mayor Washington—and in Washington—with the Corcoran Gallery and its canceled Robert Mapplethorpe exhibition, and the relations of the National Endowment for the Arts to that exhibit—have made Americans more conscious of these issues.) In any case, there is always the question whether the desired aim is to give the public the culture that it wants (the middle range of what is accepted at the moment) or should have (more sophisticated forms of culture that have just become mainstream) or to lead the way toward what it should have in the future.

Perhaps semiofficial culture is at its best, if one may say so, in supporting middlebrow culture, as when the BBC financially saved the now much loved Prom concerts, with their programs of "popular" classical music. In the hierarchical society that still persists in Britain, and was even more intensely present earlier in the twentieth century, there is the continuing problem of the patronizing and condescending attitude so frequently found in the purveyors of culture whose aim is to provide a culture that is "good" for the recipient. But in some senses it is even more demeaning for all concerned for the providers deliberately to put forth a culture that is geared to the lowest common denominator. As these studies stop in 1970, none touch on one of the most prevalent aspects of this question in Britain today: the "heritage" industry deeply intertwined with a current interest in the nature of "Englishness." On the one hand, there is the voyeuristic elitism—as well as exposure to beautiful objects—made available to the general public through the booming industry of country house visiting, and, on the other, there is an ever-growing interest in the "vernacular," both in industry and "ordinary" life, which is increasingly available in museum settings.

"Culture" has become big business, and LeMahieu is extremely useful and insightful in discussing that question. His book is primarily a powerful work of synthesis based on an extensive reading of published material, with every once in a while the use of some unpublished manuscript sources to provide a few examples. His main accomplishment is a detailed overview of aspects of how the British public spent its discretionary income on culture—culture in its wider sense, including newspapers, films, records, and radio shows at all levels. He is particularly good on dealing with how these levels are indicated, as in a fascinating section contrasting the writing of head-lines in *The Times* and the popular press. *The Times* in its style could frequently be impersonal, based on in fact a personal assumption that it was addressing someone whom one might meet in one's club. Paradoxically, as LeMahieu points out, "as new technologies helped create audiences of phenomenal size, the most effective strat-egy of communication was personal, intimate and subjective"(p. 43). The less likely it is that the author might meet the reader, the more likely it is that the prose will emanate a false friendliness. The growth of women's pages in newspapers is one example of this de-velopment. A radio presentation may have an audience of millions, yet each individual audience is minute. Ironically, in many ways "elite" culture is more of a communal experience, but on a much smaller scale, shared by several hundred or more in a theater, or quite a few people thronging a well-regarded exhibition in a mu-seum. A similar paradox exists for books: those that are bought in the millions are generally not those discussed in the publications read by "everyone who counts," a minute portion of the population, but one that tends to include those who are creating the "culture" that on a lower level is consumed and frequently enjoyed by the millions. Charlie Chaplin is something of a theme in LeMahieu's study, and he is a rare example of a cultural figure generally enjoyed at all levels in Britain, but it is surely significant that, though working-class En-glish, and Jewish at that, it was through Hollywood that he reached his great success. And of course America was the powerful influence and importer of popular culture.

High culture has its considerable influence, particularly in the world of newspapers, and design. LeMahieu discusses very well the influence of "modernism" on the world of newspaper advertising, as Victorian-cluttered advertising gave way to the more dramatic use of white space. Good design "paid," but it is never quite clear who "wins" in such a situation, the forces of commerce or the forces of art. On the whole there is no question that the public has increas-ingly received products that are better designed. But the hopes of William Morris have not been fulfilled; it does not follow that we now live in a better world. In the course of the assimilation of the modern, the modern has been tamed, and hence the avant-garde, as it should, must always appear extreme when compared to the accepted culture of the day. Perhaps LeMahieu sees the story as a little too positive. He ends with a discussion of "the strategies and paradoxes of cultural dissent"(p. 293), focused on the Leavises, the Left, and J. B. Priestley, a section that might have worked better as a postscript to his study. Yet ending with Priestley is particularly appropriate as a summation of the themes of the book: the creation of Britain during the twentieth century of a mass culture that had some hope of being both serious and humane. LeMahieu, however, may put much too much weight on Priestley's broad shoulders. "Perhaps more than any other single British figure, he represented the common culture of the decade. He appealed to all classes and regions; his work penetrated virtually all the mass media; his ideas and approach drew from both commercial and elite culture. Priestley demonstrated that cultural dissent need not be restricted to the margins of society: it could also serve to reaffirm traditional moral values for a vast public during a period of economic dislocation and rapid technological change" (p. 318). But LeMahieu does not face the hard questions about Priestley, perhaps indicating some of the limitations of what is otherwise a very impressive achievement. The politics of culture are not much discussed, and, although the war period is not very present here, it is a little surprising that there is no mention of how Priestley's extremely popular series of broadcasts, "Postscripts," was terminated because it was seen as too radical.

Talented though Priestley was, was it, as William Morris might say, "all to end with this," that the apotheosis of culture for democracy would be a sort of sub-Dickens writer who was not, with his Yorkshire radicalism, quite a member of the establishment yet was nevertheless the essence of middlebrow, an attractive common denominator, a compromise, maybe even a defeat, for what culture should mean in a "mass democracy"?

LeMahieu pays a fair amount of attention to the documentary film movement, which is discussed in much greater detail in Paul Swann's interesting study. Swann, too, concentrates on the between-the-wars period with some slight attention to wartime. It serves as a confirmation of LeMahieu's analysis of the interplay of the hopes of high culture, do-goodism, and commercial and political considerations. Not surprisingly, the irrepressible John Grierson—tactless, powerful, opinionated, hard to pin down—claims his dominant position in the documentary story, even though one senses that the author wishes to try to keep him in his place. He seems a rather odd figure, perhaps best explained as a pragmatic Scot who was determined to dominate. Grierson's emphasis was on the storyless, factual, impersonal documentary, yet it was not combined, as one might have expected, with a radical political position. Like his fellow Scotsman John Reith, the first director of the BBC, he wished to give the public what was good for it, which might be boring and would not be avant-garde. Perhaps because his most famous film, *Drifters* (1929), was about the herring industry, one has the feeling that many of his films were about fishing in high seas, which has a slight tendency to make one feel rather bilious. (Swann tells a charming and perhaps apocryphal story that the civil servant likely to authorize the money for a film was an expert on the herring industry, and so the subject was chosen to appeal to him.) In Britain, the documentary film movement was closely tied in—apparently not after many second thoughts—with the government. It started with the Empire Marketing Board. (Grierson rather touchingly thought that the Empire in British film might play the same romantic role as the West did in American film). The government at the beginning had some interest in longer and more dramatic films and invested almost the entire budget on a disastrous feature length film, *One Family* (1930), based on a Kipling story about the gathering of the ingredients of a Christmas pudding from the outposts of the empire—the dominions and colonies being played by society ladies. The mind boggles. The film cost £15,470 and earned £334. At the same time, Grierson made his best film, *Drifters*, which was shown in Britain in 1929 on the same program with *Potemkin* and which in the first reviews impressed the critics more. But the purpose of documentary films, no matter how subtly presented, was from the very beginning to make propaganda, whether for the government, first at the Empire Marketing Board and then at the Post Office, or for business. At the same time, the "Documentary Boys" deluded themselves to some degree that they could also make movies that were popular. Swann dwells comparatively little on the content of the documentary films, but he pays particular attention to their distribution and their showing outside of movie theaters.

Grierson shaped for the British what Swann calls—I don't know if the term is original with him—the "actuality" film. The documentary film, in my view, in Britain moved into its greatest period when it became less "pure," after Grierson left for Canada at the end of the 1930s. It continued to use what Swann calls "social" actors, that is, nonprofessionals who may have the very jobs being depicted, yet the photographing of them doing those jobs is especially created for the film and may even, in part, be shot in the studio, as was true for parts of perhaps the single most famous British documentary, *Night Mail* (1936). The intrinsic problem of the documentary film was that, to the extent that they were truthful about "ordinary" life, it was very hard not to be boring in most cases, even when the job was fishing in rough seas, and to the degree that they were exciting they were likely to be untruthful. And they continually ran the risk of being didactic and patronizing.

Such filmmakers as Alberto Cavalcanti, Harry Watt, and Humphrey Jennings were willing to introduce an element of story into their films and have their "social" actors reproduce experiences that they might have had. They were not like ordinary feature films. They did not explore, however superficially, character, but presented a person at the time of the film only, with perhaps just those indications of character that could be conveyed without information about the past of the individual. The documentary film came into its own during the war, when the Crown Film Unit at the Ministry of Information had at Pinewood better facilities than it had ever had before, and the war provided the drama and the romance that then gave the images a deeper but perhaps misleadingly romantic resonance. A story of sorts figured in the most popular documentary film of the war, *Target for Tonight* (1941), and in the masterpiece of the genre, *Fires Were Started* (1943). These films were less didactic than earlier documentaries. As Swann points out, their aim was to tell the public what the filmmakers thought they should know. "Toward the end of the 1930s, . . . this approach was modified into a policy of aiming films at élites and decisionmakers" (p. 178). Under the influence and danger of war, a considerable part of the gap was closed between the filmmaker and the public, although the commercial filmmaker was more likely to provide what the public wanted.

Clive Coultass considers both commercial and documentary films during wartime. He tries to preserve a balance between the older view that the elite documentary filmmakers were of greater interest and the newer populism that moves away from the "snobbish" point of view and puts greater emphasis on the commercial filmmakers. He argues convincingly that each genre informed the other; commercial films became more committed to presenting people in "real" life, and documentary films paid more attention to telling a story. The war also provided an impetus for British films to liberate themselves from the dominance of American films and to triumph after the war in the pseudorealism of the splendid Ealing comedies, which nevertheless reasserted traditional class relationships. The study is rather refreshingly old-fashioned in telling the stories, perhaps to an excessive degree, of quite a few of the films discussed without the use of any elaborate theory about them. Coultass has the interesting idea of occasionally contrasting a wartime film of the war with a more recent version of a war story, such as *The Longest Day* (1962), but he does not draw any conclusions from his contrasts. Although he recognizes the pressure in some of the films for social reform, he feels that in terms of technique and ideology the war was not that significant an influence. "There is no more misleading assumption than the one, sometimes indiscriminately made, that the Second World War caused the British cinema as a whole to take a great leap forward. In fact much of it moved at the same pace as the society it represented, conservative and divided by class-consciousness, with the war only temporarily pulling the nation together" (p. 66). Yet he acknowledges that "people of all classes undoubtedly did come together and work unsparingly beside each other in the voluntary services. For a time there was certainly a national will to survive that compelled the British to help each other, even if that sense of purpose was rapidly to vanish" (p.52).

In fact the two best-known—and splendid—commercial films of the war, *In Which We Serve* (1942) and *Henry V* (1944), were in no way challenging to the social system. *In Which We Serve* was built on a reinforcement of the class system as it traced the lives of a member of the upper class, the lower middle class, and the working class. A study of the contrasts between Olivier's *Henry V* and Kenneth Branagh's recently released *Henry V* would reveal a lot about changing assumptions and values over the last forty-five years. Coultass presents a less favorable view of *Target for Tonight* than Swann, quoting unenthusiastic reactions, but it was nevertheless a great commercial success. For Coultass, *Desert Victory* (1943) was the "pivotal British film from the Second World War, both for the national expectations it embodied and raised and also for the illusions it helped to foster" (p. 112). This study is full of information and even some points of view interestingly presented, but no conclusions are drawn other than that, under the influence of the war, British films were able to develop a realistic personality of their own and become freer of American influence. There is some sort of thesis, perhaps, struggling to get out: that the films might have been a stronger power for social reform given the role of the state, so much more powerful in wartime, and that there was a particular significance in the interplay of the documentary and the commercial lines. Swann and Coultass and Kate Whitehead, in her history of the Third Programme, all write in a rather similar affectless prose, and one wishes they were more aggressive in presenting their points of view.

Such a statement could never be made about Paul Fussell, who has given us a rich, deeply self-indulgent, idiosyncratic book, far different from the one we had been expecting of him since the publication of his masterpiece *The Great War and Modern Memory* (1975). That study has almost achieved canonical status in its assessment of the role of the First World War on the literature and thought of those who experienced it in England. One rather expected a parallel book about the Second World War. Although there are some elements that do correspond in the two studies, most of *Wartime* is a highly personal account, full of unsubstantiated obiter dicta, of one man's reaction to the war. It is a fascinating text because Fussell is an author who is well worth reading, but on the whole he does not shed too much light on topics that are of professional interest to British historians. It is as if the shattered veteran of the First World War has never really recovered from the experience, although he tried and failed to revive himself through travel as recorded in *Abroad* (1980). At the same time, *Wartime* has the feeling of being written out of the untamed imagination of the late adolescent that Fussell was when he was experiencing the war.

In one sense, however, this study is an appropriate successor to *The Great War and Modern Memory*. That book brilliantly discussed the death of illusion and its literary counterparts. And it also, in conclusion, dealt with how American writers of the Second World War were able, because of the experience of others in the First World War, to create realistic fiction, although it has only been in recent years that convention has allowed the printed word to reproduce the spoken. (Coultass points out that audiences during the war were even surprised at the use of "bloody" on the screen, and the actors in the fire-service film *Fires Were Started* commented on the total realism of the film in every particular except reproducing the everyday foulness of language.)

In *Wartime*, Fussell appears to pay the price of his earlier insight and refuses to admit that high-level ideology played an important role in the war, as in his generalization that, on the whole, only American Jews were anti-German and that the rest of the population fought the war because they were anti-Japanese, a hatred primarily based on racism rather than on any high-flown conceptions of democracy. He produces very little evidence for this sweeping generalization, other than further, rather extravagant, statements such as claiming that being asked to die for the Führer or the Japanese emperor was clearly much more effective than being asked to die for something so vacuous, in his view, as the Four Freedoms.

Exasperating as it is to read, there are nevertheless the brilliant insights and examples that one would expect from Fussell, as he dwells on examples of the "chickenshit" aspect of the war and the ways that, in his view, publicity replaced ideology. His cynical view has its virtues, resulting in perhaps a more realistic assessment of the "warm and plummy" (p. 170) J. B. Priestley than that of LeMahieu. As his pages on *Horizon*, Cyril Connolly's literary magazine published during the war, demonstrate, Fussell could well have written the book expected. He quotes the modest but, in my view, wholly admirable aim of *Horizon*: "improving upon our literary record, encouraging the young writers-at-arms who seem to find the need to write more irresistible as the War progresses, keeping them in touch with their French and American contemporaries—in short, continuing our policy of publishing the best critical and creative writing we can find in wartime England and maintaining the continuity of the present with the past" (p. 211). Fussell is right that ideology had changed from the time of the First World War. That experience, coupled with the disillusionment of the 1930s and the defeat of democracy in the Spanish Civil War, had made the commitment to the values of the democracy a matter of defending, as C. Day Lewis put it, "the bad against the worse." There were lowered expectations. Still, there was a belief that British society was preferable to German, and the situation brought out the British skill at what might be called heroic understatement, which could easily collapse into the cliché of the stiff upper lip. But at its best it achieved highly effective moments of underplayed sentimentality, as when in *Fires Were Started* the telephone operator crawls out from under the table after a bomb has fallen nearby and falling plaster has bloodied her forehead, picks up the receiver, and continues with "I'm sorry for the interruption."

Fussell also discusses the degree to which it was a reading war, with the great popularity of Modern Library and Penguin books. In contrast to the First World War, there was an understated yet powerful emphasis on maintaining civilized values, while not pretending that a horrible price was not being paid. As Fussell remarks: "Connolly laments some of the magazine's younger contributors killed in combat and while doing so comes close to locating his magazine's

bizarre focus on the highest art within the context of the most awful
horror" (p. 218). A most effective and highly popular symbol of this
sense of obligation to support civilized values was the lunchtime
concerts during the Blitz by Myra Hess, playing German music at the
National Gallery.

Fussell emphasizes the point that the horror of the war did not, as
he seems to be arguing through most of the book, eliminate "higher"
values but, rather, in contrast, might have made them more powerful. He ends his book with a discussion of the communiqué that
Eisenhower prepared if he had had to withdraw the troops from the
invasion of France. By redrafting and eliminating the passive tense,
he took on himself the blame from the failure in the phrase "it is
mine alone." "As Mailer says, you use the word shit so you can use
the word noble, and you refuse to ignore the stupidity and barbarism
and ignobility and poltroonery and filth of the real war so that it is
mine alone can flash out, a bright signal in a dark time" (p. 297).

In George Dangerfield's *The Strange Death of Liberal England*,
the discussion of Rupert Brooke at the very end changes the perspective of the book and makes Dangerfield's analysis somewhat more
praising of England than one might have expected: so, too, Fussell
ends his book somewhat differently than he began it. From the point
of view of those interested in England, one might have wished that
he had written much more on how, despite the inevitable mendaciousness, meretriciousness, and doublespeak of wartime, the values
represented by *Horizon* and Myra Hess, among others, did not disappear. Indeed, they appeared to be more important than they had
been in the past and would be in the future.

The commitment to those "higher" values, and their failure to
survive, is part of the story told in Kate Whitehead's study of the
Third Programme, the "highbrow" part of the BBC that lasted from
1946 to 1970. As she points out, the Third built on the growth of
public interest in the arts during the war. But ideas and ideology
rather disappear in her study into an institutional and bureaucratic
monograph that faithfully, one fears, reflects life in the BBC—and
the impetus to support high culture threatens to be lost in committees and red tape. (It may be a small point, but any book that uses
"liaise" five times reflects far too sympathetic an approach to the bureaucratic mind.) The subtitle of the study, "a literary history," in-
forms us that there will be no discussion of music on the Third Programme, which is a great pity. Even more vividly than words, what
music was broadcast might demonstrate how the BBC dealt with the

conundrums that Whitehead intelligently indicates were the questions for the program: At what level were the broadcasts to be? To what degree was a challenge made to taste? To what degree was taste to be shaped? And, indeed, to what degree was the avant-garde to be encouraged? As she points out, choices had to be made between an emphasis on cultural heritage or the avant-garde. And to the extent that more adventuresome fare became acceptable, it might well be hived off by the Home Service. There is interesting material here, but it is presented dully, as if it were an endless committee meeting at the BBC itself. There are flash points, as when parts of the public organize to defend the service, but it is as if the author herself becomes bored with the story, and the time from the tenth anniversary to the end of the Third Programme is hardly discussed at all.

In varying degrees, all these books take on the issue of how cultural questions interrelate in Britain with questions of class and hierarchy. Perhaps the Third Programme made these dilemmas particularly vivid. Could an audience of 12 million for Saturday Night Theatre be a "good thing?" Could an official entity such as the BBC provide "high culture?" On the whole, it did improve the financial status of quite a few writers, even if comparatively few of them were able to write in a different way for the ear than they might have for the printed word. It did enrich the cultural mix in Britain. But the BBC necessarily brought out in its employees a tendency to tell writers how to behave.

Art in many ways is and should be highly irresponsible, while the state and its servants, claiming to be answerable to the public, are not likely to be a force that will easily tolerate the necessary excesses of art. Under the pressure of war, artistic license could coexist more successfully and happily with conformity, and the times demanded a more highly directed art. In peacetime, perhaps the best role for the state is to give out the money and run.

PART TWO

WILLIAM MORRIS

7

RECENT WORK ON WILLIAM MORRIS

The year 1996, the hundredth anniversary of the death of William Morris, was an extraordinary one in Morris studies. There were innumerable exhibitions, lectures, conferences, newspaper stories, and scholarly articles. No doubt the two major publications of the period were Fiona MacCarthy's biography of Morris (appearing in 1994 in Britain and 1995 in the United States) and the completion of Norman Kelvin's masterly edition of Morris's letters. Perhaps the third most significant publication was the catalogue of the exhibition devoted to Morris at the Victoria & Albert Museum in London.

Although this listing makes no claim to be complete, it may be useful to mention the following books, all published in 1996. From the William Morris Library (Thoemmes Press) a second series, newly edited, of Morris's writings: *Journalism: Contributions to Commonweal, 1885-90*; *The Glittering Plain and Child Christopher*; *The Hollow Land and Other Contributions to the Oxford and Cambridge Magazine*; *Three Northern Love Stories and Other Tales*; *Reform and Revolution: Three Early Socialists on the Way Ahead*; and *Arts and Crafts Essays by the Members of the Arts and Crafts Exhibition Society*. Other publications of the year include David Rodgers, *William Morris At Home*; *William Morris: Icelandic Journals*; Derek Baker, *The Flowers of William Morris*; Jean Johnson and Richard Bishop, eds., *The Earthly Paradise: William Morris Yesterday and Today*; Nicholas Salmon, *The William Morris Chronology*; Richard and Hilary Myers, *William Morris: The Tile Designs of Morris and his Fellow-Workers*; Norah Gillow, *William Morris: Designs and Motifs*; and David Saxby, *William Morris at Merton*.

There has been a Morris explosion in general (quite a few other publications could be listed if one went back a few years—as well as forward) in the scholarly world, and a continuing one in the world at large, where it is likely that Morris as designer is his best known aspect. We have come a long way even since the Morris exhibition from the great Berger collection (a major lender to the V&A) in 1975 at Stanford University, although one wishes that the V&A catalogue had not made the provincial mistake of placing Stanford in Connecticut rather than in California. But the explosion is also suggestive of the present approach to Morris, which one can call a postmodernist one. The multiplicity of Morris's genius, to use a word that he wouldn't have liked, has presented a problem in the past. Then there was an attempt to present a unified Morris. That might well cause disagreement among those who had a different hierarchy for the accomplishments in his life and wished to give greatest prominence to literature, or design, or politics. What may have been his greatest claim in his lifetime—Morris the poet—is now more likely to be seen as less important than design and politics and a topic most restricted to academic interest. Norman Kelvin has, in his introduction to the last volume of the letters and in his essay in the catalogue, argued in an imaginative way for a recasting of Morris as a writer, pointing out his shared interests with early modernists and as an important precursor for them. E. P. Thompson in his epochal biographical study made politics and political ideas the integrating force. But nowadays, as in Fiona MacCarthy's biography, we are, for better or worse, more accepting of the fragmented Morris and do not see as great a need to resolve how all the parts of his multiple activities fit together.

Perhaps inadvertently, the three books I now want to discuss emphasize Morris's fragmented nature, as they are all collections of essays, only unified by sharing Morris as subject. Linda Parry's *William Morris* (1996) is a catalogue, a stunning achievement, but one that presents certain problems. Catalogues are rather hybrid publications, and one wonders how often they are read and who are their intended audience. For many who purchase them at the exhibition, they are sophisticated souvenirs, a record and a reminder. (If one were doing it properly, the best procedure would be to read the catalogue *before* seeing the exhibition, or between first and second visits but one wonders how often ordinary mortals have the time or will power to do that.) And then the catalogue itself is rather like a complicated necklace, consisting, generally, of lots of splendid illustrations. In this case almost all the objects on display are discussed, in short highly informative entries, rather like small jewels, grouped by topic, but otherwise somewhat disconnected one from another. This particular catalogue is divided into three sections—the Man, the Art, the Legacy—and then those are divided into essays by experts in the appropriate fields, six on the Man, nine on the Art, and three on the Legacy. On the whole all of the authors here serve well the needs of both professional and expert readers. (While listing the problems of catalogues, one could also mention that they are frequently quite heavy and awkward, presenting challenges while being read as well as heavy-duty transport from the location of the exhibition to one's own library!)

Having appeared to be somewhat carping, let me say that this particular catalogue is a great success, and in some ways more satisfactory than the exhibition itself, although of course the objects cannot be presented in their full richness, as they were at the V&A. As befitting Morris, a certain light tone is maintained by the reproduction throughout the text of Burne-Jones's endearing caricatures of him, the first being of Morris playing pingpong and the last of him peeing. Linda Parry, to whom one owes so much in terms of Morris studies, sets the tone in her introduction, a sketch of his life and of his extraordinary accomplishments. But she also indicates how they fell short of his hopes, as one of his titles has it, "hopes and fears," the advancement and retreat of so much that he did, that is characteristic of his brilliant patterns, his nervous energy that led him to do so many things, and to do them, or so it seems to us, on the whole so well, but in many ways never to his own satisfaction. He had reason to be discontented with his marriage, with the political organizations he was involved in, with his life. (And one is given new views in unexpected places, as in Ray Watkinson's essay on him as a painter where, characteristically, he did far more than one had thought, but also had difficulty in the depiction of women.) But if he hadn't been dissatisfied, if he hadn't been the least complacent of men, we would not have had the great range of items included in the exhibition and catalogue.

Every aspect of Morris's life is covered, but considering that the catalogue is to accompany an exhibition in what is probably the greatest design museum in the world, design is given the most attention, and within design the most important essay, a pinnacle almost in the center of the book, is Linda Parry's own on Morris's textiles. (She also writes the essay about domestic decoration.) Textiles have the longest and most beautifully illustrated catalogue entries, climaxing in carpets and tapestries. And at the exhibition itself, the most satisfactory room was the final spacious one, dominated by those objects. If it is not too cute a concept, one almost thinks of Morris as the benign but powerful lion, designed by Philip Webb in the tapestry executed by Webb, Morris, and J. H. Dearle for the Ionides family at 1 Holland Park in London in 1887.

The catalogue is excellent in presenting the immediacy of Morris, his close involvement in all that he was doing, as Burne-Jones wrote that for him: "every minute will be alive" (p. 42). As Fiona MacCarthy points out in her essay on design, there is in all that he did the immediate presence of his vision ranging from its beginnings in his workshops to his interest as a shopkeeper where he would have contact with the object's ultimate user. The exhibition rather slighted the writer and the political activist, but they are presented here in fine essays by Peter Faulkner and Nicholas Salmon. I think that Paul Greenhalgh is too gloomy is his essay on "Morris after Morris" in which he writes that Morris's "socialism has had no significant impact in the political arena during the twentieth century" (p. 363). He had much to do with the forces that led to the Labour Party, much as he might have disliked its present form, and the ideas behind what one can see as the positive parts of Britain's welfare state. In the 1960s, and even before, but particularly with a sense of the failures of state socialism, Morris's view of community and, as Thompson pointed out, his analysis of alienation, have been a compelling and influential alternative to the business corporatism that we see all around us. (Is it an amusing irony or a betrayal that, necessarily, the exhibition and catalogue were subsidized by the great media giant, Pearson, and the exhibition was opened by Princess Alexandra of Kent?)

There are other essays of note on the Businessman, the Conservationist, the Church Decorator and Stained Glass Maker, Furniture, Tiles, and Tableware, Wallpaper, Calligraphy, and the Kelmscott Press. Only Clive Wainwright, the Pugin expert, in his essay on "Morris in Context," sees fit to be somewhat snotty about the subject, appearing to suggest that his designs were rather the Muzak of the period. The catalogue sees Morris complete, and this is an invaluable publication for anyone interested in any or all of Morris's activities.

The other two publications are less important products of the year, although quite useful in their own right. Charles Harvey and Jon Press, who did the essay on Morris as Businessman in the catalogue, have made that their particular field. They turned around completely and enriched immeasurably one's understanding and appreciation of Morris's business, and specifically what role it, and other financial activities, played in his life in their *William Morris: Design and Enterprise in Victorian Britain* (1991). Valuable as the essays are in the present book—*Art, Enterprise, and Ethics: The Life and Works of William Morris* (1996)—a fair number of them have the feeling of being material that would not fit into their earlier study, and there are surprising tiny errors (a series in one paragraph has C. H. St. John Hornby of the Ashendene Press as poet laureate, and Stanley Baldwin as Georgiana Burne-Jones's son-in-law, rather than her nephew; later on the Earl of Aberdeen is promoted to a Duke). In their earlier work they had convincingly reversed the older idea that not Morris but rather his managers such as Warington Taylor and George Wardle were responsible for the success of the business. Here they make, in effect, some amends to the estimable George Wardle, reprinting with commentary what he wrote for Morris's first biographer, Burne-Jones's son-in-law, J. W. Mackail, and also Wardle's pamphlet to accompany the Morris display at the Boston Foreign Fair of 1883. One is very grateful to have detailed fleshing out of various aspects of Morris's activities, particularly in terms of business but such other aspects as his trip to Iceland and the decoration of 1 Holland Park. Particularly interesting is a discussion of Morris's awareness of the paradox of running a capitalist business though a thoroughly committed communist. Perhaps the key is a quotation from Wardle that Morris believed that "*you cannot have socialism in a corner*" (p. 108). Morris made his business marginally better than others for his workers, but he knew that such steps were not the way a better world would come into existence.

If there was anywhere that Morris thought was the earthly paradise in his own world, it was Kelmscott Manor, his rented house in the countryside. It became even more treasured for him after Rossetti ceased to be a co-tenant. *William Morris: Art and Kelmscott* (1996), edited by Linda Parry, celebrates that house, and includes the splendidly complicated way in which it, bought by Jane Morris after her husband's death, was then bequeathed by May Morris to the University of Oxford, which couldn't really handle it, and through legal steps passed it on to the residuary legatee, the Society of Antiquaries. This collection also honors a recent more-than-custodian of the house, the late A. R. "Dick" Dufty, friend to Morris scholars and author of the guide to the house, available in a new edition released in, of course, 1996. In an essay on May Morris and embroidery,

Linda Parry gives May Morris her due, and points out her independence from her father and the greater exuberance of the colors of her work. The other essays mark various aspects of Morris, with particular attention to his connections with the manor. Four houses associated with Morris are open to the public, Red House, Kelmscott House, Water House (his second home as a child and now the William Morris Gallery), and Kelmscott Manor. A sixteenth-century house, Kelmscott Manor is the oldest and the one that was dearest to him. As such it reaches back furthest and suggests the importance of historical continuity in terms of design, poetry, and politics—that a rich past could lead to a radical future—that was so important to William Morris and is so much a part of his vital legacy.

8

Two Modern Biographies of William Morris

William Morris died on October 3, 1896. The hundredth anniversary of his comparatively early death (he was born in 1834) has been marked with a great number of exhibitions and conferences. Perhaps the most significant harbinger of that event has been the publication of Fiona MacCarthy's new biography, *William Morris: A Life for Our Time* (1995). The book falls within a notable tradition. Putting aside the innumerable shorter lives and specialized studies, the standard full biographies are those by J. W. Mackail (1899), Philip Henderson (1967), Jack Lindsay (1975), and that extremely influential study by E. P. Thompson—not quite a biography and in many respects something more—first published in 1955, and then politically modified in the new edition of 1977. MacCarthy has done her own fine research, and she has, unlike previous biographers, been able to draw upon Norman Kelvin's superbly edited letters of Morris, at the time of her writing, only up to 1888, but now completed.

As we all know, the magnificent strength and great problem of Morris's life is its multiplicity. Given that most of us are poor specimens in contrast to him, and in any case have our own preoccupations, it is extremely difficult for one author to encompass all that Morris did. Perhaps MacCarthy comes as close as anyone can. One can imagine that single volumes of comparable length could be quite easily written, and some have been, on Morris as designer, writer, political thinker and activist, and printer. MacCarthy provides a sensitive story with a fine awareness of Morris's accomplishments and failures, along with a convincing portrait of the man himself. With the possible exception of the political, MacCarthy richly presents, in this writer's opinion, all parts of that great life.

What does MacCarthy mean by her subtitle, "A Life for Our

Time?" I have not been able to perform a detailed analysis of how she differs from the earlier biographers. Mackail, Sir Edward Burne-Jones's son-in-law, knew much more than he could say, and shared his father-in-law's unhappiness with Morris's politics. In the modern tradition, no information is now withheld in the present book, but in fact the two "scandals," Janey Morris's affairs with Dante Gabriel Rossetti and Wilfrid Scawen Blunt, have been known for some time. There is no new evidence that Morris's own deep affections, a lasting one for Georgiana Burne-Jones and a more fleeting one for Aglaia Coronio, were consummated. MacCarthy every once in a while uses a reference from our own times to illuminate a point, with good effect, but one wonders whether the reader in years hence—and this book should be read for years to come—will understand some of them. MacCarthy does end on a "postmodernist" note—although there is no proper conclusion—of quite wisely not trying to judge which part of Morris was the most "important." She does not impose a hierarchy of values. But the price paid is that this is a Morris who is somewhat less integrated than he might be. The impossible and almost defiant challenge that he presents is how can his multiple selves be united in a way that makes sense.

I don't think that we are given a startlingly new Morris, but there is here an emphasis on his contradictions and divisions, on conflicting psychological aspects of his personality. He is a bit of a sport, an odd man out, at the same time that he is a Victorian gentleman, fitting almost exactly into the reign of the monarch he quite detested. (It is a splendid touch that he was considered for the poet laureateship.) There is no real explanation available of why this genius should have emerged in his highly successful bourgeois family. None of its members much resembled him. Only his sister Isabella, the deaconess, shared his social concerns and seemed able to relate to the poor with ease. As he remarked to her, "I preach Socialism, you practise it" (p. 559). Fortunately MacCarthy does not pursue the once-advanced unlikely theory that his almost incestuous affection for his sister Emma might have truncated his emotions. His celebration of love, of fellowship, is powerful and deeply moving, and is made profoundly poignant by his failure to achieve those ideals in actuality. With rare exception, his friends were those of his class. His dramatic gesture of marrying a working-class girl—great and strange beauty that she was, spotted by Rossetti as a "stunner"—had on the whole unhappy results, although he and Janey achieved a certain serenity at the end. So much of his writing dwelt on the failures of love.

Although extremely well-off by the standards of the day, the Morris here is more concerned about money matters than has been previously presented. His shaky health, and its effect on his personality, is also explored: he might have had a milder form of his daughter Jenny's epilepsy. Contrary to the Thompsonian view of politics as the way to integrate Morris, MacCarthy, in the postmodern fashion, appears to be comfortable with the divided Morris and, on the whole, is quite happy to celebrate all of his parts. At the same time she makes us vividly aware of what a high personal price Morris paid for his lack of integration. He shared, I believe, the common Victorian drive to find the "key to the mysteries," one explanation for the intensity with which he took up new activities. He was a figure of his age, no matter how much he hated it, how committed he was to remove its muddle. He would be a priest, he would be a writer, he would be an architect, he would be a painter, he would be a designer, he would be active in politics, he would be a printer. At the time of his death, he was chiefly remembered in the obituaries as a writer, and at the end of his life he had had a creative burst in a new form, his prose romances. His writings were his chief claim in his own day to his considerable popular fame; paradoxically it is probably that part of his life, followed by his politics, which is now largely confined to academic study, while many of his designs still flourish in the world at large.

He tried so many paths in his attempts to achieve unity. As a designer, his aim was to create a total environment. Along the way, he was one of the most important—perhaps the most important—founding figure in eliciting our concern for the natural and the built environments. Although she doesn't say so explicitly, and I might be quite wrong in my interpretation, MacCarthy in effect seems to suggest that the political period in the 1880s that others—but far from all—have seen as the culmination of his life, was a diversion ultimately to be regretted. There might have been a little more analysis of his political ideas, of the thinker whom E. P. Thompson has called the greatest theoretician of the alienation of labor. Yet she recognizes how strong his commitment to socialism was, calling it "the rebirth, the homecoming" and citing a line written in *The Pilgrims of Hope*: "I am born again tonight" (p. 467). He plunged into the "religion" of socialism as the necessary means to integrate life and art, to create an art that would enrich life for all. Although his physical state would not allow him to continue, and he had no doubt much disillusion with immediate political possibilities, the strength of his political vision made his life more coherent, and provided a hope for himself and others that there might be a happier world. His own words of commentary are powerfully quoted, yet his political perception seems somewhat muted in this account. Nevertheless, one could hardly hope to read a better telling of a most extraordinary life.

Two impressive figures, William Morris as subject and E. P. Thompson as author, are conjoined in the immense biographical-historical-critical study *William Morris: Romantic to Revolutionary*. Both figures have gained in interest since the first edition of the book was published in England in 1955. At that time, Morris's once great reputation was no longer what it was; he seemed to be receding into the haze of the nineteenth century as yet another eminent Victorian too remote to be relevant to our own concerns—no matter that Nikolaus Pevsner, as late as 1936, had placed him among the pioneers of modern design ("from William Morris to Walter Gropius"). As for Edward Thompson, he was an obscure young historian at the start of his career, writing from a Marxian point of view, no special advantage in 1955. Unpopular politics aside, the conjunction of unknown author and unfashionable subject would have been sufficient to explain why the book was virtually ignored by the literary establishment, and dropped, as Thompson remarks in this second edition, "into an accidental silence."

But times and circumstances change. We are in the midst now of what promises to be an enduring Morris revival; and the book that was ignored in 1955 has meanwhile become something of an underground classic—almost impossible to locate in secondhand bookstores, pored over in libraries, required reading for anyone interested in Morris and, increasingly, for anyone interested in one of the most important of contemporary British historians,

Since the publication in 1963 of Thompson's masterpiece, *The Making of the English Working Class*, his reputation has been growing, and was further enhanced with *Whigs and Hunters*, a study of the Black Act against poachers of 1723. His interests, as is often the case with historians, have been moving back in time, but the centerpiece of his accomplishments is still the study of the working class coming to consciousness of itself as a class at the end of the eighteenth century and the beginning of the nineteenth. Whatever faults one may find in his work, he has the distinguishing characteristic of a great historian: he has transformed the nature of the past. It will never look the same again; and whoever works in the area of his concerns in the future must come to terms with what Thompson has written.

So too with his study of William Morris. Morris is so protean a figure, so varied in his ambitions, talents and achievements, so un-flagging in his energies, that he is difficult to encompass. A force in the Victorian age, yes; but also an innovator, an influence, a revolutionary, a precursor of the age of the modern in art and politics. As much as anyone of his time, he was a latter-day version of the Renaissance man—a compliment he would not have valued, given his hatred of the Renaissance with its emphasis upon individual genius. And yet, how else to describe a man who tried his hand, often with remarkable success, at such an astonishing variety of endeavors?

He was a prolific poet (his greatest fame in his lifetime—and he might have succeeded Tennyson as poet laureate had he not been a socialist). He was also a translator of the Icelandic sagas; the author of several prose romances (*News from Nowhere* is properly counted one of the great Utopian novels); and the founder of Morris & Co., the firm of decorators whose influence continues to be felt up to this very day, in all of whose operations he took part, from the manufacture and design of fabrics to wallpapers to furniture to stained glass. He threw himself energetically into politics and the protection of ancient buildings; and, as the founder of the Kelmscott Press, into the revival of printing as a fine art.

What Morris was unprepared to recognize was that his was truly the exceptional case. And this would have been apparent to any discerning observer: it seems to have been something one felt even at a first meeting. The young Henry James, for example, who was taken to meet him in 1869 at his house (and shop) in Queen Square, Bloomsbury, was impressed "most agreeably," and afterwards wrote to his sister Alice in Cambridge, "He's an extraordinary example, in short, of a delicate sensitive genius and taste, served by a perfectly healthy body and temper."

The problem confronting any biographer or student of Morris in all his variety is to find some unifying principle, some cohering line throughout his life, or—to call upon Henry James for a phrase once again—"the figure in the carpet." Thompson's answer, and he argues for it most persuasively, is in Morris's politics: his progression from romantic to revolutionary, beginning under the influence of Keats and ending under the influence of Marx. Earlier writers, most notably R. Page Arnot, have pointed out that the political Morris was essential and must not be submerged in folds of Morris chintz.

The arts and crafts tradition, to which Morris contributed so much, is vitally important in the English past, and present, but it cannot be allowed to take him out of politics, any more than Pevsner's placing him among the forerunners of modernism, or the enthusiasts of fine printing who celebrate the achievements of the Kelmscott Press.

It has taken quite a while for the view of the political Morris to establish itself, and it is continually in danger of being vitiated by those who quite legitimately are more interested in the literary or the artistic Morris. Four years after the publication of the first edition of Thompson's study in London—and two years before it was belatedly published in America—a contributor to the catalogue of an important Morris show at Brown University allowed himself to suggest that Morris's "outmoded socialism" was of no interest, and irrelevant to a consideration of his major achievements. Not so: one may disagree with Morris's politics; I do not see how, after reading Thompson, one can deny their importance to him, in his own life, and hence, since he never attempted a separation of the two, in his work.

For some years now one has heard rumors that Thompson was dissatisfied with the first edition of the study, that he thought it too militant and was at work on a much milder version. With the second edition in hand, it is pleasant to discover that the rumors had no substance. Thompson is one of those rare, former Communists who, although they have left the party, have not felt called upon to renounce the idealistic motives that led them into it, and who have not felt it necessary to abandon their Marxist beliefs. This is fundamentally the same book that was published in 1955, with some of the more extravagant, hortatory, and conjectural sentences excised.

The picture of Morris that emerges here shows him to be more independent of Marx than may have been the case in the first edition—a parallel thinker, as it were, though less systematic, great in his own English pragmatic fashion, in his way indeed an English Marx. A postscript has been added—primarily to review the major literature on Morris over the past twenty years—in which Thompson reveals both his own independence and that of his subject: that Morris must be seen neither as a doctrinaire Marxist nor as a jolly, nonideological Englishman who happened to subscribe to a few Marxist ideas as a kind of window dressing.

But Thompson's greatest contribution, I believe, is to uncover the figure in the carpet. Even many of those who have recognized Morris's importance as a socialist have been content to show him as a fragmented personality, writing a poem one day, designing a tapestry the next, and preaching socialism the day after that, with no relation between. Thompson presents a much more integrated and much more powerful conception. In this respect I fear that his subtitle ("Romantic to Revolutionary") may do a disservice, being more euphonious than precise. Of course there was a progression in Morris's life, but what is striking is to learn how early he was "in revolt"—a posture he would maintain to the end—having committed himself to "Holy Warfare against the age" when he was still an undergraduate at Oxford.

The age in which Morris lived (rather like our own) was notable for its shoddiness, its hypocrisy, its selfishness, its ugliness, its vulgarity and divisiveness—"shoddy is king!"—the first rank flowering of industrialism, against which in their respective ways Dickens, Ruskin, and Carlyle would wage war also. In the beginning, to be "in revolt" for Morris was to seek out a private romantic escape—in poetry, in love, and in a not especially happy marriage to the exotically beautiful Jane Burden, whose face stares out from so many pre-Raphaelite portraits, and then, moving towards a wider vision of what life might be, in the creation of beautiful things at Morris & Co. He founded the firm in 1861, and it drew upon his energies for the next twenty years. But poetry, marriage, even the firm, did not answer to the needs of his vision: a better life, not only for himself and for those who could afford the productions of Morris & Co., but for all men and women. Politics, radical politics, running counter to the drives and aspirations of Victorian England, was the logical answer for the middle-aging genius who was still, and would always be, "in revolt."

Approximately two-thirds of Thompson's study is devoted to Morris's political career: a brilliant re-creation of left-wing politics in the late nineteenth century. Ironically, it might seem that of all his protean activities, politics was the least rewarding to Morris. In the short run there was a record of failure and disappointment. He broke with the Social Democratic Federation, two years after having joined it in 1883, because it was too concerned with parliamentary politics. He broke with his own creation, the Socialist League, because it was taken over by anarchists. In the end he was left with only his own local organization, the Hammersmith Socialist Society, meeting in his London house.

Even in the long run his political career might be judged a failure: all of these organizations were to be ancestors of the present-day Labour Party and the welfare state—the world of "demi-semi-socialism," where commercialism and statism and the values of the middle class still prevail. But the impulse to be "in revolt" continued to inspire Morris—as it had, in a sense, from the beginning—and informed whatever he would do, virtually to the day of his too early death in 1896, at the age of sixty-two.

In his politics, as Thompson remarks, "the long romantic breach between aspiration and action was healed." If his vision of a transformed society, creating not equality of opportunity but a society of equals, has yet to be realized, it is not an ignoble one. "We have to make up our minds about William Morris," Thompson writes in his postscript. His book is indispensable to the task, now and in the future.

9

THE LAST OF THE LETTERS

The year 1996 is the hundredth anniversary of the death of William Morris at the comparatively early age of 62. Various exhibitions and conferences will mark the year, but few events can be as notable as the completion of this edition of Morris's collected letters (Norman Kelvin, ed., *The Collected Letters of William Morris,* Volume III, 1889-1892; Volume IV, 1893-1896 [1996]). Although Norman Kelvin generously dedicates the final volume "To all who have participated in the making of this edition," it is he who did the work and deserves the credit, although no doubt he has been considerably aided by his assistant editor, Holly Harrison. The annotations are breathtaking in their thoroughness. There are numerous illustrations, reproduced in a serviceable way. It probably would have added too many pages to include a biographical appendix in each book rather than having to follow the cross-reference to the first mention of an individual, which may well be in one or another of the volumes.

This enterprise began publication in 1984 (the hundred and fiftieth anniversary of Morris's birth); the second volume, in two parts, appeared in 1987; and now we have the concluding two volumes. The first book covered 1848 to 1880, in 659 letters; the second, ending in 1888, included 1,104 letters; and now here are a further 924 letters, ending with a letter written on September 14, 1896, shortly before Morris's death on October 3. This last letter is to his beloved daughter Jenny and deserves to be quoted in full: "Dearest own Child, I wish my hand were not so pen feeble, & then I could write you a proper letter; but as it is I must ask you let this scrawl pass. I like your letters very much darling; please write me another, & pardon me if can't answer it, or only in this fashion. Your most loving father WM. I believe I am somewhat better." (IV, 391.) This

and the two previous letters in the collection, heartbreakingly brief
and written from his deathbed, are without annotation, other than
their sources. Morris's voice is alone at the end. But throughout
these volumes the extensive annotations will be of extraordinary help
to all those in the future who wish to discover more about one of the
greatest figures of the nineteenth century. Already the fruits of the
edition have been demonstrated in the use to which the first two volumes were put by Fiona MacCarthy in her recently published new
biography.

Although Morris is always himself and one has a sense of his personality in all his letters, many are quite often purpose driven; in
most cases they are specifically practical and not introspective. In
these concluding volumes comparatively few letters—even those to
one of his oldest friends, Philip Webb, addressed as "My dear Fellow"—have the emotional charge as those letters to Jenny. And even
in those the emotion is derived more from the situation than their actual content. Jenny, an epileptic, was leading the secluded life of an
invalid. Touchingly and gallantly, Morris attempted to bring the
world to her, to tell her of his doings. May, his other daughter, had
become his business and political partner. His correspondence with
her, and with his wife, Jane, tends to be rather dispassionate, barely
reflecting the personal drama that might have been swirling about
them. At this time, May was involved in some sense with George
Bernard Shaw, yet made an unwise marriage to H. Halliday Sparling.
Morris appears to have achieved a certain serenity with Jane, even
though her lover, Wilfrid Blunt, had present business dealings with
Morris, chronicled in the correspondence between them.

One doesn't quite know what the situation might have been in the
letters he wrote to his oldest friend, Edward Burne-Jones. He generally saw Burne-Jones weekly on Sundays so they may not have corresponded much; nevertheless, one fears that many splendid letters
were lost or destroyed. In these volumes, there are just a few sentences that survive for quotation. The record is better for Morris's
letters to his closest woman friend, Burne-Jones's wife, Georgiana.
Yet virtually all of the Burne-Jones letters come to us only through
quotations selected by their son-in-law, J. W. Mackail, for his life of
Morris (1899), or from the notebook he used when writing the life.

Morris was not a great letter writer, and made no claim to be so.
He wrote to move his various projects forward. "The fact is I don't
like writing letters. I could almost wish sometimes that the art of
writing had not been invented: at any rate I wish the postmen would

strike, on all grounds" (III, 107). And it must be said that in the years covered in these letters, or to put it another way, based on what he chooses to discuss in many of the letters, his life had become, comparatively, less interesting. He is still doing more than many others possibly could, but because of his declining health he can no longer do as much as he once did. Although his opinions have remained the same, his interests have shifted. The letters certainly provide evidence that there is a total personality here, and one does not have to consider the traditional claim that one part of Morris is more important than another. An important view, largely shaped by the two versions of the biography by E. P. Thompson (1955, 1977), presented politics as the shaping force, which I find highly persuasive. Fiona MacCarthy's biography is providing us, I believe, with a more postmodernist view of Morris, eschewing the need to choose among the aspects of a multiple Morris.

Yet perhaps because of the accidents of what letters have survived, the picture of Morris that emerges here puts greatest weight on his activities connected with the Kelmscott Press, and with his buying of early books and manuscripts. That conception is accurate in the sense that these were interests of his that came to the fore in the years since 1888. Particularly with the Kelmscott Press he was fulfilling the role that he had played earlier in so many aspects of design: he was pursuing his own vision at the same time that he would have an incalculable and considerable effect on the future of that particular world. One reads in a letter of November 21, 1889: "I really am thinking of turning printer myself in a small way; the first step to that would be getting a new fount cut" (III, 124). It is fascinating to see how he deals with all aspects of producing books, such as the choice of the ink, and of course the type. One quite intriguing series of letters are those he writes to the two young Birmingham artists A. J. Gaskin and C. M. Gere, about their illustrations for Kelmscott Press editions of two of Morris's prose romances. Both projects fail, despite the care with which he comments on their work, even though Gere had made perhaps the most famous single image associated with Morris—the frontispiece for the Kelmscott Press *News from Nowhere*—and Gaskin would go on to illustrate Spenser's *Shepheardes Calender* for the Press. Morris was both demanding and considerate, but ultimately it was only Burne-Jones who could achieve the combination of timelessness and medievalism that he wanted and with whom he could be in total rapport.

Although there is no question that his activities in other areas

took less of his time than they had in the past, they were still central
to him. There are fewer letters about his role as a designer and businessman, and this would appear to be an accurate reflection of the
situation. While he was designing intensely in all sorts of ways for
the Press, for the firm his output was much less, although, for instance, in 1892 he did both the Blackthorn and Bachelor's Button
designs. Younger figures, such as J. H. Dearle, were doing most of
the new designs. At the shop in Oxford Street he relied on the Smith
brothers, and he would go from time to time to the works at Merton. He would also visit clients when necessary. To judge on the basis of surviving letters, the heroic days of the design firm were over.

His career as a writer, however, still flourished but it was not the
subject of much correspondence. He is very active in producing the
Saga Library. It is also in this period that he wrote his single most
popular prose work, *News from Nowhere*. He commented: "It has
amused me very much writing it: but you may depend upon it, it
won't sell" (III, 218). In these years too he wrote his prose romances
that tend either to be deeply admired or comparatively ignored.
There is also the little comedy in which the politician James Bryce
sounds him out as a possible successor to Tennyson as poet laureate,
a fairly ludicrous idea for he was a republican who hated the Queen.

In his introductions, Kelvin makes an intriguing argument about
Morris's connection with early modernism, perhaps most particularly in the prose romances: that they claimed an autonomy for art
that made him more sympathetic, in effect if not in thought, than
one might have expected to the Aesthetic movement and to the writers at the end of the century. His design work, including examples
from the Press, was exhibited in Brussels in 1894, along with work
by Gauguin, Signac, Redon, and Renoir. As Nikolaus Pevsner argued
controversially years ago, Morris can be seen as a profound influence upon the modern. But Kelvin would put Morris more squarely
in the group considered central in this regard than has previously
been the case. The argument is well worth further consideration.

Where Kelvin is undoubtedly completely correct is that Morris's
purpose was to serve art. He was doing so in the most immediate
and practical sense as recorded in these letters about his work at the
Kelmscott Press, and in giving himself intense personal pleasure
through the acquisition of early books and manuscripts. Creating
new books and acquiring old satisfied his sense of the book or
manuscript as a "pocket cathedral," a total work of art. Even though
his energy was declining he had the genius and the wherewithal to

satisfy himself in these endeavors. At the same time, there are enough letters here to make it absolutely clear that he had not changed his mind at all in two further areas where he has such a considerable claim to be a great figure: the environment and politics.

His letters to newspapers are present here, and they rail against what he regards as the mistakes being made, not only that threaten buildings through possible destruction but even worse when such a death is via a misguided restoration that kills the spirit of a building. Particularly intriguing, as they circle back to his childhood, are his letters on behalf of Epping Forest in which he attacks the claims of so-called experts whom he generally sees as pursuing limited and perverted agendas. The "art" of the built and natural world is destroyed by vested interests. Even more explicitly, he feels the same about politics. He supports as strongly as he can in his language the progress of socialism and is always willing to help a comrade, though he is no longer willing to enter into the intricacies of sectarianism. "As soon as there are two parties in any body I am in—then out I go" (1:1, 239). His public speaking is vastly curtailed, and his political activism largely limited to the Hammersmith Socialist Society, located next door to his London house. Yet among the strongest statements found in these volumes are those in which he argues that a true art cannot be achieved until there is a total transformation of the political system and a true socialism has come about.

Such statements are to be found in the letters that he wrote for public consumption and also in private letters to strangers who would ask about his political position. They are parallel to his political essays, which I regard as some of the finest and most powerful writing of the nineteenth century. This is found in such letters as the one of March 16, 1889, sent to a meeting held to commemorate the Paris Commune, and published in the *Commonweal* in May, in which he reiterates his commitment to Communism while recognizing the difficulties of achieving that ideal society. He wrote of his vision to the *Daily Chronicle* in November, 1893, in support of a miners' strike: "When life is easier and fuller of pleasure, people will have time to look around them and find out what they desire in the matter of art, and will also have power to compass their desires" (IV, 104). For him, art was all-important, and it could not be achieved in its proper form without socialism. These letters present the glorious dailyness of his life, but particularly in the public letters, one is reminded of his sustaining vision. One is deeply grateful to Norman Kelvin for having made so much of William Morris available.

10

WILLIAM MORRIS AS BUSINESSMAN

Charles Harvey and Jon Press's *William Morris: Design and Enterprise in Victorian Britain* (1991) is quite a stunning book. Within a small compass, it takes Morris through his comparatively short life, a story that will not be new to those who have a general familiarity with Morris. But this study puts that story in quite a new context, one that has not been investigated so thoroughly, carefully, and imaginatively before: Morris as businessman/designer.

In the course of the book, the authors demolish two standard, and quite inaccurate, generalizations about Morris. First, that Morris was a bad businessman, but thanks to Warington Taylor, the manager of the firm until 1866 (who, it turns out, was less efficient than had been thought), and later George Wardle, he was financially successful. Morris is here shown strikingly shrewd and self-aware. The second generalization, that Morris's various activities had little to do with one another, has been dubious for some time, and was most notably corrected many years ago by E. P. Thompson (who is warmly acknowledged throughout this work). Those who found Morris's socialist, indeed Communist, politics distasteful claimed, if they liked his other activities, that his politics had little or nothing to do with his work as a poet or as a designer. Those who didn't like Morris in any form enjoyed accusing him of being a hypocrite: a successful Victorian businessman who did not allow his socialism to interfere with his profits or his activities in the workplace.

The William Morris who emerges in this study is more impressive and "integrated" than ever before. Yet he is far from a sentimental hero; he is, rather, a recognizable human being, with his share of unhappiness and faults. Harvey and Press do not present a radically new pattern for Morris's life, but they present much new material, splendidly handled, on his career as a businessman. Although Morris did not become politically active until the late 1870s, his conceptions of the role of art in society, and what was wrong with British society, were formed early on. First, a bit through the interests of his tutor between Marlborough and Oxford, the Revd. F. B. Guy, a member of the Oxford Society for the Study of Gothic Architecture; then during his time in Oxford, heavily under the influence of Ruskin; and through his brief experience working with the great Gothic Revival architect, G. E. Street.

What has not been presented so carefully and thoroughly before is the actual course of the business, illustrated with useful tables and charts. The firm was founded in 1861 with several partners, most notably Burne-Jones, Rossetti, and Ford Madox Brown. Morris was increasingly the dominant figure (and his mother supplied the largest part of the capital) and the partnership became more and more irksome. Harvey and Press provide a dispassionate account of the painful buying-out of the partners in 1875, not, as is customary, automatically denouncing Rossetti and Madox Brown, but recognizing how their fame and connections, as well as talents, helped launch the firm in its early years.

This study also discusses the ways in which the various activities of the firm intertwined. At the beginning, providing stained glass was its most important activity, profiting from the great increase in church building during the period. What the authors also make clear was that the firm was not alone, that others were also doing good work. But Morris's firm rapidly became a leader in the quality of its stained glass, and as it expanded its activities (though it was never a large operation) it was highly innovative in developing a house style and "look" that has maintained itself up to the present, although the firm itself came to an end in 1940. Its success was derived from Morris's "artistic knowledge and taste, on which the whole of my business depends." Harvey and Press also demonstrate yet again that Morris was not against the machine or against subcontracting, as long as quality was not compromised. He was always perfectly happy to delegate to others both within or outside the firm once he had solved a particular design problem, although he always maintained quality control. Indeed he could easily and rapidly turn from one problem to another. He would concentrate his considerable energies intensely on one question, then put it out of his mind once he had solved it to his satisfaction. This was one reason that he could do so much in so many mediums. Indeed, his ability to "alternate" was reflected in the patterns of his designs, his poetry, his politics, and his life.

Morris was driven by the wish to create beautiful objects. But he also was determined to live at the level to which he was accustomed by being a member of the upper middle class, a rich man, thanks to his father's shrewd investment in Devon Great Consols, a copper mine. The authors carefully plot the declining income from those shares (sold in 1877) and make clear that the reorganization of the firm was also driven by Morris's need to compensate for this "rentier" income, yet without compromising quality. The firm diversified its activities and in 1881 moved to Merton Abbey in order to acquire a larger workshop. Morris also recognized the necessity to cultivate rich clients and to exploit his "celebrity" status. Morris & Co. did not design for the multitude, and had only one London retail outlet, on Oxford Street, and later one in Manchester.

Harvey and Press have made brilliant use of what records survive—alas it does not seem possible to discover very much about the workers themselves. Morris was clearly an extremely "benevolent" yet traditional employer. As he recognized, the revolution would not have come any sooner if he acted differently. One wonders if the somewhat inexpensive "Sussex" rush-seated chairs were to be found in less affluent households. The authors do not speculate to any extent on what sort of influence the firm had on improving the look of the British world—was there a "trickle-down" effect?—although they do touch on Morris's role in the Arts and Crafts movement. He recognized that a fundamental political transformation was necessary in order to bring art to the people. This was a major impetus behind his growing political involvement. In the meantime there were genuine small-scale benefits from the making of an object and the enjoyment from it. The firm's expansion and moving to Merton Abbey paid off, and thereafter Morris had the time and money for intense political activity during the 1880s.

As in every life, its rhythms change, and Morris's last eight years were dominated by the "typographical adventure" of the Kelmscott Press. William Peterson's masterly Kelmscott bibliography and history (the latter appeared too recently to be used) make the chapter on the Press a less original contribution, but here too it is made clear what a good businessman Morris was, except for possibly underpricing the Chaucer. It was also characteristic that he worked out a financial scheme that was eminently fair, so that the Smith brothers who were the managers of the Oxford Street shop might acquire an interest in the design firm in such a way that was profitable to all concerned, and would provide Morris with enough capital to indulge his final passions: the purchasing of books and manuscripts and the Kelmscott Press. (Harvey and Press weren't able to find out much about the Smiths, although they suspect they may be related to George Wardle's wife, Madeleine Smith, the famous "Not Proven" alleged Edinburgh poisoner of 1857.)

One would not have thought that new material and insights would be readily available about William Morris. Yet through a thorough and imaginative investigation of his business history Harvey and Press have provided just that and have given us cause to admire William Morris even more.

11

WILLIAM MORRIS AND C. R. ASHBEE

In the 1880s there was an extraordinary amount of activity in the world of the Arts and Crafts—not only was the term itself coined late in the decade—in 1888 by Cobden-Sanderson—but in no previous decade, as far as I know, was so much happening that could be labeled "Arts and Crafts." I would like to consider some reasons why this movement came into being then. It seems to me that the standard historical how, although true, does not really tell us why that extraordinary flowering took place in the 1880s. There is the perfectly accurate intellectual pedigree that runs from Pugin to Carlyle and Ruskin and then to William Morris. There is no need to repeat the criticism they were making of their society; their appeal for change, their distress with the dominant trends of the nineteenth century. But why was it that in the 1880s so considerable a number of people decided to do something about those appeals? True, there had been such activities earlier, but there may be historical reasons why the 1880s were the time when they achieved a new intensity and level.

It is essential to pay attention to the political context of the times. In the present historical emphasis on social history it is too easy to underestimate or neglect the important shaping role of politics. Remembering its politics can help us to understand the decade, and may provide one explanation of the impetus for the growth of the Arts and Crafts movement. (Certainly it is a mistake to look at the Arts and Crafts period as solely an episode in the history of design.) In this, as in so many other ways, William Morris provides both a lead and an example.

Let us begin with him in 1876, getting out in good Liberal fashion to agitate under Gladstone's leadership over the Eastern Question.

He had not been politically active before, although he had expressed distress with the civilization that he saw about him where "shoddy is king." Like many of his countrymen Morris was caught up in Gladstone's generous sympathy for persecuted Christians in the Balkans, and his belief that foreign policy need not be exclusively self-serving. The agitation over the Eastern Question indicated to an even greater degree than had been true earlier in the century that there might be a division between Britain's interest in the world of real-politik and the more "moral," the more proper line for her to take. This sort of division between the proper and the profitable courses would plague Britain increasingly henceforward, as her unquestioned position of world dominance came to be rivaled by other, newer, world powers, notably Germany and the United States. It is not surprising that those countries should be threatening in terms of the machine—the great farm machines that were making American wheat so cheap; and the machines and techniques that were becoming threats to Britain from German manufacture. Gladstone was taking a moral position on the Eastern Question, which appealed to Morris, and although he would shortly turn upon the Liberal leader, he continued to share with him a very similar sort of moral fervor.

The economic difficulties that Britain was experiencing in this period, the political difficulties of Gladstone's second ministry, the expansion of the electorate by the Third Reform Act of 1884, profoundly affected the nature of British politics and society. In some cases, both British design and politics were under pressure to become more "popular." Also the new voters in the land would eventually lead to a radical shift in the nature of politics.

What I find so intriguing is the parallel between the activities of William Morris—the crescendo that marked his own career both in decorating and in politics, and also marked his influence upon others—and the growing complexity of the general political situation. At the same time that he was giving more and more political talks his firm had become increasingly active, dating from its reorganization as Morris and Co. in 1875. In 1877 he began tapestry weaving. In 1879 he started weaving carpets and rugs. In 1888 he opened the works at Abbey. As the distinguished historian R. C. K. Ensor has written of Morris: "It must not be supposed that at any time he supplied any large part of the general market . . . [but] his example began to influence the firms which did, and a gradual rebirth of design resulted. On the taste of the upper classes he acted as a strong purgative. No one so effectively disillusioned the Victorians of their blind enthusiasm for machine products."[1] To an extent, because of Morris's own activities, but also for similar reasons that motivated Morris as well, British society was moving into a period of self-doubt, The doctrine of "more is better" was being questioned. It is hardly surprising that small crusading organizations should be formed in the 1880s which hoped through example and precept to work some change upon their society, both of a political and artistic nature.

The Arts and Crafts movement certainly fits into that mould. It had both an immediate purpose—the making of beautiful objects, but also a message of how life should be lived, a lesson of scale and size which is particularly attractive today. It is impressive how many of the major figures of the movement were "philosphers" later in their careers—Mackmurdo, Ashbee, Voysey—but that frequently their philosophical flights were rather woolly-minded, while their objects were wonderfully solid. Morris, almost alone, to my mind, seemed capable of combining both thought and practice in a realistic way and of course many considered him, and some still do (although fewer than used to) wildly impractical in his political thought.

But what was the more specific background of the 1880s, which made its influence felt upon Morris and his disciples, perhaps even more than they consciously realized? There is in the decade a juxtaposition of dates of the protests against capitalism and, it could also be said, against the machine—both on the political side, and the artistic. The Century Guild was founded in 1882, the Art Workers' Guild in 1884, the Arts and Crafts Exhibition Society and the Guild of Handicraft in 1888. On the political side there are the traditional dates in the growth of the Labour movement: the Democratic Federation in 1881; the Fabian Society formed in 1884; "Bloody Sunday" on November 13, 1887; the match-girls strike of 1888; the Great Dock Strike of 1889; the foundation of the Independent Labour Party in 1893. There is a significant increase in the degree of the workers' self-consciousness, a feeling on their part of being embattled—as indeed they were with the worsening economic situation of the 1880s—and this feeling was reflected in the doubling of the membership of the unions between 1888 and 1892. As was not surprising in a mature industrial society, its members were becoming more self-aware, and reflective about the industrial process. This attitude can be clearly discerned in both the Labour movement and that of the Arts and Crafts.

---

[1] R. C. K. Ensor, *England 1870-1914* (1936), p. 155.

But are these connections of accident—nice coincidences that in fact have very little significance—or are they connections of substance? Do they arise out of the same causes, and do they share similar purposes? In many ways there are resemblances between the two movements, and some of the same people were involved with both: Walter Crane, Emery Walker, and Philip Webb followed Morris politically and artistically. C. R. Ashbee called himself a socialist: but if he were so it was in a fairly superficial sense. It would be intriguing to discover, if possible, the politics of the Arts and Crafts workers, in contrast to their leaders. Some of Morris's workers followed him into radical politics but that may have been from unconscious employer pressure. As the great literary innovators of our own century have demonstrated, radicalism in one sphere does not necessitate radicalism in another. Nevertheless, major changes generally have common historical roots. Both the practitioners of the Arts and Crafts and the socialists felt they could achieve a new life, as suggested by Stephen Yeo in a very interesting article on the religion of socialism in Britain, in *History Workshop,* at least on the political side,[2] and also in the intriguing short book by Sheila Rowbotham and Jeffrey Weeks, *Socialism and the New Life: The Personal and Sexual Politics of Edward Carpenter and Havelock Ellis* (1977). Morris believed that the two worlds were inextricably intertwined. But as Sheila Rowbotham points out about Ashbee, and this would be true of so many practitioners of the Arts and Crafts, they might see their activities in the world of art as making it unnecessary for them to function in the world of politics.[3] A beautiful object might serve the purpose of helping to make a better, new life and thus obviate the need for political action.

But what was it about the 1880s which led to such a ferment of activity—political or artistic and, in some cases, both? In part, it was because of the growth of historicism: a conception of a society which grew and then declined, rather than experienced continual progress. It was no longer at all clear that the God-given intent of the British Empire was that it became more and more powerful. It is significant that it is in this period that the professional study of the past should receive a great impetus—suggesting that there was both rise and decline in the history of society, and that the present high bourgeois

---

[2] Stephen Yeo, "A New Life: The Religion of Socialism in Britain, 1883-1896," *History Workshop,* No.4 (Autumn 1977), 5-56.
[3] Sheila Rowbotham, "In Search of Carpenter," *History Workshop,* No.3 (Spring 1977), 121-33.

achievements of nineteenth-century Britain might not, perhaps should not, last forever. As the material achievements of the Victorian age were being questioned, it was hardly surprising that its artistic manifestations should be regarded with a similarly critical eye.

The first half of the decade of the 1880s was also marked by a growth in radicalism and socialism, when it seemed that they might cooperate, and when the appeal of Joseph Chamberlain was considerable. And Chamberlain might well have continued to attract left-wing voters if he had not broken with the Liberal Party over the issue of Ireland.

Indeed, Ireland cannot be neglected in attempting to assess the historical background of the Arts and Crafts movement. A great consciousness of Ireland and its culture helped to create an atmosphere sympathetic to Arts and Crafts, a sense of a more 'primitive' and Celtic culture—this was a period when increasing attention was being paid to older cultures. And there is no doubt that more heed was given to these cultures because of their growing influence upon the British political scene. It was largely questions of Ireland which brought about the disintegration of the gentlemanly code of politics which had dominated Britain at mid-century. Those who supported the justice of the Irish cause were led to doubt the sanctities of land law, to see that there might be something beyond the sacred right of contract, the pieties of the bourgeois world. Thus, the introduction of the Irish Coercion Bill of 1881 extinguished in Morris his support of Liberalism. Morris was further alienated from Liberalism by the bombing of Alexandria in 1881 and at that point he turned from Gladstone. Perhaps Morris did not sufficiently appreciate how much the coercion of Ireland and the expansion of imperial obligations distressed Gladstone himself, but Morris saw that Gladstone was not sufficiently distressed to leave his party. If the leader of the Liberal Party himself could not prevent such coercive measures, then the traditional parties were caught in the country's imperial obligations. To avoid such actions, society would have to become quite different.

Socialism and anti-imperialism are not necessary accompaniments of the Arts and Crafts world. But there is an emotional similarity—a picture of the right sort of society which both hold. The Arts and Crafts movement shared with others in the 1880s a discontent with present society, most particularly its methods of manufacture. Arts and Crafts, the trade union movement, the socialist movement were all intimately concerned with the condition of the people, both emotionally and materially. As one recent commentator on Morris has remarked, and her comment could apply equally to the political and artistic situation: "Men had become unnaturally separated from the sources and ends of their productivity, and all the daily expressions of life revealed a reductive, mechanical tension between toil and weary idleness, rather than a life-giving alternation between useful work and refreshing leisure."[4] The nature of work was at the center of these movements' concerns, and where Morris's Marxism was particularly justified. Alienation from work was the problem which the growing Socialist movement and the Arts and Crafts movement were both attempting to resolve. The Arts and Crafts movement tended to see the solution in terms of small groups and individual endeavor, and to look at the machine with a too prejudiced eye. It was one of Ashbee's considerable accomplishments that he was able to approach the machine in a far friendlier fashion than many others could. Morris did not worry overmuch about the place where the work was done (he treated his workers well, although their work itself may have been more boring than it should have been) because he felt that it would require a revolution to change such basic arrangements. But obviously his concern about the workers was one of his chief motivations, and that would be true of Ashbee as well. As Alan Crawford has written, Ashbee "was both a designer and social reformer, a maker of beautiful things and a moulder of better lives."[5] And so, in the 1880s, very similar if not exactly the same motives led intelligent men and women to question British policy in Ireland and Egypt and led some, if they had the requisite talents, into the Arts and Crafts movement.

C. R. Ashbee does, I think, provide a clear example of the similarity of impulses that made both a social and artistic reformer. John Fleming and Hugh Honour, in their *Penguin Dictionary of Decorative Arts*, in perhaps too sweeping a statement in their entry under Arts and Crafts, define it as "An attempt to revive handicrafts and improve standards of decorative design in late Victorian England, inspired by the teaching of William Morris and Ruskin. Its main organiser was C. R. Ashbee."[6]

---

[4] Barbara J. Bono, "The Prose Fictions of William Morris: A Study in the Literary Aesthetic of a Victorian Social Reformer," *Victorian Poetry*, XIII (Fall-Winter 1975), 45.
[5] Alan Crawford, "Introduction to C. R. Ashbee," in *Modern English Silverwork* (1974), p. vii. (First published 1909.)
[6] John Fleming and Hugh Honour, *The Penguin Dictionary of Decorative Arts* (1977), p. 41.

With Ashbee one has a firm sense of the context of ideas of the 1880s—of which Morris was so important a part—out of which the richest flowering of the Arts and Crafts movement took place. As Hermann Muthesius has written: "Morris was a pioneer in all areas which he incorporated into his activities. He laid the groundwork for the development which all branches of the new art movement experienced later. . . . The [arts and crafts] community was numerous enough in the first half of the eighties to form a society: the Art Workers' Guild from whose midst, since 1888, originated the series of famous Arts and Crafts Exhibitions in the New Gallery in Regent Street. . . as first historical witnesses [they] announced to the world the news of the new art that had quietly matured and now stepped from the public as a fait accompli. . . . A young generation now stood upon Morris's shoulders . . . they were the representatives of a truly original application of the arts that had developed in the twenty-five years of Morris's activity."[7] Ashbee was certainly one of those who was happy to stand on Morris's shoulders.

C. R. Ashbee was born in 1863 into a rich, cultivated, and curious home. His mother was a member of a prominent German-Jewish Hamburg mercantile family; and Charles's vacations in Hamburg, the painting lessons he took there, and his impression of small-scale yet important mercantile efforts, were significant influences on his later career. His father, H. S. Ashbee, had been a commercial traveler, descended from sound Kentish yeoman stock. Shortly after his marriage he established an independent office in London under his father-in-law's name. This rapidly became an extensive export business of its own, with branches in Manchester, Sheffield, and Bradford and, somewhat later, in Paris and Berlin. Ashbee exported machinery and goods to Europe and South America. One of his specialties was Sheffield ware, which makes his son's later disapproval of such cutlery yet another example of the contrast between father and son.

Fortunes could be made quickly in Victorian England. Ashbee senior prospered and was able to indulge himself in bookish interests. He amassed the largest Cervantes collection outside Spain. More unusually he also formed one of the great collections of obscene books, for which, under the name of Pisanus Fraxi, he wrote what was probably the most important bibliography of pornography

---

[7] Hermann Muthesius, *Das Englische Haus* (1908), vol. 1, p.98. Translated by Susan Bell.

in the nineteenth century, *Notes on Curious and Uncommon Books*, with copious extracts from the erotic works described, in three volumes. His marriage was apparently a happy one in its early years. But it steadily worsened; and he and his wife separated in the 1890s.

Despite his own bookish, if somewhat unusual, interests, H. S. Ashbee wanted his son to follow him in business. This meant that he should have no more than the conventional education—of the best sort—for a businessman of the day. A good public school (Wellington) and then into business. It was over this issue that father and son came to a parting of the ways, as Charles indicated he did not wish to go into a commercial career. At first he considered publishing; and he and his mother visited various publishers, including the family friend, Charles Kegan Paul. Perhaps on his advice Ashbee applied to King's College, Cambridge. His father gave him a thousand pounds towards his education but apparently that was the limit of his support. They were still comparatively friendly but relations strained as Charles took his mother's side in the separation and he was disinherited when his father died in 1900.

Going to Cambridge was undoubtedly very important in the shaping of his life, less for academic reasons than for the friends he made. His two greatest friends there were important ancestor figures in the history of Bloomsbury, one slightly senior to him—Goldsworthy Lowes Dickinson—the other slightly junior—Roger Fry.

Of course, every period has its innovators but I believe it is rather striking that Ashbee, Fry, and Lowes Dickinson should have been great friends—the latter two, like Ashbee, also being pioneers—the one changing art criticism and the other, one of the shapers of the idea of the League of Nations. Finding the present world unsatisfactory and redoing it is a common pursuit—particularly in the hopes of the young—but I feel there are similarities in the basic assumptions of simplifying, getting to the roots, rejecting received opinions, looking for similarities in social and artistic worlds, that characterized the new thought of the 1880s. The heart of Ashbee's undergraduate experience was intense discussion with these young men about the nature and purpose of life—a discussion which Ashbee continued with a varying cast of characters until he died. In fact, it might be said that he never outgrew his undergraduate experience. Ashbee's strength is that he was not afraid to tackle basic issues, and he believed in his capacity to do almost anything. That sort of intense enthusiasm is highly desirable of undergraduate education. But there comes a time when such enthusiasm should be more sharply focused and in Ashbee's case it frequently was not, making much of his extensive writing, both published and unpublished, somewhat soft-minded and wandering.

In his early years he thought his activities could help save the world. Cambridge and his friends worked their spell upon him. Perhaps the most important influence was a visit to Cambridge of Edward Carpenter, a prophet of the period, whom Ashbee had already met, and who preached a form of small group socialism and homosexuality that was congenial to Ashbee even though he was to marry, in 1898, and subsequently fathered four daughters. As he recorded in his diary at the time of Carpenter's visit: "He unfolded to me a wonderful idea of his of a new freemasonry, a comradeship in the life of men which might be based on our Cambridge circle of friendships. Are we to be the nucleus out of which the New Society is organized?"[8] This visit was on 20 July 1886 when Ashbee was coming to the end of his stay at Cambridge and was wondering what to do next with his life.

It was through Carpenter that Ashbee was to meet William Morris, a good deal more imposing and tough-minded figure, who would supplement Carpenter as an influence. Or rather, Ashbee's activities would be an ultimately unsuccessful attempt to combine the influence of Carpenter and Morris. At the end of 1885 Carpenter mentioned to Ashbee that he would be lecturing to the Socialist League on the subject of private property at the small lecture room attached to Morris's Kelmscott House in Hammersmith and he and Dickinson attended. After the lecture, which was delivered at one of the regular Sunday night meetings at Hammersmith, Carpenter presented Ashbee and Dickinson to Morris, who invited them to join the dinner which always took place after the talk. Ashbee has recorded the episode in his unpublished Memoirs. Dickinson and Morris had discussed first principles of socialism, and the two young men were to experience Morris at his most vehement: "'The thing is this; if we had our revolution tomorrow, what should we socialists do the day after?' 'Yes—what?' we all cried. And that he could not answer. 'We should all be hanged, because we are promising the people more than we can ever give them!'"[9] The dinner was over at midnight, but then Dickinson and Ashbee took the long walk back to Tottenham Court Road with Bernard Shaw, continuing the conversation. Shaw

---

[8] C. R. Ashbee, *Journal*, July 1886; Ashbee Papers, King's College, Cambridge.

[9] C. R. Ashbee, *Memoirs*; Victoria & Albert Museum, vol. 1, pp. 19-20. (Written between 1938-40; based on his journals of the time.)

also felt that if the revolution came, all the leaders of it would be killed by their followers. "We shall have conjured up such a power that in seeking to guide it we shall be swallowed up ourselves."[10] Ashbee heard Morris lecture again six months later at the Fabian Society, when he was again down from Cambridge—in fact his college career was over. This time he heard Morris on the Aims of Art and recorded his impression in his *Journal*: "Grand old Morris in his peacock blue shirt as bluff and as powerful as ever. I have a lurking belief that his indictment of modern Art is true."[11] It was a powerful lecture, arguing persuasively for the need for pleasure in all work, whether artistic or otherwise. Morris stated that the need for man was to control the machine rather than the other way round, and he pointed out the connection, as he saw it, between industrial slavery, commercial slavery, and the degradation of the arts. Morris's aim was to abolish the curse of labor, both in manufacturing and in the world of art. As he concluded his lecture: "Everywhere—in State, in Church, in the household—we must be resolute to endure no tyranny, accept no lie, quail before no fear, although they may come before us disguised as piety, duty, or affection, as useful opportunity and good-nature, as prudence or kindness. The world's roughness, falseness, and injustice will bring about their natural consequences; but since we inherit also the consciousness of old resistance to those curses, let us look to it to have our fair share of that inheritance also which, if nothing else come of it, will at least bring to us courage and hope, that is, eager life while we live, which is above all the Aim of Art."[12]

Ashbee's wish then was to become an architect and he would indeed achieve a certain distinction in this field.[13] He apprenticed himself to G. F. Bodley, an eminent architect of the time, and took up residence in Toynbee Hall, the first Settlement house in the East End of London. Idealistic university men tended to live there, to be close to the poor whom they tried to assist, while pursuing careers of their own as well. (Some years later being at Toynbee Hall would form an important part of C. R. Attlee's conversion to socialism.) Ashbee began holding classes on Ruskin and gave lectures on his work and related topics at Toynbee Hall and elsewhere.

---

[10] Ibid.
[11] Ibid., p.24.
[12] William Morris, *Collected Works* (1915), vol. XXIII, pp. 96-97.
[13] Alan Crawford, "Ten Letters from Frank Lloyd Wright to Charles Robert Ashbee," *Architectural History*, XIII (1970), 73-76, lists Ashbee's architectural accomplishment.

Ashbee's experience at Toynbee Hall and his direct observation of the poor and their intense economic distress made him feel a need to do something. He was inspired to form a Guild of Handicraft, which would manufacture goods in some sort of cooperative scheme, and a School of Handicraft which would train men and boys from the East End as artisans, thus fulfilling some of the purposes of the settlement house. He saw himself as practicing the role of the artist-craftsman in a way envisioned by Morris and he sought his blessing.

Morris himself had profound doubts of the efficacy of such organizations. He was at his most political during the 1880s and a committed Marxist socialist; he believed the changes needed in society were much more sweeping than could be brought into being by such organizations. He did not regard his own firm as a serious vehicle of social change; it had been formed before his political ideas were so important in his life. Morris did not worry overmuch about the contradictions between his life as a businessman and as a socialist because he did not believe anything so small as one business could either bring about or delay changes that he regarded as so highly desirable and inevitable.

But as a designer who ran a firm, as a social thinker, and as a man who was regarded as a sage, he could not avoid being sought after for advice, and to have his example taken, as it was by Ashbee and others, as a shining one to be imitated. Morris did not encourage this adulation. He informed those who were seeking his advice that their activities were too small-scale to make any difference. Ashbee went to see him on 3 December 1887 and wrote of the interview: "William Morris and a great deal of cold water! Spent last evening with him by appointment—à propos of 'Art Schools.' He says it is useless, and that I am about to do a thing with no basis to do it on. I anticipated all he said to me. If I could draw him it would be thus—a great soul rushing through space with a halo of glory around him . . . I could not exchange a single argument with him till I granted his whole position as a socialist and then said: 'Look, you, I am going to forge a weapon for you;—and thus I too work with you in the overthrow of Society.' To which he replied, 'The weapon is too small to be of value.' How hard it is for a great mind to set itself to see the simple point of a lesser. Were men of his metal, we should need no weapons."[14]

---

[14] C. R. Ashbee. *Memoirs*; Victoria & Albert Museum, Vol. 1, p. 45. In the manuscript version at King's College, Cambridge, such a drawing of Morris by Ashbee can be found.

Ashbee did not allow himself to be deterred by Morris. In June 1888 he established his Guild and School, which remained at Toynbee Hall until 1891 when Ashbee moved them to the eighteenth-century Essex House, also in the East End of London. By that time the School was already in a precarious financial position, which steadily worsened, and it ceased operation in 1895. But the Guild itself flourished and produced and sold a wide range of artifacts, mostly designed by Ashbee, among them works in wood and various metals, most notably silver.

The Guild, which Ashbee regarded as "a protest against modern business methods, against the Trade point of view, against the Commercial spirit,"[15] functioned on cooperative principles, although it seems clear that Ashbee himself dominated it. It prospered in its early years, in large part because it could make goods on commission, often extremely handsome, of comparative simplicity, in a sort of restrained art nouveau style—which Ashbee thought he hated. When times were slack, the Guildsmen, being in London, could work elsewhere. It was Ashbee's view that the Guild owed its origin to the socialist movement, the movement for technical education, and to the revival of English decorative art that had been sparked by Morris and Co. But in spite of the Guild's initial success, Ashbee wished to improve it, and the way he chose to do so turned out to be a crucial factor in its downfall. He believed that it should move to the country. London was becoming filthier, the country always had a strong attraction—it was also the influence of Carpenter, and that Morris's factory was in the country, though very close to London. In 1902 the Guild, on a divided vote, decided to move to Chipping Campden in Gloucestershire, and a group of about fifty guildsmen, and a further hundred of their families, made about a ten percent unwelcome increase in the population of Chipping Campden. They did not all stay; indeed quite a few members did not come at all.

Ashbee did practice profit-sharing, and saw the Guild, at least in early years, as a move against capitalism. The Guild also shared with other movements of the period the need to recapture the past through songs and drama, and at Chipping Campden, through returning to the land it also partook in the antiurbanism that was such an important force at the end of the nineteenth century. "The exodus to Campden in a sense was Ashbee's masterpiece, the perfect culmi-

[15] C. R. Ashbee, *An Endeavour Toward the Teaching of John Ruskin and William Morris* (1901), p. 20.

nation of the Guild Idea . . . Campden was a place of exceptional beauty, very English in its character, with its great church tower and its gently sweeping High Street. It seemed to be the absolute antithesis to Whitechapel: ideal socialist dream city, Ashbee's City of the Sun."[16]

Even though the Guild had a showroom in London, the distance from the capital and the added expense of transport, combined with a recession in trade, put the Guild into continual financial jeopardy and in 1908 it was forced to dissolve. Many of the Guildsmen, including Ashbee, remained in the area, assisted by the American philanthropist, Joseph Fels of Fels Naptha soap, who bought some land for the surviving Guildsmen so that they could combine their dream of living off the land while pursuing their decorative art. Ashbee himself remained in the Cotswolds until 1917. He restored quite a few of the local houses, and the preservation of the charm of the town owes a considerable amount to him. But his Arts and Crafts dream was over; he had a further period of prominence as the city planner for Jerusalem from 1918 to 1922; he then retired, moved to his wife's house near Sevenoaks in Kent, where he lived until his death in 1942.

The Arts and Crafts movement must be seen not in isolation but as part of the late nineteenth century questioning of the values that had shaped that century. The central role of William Morris does not mean that every socialist has also to be a believer in the Arts and Crafts. But there are, I believe, important similarities between the two movements, both coming into prominence in the same years. Far more than the traditional politicians and artists of their period, both socialists and practitioners of the Arts and Crafts wished to create a new design for life.

---

[16] Fiona MacCarthy, "C. R. Ashbee and the Guild Idea," in Alan Crawford and Fiona MacCarthy, *C. R. Ashbee & the Guild of Handicraft* (1981), p. 10. See also Fiona MacCarthy, *The Simple Life: C. R. Ashbee in the Cotswolds* (1981), and Jan Marsh, *Back to the Land: The Pastoral Impulse in Victorian England from 1880 to 1914* (1982).

12

MARTIN CONWAY

The history of the foundation in 1888 of the National Association for the Advancement of Art and its Application to Industry brings together in curious conjunction certain public-spirited, philanthropic, art-loving citizens of Liverpool, an ambitious young art historian who was briefly in residence there, an impressive number of leading figures in the British art "establishment" of the period, and trailing in the rear, some obscure, not to say invisible, industrialists and manufacturers who were meant, in theory anyway, to be the chief beneficiaries of the Association.

At the outset one should note that the 1880s in Britain were marked generally by efforts to adapt to new needs and aspirations. Such efforts were most conspicuous, perhaps, in politics, where the Liberal and Tory parties were attempting to come to terms with the implications of the Third Reform Act of 1884, and radical political groups were growing more active. But there was a comparable striving in the arts, along a line ranging from the most rarefied and theoretical down to the most immediate and practical. The National Association for the Advancement of Art and its Application to Industry was one such attempt, an ambitious and intriguing scheme that takes its place—if only for a brief time—within the movement to bring the world of art, particularly "practical" art, into a more integrated relation with industrial and domestic design, and so become a more viable part of British society.

The central figure in the movement, of course, was William Morris, poet, artist, businessman, Marxist Socialist, who by the 1880s was convinced that neither traditional politics and art, nor the traditional separation of art and politics, would answer the needs of the age. The National Association was only one of the organizations formed in the 1880s that owed a great deal to his inspiration, and to his belief in the importance of the social role of art. Among the more notable were the Century Guild, begun in 1882, in which the chief figure was A. H. Mackmurdo; the Art-Workers' Guild (1884) and its offspring, founded in 1888, the Arts and Crafts Exhibition Society (for which the enduring, pervasive term "Arts and Crafts" was coined by T. J. Cobden-Sanderson); and the Guild of Handicraft, founded by C. R. Ashbee in the same year. Only the Art-Workers' Guild still survives, and the shortest life—a mere four years—was that of the National Association.

Yet in theory at least it was the most ambitious of them all, having modeled itself on the British Association for the Advancement of Science. Like its model, it planned to hold a large annual meeting in a provincial city, which would focus the attention of the country upon the latest developments in the application of art to industry. In essence, this was not a new idea. The relation of the fine and the practical arts suggested by the Association's name had been a concern in Britain—not least in Liverpool—throughout much of the century. The British had felt, and continued to feel, that their design, beginning with common objects of manufacture, was on a lower level than that being produced on the Continent, and somehow must be improved. A legitimate, even admirable concern; but it also proved to be one of those issues which inspire the British to form organizations and institutions to deal with them, and then, as if by instinct, to endow them with class connotations. Although Britain achieved its commanding position in the world thanks to its prodigious development following upon the industrial revolution, trade and industry have always had a difficult time in being accepted socially. Similarly, between design and industry there has always been an uneasiness in the relationship of the craftsman to the artist. If the National Association had fulfilled the name announced in its title, it would have struck the ideal balance, but in the working out—the inevitable consequence of the procedures and machinations that brought it into being—balance was the first casualty. The scales were weighted precisely as one might have predicted, with the result that the Association had no real reason for existing; the surprising thing is not that its life was so brief, but that it should have lived as long as it did. Its success might have been inspiring; its failure is instructive.

I

An odd combination of circumstances was responsible for the existence of the National Association. Liverpool in the later years of the nineteenth century had been enjoying something of a cultural flowering, thanks to the generosity of certain of the great local mercantile families, among them the Walkers and the Rathbones. Thus, in 1872 the Walkers had endowed the Art Gallery that bears their name and was presently to become one of the most distinguished museums in the country. Six years later, at a public meeting in which the Rathbones prominently figured, a resolution was passed that there should be created an institution "to provide such instruction in all branches of liberal education . . . [and] to give such technical instruction as would be of immediate service in professional and commercial life."[1] It was this sort of interest in the practical dissemination of knowledge that in due course would lead the civic worthies of Liverpool to support the Association. The Rathbones, especially William, the head of the family, played leading roles in the founding of the college that was the logical, practical sequel to the resolution. Money was raised and in 1881 Gerald Rendall was appointed Principal; in January 1882 the institution opened as a University College; two years later it was made a component of Victoria University, centered in Manchester. In October 1903 it achieved independent status as the University of Liverpool.

It was the college that brought William Martin Conway to Liverpool, and it was Conway, in rather a umbrageous relationship with Philip Rathbone, the youngest brother of William and chairman of the Walker Gallery from 1886 until his death in 1895, who was a prime mover in the founding of the National Association. Conway is an intriguing and perhaps characteristic figure of late-Victorian England, a man of intelligence, power, charm, and many gifts, none of which he seems ever to have fully realized, except perhaps for his pronounced gift for self-advancement. In his time he was well known as the author of many books on art and on mountaineering. Perhaps his greatest contribution to the world of art was his early belief in its usefulness of photographs for comparative study, and his formation of a vast collection of more than 100,000 photographs of paintings, which he gave to the Courtauld Institute. In 1895 he was knighted, ostensibly for his mountaineering feats, but in fact to help him in his

---

[1] *University College and the University of Liverpool, 1882-1903* (1907), pp. 4-5.

attempt—unsuccessful, as it turned out—to win a parliamentary seat at Bath for the Liberals. He did hold, as a Unionist, the Combined Universities seat from 1918 to 1931, and in that year he was created Baron Conway of Allington. He died in 1937. Although he "had willingly accepted [the creed he had first learned at Cambridge] that the pursuit of historical truth for its own sake was a sufficient purpose in life; and had unconsciously assumed, with all Cambridge and most of England, that achievement was to be measured by the estimation of one's peers and not in terms of money,"[2] he never had quite the means to support his way of life, which was not austere, and had to rely on his wealthy American wife, Katrina Lambard, and her stepfather, Manton Marble, figures from the world of Henry James. Conway was on very close terms with Marble, and it was he who pushed him toward a quest for money and success, both of which he achieved, as the world, if not Cambridge, measures such things.

Conway was born in 1856, the son of a well-known churchman, William Conway, a canon of Westminster Abbey. He attended Repton, and then, after some unpleasantness about the question of whether he had cheated on his entrance examination, Trinity College, Cambridge. His Cambridge associations were to be crucial, particularly the example of Henry Bradshaw, the librarian of the university, a scholar of small production but great influence who persuaded Conway to favor serious scholarship rather than "appreciation." Yet another influence upon him was John Ruskin, both in turning his interests toward art, and toward the Alps, though it must be said that even in the latter respect there was a slight sense of his never quite achieving the heights of his pursuit; he was "a mountaineer who preferred the passes to peaks."[3]

In 1882 Conway had met Gerald Rendall at Trinity, who urged him to put in for a chair of Fine Arts at the new college that Rendall was to head in Liverpool. In May he presented an impressive batch of testimonials by such eminent Cambridge figures as Sidney Colvin, Henry Bradshaw, Charles Waldstein, and Oscar Browning, but it was decided to make no appointment at that time. Conway, however, was sufficiently inspired to continue to prepare himself for the post, whenever it might become available, and gave a number of lectures on art under the auspices of the Cambridge University Extension movement.

---

[2] Joan Evans, *The Conways: A History of Three Generations* (1966), p. 87.
[3] *The Concise Dictionary of National Biography, 1900-1950* (1961), p. 96.

The next year he came to Liverpool to deliver a lecture, and it was then that he became acquainted with members of the Rathbone family. William, the head of the family, had, as we have seen, played an active role in the founding of the college. He had insisted that religious questions not enter into appointments, and the money that had been raised (much of it his) be used first for the hiring of professors, with an emphasis upon youth, before being spent on buildings. (The college in fact opened in a disused lunatic asylum.) He and his two brothers gave the money for the King Alfred Chair of Modern Literature and English Language; three other businessmen endowed the Gladstone Chair of Greek; and Lord Derby, a Chair of Natural History along with other professorships. There was also some money for a Roscoe Chair of Art from admirers of the early nineteenth-century Liverpool figure, William Roscoe, who, unsuccessful as a banker, was also a poet and a botanist, but is best remembered as a historian of the Renaissance. At first the money was used to provide occasional lectures on the arts, but in 1885 it was decided to use it to establish a Chair of Art. Early in 1885, Rendall wrote to Conway with advance information on the chair; on 25 March the registrar made the formal offer to him of the Roscoe Professorship, with five years' tenure, for £375 per year, plus two-thirds of any fees, with a minimum guaranteed of £400. Residence in Liverpool was required, but Conway secured the right to travel abroad in the spring term in order to see the great European works of art.[4]

Early on, Conway recognized the importance of Philip Rathbone in the artistic world of Liverpool, but his attitude toward him would always be patronizing and boded ill for any joint ventures. "He trundles the Art Machine about Liverpool," Conway wrote his father-in-law, "and generally works public galleries and the like."[5] But this hardly does justice to Rathbone. Not only was he chairman of the Walker Gallery, he was active on the City Council's Museums and Art Committee, and he and Alderman Samuelson were the chief arrangers of the annual Autumn Exhibition. He was a supporter of the Pre-Raphaelites and William Morris, and, as his niece Eleanor Rathbone wrote of him, he favored

---

[4] Conway Papers, Cambridge University Library, dated pre-March 1885, in a different hand; 25 March 1885, P/68; draft, Conway to Registrar, 12 April 1885, P/60. Hereafter referred to in the text as CP. The abbreviations in the letters have been regularized.

[5] CP, Conway to Marble, 25 November 1883, F/10. Evans, *Conways*, pp. 85-86.

every development in art which seemed to him to show individuality, spontaneity and growth. His choice of pictures for the public galleries sometimes tried the faith of his fellow-citizens, though it was generally admitted that he and his colleagues succeeded in making both the permanent and the annual exhibitions perhaps the best interesting and representative in any provincial city. He believed in strengthening corporate life and in quickening civil patriotism, by appealing to men through their senses and making the visible city a place to be proud of. Every institution and project for fostering the artistic life, or for improving its architecture, or for giving it beauty and dignity in any form was sure of his sympathy.[6]

Conway and Rathbone were thrown together willy-nilly; it seems a pity that Conway, the Londoner, could not have been a little more tolerant of the older man's "provincialism" and a little more willing to acknowledge his genuine concern with art. A degree of rivalry was also involved. For, as it worked out, Conway was to be a professor without students, and his role was more of a general cultural factotum for the city. Most of the lectures to the Liverpool Arts Club were his; he gave many other talks as well as three public lectures a week as Roscoe Professor. One would have thought he might find his life congenial, but it was not sufficient for his nervous energy, nor was he especially happy in provincial Liverpool. As early as February 1886, he put in for the Slade Professorship at Cambridge, with a testimonial from seventeen professors from Liverpool recommending him but saying how much they would regret his leaving (CP, O/17). On that occasion, he lost the chair to J. Henry Middleton. Nevertheless, the following academic year, in March 1888, he decided he could no longer stay in Liverpool, and on 17 March tendered his resignation on the grounds that he could not perform both his professional and literary work. He had given his last lecture on 14 March.[7]

---

[6] Eleanor Rathbone, *William Rathbone* (1905), pp. 460-61. Philip Rathbone's children continued his traditions: one son, Harold, founded the Della Robbia Pottery and another, Edmund, an architect, ran The City Beautiful Wayside Café. (John Willett, *Art in a City* [1967], p. 56.)

[7] CP, Conway to Chairman, University Council, draft 17 March 1888, P/98. One should note here the future history of the chair: Conway was succeeded by the very lively R. A. M. Stevenson, cousin of Robert Louis Stevenson, and author of an important book on Velázquez; Stevenson would keep the post until 1892 when he went to London to become art critic of the *Pall Mall Gazette*. In 1895 the Roscoe fund was used to help establish the first School of Architecture and Applied Arts at a university, hence using the money for a purpose consistent · with the National Association itself. See R. F. Bisson, *The Sandon Studios Soci-*

II

Conway devoted the remainder of 1888 to the establishment of the National Association for the Advancement of Art and its Application to Industry, dividing his time between Liverpool and London. In the capital he scurried about, seeing "important" people, and attempting, as was the common practice, to capture decorative names and powerful figures of the period, less for what they might do than what they were, as window dressing for the organization; and he did succeed in gaining a smattering of peers and politicians. In fairness to him, it should be added that he also addressed himself with some care and thought to what was to be special to the association: the presence in it of the artists themselves. But there is no evidence—beyond the mercantile interests represented by the second or third generation of Liverpool worthies—that he even tried to see the great manufacturers whose support would have been essential to fulfill the main purpose of the organization. A group dedicated to bringing artists and manufacturers together might not have succeeded in any case, but it had practically no chance to succeed when Conway neglected those who might have both funds and interest to support such an enterprise. Those "diffident feelings" about trade and industry, so endemic in Britain, permeated even an association allegedly devoted to removing such barriers. And this was particularly true when the main organizer was as ambitious and snobbish as Conway himself.

In later life, writing his memoirs, Conway chose to present the origin of the Association in an utterly frivolous vein, perhaps because it had collapsed after so promising a beginning. There he writes that it came into being as a protest against the attitude of the city fathers of Liverpool toward Stirling Lee's bas-reliefs in St. George's Hall, the central architectural feature of the city. Lee, in the second of the first six reliefs, had depicted Justice as a nude pubescent girl. Without seeing the offending panel, the Finance Committee of the Council broke the contract with Lee, and in 1890, Philip Rathbone, who had originally suggested the decoration himself, paid for the further four panels. Conway chose to remember that when the public quarrel started about the nude girl, he "took a bold resolution. I suggested that an Art Congress should be held in Liverpool, intended to be the first in a series of Congresses to fulfill for Art the function performed for Science by the British Association." At the end of his life, Lord Conway of Allington would have us believe that a national organization to which he and others devoted so much of their time, had its inception as a gesture to shame the city fathers. And it is quite true that in 1890, at the second annual meeting of the Association, in Edinburgh, an elaborate motion of censure, with many distinguished signatures, was passed, deploring the treatment of Lee's "nude girl." Thereafter, with honor done, Lord Conway claimed that he lost interest in the entire enterprise.[8]

But the lordly memoirs of 1932 do not parallel too closely the realities of 1888. In fact, the idea of the Association had been present in conversations between Philip Rathbone and Conway for some time, and there seems to have been a question as to who originated the idea. Conway claimed it for himself, writing to his father-in-law in April 1888; "The idea so far took root in the mind of Philip Rathbone, to whom I communicated it a year or more ago, that a few months back he gave expression to a bungled form of it as an original motion of his own. He asked if I would help him, & I agreed" (CP, Conway to Marble, 22 April 1888, F/75). Presumably he is referring to a meeting of the Committee of the Liverpool Art Club held in the previous November, at which Philip Rathbone had proposed a resolution that was passed and signed by representatives of Liverpool cultural groups, that there should be consideration of "questions concerning the education of artists and designers, the right relations of various Arts and the right employment of the power of public and private patronage, the facts of Art history."[9]

Conway may well be accurate in presenting himself as the originator of the idea; but there is little evidence that before this time he had been deeply troubled by the state of the arts in Britain, and their relation to industry and commerce. In any event, he and Philip Rathbone met on 11 March 1888 and agreed on a plan of action (CP, Diary,

[8] Lord Conway of Aldington, *Episodes in a Varied Life* (1932), p. 85.
[9] CP, H. E. Rensburg, *Report of the Initiatory Proceedings for the Foundation and First Congress of "The National Association for the Advancement of Art and Its Application to Industry,"* June 1888, Y/18 (Conway's diary for 1888). The signers of the resolution included the presidents of the Art Club, the Kyrle Society, the Liverpool Academy of Art, the Art-Workers' Guild of Liverpool, the Architectural Society, the Society of Painters in Water Colours, and the donor of the Walker Art Gallery.

1888). They persuaded the Lord Mayor to call a town meeting on 21 March to launch the project, and in some respects the meeting was a success: £1,000 was raised for local running expenses and publicity. But Conway felt that Rathbone had failed properly to organize the meeting, that the resolutions presented there were wrong, and that the speakers had not been wisely selected. By his own account it was he who had the mayor ask Rathbone to present the project while be himself went around the room asking speakers to support it. Rathbone, Conway complained, "made a speech sufficient to damn any scheme. The other speakers knew nothing about the affair & the whole thing went as badly as could be" (CP, Conway to Marble, 22 April 1888, F/75a). Still, a committee of 172 was selected at this meeting and a resolution was passed stating that "considering that scientific inventions and the perfection of machinery have largely displaced unskilled labour and reduced the demand for skilled labour, the introduction of special education in the artistic handicrafts has become necessary to the future welfare of the country, and it is therefore desirable that a Congress should be held to consider the whole question." The General Committee elected an Executive Committee of 25, more or less of Conway's choosing. At its meeting of 18 April, it was decided that "an important Association such as the one contemplated must necessarily be of a national character and its birth must, therefore, take place in the metropolis—the seat of acknowledged authority, and the centre of National effort" (CP, *Initiatory Proceedings*, June 1888, Y/18). At this meeting Conway was appointed to be the man to go to London. As he wrote, "London has yet to give birth to the Art Association which Liverpool was to receive."

It is one thing to believe that an organization should exist, and another actually to bring it into existence. Despite his comparative youth—he was in his early thirties—Conway was experienced in the ins-and-outs of the art world. He had been an unsuccessful applicant both for the chair he now held, although at that earlier time it had been given to no one and remained vacant, and for the Slade Professorship. He knew who counted; most importantly he was on friendly terms with Sidney Colvin, formerly Slade Professor at Cambridge, director of the Fitzwilliam Museum there, and now keeper of prints and drawings at the British Museum. Colvin had supported both Conway and Middleton as his successor and he may have turned the scale in favor of the latter. Conway knew that he needed strong local support in Liverpool, as the plan was to hold the first meeting of the

Association there, but at the same time he wanted to create a national organization which would have its headquarters in London and for that he needed a wider network.

He came down to London on 19 April, and started a whirlwind of activity, in place of his usual European travel. From his diary and letters to Marble emerge a picture of the creation of the organization, beginning with his notion that it should "meet for a few days once each year at some provincial town, have a presidential address, be divided into sections with sectional Presidents (Architecture, Sculpture, Decorative Arts, Art History, etc.) who will open also with addresses." On 20 April he went to see Sidney Colvin, although he did not completely trust him after the vexing matter of the lost Slade Professorship, and secured his promise "to preside over Art History so as not to have him for an opponent."

The same day he also called upon Sir George Scharf, the director of the National Portrait Gallery. But his most important meeting was the next day with Sir Frederic Leighton, then president of the Royal Academy, whom he wanted to consent to be president of the Association. The new organization, then, would be as respectable as possible. The Academy was very leery of alliances, and was continually feeling itself besieged by the "lesser arts." The formation of the Art-Workers' Guild of 1884 had, in a sense, been a move against the Royal Academy. In 1888, when the Arts and Crafts Exhibition Society held its first exhibition, it was practically in explicit rivalry to what it considered the restrictive policies against the decorative arts of the Academy. But Conway was adept at using both blandishments and threats. "He [Leighton] . . . utterly refused to preside. I . . . suggested that the meeting would be held, might be made a power for good," and then allowed a veiled threat to appear. The meeting

might also be made an engine for "dynamiting the *Academy*"! I turned the subject then & about 5 minutes later returned to the charge & put it straight to him that it was his manifest duty & business to preside. He then discussed what he should say, who should be the sectional presidents, at what date the meeting should be held, & I left him after 2 1/2 hours with a provisional consent to come down & deliver the presidential address provided suitable support is found to worthily fill the sectional chairs. That was all I asked him. I am now using his name to get Herkomer, Walter Crane, Poynter & a leading architect.
(CP, Conway to Marble, 22 April 1888, F/75a,b.)

The picture that Conway presented of Leighton more than forty years later in his memoirs was slightly different, and more cynical.

Although Leighton's official argument was that art could not be fur-
thered "by any public effort," it was clear to Conway that he was
fearful of there being created an organization that "might voice the
rather wide-spread criticism of the Royal Academy that was then
finding utterance through the mouths of the younger generation of
artists." Conway goes on to remark: "Luckily it happened at the
moment that Leighton had a very large picture, newly finished to
sell. Liverpool was thinking of buying it, I think that consideration
turned the scale, but in assenting to serve he stipulated that the
Academy should not be attacked" (Conway, *Episodes*, pp. 85-86).

Conway's diary continues to record his somewhat frenzied activities, bolstered now by the immense advantage of Leighton's name.
On 24 April he saw Humphry Ward, the art critic for *The Times*
(whose wife's novel, *Robert Elsmere*, was the sensation of the year),
and Colvin again. On the 25th he called on Edward Poynter, the
painter, Albert Gilbert, the sculptor, and John Ruskin, to ask his
blessing for the enterprise, and with whom he also arranged to have
breakfast the next day. On 28 April he wrote a second letter to Marble, extremely pleased with his fast progress.

I have got Sir F. Leighton's promise to be general president. I have also got
the following sections thus presided over—
> Architecture: Prof. Aitchison of the RA
> Sculpture: Alfred Gilbert, A.R.A.
> Painting: Alma Tadema RA
> Art Hist.: Sidney Colvin

Decorative and Industrial Art remain unfilled & will remain till Walter
Crane returns from Greece.

Having done exceedingly well in less than two weeks, Conway
now turned to his project to make the organization national in
scope, and, he hoped, to secure his own future as a considerable figure. The concept of the Association had been born and supported in
Liverpool and owed a great deal to the spirit of the city. Yet Conway
clearly was not going to allow it to be based in the provinces. His
letter to Marble continued that he had visited

the Duke of Westminster to ask him to . . . become permanent President of
the Central London Committee. If he says yes, I shall get him to call a
meeting at Grosvenor house . . . & there I shall get myself elected permanent Hon. Sec. of the Association . . . I shall thus be placed in a permanent
position of equal influence (or even greater) to that of Prof. at Liverpool,
only it will not (after the first meeting) involve much work. . . . The great
danger now is that Liverpool may hear that I am in reality getting the cen-

tral Association organized in London. They will not be pleased if they think that they have played cat's paw for London. Once the London Committee is organised under a Duke, of course it does not matter, because the titles one can get into the gen. committee will comfortably swamp provincial jealousy & turn it into toadyism. . . . The Duke of W. may refuse. That will cause delay. Then I shall have to go to Lord Derby. He won't be so good because he is of course very Liverpool & sensitive to Liverpool feeling. With him as president the central organisation will never grow to be free from Liverpool influence & even control.

(CP, Conway to Marble, 28 April 1888, F/76.)

Conway had convinced himself, perhaps correctly, that a meeting at Grosvenor House, chaired by the Duke, was essential to his plans; he was determined to succeed. He recorded his efforts in a letter to Marble, which ends on the triumphant note: "Had a very pleasant talk [with Westminster], got him to promise to hold a meeting at Grosvenor House on the 9th of June. 'But' he said 'it must be a good meeting.' I have now got to get that up" (CP, Conway to Marble, 5 May 1888, F/77).

Walter Crane wrote Conway on 3 May agreeing to be president of the Applied Art Section, so Conway had established a strong connection with the Arts and Crafts world. Crane registered a mild suggestion for wider internal democracy: "I think the plan of electing the officers by as wide a suffrage as possible would strengthen the basis of the congress very much" (CP, Walter Crane to Conway P/105). This sort of issue was much on Crane's mind. In the formation of the Arts and Crafts Exhibition Society, of which he became president, it was decided that the selection jury would be elected, specifically in contrast to the appointed juries of the Royal Academy. But the good news from Crane was offset by a note from Leighton on 12 May that he felt he was unfit to do a formal speech. Eventually, however, Conway prevailed upon him and he did deliver the presidential address.

Conway also heard from George Howard, who would succeed as the Earl of Carlisle the following year, a talented painter and one of the leading patrons and friends of William Morris. Howard regretted that he could not attend the meeting at Grosvenor House and then went on to express some of his concerns about the Association. He seemed to sense the lack of practical concern in the enterprise, and feared that it would concentrate too much on general art appreciation, of which, he felt, there was

a very great deal too much already. I do not think that any permanent good

is to be done by telling people what they ought to like & what they ought to buy; if they follow your advice you may give a temporary impetus to a demand for good work; but a demand which is not founded on any want that is felt by the people who make it, themselves, will not have any character of permanence. . . . I would rather see people buy bad pictures because they like them, than good ones because they think that is the right thing to do.
(CP, George Howard to Conway, 12 May 1888, P/1033.)

On 14 May Conway returned to London from Liverpool and the following day had a further consultation with Westminster about the June meeting. On the 16th there was a meeting of the Sculpture Committee at the studio of Stirling Lee, on whose behalf, in a sense, the entire Association was being formed. On 24 May he had an important meeting. "Called Macmurdo [sic] & made arrangements." A. H. Mackmurdo is now recognized, thanks to the work of Nikolaus Pevsner, as one of the founders of the modern movement, because of the advanced nature of his designs for furniture, crafts, and buildings and because of his establishment, with the assistance of Selwyn Image and Herbert Horne, of the Century Guild and its publication, the *Hobby Horse*. With Mackmurdo, Conway was bringing in a sophisticated leader of the Arts and Crafts movement. Later Mackmurdo was also perfectly willing to take credit for the Association, although there is little evidence that what he states as the achievements of the Association actually happened. "As one of the honorary secretaries of this association [which he became at the time of the Liverpool meeting] I was enabled to bring together in congress . . . the best known master-craftsmen, artists and decorators. These meetings gave them the opportunity of addressing the public, and in particular, the manufacturers, with a view to some better understanding of the relation of industry to life." But this is argumentation long after the fact, and there is no record of how many, if any, manufacturers were actually present at the three meetings.[10]

The success of the venture now hinged on the meeting at Grosvenor House. The Duke of Westminster did not appear entirely to un-

---

[10] A. H. Mackmurdo, "A History of the Arts and Crafts Movement," manuscript, K1037, Mackmurdo Collection, William Morris Museum, Walthamstow, p. 208. Mackmurdo would edit what appears to be the one publication, other than the three volumes of *Transactions*, of the Association, and its last gesture, published in 1892. It is entitled *Plain Handicrafts, Being Essays by Artists Setting Forth the Principles of Design and Established Methods of Workmanship: A Guide to Elementary Practice*. It had a preface by G. F. Watts and essays by W. R. Lethaby, May Morris, and Ernest Gimson, among others.

derstand the main purpose of the Association: he announced from the chair that he "would be very glad to assist in any way he could the endeavor to make art more popular with the masses of the population." Conway had recognized the considerable extent to which the idea of the organization stemmed from William Morris and had persuaded him to move the founding resolution: "That in view of the problems presented by the present conditions of art and industry in this country, it is advisable to form an association to be called the National Association for the Advancement of Art and its Application to Industry for the purpose of holding an annual Congress in different parts of the country to discuss all questions of a practical nature connected with the furtherance of art." The motion was seconded by Edmund Gosse and supported by Sir Charles Newton, a distinguished archeologist, who saw the association as a means for provincial cities to "emulate Oxford and Cambridge in embellishment." It was left to Walter Crane to introduce a political note in his statement that under present conditions in factories making such goods as carpets it was impossible to produce works of art. He felt that "what they had to do was to turn their artists into craftsmen and their craftsmen into artists" (*The Times*, 9 June 1888). Conway recorded in his dairy that the meeting was a great success, that he had spoken, as had Philip Rathbone, John Dun, the honorary Treasurer, from Liverpool, and Oscar Wilde. There were approximately 400 there, and Conway had every reason to feel satisfied. That evening he left to spend most of the rest of the month on the Continent.

At about this time the prospectus for the new organization was issued; it represents Conway's work in the committees listed and the ideas put forth. There was the president, Sir Frederic Leighton, supported by an array of vice-presidents: Earl Derby, Earl Pembroke, Earl Wharncliffe, Lord Ronald Gower, Viscount Hardinge, Lord Dorchester, Sir A. H. Layard, A. J. Balfour, David Plunket, Sir Coutts Lindsay, Sir Andrew Barclay Walker, Sir John Millais, and R. S. Halford. On the Central Committee there was a mixture of national and Liverpool names: Eustace Balfour, Cyril Flower, Edmund Gosse, Hubert von Herkomer, George Howard, C. Leland, F. J. Leslie, Rev. V. J. Loftie, A. H. Mackmurdo, Cosmo Monkhouse, E. J. Poynter, P. H. Rathbone, H. E. Rensburg, George Scharf, H. H. Statham, R. A. M. Stevenson, and T. Humphry Ward.[11]

---

[11] Secretaries of the various sections were A. H. Mackmurdo for Architecture, George Simonds for Sculpture, George Clausen for Painting, Lionel Cust for Art History, Mervyn Macartney for Applied Art, and Philip Rathbone for Encour-

The prospectus then enunciated the aims of the Association. They included discussion of

problems of a practical nature connected with the welfare of the Arts, Fine and Applied. . . . Machinery, by making less immediate the contact of the artizan with the object of manufacture, and by its tendency to specialise the artizan's work, has rendered obsolete, so far as many industries are concerned, the old traditions of design, and these have not as yet been replaced by new. . . . The adaptation therefore of artistic design to modern methods of manufacture, and the cherishing, or rehabilitation, of many crafts which are independent of machinery, and which the individuality of the workman's touch is an essential feature, are matters of high importance at the present time.

The welfare of the masses of our people largely depends upon the commercial superiority of England. That commercial superiority cannot be maintained by the fact of bygone priority or exclusive possession of labour-saving inventions. . . . It is by excellence of make and superiority of artistic design that the manufacture of any country will henceforward attain prestige and command markets. But the artistic quality of a nation's manufacturers, and its prosperity through the Applied Arts, depends upon its high level of excellence in the Fine Arts. The education of artists and artizans, the maintenance and development of museums of all kinds, the steps taken to elevate the taste of the people, the amount and intimacy of the contact between the higher and lower order of artists and craftsmen, the encouragement which governments and municipalities, in the mere exercise of their ordinary functions, may be able to give to the forces of artistic production—these, and like questions, are thus involved in the industrial problems placed before us by the inexorable progress of events.[12]

III

By the end of June, Conway was back in London continuing to organize. He saw quite a bit of Mackmurdo there, and met the secretaries of the various sections at his office. On 3 July Conway devoted himself to hunting for London offices for the Association, and settled on 22 Albemarle Street. (The Liverpool headquarters were at the Walker Art Gallery.) But if the London side of things was going along smoothly, progress in Liverpool seemed to be slowing down.

---

agement of Art. A. J. Mundella, the prominent Liberal politician, was president of the Encouragement of Art section.

[12] *Transactions* (1889), pp. viii-ix.

Perhaps it was summer doldrums, or perhaps the Liverpudlians were more conscious than Conway realized that they were being bypassed. On the first of August there was a *cri de cœur* from H. E. Rensburg who, along with F. J. Leslie, was one of the two local honorary secretaries. Rensburg maintained that Conway had deserted Liverpool and that the scheme was in danger of foundering because of his withdrawal.

> If this were a thing that people here understood, a committee might do the work but where it concerns a movement for which the enthusiasm is to be manufactured the guiding spirit of one who devotes himself ENTIRELY to the object is wanting.—I am doubtful whether anyone now connected with the thing would have joined the movement if it had not been understood that you would be the guiding spirit—I must confess that a feeling of disappointment and I might almost say alarm has taken possession of us all since we found that you decided virtually to leave Liverpool.
>
> (CP, H. E. Rensburg to Conway, 1 August 1888, P/107a.)

Conway was, however, determined both that the Congress would be a success, and that he would be able to preserve his distance from Liverpool; indeed, he was in the process of moving to London. The Association was his way of projecting himself out of provincial life.

The Association received the ultimate accolade of a favorable editorial in *The Times* in August, welcoming the youngest of the friendly rivals to the British Association. "If this is not one of the great ages of art, it is at least an age in which there is more art production and more talk and writing about art than has ever been known before. . . . The new Association will, let us hope, do much to help the concentration of effort, especially in the direction of industrial art" (*The Times*, 17 August 1888).

In the same issue Conway published a letter which appealed for manufacturers to come forward: it was his only plea. Conway knew the art world, but there was little apparent effort on his—or, as far as one can tell, on anybody else's—part, except for this one letter, to reach out to the world of industry. Mackmurdo had formed the Century Guild, and the Art-Workers' Guild had come into existence in 1884, both in large part because craftsmen felt that they did not have sufficient connection with the world of manufacture. Morris & Co. made its own goods, or done on contract by other firms. The Arts and Crafts Exhibition Society would insist that both designer and manufacturer be indicated on the goods displayed. Morris believed this to be a gesture of little significance, but it did at least represent a felt need to have both designer and manufacturer recognized as participants in the industrial life of the country. The sense of a gulf between industry and design could not be more acute. The drive for the Association had come from artistic circles, supported by municipal figures, yet the divisions between city fathers and artists were greater in Liverpool at the end of the century than had been earlier (see Willett, *Art in a City*, p. 66). Perhaps Conway's greatest failure, assuming he was genuinely interested in the ultimate success of the organization, was not to have cultivated the industrial and commercial connections of the men of Liverpool, and to have made sure that of the 1,000 who came to the Liverpool meeting, a considerable number should have been manufacturers. That element did not materialize to any noticeable degree. An easily overlooked letter to *The Times* (17 August 1888) asking for support hardly suggests an earnest attempt to reach the manufacturers, men no doubt of excellent character and certainly men of means, but less glamorous, less suitable, say, than the Duke of Westminster, or the Earl of Derby, or that titled, serious, accomplished, excruciatingly saccharine painter, Lord Leighton. Conway felt the pressure was upon him. Writing to Marble in August from Liverpool he explained that he was not sure whether he would be able to join the family on a tour in the west of England. "If only I should not in the public eye be credited with the failure or success of this Congress I could let it slide; as it is my own reputation is at stake and I am forced to make sacrifices which are decidedly unpleasant."[13]

The date for the opening of the Congress had been fixed for Monday, 2 December, and with the coming of autumn Conway found himself under greater pressure. His diary records many notations of meetings held in London and Liverpool; and there are pasted-in clippings of paragraphs in various newspapers about the forthcoming Congress. Later in November there was a last major crisis. Before then, plans seemed to have gone forward with only the normal confusion attendant upon such enterprises. Very few letters survive of the many that must have been written There are some from George Clausen the honorary secretary of the Painting section, about the papers which were coming in, and in part concerned with

---

[13] CP, Conway to Marble F/78, n.d. (?August 1888). There does not appear to be any surviving record of membership figures or money received from subscriptions. In June Rensburg had raised the question with Conway of what fees should be—perhaps a guinea for membership and a 1/2 guinea fee, later changed to a guinea, to attend the meetings. (CP, Rensburg to Conway, 25 June 1888, P/106.a.b.)

an unsuccessful attempt to have Whistler give one of his "Ten O'Clock" lectures. Another problem Clausen raised was the difficulty of getting papers from artists whose natural medium was elsewhere: "The men are very shy of pen and ink" (CP, Clausen to Conway, 25 and 27 October 1888, P/111,112). Similarly George Simonds, serving as Secretary for the Sculpture section, complained about the difficulty of getting prompt answers to anything (CP, Simonds to Conway, 23 October 1888, P/110).

Then the Congress almost came apart over a late Victorian manifestation of Sabbatarianism: could the question of whether museums should be open on Sundays even be discussed? There was a proposal to do just that in the Art History and Museums section. The mayor, Edward H. Cookson, announced that such a discussion was impossible; it was yet another instance of a clash between provincial sensibilities and metropolitan interests that might have been avoided if Conway had been more responsive to the former and less exhilarated by the latter. There was a sense of panic over the issue, particularly as it arose less than two weeks before the Congress was to begin. One can only imagine what Conway had telegraphed to Rensburg to which the latter felt obliged to reply on 23 November: "I received two telegrams from you today which I must refuse to regard as serious. The one I received from Mr. Dun was more to the point and in accordance with its content I have called a Meeting of the Liverpool Executive Committee for Monday next." Rensburg goes on to say that he has put off the Mayor by telling him that as the Central Committee was in London his communication had been forwarded to Conway to be taken up with that committee. Rensburg urged moderation upon Conway and "worldly wisdom." He did feel that the question of Sunday opening "is not strictly an Art Question" and he reminded Conway that at the initial town meeting it had been mentioned, and the town's leaders had been assured that no controversial questions would be discussed.

Considering the constitution of the Liverpool Corporation and their conscientious views to the contrary, and furthermore the dangerous element of Orangemen in the Liverpool population, I can even go so far as to sympathize with the Chief Magistrate of the City who is bound to avoid countenancing anything that would give offense to the majority of his council representing the majority of the citizens of Liverpool.

Rensburg suggested that the question be discussed outside of the Congress. "To make this question the 'to be or not to be' of the Congress or even of a Section of the Congress would be a proceeding unworthy of responsible men who profess to have the Advancement of Art at heart." He feared that if the Mayor resigned over the issue, the "Orangemen" would cause a riot at the meeting. Fearful that Conway himself might abandon the Congress, he ends his letter, "Pray consider all this, and do not run away from the first difficulty that presents itself by resigning" (CF, Rensburg to Conway, 23 November 1888, P/119 a,b).

Reasonable as the tone of Rensburg's letter was, in fact he had somewhat exaggerated how seriously the issue was actually taken, although Colvin and the secretary of the section, Lionel Cust, had both threatened to resign if it were not discussed. Conway hurried about London talking to a deputation from Liverpool, and seeing Walter Crane, Leighton, and Colvin. On 24 November, Colvin wrote a letter stating in clear terms that the question must be discussed, and that not to do so would reflect the small-mindedness of Liverpool.

It seems a great pity that the Sunday opening question should have been dragged into so much prominence. . . . It is only one of many questions which must come up as a matter of course in any discussion on the administration and practical usefulness of museums. The view that it is not an art question, but a religious question, and therefore one that must be put aside, is surely quite untenable. . . . If anything in the particular circumstances or temper of Liverpool makes the discussion of the subject on these conditions unwelcome, there is only one thing for us to do, and that is to withdraw from the Congress altogether, and leave the discussion of art museums, their organization, administration and usefulness for a future meeting of the Association at some centre where these difficulties do not exist.[14]

On 27 November the Mayor resigned as chairman of the Liverpool Committee, and Sir James Picton and Alderman Samuelson replaced him. On 1 December there was a great row in the newspapers, and Colvin came down with what may have been a diplomatic illness. "I am afraid that it is out of the question for me to prepare and read the promised paper: and very much afraid that I may be told I must seek quiet and country instead of going to the Congress at all" (CP, Colvin to Conway, 1 December 1888, M/9). But the issue was smoothed over and a last difference between Liverpool and London

---

[14] Colvin to Dun, 24 November 1888, M/8a,b. The two papers in question were "The City of Birmingham Museum and Art Gallery: Its Development, Its Work and Its Sunday Opening," by Whitworth Wallis, and "The Desirability of Making a Fuller Use of the English Sunday for the Advancement of Art amongst the Industrial Classes," by J. Pyke Thompson.

was resolved. Lionel Cust gave an address in Colvin's place and the two controversial papers were presented.

The Congress went very smoothly and was a great success beginning with a musical evening party, given by Rensburg. The speakers, presidents, and secretaries were entertained as houseguests at various Liverpool homes. An invitation was received from Edinburgh to act as host for the Association's meeting the following year. Conway could feel content with his inaugural work, and on 7 December he left on a six-month-trip to Egypt.

There were to be three congresses in the history of the Association—Liverpool in 1888, Edinburgh in 1889, and Birmingham in 1890. The ambitions of Martin Conway as they united with the seriousness of some high-minded men from Liverpool had resulted in the founding of the National Association for the Advancement of Art and its Application to Industry. It is indicative of the concerns of the decade that some of the most creative figures in the land, among them William Morris, felt deeply enough about the issues of art and society, and their relationship to each other, to write papers for the new organization and to come to discuss them in December 1888 in Liverpool. At the time, it seemed that something significant had occurred, and, symptomatically at least, it had.

And yet, in the end, it is to Conway's aspirations that one must look if one is to understand both the founding of the organization and its dissolution. For it was he who saw to it that "Art" was richly represented and "Industry" hardly at all. In 1890, the last year of the National Association's abortive career, William Gladstone, in whom idealism and realism were most astonishingly conjoined, remarked that "the industries of the country will derive enormous advantage from the cultivation of art. Beauty is an element of immense pecuniary value."[15] Realism of the Gladstonian sort, as well as his idealism, was quite beyond William Martin Conway. In his letter to *The Times* in August 1888, Conway had written, "The chief difficulty is that of putting ourselves in communication with the large body of manufacturers . . . who have been led by the necessities of their daily work, to face the problems of industry in its relation to art. We know that there are many such men willing to assist, and capable of able assisting, in the work we have in hand; but unless they put themselves in communication with us we shall scarcely be able to

---

[15] William E. Gladstone, *The Speeches of the Rt. Hon. W. E. Gladstone, 1881-1891* (1902), pp. 303-4.

reach them." In short, and how characteristically, the burden had been shifted from art to industry. They must put themselves "in communication"; otherwise, we shall not be able "to reach them." The aspirations of Conway had led him, ever so eagerly, to the portals of the Royal Academy and Grosvenor House. Manufacturers, however, were to be encountered only in the columns of *The Times*; there is no evidence of his having ventured into the precincts of a single factory.

13

WILLIAM MORRIS AND BLOOMSBURY

There is very little mention of William Morris in the Bloomsbury corpus. Although he hated his own age, which he saw as the age of shoddy and of mumbo jumbo, he was nevertheless in so many respects a Victorian. He was not a likely candidate for Lytton Strachey's *Eminent Victorians* of 1918 but in certain ways he resembled those figures in his energy and the scope of his activity. Although he hated both periods, he could be called a Victorian Renaissance man. His first official biography, published in 1899, by Edward Burne-Jones's son-in-law, J. W. Mackail, was somewhat in the life and letters genre that Strachey hated, although it was in many ways a useful and satisfactory two volumes. Mackail did tend to de-emphasize the political side of Morris and it was hardly surprising that he did not reveal Jane Morris's infidelities. They did not become common knowledge until fairly recently, under the influence of the nothing hidden biographies, ironically inaugurated by Michael Holroyd's biography of Lytton Strachey of 1968.

There are, however, many parallels, and indeed continuities, between William Morris and Bloomsbury. And my hope is that considering them may cast some illumination upon England and its history. There are political similarities between Morris and his friends and Bloomsbury with, indeed, Morris himself being further to the left of most of Bloomsbury. Morris was proud of being a Marxist. The literary critic Jane Marcus to the contrary, Virginia Woolf was not a Marxist. But she was much more of a feminist than Morris. His attitude toward women has created some problems for his admirers who, largely ignoring the significance of historical context, wish to see him as completely up to date. It is true that in his great work, *News from Nowhere*, he tends to emphasize what he sees as the affinity of women to domestic tasks. And he has been accused in the interesting book by Anthea Callen, *Women Artists of the Arts & Crafts Movement* (1979) of, on the one hand, putting women on pedestals, and on the other making them do what she sees as the most boring task in the arts and crafts world: embroidery.

In his own life and in his own thoughts about women, he was a firm believer in their equality. In his ideas about love and sex he was very similar to Bloomsbury, as he believed that individuals need to follow their inclinations, although that did not prevent him feeling pain over his wife's infidelities, much as Vanessa Bell was better in theory than practice in coming to terms with Duncan Grant's homosexuality. Morris worked closely with Marx's daughter, Eleanor, although ultimately they disagreed over politics, and his own daughter May was a full colleague. And most importantly, and in this he was very similar to Bloomsbury, and even more so than they, ahead of his time, he believed that passions have to be given their due, even at a personal cost to another relationship, including that of marriage. He made no objection to his wife Jane going her own way and with quite considerable personal pain, he accommodated himself to her affair with Dante Gabriel Rossetti. Like Bloomsbury, he was much more aware than most of his contemporaries of the role of the sexual drive in human relationships. He expressed this in a powerful way in his poems and stories. Many of his stories take place in a medieval or archaic past, a factor that helped make them very popular in their time; it now makes them less accessible to the modern reader. (And Bloomsbury made an important contribution to this change of style and content.) His mode of expression was far different from Bloomsbury's, but there were much greater similarities of ideas than one might expect.

Leonard Woolf was a socialist and even a Marxist in his 1920 study, *Empire and Commerce in Africa*. But as far as I can tell he has nothing to say about Morris. In the index for the *Collected Writings of John Maynard Keynes*, a Liberal and politically closer to the center than Woolf, there is no listing for Morris. Yet Keynes shared with Morris a conviction that the point was to create a better society and that economists and politicians were servants of that goal. Keynes was, to a considerable degree, interested in the role of art in society. Like Morris, he was an avid collector although with different interests. In part because of his commitment to the career of his wife, the ballet dancer Lydia Lopokova, he established the Arts Theatre in Cambridge. But most importantly, he was the creator of the Arts

Council, the government supporter of the arts in Britain, which was founded during the Second World War. He may have led it away from its more Morrisean proclivities to support the applied as well as the fine arts, but he imbued it with a deep sense of the interrelationships of art and society, that the one could not flourish without the other. Thus one might say that the achievements of art are the purposes of society, but that they cannot be accomplished unless there is the right sort of state. There, of course, Keynes and Morris differed as Keynes favored a powerful Liberal state while Morris was for local but total socialism. But both believed that art was the highest value of civilization and that it could only be achieved if society itself were radically changed.

I want to briefly consider if there is any evidence of connections between Morris and Bloomsbury in the writings of Virginia Woolf. Of course she did write the biography of Roger Fry (1940), and it is with Fry that there are the greatest continuities between Morris and the Bloomsbury Group. In her letters and diaries, and in the collected essays, now published up till 1924, there are comparatively few mentions of Morris, but those that are there are quite intriguing. She clearly thought of Morris and his friends, with their multiplicity of activities, as somewhat similar to the Bloomsbury group, and in a rather nice modest way. As she wrote in her diary on May 31, 1928: "I walked Pinker [her dog] to Grays Inn Gardens this afternoon, & saw—Red Lion Square: Morris's house; thought of them on winters evenings in the 50ties; thought we are just as interesting."[1] There is the parallelism that the Morris group began as a group of friends at Oxford, not all that dissimilar to the crucial role that the group of friends at Cambridge played in the history of Bloomsbury.

Indeed, in her early unsystematic journals, which are more jottings than the later, great diaries, there is an interesting comment, again inspired by walking a dog, this time Gurth, on the Mackail biography of Morris, which she might have had a further interest in as she and her sister Vanessa, the painter, had an acquaintance with Philip Burne-Jones, the artist's son. "Finished the life of Morris—a very interesting book, & a great man—so much superior as a genius to B.[urne]-J.[ones] but curiously inhuman." It is a tantalizing remark, as Bloomsbury, based on the philosophy of G. E. Moore, was to make such a point of personal relations. There is an intriguing juxtaposition in the diary as just before her remark about the biog-

---

[1] Anne Olivier Bell, ed., *The Diary of Virginia Woolf* (1986), III, 186.

raphy she wrote, "Read my review book, which might have been better."[2] She had just started reviewing in 1904, when she was 22, for the *Guardian*, not the eminent Liberal paper but a small circulation ladies' Anglican journal. The review (only the fifth piece she had written for publication) and the book that she was likely to be referring to was W. L. Courtney's *The Feminine Note in Fiction*, which, she pointed out in a quite gentle fashion, she found rather patronizing and obtuse.[3] In a sense, if it is not putting too much weight on this casual journal entry, the two worlds of Morris and Bloomsbury are meeting in her jottings: Virginia Woolf is heralding her major concerns as a novelist and a critic, aspects of being a woman writing in the twentieth century for which there is very little precedent in the writings and works of William Morris. Yet she is building on and rebelling from the world of the late Victorians, as represented by her father, Sir Leslie Stephen, and William Morris as well, with whose work she was clearly quite well acquainted. That Morris was representative of the world of her father is made very clear in her Memoir Club essay describing the great break of 1904 when the four Stephen children left their deceased father's house in Kensington for 46 Gordon Square in Bloomsbury: "Instead of Morris wall-papers with their intricate patterns we decorated our walls with washes of plain distemper."[4]

In 1915 she wanted to borrow from Margaret Llewelyn Davies a copy of Morris's *The Pilgrims of Hope*, his long political poem of 1886 on the Paris Commune, which she had read about in *The Times*. "It sounds magnificent."[5] But there is no record of whether she actually read it and what she thought of Morris's politics. Her sense of the division between her age and that of Morris's is suggested in a review she wrote for the *Times Literary Supplement* in 1918 of a reminiscence by Belfort Bax, a political colleague and collaborator of Morris's (and a noted misogynist). She writes that his book "produces a curious sense that the mid and late Victorian age, so near ours in point of time, is already distant and different enough to be summed up and judged as we sum up and judge the lives of the dead. As we read we feel ourselves exalted almost to the rank of the

[2] Virginia Woolf, *A Passionate Apprentice: The Early Journals, 1897-1909* (1990), ed. by Mitchell A. Leaska, p. 221.
[3] Andrew McNeillie, ed., *The Essays of Virginia Woolf* (1986), I, 15-17.
[4] Virginia Woolf, *Moments of Being* (1976), p. 163.
[5] Nigel Nicolson and Joanne Trautmann, eds., *The Letters of Virginia Woolf* (1976), II, 60.

impartial observer to whom the England of the nineteenth century will appear as the Rome of the year 116 appears to an observer of the present day. . . . [His book] is very sincere, very plain spoken, and very much in earnest . . . the drastic moral tone of Mr Bax's generation." She goes on to pinpoint the crucial stylistic differences between Bax's age and her own, as in Keynes's famous remark bemoaning the agonized high seriousness in which Henry Sidgwick declared that he didn't believe in Christianity. As Woolf wrote in this review: "The moral earnestness which replaces and demolishes a too-easy credulity is bound in retrospect to seem a little excessive. Even when they took upon them[selves] to chide prigs or to denounce asceticism, one feels that the ghosts of the Evangelicals have inspirited them rather than a pure delight in the joys of the senses." It is true that Morris was deadly serious in his hatred of his age, and of the Evangelical spirit (from which Virginia herself had descended as a great-granddaughter of a member of the Clapham Sect). But Morris was more of a bridge to the modern age than Bax might have been in that he was not overly encumbered with earnestness and believed in the enjoyment of sensuality. In that, too, in some senses, he was similar to Bloomsbury, as some of its members were better in advocating sensual pleasure in theory than in practice, although some did manage to do both![6]

Morris was a presence in her life, but it would be misleading to suggest that he was a major figure. In February 1940, she mentions an inclination to write about Morris but is not any more specific than that. And in July she wrote to John Lehmann how much she is enjoying, a bit improbably, Morris's *Chants for Socialists*.[7] It is somewhat intriguing that both remarks are in the context of John Lehmann, as the first occurs in the midst of an account of a meeting with him and his contemporaries, as if Morris were a bridge to their (more than her) intense and immediate interest in the politics of the 1930s. But one last significant mention of Morris I've found in her writings provides a significant link between the world of Morris and the world of Bloomsbury: the painter and art critic Roger Fry. In July 1935, she had gone to Bristol to open a memorial exhibition of Roger Fry's pictures—he had died the previous year. "I can't describe the horror of Bristol on Friday—200 stout burgesses, crammed and dripping, and having to talk about art after losing my

---

[6] Andrew McNeillie, ed., *The Essays of Virginia Woolf* (1987), II, 261-64.
[7] Bell, *Diary* (1984) V, 264; Nicolson, *Letters*, VI, 408.

way in the most hideous of all towns—but its too hot." But seeing Morris's house on the way back to London provided a welcome relief. "But we cooled down at Lechlade, and saw Kelmscot today— why dont we all live in a silver great manor house, and sit on the Thames banks, and watch the moon rise, as I did last night—it was incredibly lovely—like a rose petal in the sky."[8]

The most obvious possible connection between Morris and Bloomsbury is, as I have suggested, through Roger Fry, although it is frequently rejected out of hand. On first blush, if one looks at designs by William Morris and parallel designs by the Omega Workshop, which functioned from 1913 to 1919, having been founded by Roger Fry, there is a sense of very little similarity, at least superficially. What I would like to suggest, however, is a rather parallel argument to that made in Nicolas Pevsner's influential and still controversial study *Pioneers of Modern Design: From Morris to Gropius*, that in fact Morris helped lead to modernism. Bloomsbury was, I believe, a crucial force in the making of that modernism in Britain and elsewhere, and Morris was an extremely important factor in that making, although that may not be immediately obvious.

To anticipate a main point, both Morris & Co. and Omega believed in the intertwining of life and art. But in Morris's case it was a matter of the worker, the crafts worker, infusing art with those values. In the case of Omega, it was somewhat the other way round, in that the designers were artists and designers first, and not workers at all although they were engaged in commerce. Omega was designed to fill one's ordinary surroundings with art, as was Morris & Co. but its original purpose was to provide income for artists. Most of Omega work was done outside the workshop; more of Morris work was done outside the workshop than one might expect but still probably the majority of the production was done "in house."

Roger Fry might perfectly well have been a disciple of William Morris. Older than most of the members of Bloomsbury, he was born in 1866 and went to King's College, Cambridge, where he studied science and was an Apostle. His greatest college friend was C. R. Ashbee who, with his Guild of Handicraft founded in 1888, became a leading disciple of William Morris, one of those crucial organizations that did so much to spread the influence of Morris's conceptions of the Arts and Crafts. Ashbee attempted to secure Fry's help in the Guild, as one of the wellborn young men who were trying

---

[8] Nicolson, *Letters* (1979), V, 415.

to improve the world in the East End, in this case through Arts and Crafts. But as Fry wrote to Ashbee in 1887: "I don't see my way to action yet." Although he wouldn't commit himself completely, he did help out by assisting in a class to teach boys how to decorate.[9] The mood of the enterprise is captured by the book Ashbee wrote in 1892, *From Whitechapel to Camelot*, which was illustrated by Fry. Also, in 1893, Fry painted the fireplace for the "Magpie and Stump," the house that Ashbee built as an office, a showroom, and a home for his mother at 37 Cheyne Walk. Fry, like Ashbee and E. M. Forster, and the King's College don Goldsworthy Lowes Dickinson, were influenced by meeting Edward Carpenter. Fry and Ashbee did so in 1885 at Morris's Hammersmith Socialist Society at a lecture held in its meeting room next to Morris's London house. Later, Carpenter visited Cambridge and Fry and Ashbee visited his home at Millthorpe. The issues that these young men considered were inevitably the relations between art, labor, and the nature of society and also, given Carpenter's own commitment to homosexuality, more modern views of sexuality, which would become such an important part of the life of Bloomsbury. (Both Ashbee and Dickinson were in love with Fry. As far as one knows, Fry was a heterosexual, but he did indulge Dickinson's passion for him to some degree. As Dickinson wrote in his autobiography, written in 1927 but not published until 1973, forty years after he died, "In the academic year 1887-8, which was his [Fry's] last at Cambridge, we lunched and breakfasted every day together, and every night I used to see him to bed and then kiss him passionately. The feeling of sex was now strong, but I did not indulge it, and should have thought it wrong to do so. There recurred also the old childish, I suppose really infantine, tick about boots, and I used to lie on the floor and get him to put his feet on me."[10] One has a sense of being halfway on the road to Bloomsbury, from late Victorian fetishism to a belief in sexual fulfillment.)

Morris does not figure at all in Fry's selected published correspondence but there is mention of him in some of his public pronouncements. His was the immediately preceding generation and Fry thought of himself as quite different, but he could not have avoided

---

[9] Quoted by Fiona MacCarthy, "Roger Fry and the Omega Idea," *The Omega Worskhops, 1913-19: Decorative Arts of Bloomsbury* (1983), p. 9 (Fry to Ashbee, 22 Oct 1887). It's interesting that MacCarthy went on to write the latest considerable biography of Morris. For Fry teaching, see Alan Crawford, *C. R. Ashbee* (1985), p. 36.
[10] Dennis Proctor, ed., *The Autobiography of G. Lowes Dickinson* (1973), p. 90.

discussing and being intensely aware of Morris through Ashbee's discipleship. Indeed, in April 1889, when Morris came to Toynbee Hall to deliver, for the first time, for Ashbee's Guild of Handicraft, his lecture on Gothic Architecture, it was Fry who was in charge of the slides. As Morris wrote to Ashbee: "I was depending on Mr Fry for all the absolutely necessary slides. . . . By the way you must understand that I know nothing about such things so I hope you will get some one to help me. I will come (and thanks) to dinner: but I must certainly be on the spot before the lecture begins so as to arrange properly."[11] Doing slides for the great man is not necessarily an intellectual connection but if Fry wasn't too worried about working the slides, he must have absorbed the lecture. It is somehow a nice touch that this was the lecture, in a later version, that was actually printed during the Arts and Crafts Exhibition in 1893. Fry did not necessarily agree with Morris that Gothic was the only really acceptable style, particularly as he was rather fond of the baroque, which Morris probably disliked as even worse than the Renaissance style.

Fry was also influenced by J. H. Middleton, Slade Professor at Cambridge, the archeologist and architect, socialist, and friend of Morris's, who advised Fry to be an architect. After leaving Cambridge Fry was able to persuade his father to allow him to pursue a career as a painter. He also increasingly devoted himself to art criticism, and became, according to Kenneth Clark, the most important British art critic of the twentieth century, the equivalent to Ruskin. Like Morris, Fry had extraordinary energy and was active in many areas; and sadly, like him, he also died comparatively young, at the age of 68 in 1934. Fry became, under the tutelage of Bernard Berenson, a major art critic and, using the methods of Morelli, could participate in the authenticating of old masters, making them viable objects to sell to newly rich Americans. At the same time, he pursued his career in English artistic circles, becoming a habitué at the home of the painters Charles Shannon and Charles Ricketts, as well as a friend of the art dealer and critic, Robert Ross. Both Ricketts and Ross would eventually deeply disapprove of his enthusiasm for the Post-Impressionists. He also was active with the comparatively avant-garde group of British painters as a member of the New English Art Club.

---

[11] Norman Kelvin, ed., *The Collected Letters of William Morris* (1996), III, 49-50 (April 6?, 1889).

He was also in the circle of the second generation of the Arts and Crafts movement, not only Ashbee but also A. H. Mackmurdo of the Century Guild. The Guild served as one transition to the modern movement in its elegant furniture. It was through the Century Guild that Fry met his wife Helen Coombe who had been involved with A. H. Mackmurdo, the leader of the Guild. Her most notable Guild effort, the decoration of a harpsichord, has connections with William Morris. It was an instrument built by Arnold Dolmetsch, the rediscoverer of ancient music but even more important for his insistence that the music be played on period instruments. He was very much in the spirit of Morris, and played to him on the virginals as he lay dying. Fry attended Dolmetsch concerts of early music at the Century Guild at 20 Fitzroy Street, around the corner from 33 Fitzroy Square where he was to establish the Omega, years later, in 1913. (Adrian and Virginia had moved to 29 Fitzroy Square when Vanessa married in 1907 and were there until 1911.) Helen did the decorations on the so-called Green Harpsichord, which in fact was being completed, at Morris's suggestion, for display at the Arts and Crafts Exhibition of 1896. The other two most important members of the Guild did work on it as well: Selwyn Image, its medievalesque inscription, and Herbert Horne, the Roman lettering; Fry closely advised on the scheme and it reflected his taste at the time. (In fact, Helen referred to the harpsichord as her and Fry's child.) The private view for the exhibition, sadly, was on the day that Morris died, October 3, 1896. Fry and Coombe married two months later. This was the advanced art of the time, and yet one can see how far art had developed by contrasting this harpsichord with another with highly abstract designs and a modern figure that Fry decorated twenty-two years later, in 1918, also a Dolmetsch harpsichord. Building on the Arts and Crafts, the modern movement had arrived.

One can also see in a similar way how Morris led to architectural changes that were precursors of modernism. For neither Morris nor Fry was architecture a major activity, but both recognized its crucial importance, Morris viewing it as the greatest of the arts that united so many of his interests and provided the setting for his works. His own architectural taste aimed at a certain timelessness in style, as in the highly important Red House which Philip Webb built for him in 1859 and which he and his friends decorated, the experience (along with the furniture he designed for his first London residence in Red Lion Square) that led to the founding of his firm. Similar simplicity, at a very high level, was to be found in his favorite home, his country house, Kelmscott Manor, built in the late sixteenth and early seventeenth century. Even his comparatively nondescript later London residence, the late eighteenth century Kelmscott House, had a certain elegant simplicity attractive to our taste today. One can also sense this evolution in two houses that A. H. Mackmurdo built for his family in Enfield, an outlying district of London, Halcyon House of 1873 for his mother, a perfectly pleasant combination of Queen Anne and Gothic Revival, and then approximately ten years later Brooklyn, for his brother, is a recognizable modern house.

In a similar way, the only house that Roger Fry built, for his family, Durbins in Guildford, in 1908, appears to be a modern house in its eschewing of an historical style. Fry wrote about this house (which he would have to sell when Omega went bankrupt in 1919) much as Morris might: "What if people were just to let their houses be the direct outcome of their actual needs, and of their actual way of life. . . . Wouldn't such houses have really a great deal more character, and therefore interest for others, than those which are deliberately made to look like something or other. Instead of looking like something, they would then be something. . . . It is through the artist's sense of proportion and his feeling for the plastic relief of the whole surface that a work of mere utility may become a work of art. . . . The artistic or architectural part of this house was confined, then, merely to the careful choice of proportions within certain fixed limits defined by needs, and neither time, money, nor thought were expended on giving the house the appearance of any particular style. . . . It does not require genius or even an extraordinary talent to make a genuine and honest piece of domestic architecture which will continue to look distinguished when the last 'style' but one having just become *démodé* already stinks in the nostrils of all cultured people."[12]

When these changes happen, it would appear that there is a considerable break if one is close to them. Of course one of the clichés of the historian's trade is change on the one hand, continuity on the other, and continuity is more likely to be seen in the *longue durée* than in the short term. It is clear that there are dramatic differences between the work of the Morris firm and the Omega Workshops. That difference is also reinforced by the fact that Ashbee, Fry's Arts and Crafts contemporary, heartily disliked the Omega work. And as

---

[12] Roger Fry, "A Possible Domestic Architecture" (1918), in *Vision and Design* (1920), pp. 179-83.

I've mentioned, Morris and his colleagues began as craftspeople and Fry and his colleagues began as artists. Yet much as Morris went to Leek to learn about dyeing, so Fry went to the potter George Schenck and to a pottery in Poole. As Virginia Woolf wrote in her biography of Fry: "Soon a row of hand-made pots stood on the studio floor. [Then quoting Fry] 'it is fearfully exciting . . . when the stuff begins to come up between your fingers.'"[13]

The standard view is that Omega owed little or nothing to Morris.[14] Bloomsbury liked to bow more toward the Continent, and connections are more likely to be seen with the *Wiener Werkstätte* and Paul Poiret's *École Martine*. Also there was the dramatic intervention of the influence of the Post-Impressionists, introduced to Britain (and the term coined) in Fry's epochal exhibition, "Manet and the Post-Impressionists" in 1910 when, according to Virginia Woolf, human character changed. Omega was certainly post-impressionist in appearance. Also, Fry saw the work of Omega as apolitical, unlike Morris. The writers on Omega make, in my view, a double error in the political sphere. Fry's excellent modern biographer differentiates the two groups, writing that "unlike William Morris's firm, the Omega had little underlying political motivation."[15] Morris's firm had no underlying political motivation at its founding in 1861 or its refounding in 1875 and even when Morris was at his most political in the 1880s the firm as such was not political, even though its implications might be. If anything, one might argue that Fry was more aware of the relation of art to politics at the time of his founding of Omega than Morris had been, as he had just published in 1912 his essay on "The Artist and the Great State" in the collection entitled *Socialism and the Great State*, along with essays by such eminent figures as H. G. Wells, who had asked Fry to write the piece. There he made it clear that he was not a socialist and feared the role of the state in art. On the other hand, he felt that there was a better chance in a socialist state that there might be genuine values and a decrease of wasteful and purposeless work.[16] He shared with Morris a hatred of "muddle" and "shoddy" and of the role of the "swinish rich" in the world of art and design. Morris and Fry also shared an intense disdain for the taste of those whom Fry called the "Custard Island-

---

[13] Judith Collins, *The Omega Workshops* (1984), p. 100.

[14] See Judith Collins and Isabelle Anscombe, *Omega and After* (1981).

[15] Frances Spalding, *Roger Fry: Art and Life* (1980), p. 178.

[16] Republished as "Art and Socialism" in Roger Fry, *Vision and Design*, pp. 36-51.

ers." Subsequent commentators also make the error of assuming that Morris's design followers shared his politics; in fact those who did, such as Ashbee in his fashion, were the exception rather than the rule.

Indeed, the prospectus for the Omega workshops reads much like a Morris document: "Until the 19th century (with the possible exception of the Roman Empire) men used for daily life objects which expressed the joy of the creator and the craftsman and conveyed a corresponding delight to the user. . . . [Modern industrialism] has indeed effected a complete divorce between art and industry to the harm of both. . . . Nor have there been wanting attempts to rectify [the situation], of which the most notable was that of William Morris. . . . The most recent movement in art, which may be described under the inclusive title of Post-Impressionism, has brought the artist back to the problems of design so that he is once more in a position to grasp sympathetically the conditions of applied art."[17]

It is true that Morris, unlike Fry, was much more interested in nature in his designs, but Morris's designs were far less slavish to nature. They were, in my view, precursors of modernism in their interest in flat pattern and a comparative feeling of abstraction. Fry was quite wrong when he wrote that Omega, unlike Morris, "would be less ambitious than William Morris, [it does] not hope to solve the social problems of production at the same time as the artistic."[18] In fact, Morris recognized that the social problems could not be solved through art, but rather the problem was the other way around; it was necessary first to solve society's problems.

Fry did not deny Morris's importance. In the introduction to an exhibition in 1914 of "Twentieth Century Art—A Review of Modern Movements," which of 414 works on display, Omega had 80, the introduction, written under Fry's influence, stated: "In decoration a new style has come, and this shows the first forward move in this country since William Morris and the 'arts and crafts' movement. . . . In design this new style shows affinities with Byzantine Art and with much savage art of the present time. [In this it differed to a degree from Morris, although, as I've suggested, Morris, comparatively, was moving toward abstraction. The quotation continues] it avoids the heavy metallic crudity of the colour schemes of the mid-Victorian period and the sophisticated timidity of the 'art shades'

---

[17] Christopher Reed, *A Roger Fry Reader* (1996), p. 198.
[18] Collins, p. 30. No source given.

that followed in the eighteen-eighties and nineties."[19] In this it was similar to Morris.

Roger Fry and the rest of Bloomsbury did have a close affinity to Morris, in that both recognized the supreme importance of the domestic, and its radical implications. The Charleston Farmhouse in Sussex, the home of the two most important Bloomsbury artists, Vanessa Bell and Duncan Grant,[20] fulfilled the ideal as enunciated by Morris in 1874: "Suppose people lived in little communities among gardens and green fields, so that you could be in the country in five minutes' walk, and had few wants . . . and studied the (difficult) arts of enjoying life, and finding out what they really wanted: then I think one might hope civilization had really begun."[21] In England there is an extraordinary emphasis on the domestic, and both Morris and Bloomsbury emphasized to an intense degree its importance. Think of Virginia Woolf's *A Room of One's Own*. It seems to me that the rooms in Charleston on the Sussex Downs, the sort of place suggested in the quotation from Morris, have taken Morris's conceptions and given them a modern idiom. Omega began in 1913 when it seemed, in a pre-1914 world, that perhaps a new sort of society might be possible. The First World War put an end to that optimism, but gave greater emphasis to the private values of Bloomsbury that could be pursued at Charleston (which began as a refuge where Duncan Grant and David Garnett could do agricultural work as alternate service—surely Morris would have deeply disapproved of the First World War), where Keynes denounced the result of the war while writing there *The Economic Consequences of the Peace*, and where Clive Bell wrote *Art*. It was here that there could be what the daughter of the house, Angelica Garnett, has called "the earthly paradise," although her autobiography, *Deceived with Kindness* (1984), demonstrates that even there, there might be a serpent in the garden.

In a review of Andrew Graham-Dixon's book and television series, *A History of British Art*, James Hall remarks, in disagreeing

---

[19] Ibid., p. 91.

[20] For this approach I am indebted to the work of Christopher Reed. See Christopher G. Reed, "Re-Imagining Domesticity: The Bloomsbury Artists and the Victorian Avant-Garde," unpublished Yale University Ph.D. dissertation, 1991. See also Christopher Reed, "'A Room of One's Own': The Bloomsbury Group's Creation of a Modernist Domesticity," in idem, ed., *Not at Home: The Suppression of Domesticity in Modern Art and Architecture* (1996).

[21] Quoted in Peter Stansky, *Redesigning the World* (1985), p. 50.

with Graham-Dixon's attacks on Morris that "Morris did change the world. His belief that everything in society, from wallpaper to lampposts, should be well and simply designed, with form expressive of function, is one of the more radical and fertile ideas of the nineteenth century. Graham-Dixon admits as much in the final programme of the series when discussing the interior decoration of Charleston, but he neglects to name the principal source of that idea and thus air-brushes Morris out of history."[22] If the revolution is in the domestic, the personal is the political, then there is a continuum from Morris to Bloomsbury.

The reality may not achieve the dream: but Art and the Good Life, that was the dream of Morris, the dream of Bloomsbury, and both had hopes of achieving it. As Christopher Reed has written: "What gave coherence to the two movements [Aestheticism and the Arts and Crafts] was their connection of aesthetic and social reform through the re-imagining of the look of daily life. . . . The objects of daily life reveal and perpetuate the social and moral conditions of their creation."[23] Morris helped make Bloomsbury possible, although, as an immediate ancestor, Bloomsbury paid him comparatively little attention. Bloomsbury wished to live lives that were deeply imbued with art, yet in ways that were not overly attenuated and refined. That is what it aimed for at Charleston. In my view, it would not have been possible if Morris had not pointed the way.

---

[22] James Hall, "Patchwork Phoenix," *Times Literary Supplement*, June 7, 1996.
[23] Reed, *A Roger Fry Reader*, pp. 167-69.

PART THREE

BLOOMSBURY

14

BLOOMSBURY IN SUSSEX

Bloomsbury has always been associated with place; indeed one can say that this has almost been inevitably true of English literature—probably other literatures too—but in England in its own special way. City and country has always been a great, and contrasting, theme in English literature, as in English lives, with a deep affection for the countryside and the desire to have a country home. In London itself many of the English living there wish (and many succeed) to have a garden, a bit of country in the city. Houses as such have always played an important part in English literature, in specific works and in the lives of those who wrote them. So too has this been intensely true with the Bloomsbury group and its two central members.

Both of them of course are quite well known—the writer more than the artist, perhaps—the Stephen sisters, but to give them their better known married names: Virginia Woolf and Vanessa Bell. The sisters themselves are the subject of two recent books, Diane Gillespie's *The Sisters' Arts: the Writing and Painting of Virginia Woolf and Vanessa Bell*, published in 1988, and Jane Dunn's *A Very Close Conspiracy*, published in 1990. I wish to tell a somewhat different story, about the houses in Sussex that were ultimately their country homes, and increasingly their main residences, Vanessa Bell's Charleston Farmhouse, and Virginia Woolf's Monk's House, as well as the two Sussex houses associated with them earlier, Little Talland House and Asheham. (Incidentally both Charleston and Monk's House are open to the public, the former as a Trust on its own, and the other as part of the National Trust.)

I will not discuss the contrasts between the sisters in all their aspects, but rather the relation between the two houses, similarities and tensions. Perhaps there will be implications about the differences between the way of the writer and the way of the artist. At the same time, I will attempt to tell the story of Bloomsbury in Sussex, that area on the South Downs near Lewes and not very far from Brighton which, since the early part of this century, has been associated with the group, and has been called Bloomsbury-by-the-Sea in contast to Bloomsbury in London.

My own interest in Bloomsbury began in the early 1950s when, on a summer trip to England, I was taken by a graduate of King's College to visit it at Cambridge, the college being closely associated with the group. I think maybe the desire to know more about where I had visited helped steer me to Bloomsbury, and I wrote a senior essay at Yale that was partially about Julian Bell, Vanessa Bell's son and Virginia Woolf's nephew, killed tragically in the Spanish Civil War where he was serving as an ambulance driver. When I applied to study at King's I mentioned my interest in Bloomsbury and those who read my application were amused at this brash American. For them, the members of Bloomsbury were their friends, not a subject for study. In any case, I did a second B.A. in history there, and did not return to my interest in Bloomsbury until some years later. Since then, I have been revisiting the subject from time to time. Virginia Woolf was hardly unknown in the 1950s, but the first study of the group as such had just been published then, the first hint of the avalanche that was to come.

There does tend to be a difference in approach between Britain and America in Woolf studies. I call the American scholars of Woolf Lupines and the British Woolfians—and my attempt is to steer a middle course. One bone of contention between them is over the subject of sexual abuse, such a matter of concern nowadays. No one questions that Virginia's older half brothers, George and Gerald Duckworth, went far beyond proper behavior, Gerald examining her private parts when she was six and George coming in to embrace her at the end of the day—one doesn't know how far he went—when she was in her late teens. Virginia has won the war against her half brothers and the common view of them is as insensitive and dumb oafs. Certainly they did not act properly but they had more interesting careers than one might expect: Gerald founded a publishing house, Duckworths, that still exists, and George was the longtime secretary of the Royal Commission of Historical Monuments and was made a knight.

Family obviously has a lot to do with where one lives. Julia Stephen, the mother of them all, died in 1895. Vanessa and Virginia remained with their father, Sir Leslie Stephen, in the grand house in Kensington until his death in 1904. Then the four orphans, the two sisters and their brothers, Thoby and Adrian, proposed to move to respectable but unfashionable Bloomsbury (hence some years later giving birth to the name of the group), the area in London around the British Museum. The Duckworth brothers disapproved because even though their half siblings were in their twenties, they would be unchaperoned. Gerald was off on his own, having established his publishing house in 1898. George lived with the others in Kensington. He had served for ten years as an assistant to George Booth in his great survey of London; at this point, 1904, he was a private secretary for the eminent rising Tory politician, Austen Chamberlain. George very likely would have gritted his teeth, and insisted on joining the four young Stephens in Bloomsbury if he had not, in September 1904, made an aristocratic marriage to Lady Margaret Herbert, a daughter of the Earl of Carnarvon. On their marriage, they settled at Dalingridge Place, near East Grinstead, in Sussex. Later, Virginia was on sufficiently good terms with George to spend two months at his house in Sussex recovering from her suicide attempt in 1913. Yet even in these years she preferred to avoid him. And she did come to dislike the Duckworth brothers more and more as time passed. The point of this disgression is that as far as I know, with one slight exception, this was the only family connection with Sussex before 1910. But I don't want to make too much of it. It may well have been that Sussex, a county close to London, simply was a logical choice to look for a place in the country. Roger Fry, who knew Edward Perry Warren, an eccentric American art collector living in Lewes, may have mentioned the area to Virginia—they were just coming to know one another in 1910. But it may have been pure chance that led her to visit Sussex, when she had it in mind to find a house in the country.

There were other possibilities for a holiday home but they were too far from London to be practical for young people beginning to make their careers and needing to be close to those who might commission works from them. Growing up, the Stephen children had adored Talland House in St. Ives in Cornwall where they spent family summers, and which Woolf would later immortalize in *To the Lighthouse*. But it was too remote. And though the Bell family and Virginia had also had enjoyable holidays in Dorset at Studland, remembered in the snapshots Vanessa took, and in her painting of

1912 of Studland Beach. But even Dorset was a little too far as a practical choice. For whatever reason, in December 1910 Virginia was in Lewes looking for a place. Thirteen years earlier, the Stephens had spent a two-week holiday in nearby Brighton at Eastertime right after their half sister Stella's wedding (she was to die tragically the following July) which included some bicycling around Lewes. Yet Virginia, in her diary of the time, gives no indication that this is where she would like someday to have a place in the country. But all three holiday locations had in common a proximity to the sea.

1910, particularly December, based on Virginia Woolf's famous remark of 1924, that "on or about December 1910 human character changed," was a crucial year and month for Bloomsbury. In terms of Sussex that statement is absolutely true. 1910 had been a busy and not happy year for Virginia, with a nervous breakdown in the summer, and after her recovery a new name for, and dedication to working on, her first novel, *The Voyage Out*, which would not be published until 1915 by her half brother's firm.

Virginia and her younger brother, Adrian, went to the Pelham Arms in Lewes on Christmas eve, 1910. Perhaps they wanted to be away from London at Christmas when the city tends to close down or perhaps they found Clive and Vanessa and their two sons too much of a unit that might exclude them at the holiday time and in any case the Bells had gone to his family in the country at the manor house at Seend in Wiltshire. The Bells had been deeply solicitous of Virginia during the year, looking after her at a holiday at Blean near Canterbury and at Studland, but there were tensions between them as Vanessa had not totally forgiven Virginia for her flirtation with Clive a few years before, although by 1910 it had become less ardent. Even so, Clive did write to Virginia about the possible acquisition of a place of her own: "Will you have a little spare-room in your cottage and invite me to sleep in it often? If so I'm all in favour of the purchase." Virginia wrote to her sister from Lewes on Christmas day, about herself and her brother: "The eccentricity of our appearance is magnificent. Adrians hair flows like a crazy poets; then we bought him a Harvest hat for a shilling, a strawberry roan colour suited for an August afternoon. I wear a bright purple cloak, over my red dress, with a small black toque. . . . Yesterday by the way (Adrian will tell the story) I got past the ticket inspector with a dog ticket. Hans had mine. . . . We have just discovered that one can telephone from here; Duncan [Grant] can be talked to for two pence. Adrian comes up beaming, from Love, I suppose. I withdrew discreetly." But she also reported on her house hunting. "As usual, I am violently in favour of a country life. . . . I like looking out places on the map; already I have bought two guides and planned several expeditions. The country is very beautiful." She assures Clive that if he and Vanessa really would come to stay, she would buy a cottage. By New Year's Day she had come very close to committing herself; she wrote to her close friend Violet Dickinson that she "may be going to take a cottage in the neighborhood. It is a very ugly villa; but underneath the downs, in a charming village [of Firle]." That was a very accurate description of the house, which she called Little Talland House, in memory of the Talland House of St. Ives. The rent was £19.10 a year. On New Year's Day she wrote to Lady Ottoline Morrell "I am very much tempted to buy a house here. One has the most lovely downs at one's door, and there are beautiful 18th century houses, with Corinthian pillars inside, oak panels, and marble mantelpieces." Probably the ugly house was thought of as a temporary base from which to look for something more permanent.

During 1911 she spent a fair amount of time at Firle, and invited her friends and relations there, and was enjoying it: "a starlight walk upon the downs, a horse nibbling and taking one for a great white sheep, a flock ringing bells, startled birds and the sea too." She wrote to Molly MacCarthy: "The villa is inconceivably ugly, done up in patches of post-impressionist colour." She was pleased to miss a visit from George and Margaret Duckworth: "Thank God I was out, having fallen into the canal. Margaret was heard to say she'd never seen a prettier house."

Whatever the quality of the house, Virginia was becoming increasingly enthusiasic about the area. Leonard Woolf, now back on leave from the civil service in Ceylon, would come to stay, with others. It was an active time in her personal life: Walter Lamb proposed to her during 1911, then in December, Sydney Waterlow proposed, and in January 1912, Leonard. She turned them all down but would change her mind about Leonard in the Spring. And she also changed house; at the end of 1911, she transferred her lease on the house in Firle to a Cambridge friend of Leonard's, Robin Mayor. She now went to the second Bloomsbury house in Sussex. This was Asham or Asheham, quite close to Firle, not in a village but on its own, although with some cottages nearby. Asham is apparently the correct name, going back to the twelfth century meaning valley of asses, but the longer spelling was more common when Virginia lived there.

It is the one Bloomsbury-in-Sussex house that no longer exists, having been quite recently demolished. There was an intriguing debate about its demolition, and I was one of those who wrote a letter to the local authority protesting against it happening. But perhaps the location had already been so ruined that the poor house needed to be put out of its misery. The house was derelict then but presumably could have been restored. The issue was whether, because of its place in Bloomsbury history, it should be saved. Although the house remained, all around it had changed. Worst of all, the development of a cement works next door caused fumes, toxic dust, and other horrors, from 1932 on. Virginia referred to the perpetrators as "these damnable buggers" and that "this kind of outrage is among the real sorrows of life." Hills had been built up (although covered with growth) and plunged the house into a small valley with no view when earlier it had looked over the downs to the sea. The barn opposite the property is being converted into a youth hostel for walkers and cyclists on the south Downs and will incorporate elements of the demolished house and a display about Bloomsbury. So in some sense the tradition continues.

In many ways it could be argued that Asheham, however intermittently occupied, was the most significant of the Bloomsbury houses in Sussex. It was the single base, a place for the unity of the arts, where Virginia could write and Vanessa and her friends could paint, in the early and most intense years of Bloomsbury before the First World War. This was the time when the group had just secured, in 1910, the adherence of Roger Fry and E. M. Forster. Since Vanessa's marriage in 1907 the sisters had lived separately, although close by, in London. But they would frequently be together at Asheham. It was here, in December 1915, that Carrington crept into Lytton Strachey's bedroom, planning to cut off his beard in revenge for his attempt to kiss her when, as his eyes opened, she fell in love with him, despite his homosexuality, and they spent the rest of their lives together. It was here that Vanessa painted rather post-impressionist portraits of her sister with her face interestingly verging toward the blank—the artist in paint commenting on the artist in words?

Asheham was discovered by Leonard and Virginia in the Fall of 1911 when they were on a walk in the Ouse Valley. Immediately responsive to it, she leased the house for five years. Quentin Bell in his great biography of his aunt desribes it as "a strange and beautiful house in a lonely and romantic situation a few miles to the west of Firle." Leonard called it "romantic, gentle, melancholy, lovely." Virginia was there, in the end, for seven years, and it was the great prelude to the two major houses. The house was inhabited fitfully all through the year, not just the summer, but for the major holidays of Christmas and New Year's, numerous weekends and at times for weeks at a time. The house, apparently built around 1820 by a Lewes solicitor, Mr. Hoper, whose descendants still owned it until the mid 1920s, had two drawing rooms on the ground floor and a pavilion which was turned into a studio. There were four principal bedrooms upstairs and servants' rooms. As Richard Shone has written: "the view . . . was one of its glories, taking in the pastures of the Ouse Valley, across to the villages of Rodmell and Iford and the Downs beyond." There was also a belief by some that the house was haunted, which Virginia drew upon in her early short sketch "A Haunted House." Lytton Strachey described a visit in a letter to Lady Ottoline Morrell: "Conversation, as you may imagine, eddied and swirled unceasingly . . . but I managed to survive, and actually at the last moment succeeded in winning 30/- from them all at poker." Although Virginia had the lease, Vanessa frequently rented it and entertained there, notably when Virginia was away on her long honeymoon trip and for six months during her very serious breakdown of 1913. By 1916 Vanessa and Duncan Grant, as we shall see, had established themselves at nearby Charleston, and the Woolfs were the sole occupants of Asheham. They had guests but with the advent of the First World War (and during it one could hear the guns from France); with Virginia's breakdown; with the contrast in style of the two sisters—the three remaining Asheham years were more austere and quieter; not in the more exuberant manner of before the war. Then they were all younger, and personal and sexual arrangements were being sorted out. It was before the Bloomsbury figures had become better known, recognizable as "figures." Then, much to the Woolfs' distress, in 1918, Hoper, the owner of the house, informed them, giving them a year's notice, that he wanted the house for his bailiff.

In the meantime, in 1916, Vanessa Bell had come to Charleston, where she would spend a great deal of her time, alternating with London and long holidays in France, until her death in 1961, and so did the painter Duncan Grant until his death in 1978. The two of them had started painting together about 1912, and designed together for the Omega Workshops from 1913 to 1919. Grant had become very much part of the Bloomsbury circle, as a painter, as a first cousin of Lytton Strachey, as the beautiful young man whom Lytton, John Maynard Keynes, and Adrian Stephen were all in love with.

Vanessa would fall in love with him as well, and it was the most important attachment for the rest of her life. They lived together a good deal of the time at Charleston, had a child together, Angelica, born at Charleston on Christmas day, 1918. Yet Grant's primary commitment was homosexual and he had a series of lovers, many of whom became good friends of Vanessa's, although she was disturbed when one of them, the novelist David Garnett, married Angelica, 26 years younger than he, as his second wife.

Vanessa was famously apolitical and once while at Lady Ottoline's country house, Garsington, turned to the man sitting next to her, who happened to be the prime minister, Asquith, and asked him what he did. But the war did impinge upon her to the extent that she wanted to help Grant and Garnett to do agricultural labor as conscientious objectors when conscription was introduced in January 1916. It was a choice of doing that or going into military service. Duncan's father, a retired major in the army, although disapproving of his son's position, was managing an estate, Wissett, in Suffolk and didn't object to Duncan, and Garnett, whom he referred to as "your friend Garbage," working on the land there. They were called up by the Conscription Tribunal where Philip Morrell, Ottoline's husband, an M.P. who opposed the war, John Maynard Keynes, then holding a major position in the Treasury, and Adrian, then a barrister, represented them. But this galaxy did not impress the board in Suffolk; perhaps it was counterproductive. The Board ruled that they could not work on their own, but would need to be employed as farm laborers. Because of Asheham, they were more likely to know farmers who would be willing to employ them in Sussex. Virginia had found a house that might do: Charleston. It had been a farmhouse which had then served as a boardinghouse, presumably for simple country vacations. It was owned by Lord Gage of Firle Place and in fact continued to be so until 1981. Adrian, also a conscientious objector, and his wife Karin were interested in it but Virginia preferred that Vanessa take it. She must have mentioned it to her before the first time the house appears in her letters in May 1916: "I wish you'd leave Wissett, and take Charleston. Leonard went over it, and says its a most delightful house and strongly advises you to take it. . . . It has a charming garden, with a pond, and fruit trees, and vegetables, all now rather run wild, but you could make it lovely. The house is very nice, with large rooms, and one room with big windows fit for a studio. . . 4 miles from us, so you wouldn't be badgered by us." In August Vanessa came to look for herself and was not overwhelmed but she may have been taken by the quality of the light and the setting on the way to Firle Beacon. She came again a few days later, after she secured a promise from a farmer of work for Grant and Garnett, and she agreed to rent. On September 24 Virginia wrote to Vanessa to reinforce her decision: "Leonard says that there are certainly 8 bedrooms, probably more, and very good ones, two big sitting rooms on the ground floor and one small one; and very good large rooms on the first floor. He says the garden could be made lovely—there are fruit trees, and vegetables, and a most charming walk under trees. The only drawbacks seemed to be that there is cold water, and no hot, in the bathroom, not a very nice w.c., and a cesspool in the tennis court. . . . I do envy you, taking a new house—Nothing in the world is so exciting." She concluded her letter: "I'm sure, if you get Charleston, you'll end by buying it forever. If you lived there, you could make it absolutely divine."

In October it was settled: Vanessa, Duncan, David Garnett, and her two sons moved in. Virginia was absolutely right, and with the two houses Bloomsbury-by-the-Sea was established. Vanessa was devoted to her painting but did not achieve the same fame as her sister as a writer. But more so than her sister, her work of art was her life, with her children and the creation of an "earthly paradise" at Charleston, a project that started in 1916 and continued until Duncan's death in 1978.

The house was a considerable challenge, with water needing to be pumped and heated by wood, and there was no electricity until 1933. But eventually the house began to take shape, pulsating with the richness and fecundity of existence. Vanessa resented how much time had to be given to the house and how it kept her away from her painting. She was a painter with a growing reputation, as was Grant, and they continued to exhibit. In her diary for April 1, 1930, Virginia wrote: "Nessa is at Charleston. They will have the windows open; perhaps even sit by the pond. She will think This is what I have made by years of unknown work—my sons, my daughter. She will be perfectly content (as I suppose)." But in terms of art and continuing fame, there is no question that the far less psychologically secure, the suicidal Virginia, has had the far greater triumph. As so frequently happens in families, there was intense love but also a certain rivalry between the two. One feels that the very heart of Bloomsbury was the two sisters. Virginia played the role of the jolly aunt who would come over to Charleston to amuse, as she suggests in the preface to *Orlando*. In the children's paper in the mid 1920s they recorded the case of the disappearing aunt. "It appears that for some whim she decided to eat her tea under a hay stack instead of in Charleston dining room. The difference, however, is not great, and it is even possible that she mistook the one for the other." But as the children grew older, the role might become a little oppressive. She wrote in her diary in 1934 about visiting Charleston that she was "thoroughly irritated . . . with myself for being a good fairy Aunt. Lord how that role can bore me—how unreal it is—& why do I act it?" But this was likely to be a momentary regret in what was generally a very happy relation.

There were compensations for living in a calmer atmosphere. Virginia recorded in her diary an earlier visit in March 1919: "Charleston is by no means a gentleman's house. I bicycled round there in a flood of rain, & found the baby asleep in its cot, & Nessa & Duncan sitting over the fire, with bottles & bibs & basins all round them. . . . . By extreme method & unselfishness & routine on Nessa's and Duncan's parts chiefly [the cook was ill], the dinner is cooked, & innumerable refills of hotwater bottles & baths supplied. One has the feeling of living on the brink of a move. In one of the little islands of comparative order Duncan set up his canvas, & Bunny [Garnett] wrote a novel in a set of copy books." Certainly Virginia preferred Asheham, as she wrote in her diary in May: Asheham "compares very well with Charleston; indeed I've never come back to it without the feeling of being incredulous as one perfection was added to another. . . . I got over to Charleston, though; & had a night & morning alone with V.—so far as she can ever be alone. There was Pitcher, the new gardener; Angelica; Julian & Quentin of course; the new nurse; & a fire which wouldn't burn. Indeed living is fairly bare at the moment. . . My life, by comparison, seemed padded at every turn."

But as we know, the Asheham paradise was not to last. In June, the Woolfs bought, for £300, the Round House, a converted windmill, on the walls of Lewes Castle, with a nice view;"the general oddity & character of the whole place were the result of finding something that would do, that one could conceive living in, that was cheap." But then a little less than a month later they bought in nearby Rodmell another house, Monk's House ("a name I hope to write many thousands of times before I've done with it"). In the pages of her diary she tells the dramatic story of the acquisition of Monk's House, how she and Leonard saw a notice of its forthcoming auction as they went up to the street in Lewes to see the Round

House. They went to examine Monk's House; they found the building and the view acceptable but the garden magnificent: "the size & shape & fertility & wildness of the garden. There seemed an infinity of fruitbearing trees; the plums crow[d]ed so as to weigh the tip of the branch down; unexpected flowers sprouted among cabbages." They knew the house from walks already and Leonard much admired its owner, "a great character" and a mainstay of the village. "They have died out with the earth closets in the laurel shrubberies. I am glad that I knew them and for a short time lived in the village among them." Monk's House too, like Charleston at this point had no water, gas or electricity. It had eight or nine rooms which, by tearing down thin partitions, were made into six. Virginia's diary in July 1919 tells the excitement of the auction and acquiring the house for £700, £100 less than they were willing to go. "I purple in the cheeks, & L. trembling like a reed."

They moved to Monk's House on September 1, 1919. Virginia would be there until 1941, when she drowned herself in the river Ouse a five minutes' walk from the house across a meadow. Leonard lived on there until his death in 1969. Monk's House was said to be a fifteenth- or sixteenth-century house that had been used as a retreat by the monks of Lewes priory, although Leonard did not believe the story. The name "Monk's House" was bestowed upon the house for the first time in the posting for the auction. Leonard did research into the history of the house, tracing it back to 1707. Only three different families had lived there between then and the Woolfs' purchase. The house was somewhat modernized while they were there, with plumbing much improved in 1926. Part of the previous year, Virginia had devoted herself to journalism, specifically to pay for these improvements. Two further rooms added on in 1929 were financed by *Orlando*. The house gave them great pleasure; Leonard worked hard in the garden, producing a place of beauty.

Virginia liked to play up the inferiority of Monk's House to Charleston, claiming, despite Vanessa's protests to the contrary, that she had been very critical of it when she, Duncan and the children stayed there while Virginia was abroad. Vanessa wrote to her from Monk's House "Did I say I preferred Charleston to this? No, of course you've made it up. So I shall say nothing, except that I think both houses suitable to their owners." She also consulted her sister about decoration. Virginia wrote in 1926 "I do not like to insinuate that your genius with the brush and the pot is badly required: but so it is; and I have purposely left several bare beams in the drawing rooms, should you feel inspired. I will say this: it has the makings of a most peculiar and I think comfortable, charming, characteristic, queer resort; but a paralysis attacks my vision when directed to practical details. What curtains? What chair covers?" Virginia liked to tease—perhaps an understatement. She continued: "Would I be allowed some rather garish but vibrating green and red lustres on the mantelpiece? Showers of glass, shaped like long fingers in a bunch—you know my taste that way. Also I want to buy a ship in a glass bottle: also a mother of pearl and wooden platter."

How different were the houses? Both were places where there were great creative achievements in which the most important figures were Vanessa and Virginia, although Duncan and Leonard painted and wrote respectively themselves to no mean degree. Both houses had their visitors, although more at Charleston and more lived there; there was more room but it also differed in the spirit of the place. Particularly in the 1920s, it had more the feeling of a commune, particularly with the three children and the constant coming and going, while for the Woolfs, Monk's House, despite frequent visitors, was more a place of retreat. Vanessa, the daughter of Sir Leslie Stephen, was an articulate woman, as her letters show, but hers was the way of the painter, and one who on the whole painted domesticity. Hers was the world of sensuality. She was unrestrained. Virginia was much more sensitive and although she reveled in gossip and invention, was an intense intellectual. Whether rightly or wrongly, they had ultimately decided for the sake of her health that she should not have children. Whether because of the molestation by her half brothers or for other reasons, it was thought that she was sexually frigid. She had attracted proposals when young but her commitment to Leonard was not notably passionate, although they became a couple deeply devoted to one another. So it was not surprising that on the whole Charleston was a house of sensuality and Monk's House of austerity. Charleston was larger and perhaps more welcoming, although somewhat more isolated, not being in a village.

Is the difference between the houses reflected in the rooms themselves? That sort of judgment is hard to make, particularly as so many of the furnishings at Monk's House were designed by Vanessa and Duncan. Probably the grandest room in Charleston is Duncan's studio, added in 1925 based on plans made by Roger Fry. Its most impressive feature are Duncan's caryatids below the mantel shelf of the fireplace. There is also his screen from the Omega Workshop. And one is reminded that there is a grand lineage in the Bloomsbury group, although in this case not quite of blood, in that the walnut early-nineteenth-century Cabinet had belonged to Thackeray, the father of Leslie Stephen's first wife, and within it one can see a plate designed by Vanessa. The other large room at Charleston is the garden room. It is famous for its literary associations, for here Lytton Strachey read from *Eminent Victorians* and Desmond MacCarthy explained *The Waste Land*, published by the Woolfs' Hogarth Press, to Clive Bell and Duncan Grant. This room once contained pictures by Picasso, Gris, Vlaminck, Matisse, and Rouault. Now it has on loan a small Matisse that Fry bequeathed to Vanessa. The sitting room of Monk's House is much more austere and with furniture from the seventeenth to the twentieth centuries. The table and chairs were designed by Vanessa and Duncan, commissioned by the Woolfs. Virginia had commissioned Duncan and Vanessa to the extent of £100 to design furniture for this room and complained that Vanessa did not charge the full amount. But one can sense the awkwardness of the situation: Virginia wanted to help a less prosperous and older sister (as well as being happy to have the decoration) but it must have rankled a little. I do think it is quite striking, considering that so many of the objects and paintings at Monk's House were done by Vanessa and Duncan, that the feeling of the rooms should be so different.

I've attempted to say something of Bloomsbury's life in Sussex, the three houses that Virginia Woolf lived in there, the second shared to an extent with her sister, and the one house dominated by Vanessa. Although it is not true, as it is frequently said, that no inch of Charleston was left undecorated, it was certainly far more of a creation than Monk's House. It was the house of artists, not a house of writers. Vanessa both reveled in her creation and resented the time it demanded of her. Much more than her sister, she created a world of paint and decoration, of children, of visitors, of life, at Charleston. She had great talent but less than her sister's. Good as she was, I do not believe that she would have been a greater artist if she had devoted less time to creating the world of Charleston. It is harder to say whether Virginia would have been a lesser figure if she and Leonard had decided to take what Leonard saw as the psychic risk of having children. As her diaries and letters demonstrate, she was deeply involved with the world; she was hardly a recluse. Comparatively primitive as Monk's House might have been, particularly in its early years, she (as did Vanessa) had servants and she had Leonard. She had time for her art. Did she choose art over life? Did the commitment, after the completion of *Between the Acts*, over-strain her and help lead to her suicide? These are issues that cannot be resolved, but through their country houses I've attempted to come closer to the lives of two extraordinary women.

15

S. P. ROSENBAUM ON BLOOMSBURY

S. P. Rosenbaum's *Victorian Bloomsbury: The Early Literary History of the Bloomsbury Group* (1987) is an immensely useful book, an essential "survey" for anyone who wishes to go on to further study of the antecedents of the Bloomsbury group, or wishes to know about its origins and earliest years. It emphasizes the connection of the group with Victorian forebears. The theme is not new, and Noel Annan in his studies of Leslie Stephen (1951; revised edition, 1984) made very clear the continuities of the intellectual aristocracy, stretching back to the Clapham Sect: the similarities of seriousness and high-mindedness. But it is still more common, I believe, to think of the group as in rebellion against Victorianism—which indeed to some extent it was.

In the context of this study, it might be too easy to tend to forget the ways in which the group was in rebellion against the pieties of the past. There should be a few more reminders of the sort Rosenbaum offers when he remarks on the importance for Bloomsbury of Samuel Butler's *The Way of All Flesh* (1903): "More than any other contemporary work it smashed the moral, religious and educational icons of the Victorian patriarchy."

The group itself when looking back tended to have mixed feelings about its coherence, and its origins, but Rosenbaum demonstrates effectively the extent that its members shared ideas in common. He discusses Bloomsbury's descent from the mainstream of Victorianism, pointing out how much it owed to those great intellectual and social movements: evangelicalism and utilitarianism. True, Bloomsbury itself was not religious, and would not tolerate the endless worry with which late Victorians rejected God. G. Lowes Dickinson gave a paper to the Apostles, "Shall We Elect God?" to which the answer was no; nevertheless God appeared as an attractive figure in the discourse. (An example of Dickinson's relentless fairness.) But Bloomsbury certainly believed in seriousness, and there were remnants of the evangelical tradition in its commitment to truth and in not hesitating—perhaps enjoying?—to tell the truth to one another, painful though it might be. As Rosenbaum points out, there was also a Quaker tradition in the group, perhaps reflected in their willingness to sit in silence if no one had anything worth saying. As is so frequently the case, they were much more in the traditions of their parents than they would have liked to believe.

Rosenbaum also makes clear how much the group owed to utilitarianism, but it was a utilitarianism greatly transformed by Cambridge philosophers. This study is quite splendid in showing the interconnectedness of the group and explaining how it could be both so committed to rationality, but also, perhaps surprisingly, shot through with Platonism and even mysticism. The famous theme of *Howards End* (1911), "only connect" the prose and the passion, the rational and irrational, can now be seen not only as a special quality of E. M. Forster, but shared by the rest of the group, to a degree in the philosophy it learned at Cambridge, encapsulated, perhaps, in the "moments of being" emphasized by Virginia Woolf.

Rosenbaum tells us of the group's experiences, mostly, admittedly, the men's, with a full discussion of their time in Cambridge. There is some attention to the growing up of the Stephen sisters, but the emphasis here is on the shared experience at university. (Of course the group would take on its London existence through the sisters, in the traditional womanly way, providing a salon for the men, but, most notably in its willingness to discuss sex in mixed company, their gatherings lost most resemblances to a proper Victorian at home.) The group's education at Cambridge was primarily from one another, and from the dons who were members of the Apostles. They did not, on the whole, do that well in their examinations. Rosenbaum is illuminating on the contrasts between King's and Trinity, the Cambridge colleges the men attended, King's being more aesthetic and Trinity more severe. (And the book is appropriately bound and jacketed in King's purple.) He tells us about their studies, their readings, their early writings. His own readings in all the areas of interest to Bloomsbury are prodigious in themselves, and he has drawn from a wide range of sources. The bibliography and references are extremely handy for further investigation. He ends with a brief discussion of Bloomsbury writings at Cambridge. On the whole their efforts were rather disappointing, and the section reads more like an appendix than part of the text. On the other hand, it makes Bloomsbury a little less daunting to discover that their juvenilia is less impressive than one might have expected.

Perhaps the most important part of the book is the penultimate chapter dealing with Cambridge philosophers, those dons who were senior members of the Apostles. The magical moments happened when Keynes, Lytton Strachey, and Leonard Woolf were undergraduate members. (Forster and Roger Fry had been elected some years before.) Rosenbaum provides a brief exposition of the ideas of J. E. McTaggart, Bertrand Russell, and G. E. Moore. Although Keynes was the most adept at philosophy of the group, Rosenbaum tends to agree with Woolf rather than Keynes that quite a few of the ideas of the philosophers, particularly of course those contained in the canonical book for Bloomsbury, G. E. Moore's *Principia Ethica* (1903), were extremely important for the future of the group. But Rosenbaum may give these young men a little too much credit. Were most of the group sufficiently philosophically sophisticated to operate at the level Rosenbaum does himself in his discussion of the philosophers? But in a non-technical sense, the continual tension between appearance and reality can be seen as the enduring and central question for Bloomsbury, and that question was largely derived from the Cambridge philosophers.

This valuable volume of the early literary history of Bloomsbury before it was Bloomsbury is important for what it tells us of the group's origins, what Bloomsbury owed to its own intellectual and personal past, to its time at Cambridge, and to the older generation there. We can now clearly see why "Victorian" and "Bloomsbury" can legitimately if perhaps somewhat surprisingly come together in the title of this study.

S. P. Rosenbaum's *Edwardian Bloomsbury: The Early Literary History of the Bloomsbury Group* (1994) is the second volume of a formidable enterprise, and part of a series of publications by the same author that may entitle him to the position as the leading scholar of the Bloomsbury Group. He started on a comparatively small scale in 1975 with a valuable anthology, *The Bloomsbury Group*, supplemented in 1993 with a second selection, *The Bloomsbury Group Reader*. In 1992 he published an edition of the manuscript of *A Room of One's Own*, entitled *Women and Fiction*, based on the manuscript that he had discovered in the library of the Fitzwilliam Museum, Cambridge. But most important has been the present enterprise of which this is the second volume, taking the Group from 1903 through 1910. The first volume, *Victorian Bloomsbury*, concentrated on the origins of the Group and the experiences of its men at Cambridge, with particular emphasis upon Cambridge philosophy. Rosenbaum then hoped to complete his study with one more volume, but we are now promised a third, *Georgian Bloomsbury*, which will take the Group through the First World War.

One assumes that volume three will complete the early literary history, as after 1918 the Group became far better known. They were in fact in those years somewhat less cohesive, though seeing a great deal of one another, and the golden years as a Group are probably in the eight years to be dealt with in the book to come. The time of its greatest reputation will still be in the future: after 1918 their productivity became so considerable that it would be a task, should anyone undertake it, requiring innumerable volumes to discuss their writings with the thoroughness of the present work.

The subtitle is to be taken quite literally. When appropriate, Rosenbaum alludes to later work, demonstrating his extraordinary command of the writings of the Group as well as of the critical literature. Even though the painters of the group, Vanessa Bell and Duncan Grant, play a role, as they must, there is virtually no discussion of their work or the less significant paintings by Roger Fry. Fry's prose is given a chapter but as it is more significant for art history than as literature, he is not studied in the same detail. Rosenbaum also appears slightly less at ease with the writings of Leonard Woolf, who was a civil servant in Ceylon during the period of the book and hence away from the main action. Rosenbaum does discuss his fiction—*The Village in the Jungle* and *Stories from the East*—but he is far less of a literary character than the other writers considered, and it doesn't quite work to use the relevant volume of autobiography, *Growing*, written many years later, as a major text of his Ceylon period, when virtually all other writings considered are contemporary with their time. The work of the greatest twentieth-century economist, John Maynard Keynes, is not discussed. It is a legitimate decision to exclude him, even though he would have provided further evidence for Rosenbaum's major theme: the great influence of the philosopher G. E. Moore.

Except for E. M. Forster, who published four of his five novels at quite an early age, and Roger Fry, who was quite a bit older, the other members of Bloomsbury were hardly known throughout this period. The third volume will herald their later fame to a much greater degree, as Virginia Woolf published her first novel, *The Voyage Out*, in 1915, and Lytton Strachey burst upon the world with *Eminent Victorians* in 1918.

It is very impressive, however, to how great a degree Rosenbaum has managed to write with freshness and insight about Forster's novels, no matter how much they have been analyzed before. His concluding chapter on *Howards End* appears to me to be a tour de force. I would not, however, assent completely with his claim that *Howards End* is the essence of Bloomsbury. It seems to me to give much more play to the mystical and have much more respect for the world of the Wilcoxes than Bloomsbury generally tolerated. Forster's relationship to Bloomsbury in any case has always been somewhat tangential, and it was not, I believe, until the end of 1910 that Forster met the Stephen sisters. Other than a rather evenhanded review by Clive Bell of *Howards End*, Bloomsbury did not appear to take much notice of its publication at the time, even in its correspondence. And, as Rosenbaum notes, Woolf's and Forster's attitude toward one another's fiction would show in the future some streaks of ambivalence.

In the light of Rosenbaum's first volume, and its emphasis upon Cambridge, the chapter here on *The Longest Journey* is particularly interesting. Its title is significant, "The Refutation of Idealism," placing emphasis on the novel's concern with philosophy more than, as I see it, being a young man's *bildungsroman*. It is true that Ansell and the cow are quite important in the novel, and that many parallels can be found with Moore's philosophy. No doubt Forster was heavily influenced by the Moorean "atmosphere" at Cambridge, particularly among his fellow Apostles, but he was no longer an undergraduate at the time of the publication of *Principia Ethica* in 1903. Its emphasis on the reality beneath appearance, on a sophisticated utilitarianism that wishes to shed the practicality of its nineteenth-century origins, while at the same time not being as removed from the world as Whistlerian aestheticism, is extremely important for Forster and the other members of Bloomsbury. Yet as Rosenbaum tells us, Forster never read Moore, though of course that does not prevent influence. Indeed, in both volumes Rosenbaum seems to me to be perhaps a little overanxious to argue the importance of the influence of Moore. He is, however, absolutely right about Moore's significance as the unifying intellectual factor in early Bloomsbury.

But the greatest contribution that this study makes is in its splen-

did discussion of the comparatively "unknown" writings of Bloomsbury, the short works, mostly essays and reviews, that Bloomsbury
wrote in its apprenticeship. One major figure, Desmond MacCarthy,
never really moved further, despite the highest expectations. The
Court Theatre, 1904-1907 of 1907 was his only proper book, his
other volumes being collections, as even his first one was to a degree.
Rosenbaum brings into play the complicated world of Edwardian serious journalism, most particularly MacCarthy's connections with
the *Independent Review*, the *New Quarterly*, and the *Speaker*, Bell's
and Fry's with the *Athenaeum*, and Virginia Woolf's with the *Times
Literary Supplement*.

Almost all of Virginia Woolf's early work has now been published, most importantly in the fine ongoing series edited by Andrew
McNeillie. Even so, Bloomsbury's shorter writings have not been
discussed critically with the acumen and thoroughness that they receive here. It is a substantial challenge to expatiate in a coherent and
convincing way about a series of short writings, without reducing
the series to one thing after another.

The argument about Lytton Strachey is particularly intriguing as
it demonstrates that it took him far longer to be iconoclastic than
one might have thought. In his private life and conversation, he was
quite unconventional, but as a writer he was doubly caught in family
tradition. It was not until 1910 that he abandoned the attempt to
turn his failed dissertation on Warren Hastings into a book loyal to
the family commitment to India, and most of his early writing was
for the family journal, the *Spectator*. Yet these writings were significant, and Rosenbaum carefully considers the long manuscript of the
dissertation, where Strachey was not yet able to put his two worlds
together, those of appearance and reality: "Looking back from *Eminent Victorians* and his later works, one might see in Strachey's Edwardian Cambridge texts a divorce of the outer from the inner. His
dissertation is almost exclusively concerned with the manifestations
of Hastings's action, whereas his essays for discussion societies are
mostly about states of mind."

Although the world of painting is not his concern, Rosenbaum
ends this study with a mention of Roger Fry's famous "Manet and
Post-Impressionism" exhibition, one of the reasons that Virginia
Woolf wrote in 1924 that "on or about December 1910 human
character changed." The next volume will deal with the effect of that
exhibition upon the Group's writing and much more, I am sure, of
its early literary history.

16

BLOOMSBURY BOOKS

The number of books dealing with Bloomsbury lives—major, minor, and marginal—seems to increase proportionately, not to say perversely, as the material upon which they are based grows thinner, paler, and more familiar. What in the world is left to say of any significance, whether of Goldie or Lytton or Clive or Carrington, that we have not heard already, at least once?

Studies in Virginia Woolf flourish on a truly international scale. Having survived the attacks of her detractors, who once were numerous and audible, she has become the beloved possession of her admirers. The chairman of an eminent English department was heard to remark that one-third of the job-seekers he interviews are in American literature, one-third in English literature, and one-third students of Virginia Woolf.

No matter that this is a slight exaggeration, and no matter, either, that a mandarin, sometimes snobbish writer of genius has been transformed into a not altogether inappropriate hero for women's liberation. The fact remains, students of Virginia Woolf have, on the whole, their priorities right. Most of them are interested in what she wrote: her writings have pride of place. Which is not to say that they are indifferent to the history of her life, and do not hesitate to make of her a symbol of the dilemma and equivocal position of the woman writer. This was, after all, an awareness that Virginia Woolf herself acutely shared, and wrote about in *A Room of One's Own* and *Three Guineas*. Yet one can imagine the tough, wonderfully exaggerated remarks, verging upon cruelty, that she might have made about many of those who now are devoting themselves to her with such passion. But gratittide was not one of her famous virtues.

My own view is that Virginia Woolf, however much a central fig-

ure in Bloomsbury, is coming to occupy a category of her own, like
E. M. Forster's, apart from Bloomsbury, in which she will continue
to exist as a major writer of this century, whereas most of the lesser
Bloomsbury figures will dwindle away to mere names, turning up
and footnoted in her diaries, and in the chapters of literary history
devoted to the Age of Virginia Woolf.

Bloomsbury, that famous group of friends of unequal gifts, suffered, or rather, enjoyed an intense self-consciousness. It had much
pleasure and spent much time in attempting to define itself, and had
great sport in refuting the definitions of outsiders. It even enjoyed
asking the rhetorical question, whether or not there was such a thing
as Bloomsbury at all. In Professor Rosenbaum's voluminous collection of documents, and in Mr. Gadd's brisk canter over familiar ter-
ritory, and indeed, wherever Bloomsbury is discussed, there is the inevitable genealogy, and the inevitable litany of names (Leonard, Virginia, Vanessa, Clive), and then, too, the inevitable litany of addresses, among the squares of the Bloomsbury district of London in
the years before the First World War.

There was "Old," "Ur," and "Young" Bloomsbury—a growing
group of friends, marching along the avenue (to use Quentin Bell's
image,) reshaping from time to time. If I may add a litany of my
own, I would submit, with all the possible "ifs" and "buts" of quali-
fication, that the figures at the center were the novelist Virginia
Woolf, the economist John Maynard Keynes, the biographer Lytton
Strachey, the social critic Leonard Woolf, the art critics Roger Fry
and Clive Bell, and the painters Vanessa Bell and Duncan Grant.
Slightly to one side, but very much their friend, was E. M. Forster.
(His peripheral relation to Bloomsbury is perhaps suggested by the
fact that he left their parties early, before the fun began, to return
each night to his mother in Weybridge, Surrey.) It is important, if
one is to understand the transformations in English art and society in
the first three decades, to know about their work and their lives, but
in the latter regard the degree of detail we are getting about them
now is perhaps getting out of hand: what does it matter, really, in
any significant way, whether or not Lytton Strachey had an erection
while kissing David Garnett?

Bloomsbury lives, separated from Bloomsbury works, are not all
that interesting; and the ordinary reader, as opposed to the addict
(for whom yet another account of hijinks in Gordon Square is
equivalent to a "fix"), has to be sure that the steadily growing literature about Bloomsbury does not obscure the works themselves.

David Gadd's *The Loving Friends* is a useful little guidebook, a sort of program with the names and characters, and a description of what Paul Levy calls the "Bloomsbury Gavotte": that is, who was sleeping with whom, and when. As a former director of Army Education, Gadd writes in a straightforward and biographically useful way. His narrative is a summary of the lives, drawn largely as he says, from Quentin Bell's biography of Virginia Woolf, and Michael Holroyd's of Lytton Strachey, and it makes a perfectly agreeable light read. Gadd does interject an occasional literary judgment or comment into his story, but on the whole, this is quite a wrong-headed book, however handy it might be as a short summation. He believes, contrary to the views of Bloomsbury and most other artists, that the life of the artist counts for more than his art, and in the case of Bloomsbury one can only infer that the Gavotte matters more than the work of the group. "Human beings," he writes, "are less available than their works and always more complex and exciting. There is infinitely more in Lytton Strachey than in *Eminent Victorians*, and Roger Fry's aesthetics are dull compared with Roger Fry. This book then is concerned with people who happened to be writers and artists rather than with the work by which they are well known."

So be it, but the attitude strikes me as wildly askew. It is not as though Gadd were writing fiction, inventing as a character an author named Hilary Strachey, among whose works was an imaginary book called, say, *Those Mad Victorians*. The fact is—the crucial fact, really—is not only that *Eminent Victorians* exists as a work of history, but is itself historically valuable. Cyril Connolly, in *The Modern Moment*, points out very justly that Strachey "struck the note of ridicule which the whole war-weary generation wanted to hear," and of *Eminent Victorians*, "It appeared to the post-war young people like the light at the end of a tunnel."

One is not calling into question the value of literary biography: it can be fascinating and important, exemplary and interesting, in rare cases even a work of art, but not an end in itself. G. E. Moore, the philosopher whose influence upon Bloomsbury was so pervasive, advocated the value of life and art in a mutually enriching relationship. Life is not notably enriched by a description, without much analysis, of the lives of an artistic group in England. Rather, it will be enriched by the degree to which the works, perhaps illuminated by the lives of their creators, survive. If they do not merit survival, then the reading of *The Loving Friends* becomes a form of entertaining and quite harmless voyeurism. Gadd himself is aware of the limitations of the life-without-the-art approach, though he does not appear to apply them to himself. In his nice sketch of Lady Ottoline Morrell, he remarks that she was "for all her remarkable qualities, a woman without talent or taste . . . whose worshipful reverence for artists was never modified by understanding or critical sense. When, in her memoirs, she writes of the artists she knew, she has nothing to say of their work. . . . Not a word of writing or painting; they might as well have been stockbrokers."

Bloomsbury itself, committed to the ideal of absolute honesty in personal relations, did not particularly relish the interest of the outside world. Significantly, its most honest writings about itself came at the meetings of the Memoir Club, which gathered together from 1920 to 1956. It is in the essays for delivery to the club—a number are to be found in Rosenbaum's collection—that one encounters biographical and autobiographical Bloomsbury at its best. Like the upper-class English that they were, they set great store on privacy, and shared that English love of forming small organizations. This had been true of the male members of the group since their undergraduate days at Cambridge, when most of them had been members of that most secret and high-toned of secret societies, the Apostles; and indeed, one might even argue that Bloomsbury was, perhaps unconsciously, an attempt to re-create the Apostles on a larger, more sexually diversified, and vastly more sophisticated scale in the great world. I stress the word English, for Bloomsbury was not quite as revolutionary as it appeared or may have liked to think itself: rather it followed out the verbal implications of what had been the style of English upper-class life even during the previous century. Much of its intellectual and sexual Gavotte it wanted to keep to itself. It believed in the freedom of private life—without hypocrisy, but without proselytizing. However tempting it may be to update Bloomsbury and present its members as our contemporaries, one suspects they might have been offended by the rash of revelations in progress: they were neither gurus of permissiveness nor firm believers in the right of the hoi polloi to know.

Reading the Memoir Club papers, one discovers again, in a peculiarly intimate way, the fascination of Bloomsbury. So that it comes as something of a surprise to be told by David Gadd—with perhaps a nice and venturesome disregard for received opinion—that "In many ways, Carrington is the most fascinating personality in the whole Bloomsbury story." A minor painter of authentic talent, a bisexual whose affair with Gerald Brenan in all its craziness is candidly told in his autobiography, *Personal Record*, Carrington—to resume the story briefly—was the mistress up-to-a-point of the homosexual Lytton Strachey, whom she adored, and the wife of Ralph Partridge, of whom she was fond. (Partridge also happened to be Gerald Brenan's best friend, and Strachey found him most congenial.) So long as Strachey lived, Carrington was in residence at his house, Ham Spray, to take care of him, and a month after his early death, unable to bear life without him, she chose to kill herself. *Carrington: Letters and Extracts from Her Diaries*—is moving to read, particular the last entries from the diaries, but not even a writer as skillful as Brenan is able to evoke her fascination as it appears to have caught Mr. Gadd's fancy in retrospect.

It is the Carrington love story that gives Brenan's *Personal Record* its coherence, and while it does tend to slacken a bit after he ceases to be involved with her, his account of his marriage to Gamel Woolsey has a peculiar interest of its own—he seemed to have a propensity to have his major involvements with women who were emotionally more committed to prominent writers than to himself (in Gamel Woolsey's case, the writer was Llewelyn Powys).

The publication of *Personal Record*, which is never less than interesting and sometimes in its descriptive passages very beautiful, is a consequence of the "new honesty." Brenan originally had intended that it should appear posthumously: he felt that the revelations of his many sexual adventures, mostly with nonliterary ladies, would have to wait until after his death. But judged by the standard of the present, there is nothing here to give offense, and much to give pleasure: one is grateful to learn more about Brenan and his life in Spain, beyond what he has already written in *South from Granada* (1957), and for the further light cast upon *The Spanish Labyrinth* (1943), his masterpiece and one of the great historical studies of this century.

It would seem that most of Brenan's life has been devoted either to avoiding loneliness in England, or in seeking it out in Spain. The Bloomsbury connection, after Carrington, proved a slender but enduring one. Scattered through *Personal Record* are vivid glimpses of Bloomsbury, and ruminations it has inspired; and in Professor Rosenbaum's collection there are reprinted some memorable accounts from *South from Granada* of the visits made to Brenan in Spain by the Strachey ménage, and at a later time, by Leonard and Virginia Woolf.

One has the sense, reading this memoir which brings him to his eightieth year, that Brenan, as with so many of the Bloomsbury figures, and in spite of all their difficulties, has remained in control of life. Between poetry and worldliness, a balance has been struck.

In none of the group, I think, was that balance more dramatically evident than in John Maynard Keynes, the subject of a collection of original essays edited by his nephew. It is rather a mixed bag, best suited to those already familiar with the work of the great economist; for those who are not, it is a less than ideal introduction, and such readers would do well to go back to Roy Harrod's biography. But even if one makes no more than an occasional dip into contents, one becomes aware of Keynes's extraordinary energy and ability, his arrogance and generosity, his splendid service to the arts. The personal figure is a little too fragmented in these essays, but Keynes the economist, in his strengths and weaknesses, and his genius, emerges vividly enough, and there are interesting glimpses of him as teacher, collector, and public figure. Keynes was Bloomsbury's "bridge" to the outside, public world—rather an odd place for a Bloomsburyan to be, and there was, from his more private friends, an ever so faint uncertainty as to the suitability of his achievement, along with an ever so faint pride in its unmistakable magnitude.

I have already referred to Rosenbaum's collection of documents, *The Bloomsbury Group*. As an introduction, next to reading the works themselves, it can hardly be bettered. Here is Bloomsbury on Bloomsbury, including pieces otherwise hard to come by, such as Virginia Woolf on her sister Vanessa Bell in an art catalogue of 1930, Bernard Shaw on Clive Bell, and Leonard Woolf on Strachey (both from the *New Statesman*), T. S. Eliot on Virginia Woolf (from *Horizon*), and best of all, a paper by Vanessa Bell, written for the Memoir Club in 1951, on Bloomsbury, which has never before been published. One is reminded here of the immense variety of Bloomsbury, and that, as friends, they were more than capable of criticizing one another and not pretending to like one another's work when they did not. With all the emphasis on personal relations, it is salutary to discover how cold they could be, to outsiders and to each other. Who said: "In Bloomsbury one hesitated to say anything true or profound unless it was also amusing. In my experience what is amusing is very rarely true or profound, and what is true or profound is hardly ever amusing"? No, not F. R. Leavis, that avowed enemy of Bloomsbury, but Leonard Woolf in a paper delivered to the Memoir Club in 1951. Yet there is ample evidence in Rosenbaum's pages that Woolf was wrong: Bloomsbury could often be true, profound, and amusing. Also: silly, exasperating, and dull. Gertrude Stein characterized the group to Edith Sitwell as "members of the Young Men's Christian Association—with Christ left out, of course."

What does it all matter? It now seems trivial that in 1906 Strachey caused a revolution in relationships by writing to Clive Bell as "Dear Clive," so that close male friends began calling one another by their first names rather than surnames. Or that in 1908 he caused a revolution in conversation by pointing to a stain on Vanessa Bell's dress, and asking her, "Semen?" It is hard to imagine how stultified by convention English and Western society was in the years before the First World War. The far more important artistic changes developing in those years needed the sort of ice-breaking that Bloomsbury represented.

The justification for the Bloomsbury industry, provided that it doesn't get out of hand, is that it should help us better to understand and to discriminate among the group's works and achievements, and even their failures. Rosenbaum assembled this important collection of documents as a preliminary for his own literary study of the work of the group; and one can appreciate the need of knowing the material contained in his anthology in order to judge their greater achievements. But it is those achievements that must be kept continually in mind. They should eclipse the lives, and if they do not, then from both Bloomsbury's and our point of view, the lives are not worth rediscovering.

17

LEONARD WOOLF

Leonard Woolf had no belief in the afterlife or personal immortality, but he left an enduring memorial in the autobiography he started to write as he was turning eighty, and whose fifth and final volume he completed just before his death at the age of eighty-eight. Each volume has the characteristic charm and power of his prose and personality; a rigorous discursiveness that gives the work its special quality of free association, or better yet, of free conversation, combined with an extraordinary tough-mindedness. But the "wandering effect" is deceptive, for almost every word, every incident, is made to count in the extraordinary unfolding of an extraordinary life. Given his fascination with figures—how many copies of Virginia Woolf's novels have been sold? how many hours has he worked for political causes?—one can imagine Woolf himself adding up his words as he came to the end of each brief volume. Few words have been wasted in rhetorical flourishes or self-dramatization, and that is characteristic of him too. The sense of adding up accounts, which he enjoyed doing as a colonial officer in Ceylon after he came down from Cambridge, and which he enjoyed doing as a founder and owner and jack-of-all trades of the Hogarth Press, is pervasive here. He is rendering an account of his own life, and to some extent of the lives of others. A humane man whom experience has purged of illusions, he can be hard in his judgments on others, but no harder than he is on himself.

Woolf was a man of varied accomplishments: the author of twenty-four books and the publisher of many more (among them the collected works of his wife, Virginia Woolf, and the collected works of Sigmund Freud); the editor of the *Political Quarterly*; a director of the *New Statesman*; a political philosopher and an active worker for the establishment of the League of Nations. Yet it is the character of the man himself, as the husband and one is tempted to say the curator of a woman of undoubted genius, and in his own right as a representative of an aspect of English life that has vanished into history, that he commands our interest and promises to endure.

It can be said of Woolf that he was among the last survivors of the English Enlightenment. Humane and civilized themselves, they believed in the values of civilization. For them, barbarism and its values—more properly, its non-values—were the enemy. Too skeptical to be Utopians, they were believers in the idea of human betterment, the possibility that a more humane and decent society might come into being. History, or barbarism, willed otherwise. Speaking of the political and historical climate of 1939, Woolf comments, "The world had reverted to regarding human beings not as individuals but as pawns or pegs or puppets in the nasty process of silencing their own fears or satisfying their own hates. It was impossible even for that most savage of all animals, man, to torture and kill on a large scale peasants, fellow-socialists, capitalists, Jews, gypsies, Poles, etc. if they were regarded as individuals; they had to be regarded as members of an evil and malignant class—peasants, deviating socialists, capitalists, Jews, gypsies, Poles. The world was reverting to, or had reverted to barbarism."

This emphasis upon the individual—that is, the human being—as opposed to the unit, the mass, the class, so convenient for incineration or saturation bombing—this emphasis is the mark of civilization, and of the philosophy that Woolf imbibed at Cambridge. It was a philosophy derived chiefly from G. E. Moore, and it placed the greatest importance upon personal relations, but wholly without the distortions of sentimentality. Individuals were to be truly valued, which meant that they were to be seen without preconceptions and as closely as possible to what they were—not necessarily an edifying sight. At the same time one was to subject oneself to equally candid and unsparing scrutiny. Fortunately this proved in the working-out less portentous than it sounds. For there was always, as there is in England, a saving grace of comedy. The seriousness of the enterprise must never be taken too seriously; and English pragmatism would never allow for the idiocy, not to say the barbarism, of the Teutonic "blood-brotherhood," which was presently to darken the world. It was a philosophy that valued the personal and also, when it was transported by Woolf and his Cambridge friends to Bloomsbury, admirably designed to deflate pomposity and pretension. There is nothing quite so effective in that regard as to be asked, "What exactly do you mean?"

Certainly the self-portrait drawn in his autobiography conforms to the man I met in the summer of 1962. William Abrahams and I were just beginning our study of Woolf's nephew, Julian Bell, for our book *Journey to the Frontier*. We went to see him in his intimate, cold office, a cubicle off a passage at Chatto and Windus, the publishing house with which the Hogarth Press had become affiliated after the war. He himself, with his white hair and skin, conveyed a sense of colorlessness increased by the fact that the room was skylighted, and all was bathed with a certain arctic light on a cold June day in London. His attitude toward Julian, his wife's beloved nephew who had been killed in the Spanish Civil War, was characteristic. Clearly he cared for him, but he was not about to abandon his critical sense. His view of Julian's virtues and defects, although premised on the affection due to a nephew, was truthful and hardheaded. For the very reason that individuals were so important, the perception of them was not to be clouded by any false sentimentality. In its effect, his conversation was like his autobiography: it gave the appearance of being discursive, but as it went on, each touch added up to a picture of Julian as be remembered him. The comments were put in what seemed to be an erratic way, much as a painter might daub on his color, but it was the best way for him to create a portrait. Having begun by saying he had little to tell us, he ended by telling us a good deal. We were never to meet again, but we corresponded. His letters were succinct and to the point, and always sent in used envelopes, in what I imagined to be a sign of Gladstonian parsimony, but may actually have come from the habit of saving paper during the Second World War. In these exchanges he revealed a keen editorial sense along with the shrewdness of a man of business. We had wanted to use extensive quotations from Virginia Woolf's unpublished memoir of Julian; he only allowed us to use about half of what we had originally asked for. He was right, editorially, for he forced us to rely on our own words, and not on another's, to gain the effect we wanted. Also, by limiting the amount of hitherto unpublished material by his wife to appear in print, he was, as he pointed out, protecting the economic value of her words. After our book was published, he sent a warm, but brief note of praise, and listed a few errors. In all respects, that, too, was characteristic.

I hadn't meant to go on so long about my small connection with Leonard Woolf, although it seems appropriate when writing about the final volume of his autobiography to remember one's own contact with the man, particularly when he was a man who was so much of a piece, so consistent in his style, so eager to be a part of life, and yet to handle it on his own terms. His pleasure in his many activities—there was no question ever of his "retiring"—continued to the day of his death. This last volume is in many ways a Stoic's ruminations about death, a counterpart to that book which stands out oddly among his list of publications: *A Calendar of Consolation: A Comforting Thought for Every Day in Year.* One would not have anticipated that subtitle, with its air of the vicarage, but Leonard Woolf never felt obligated to do what was expected of him, and in any event, many of the quotations are cold comfort indeed. (On the very first page one is brought up short with Swift's "A nice man is a man of nasty ideas.") As E. M. Forster has reminded us, death kills but the idea of death gives life. And Woolf accepted all along that it must end in the grave, or more precisely, as ashes buried at the base of two interwined elms called Leonard and Virginia in the garden of his home, Monk's House, in Rodmell. (But one of the trees—he does not tell us which—was blown down during the Second World War.) The idea of death gives a punctuation and a power to one's years, particularly when they have been so considerable that one can write an autobiography that begins in 1880 and ends in 1969.

When he was a small boy, he had to drown three newborn puppies, and the blind, tiny creatures struggling for life in the bucket conveyed to him a vivid sense that in everything there is an "I" which deserves respect. Every animal, and every person, has, he believed, a "magnetic field" which gives it the impression that it is important and what it is doing is important in the world. This must be respected, even if ultimately the world is a folly and any attempt to improve it almost inevitably futile—as he judged his own 200,000 hours of work for the Labour party and affiliated causes to have been. His attitude, a compound of realism and stoicism, encouraged him to cope with whatever came his way. He behaved as though he were "invincible, indefatigable, and imperishable," and he knew that he would continue to have his eggs and bacon for breakfast, no matter what happened, even as he was getting hold of poison so that he and Virginia could kill themselves if the Germans invaded England in 1940. (Not as paranoid a notion as it may seem. After the war it was learned that he and his wife had been on the Gestapo blacklist.)

But the last impression, I believe, that Leonard Woolf would want to give was that such an attitude was easy, or unearned. His own death came to him in good time, and he rather enjoyed the prestige that mere survival gives to one. But in March 1941 his wife chose to drown herself, to escape the onset of madness, such as she had suffered from during the First World War, and whose recurrence she feared might prove permanent. Although he was able to cope with the event, the most tragic of his life, in his own style—and writes of it with a directness and austerity that are deeply affecting—there is no doubt that it was a lasting blow to his head and heart.

His long approach to death thereafter—which, essentially, the rest of this final volume is about—owed much to Bloomsbury, and to the Enlightenment out of which it had sprung. But paradoxically, though he was at the heart of Bloomsbury, he was not of it heart and soul—his own strength came, he felt, from what he considered the Judaic tradition, his father quoting Micah: "What doth the Lord require of thee, but to do justly, and to love mercy, and to walk humbly with thy God." Like George Eliot he rejected God, but grasped justice and mercy. And he felt a kinship, too, with Montaigne, from whom he took the title for his concluding volume, sharing with him a hatred of selfishness, and a belief in the "I" as it sets out on its journey through life. In his own case it was a journey marked with regret for what the world had become after 1914, for what the world had arrived at after 1939. "Downhill All the Way," as he titled his next-to-last volume. And yet, significantly, it is "The Journey Not the Arrival That Matters."

18

E. M. FORSTER

P. N. Furbank has written a biography of E. M. Forster not likely to be superseded for years to come; and besides a plenitude of fascinating stories that make his long book so agreeable to read, he has provided the means by which one can come to terms with Forster, to try to cope with the somewhat uneasy but intense admiration that he still can inspire in the sympathetic reader.

As in Quentin Bell's biography of Woolf, so here too there is complete frankness. Furbank quotes on the title page a letter from Forster to his friend T. E. Lawrence in 1928: "But when I die and they write my life, they can say anything." And one feels, except for the rare instance where tact for the living has intervened, everything needful in this curious life story has been candidly said. Furbank seems admirably equipped for the task for which he was chosen by Forster himself, and he has made admirable use of the prodigious amount of material—letters, journals, commonplace books, etc.— that were placed at his disposal. He is an accomplished literary critic; he has written enlightening studies of Italo Svevo and Samuel Butler. He knew Forster well in the later years of his life, but has maintained an enviable poise between affection and detachment—his chapter, "E. M. Forster Described," giving a picture of him from 1947 when they first met in Cambridge, is particularly effective.

Indeed, if one has an objection or regret, it is simply that Furbank has chosen not to exercise his critical gift more fully. One would have welcomed more of Furbark on Forster's novels, the raison d'être, after all, for a life of Forster. But this is the age-old dilemma of the author of a literary biography: whether to emphasize the life, or the novels that come out of the life. Furbank has opted for the former, and his major contribution is biographical.

I think he has chosen wisely. The facts of Forster's life tell so much about his accomplishment, about English society in this century, and perhaps also something about homosexual "closetry." The essential problem for the biographer is the comparative quiet of the life. Forster wondered himself whether there was enough in it to justify a biography. There is the further problem that the novels that constitute his permanent contribution to literature belong to the brief, relatively early, and quite separate periods in his long, long life. Between 1905 and 1910 he published *Where Angels Fear to Tread*, *The Longest Journey*, *A Room with a View*, and *Howards End*. Then, in 1924, he published his final novel, and what is generally thought his masterpiece, *A Passage to India*. *Maurice*, the one novel of his to deal specifically with homosexuality, was written in 1913 when his knowledge of the subject was still theoretical, and was not published until 1971; of greater psychological than literary interest, it occupies a minor place in the canon.

In short, the line of the life is not at all what one finds in an archetypal literary biography: the youthful apprenticeship, the productive middle years, and then, the serene final productions of a distinguished old age. Yet I suspect that it is the absence of those traditional properties that helps account for the unfailing interest of Furbank's biography. Given its unlikely hero, and the unlikely circumstances in which Forster came to maturity and fame, this is a success story that, in the light of conventional wisdom, ought not to have been a success.

E. M. Forster was born in 1879 into the upper middle class, descended on his father's side from the Thorntons, formidable members of the evangelical Clapham Sect (which also figures in Virginia Woolf's background), who in the early nineteenth century made money, worked to reform the established Church, and agitated against the slave trade. Forster hardly shared their preoccupations, but in his fashion he was as morally earnest and as firm-minded as they. It was the £8,000 that his great-aunt Marianne left him (and which he repaid, so to speak, in his biography of her in 1956) that allowed him to travel and to work as he wished when he came down from Cambridge in 1901. (As we will see, travel and work would always be significantly connected for him.) His mother's side, with the whimsical name of Whichelo and an un-Thornton-like complement of clerks and governesses (though very nice and most artistic), was far less well-off.

Aunt Marianne ("Monie") made a match between her protégée,

Lily Whichelo, and her favorite nephew, Edward Morgan Llewelyn Forster, a young architect. They were married in 1877 and promptly started a family. The first child died at birth; the second was born on the first of January, 1879, and registered as Henry Morgan Forster. But two months later, at the baby's christening, there was a muddle about his name, wonderfully symbolic for an author who was to elevate the muddles of everyday life to an artistic principle. Edward the father, in a fit of absent-mindedness, when asked by the verger what the child's name was to be, gave his own. This the verger wrote down. "When the clergyman asked the same question, Lily's mother, who was holding the child at the font, merely pointed to the paper in the verger's hand. And so, to her horror, Lily heard the child christened 'Edward'; he had been registered one way and baptized another."

But this tiny crisis—of such, so often, is the stuff of Forster's fiction—soon gave way to one that was truly serious, indeed tragic in its consequence. The young father fell ill soon after the birth of his son. He suffered from a chronic cough, and not until several months later was he officially diagnosed as in an advanced state of consumption. By October 30, 1880, he was dead. The infant Edward Morgan was then 22 months old.

In a post-Freudian age the significance of the event requires no elucidation: if it doesn't explain all, it explains a lot in the life that followed. Lily Forster, though she had opportunities to do so, chose not to remarry; instead, for the remainder of her long existence—she died at 90 in 1945—she devoted herself to her beloved son. Morgan's childhood was spent among ladies, most of them elderly, who doted on him—his hair was curled Fauntleroy-fashion at Monie's insistence; he was nicknamed "the Important One"—and it was a singularly happy time in his life. An observant child, such as he was, listening and watching, can learn a great deal when the tea is poured, and it seems fair to conclude that Forster's remarkable sensitivity in his novels to the lives and roles of women as social beings had its beginning then.

The bliss of childhood ended in a traditional English upper-class fashion when he was sent off to prep school (Kent House) and public school (Tonbridge), and, in a way that brings to mind such articulate victims of the system as George Orwell, Osbert Sitwell, and Winston Churchill, he remembered himself as being miserable. The unhappiness rankled, and much as Orwell, shortly before his death, was paying off scores against St. Cyprian's in "Such, Such Were the

Joys," so Forster was writing in *The Spectator* in 1933—a mere half
century later—"School was the unhappiest time of my life."

But then, he entered King's College, Cambridge, and it was bliss
all over again—though, of course, in a different way. As a child he
had lived among women; now he lived among men. Attractive contemporaries—most notably his fellow Apostles—and sympathetic
dons, such as Goldsworthy Lowes Dickinson and Nathaniel Wedd,
encouraged his intellectual development, but one feels that he
learned most—most that in the end would serve his art—by watching and listening. His friend and fellow Apostle, Lytton Strachey,
"coined the name 'the taupe' [i.e. mole] for him, and this was apt; he
was drab-colored and unobtrusive and came up in odd places and
unexpected circles." He was still the observant child, grown older.
As a boy at home, amid the rustle and long skirts and the rattle of
teacups, he had learned about women; now, in the miniature world
of the university, he learned about the lives and roles of men as social beings, enrichers of the spirit and disturbers of the peace.

Some things he didn't learn about: passion, for example, especially as it had to do with the mysterious, indescribable, unsocial,
physical union of men and women. Passion was much talked of in
Apostolic Cambridge in the 1890s, but not much acted upon; and although Forster was decidedly an odd fish, he was not all that odd,
judged by the standard of the day and place, in not knowing until he
was 30 what copulation between men and women actually meant.
(And even then he was no more comfortable than most novelists of
either sex at finding a place for it in his fiction.) Leaving Cambridge,
what he knew best was something that could not be taught—in Furbank's words, "a super-quick sensing of immediate sensations,
and—in flashes—an extraordinary sweep of human understanding."

To this point in Furbank's biography, a reader unfamiliar with
Forster (assuming such a reader to exist) might well wonder how it
was all going to come out. For that matter, just such a question must
have occurred to Forster's friends at Cambridge. Each year hundreds
of sensitive, shy, intelligent young men, no more notable than the
taupe, come down from the universities and live their lives, and leave
no mark upon the world. Why should this not happen also with
Morgan? Here the life becomes of gripping interest, for Furbank is
now able to bring forward his two commanding themes: Forster's
discovery of his literary vocation, and his recognition of his sexual
nature.

After leaving Cambridge he traveled with his mother to Italy, and on a visit to the Amalfi coast, staying at the Hotel Palumbo in the enchanting, hilltop village of Ravello (where I am writing this review), he walked through the silent woodlands to the Vallone Fontana Caroso. Here he was to have the decisive experience of his life, as an artist. Into his head there flashed the idea of a short story which he would write down, later that day at the hotel, "The Story of a Panic," and which subsequently appeared in *The Independent*. But more importantly, at that spring in the hills above Ravello, he had a kind of epiphanal experience: a recognition of the imaginative power that was his—that, as Furbank puts it, "He was able, imaginatively, to respond to the 'greatness' of life . . . he knew now for certain that he was a writer."

Although thereafter there was a certain amount of desultory casting about for something "worth-while" to do—"You ought to get study or employment," the historian G. M. Trevelyan wrote to him in brisk, no-nonsense accents, and he did intermittently do a little teaching and tutoring—there was no turning back from that epiphanic incident at the Fontana Caroso. He was meant to write, he intended to write, he did write. Like Lily Briscoe in *To the Lighthouse*, he had had his vision, and the vision inspired a remarkable outpouring. Between 1904 and 1912 there were four novels, a collection of stories, and a good deal of casual journalism that remains, these sixty years later, fresh and interesting.

Two of the novels, *A Room with a View* and *Where Angels Fear to Tread*, are set largely in Italy—observant as always, plucking in details and backgrounds, he had put his year abroad with his mother to good use. *The Longest Journey* and *Howards End* are rooted deeply in the England he knew. In all these early novels, social observation of a sharp, sometimes feline sort is merged with an unexpected poetic and visionary quality. He sees more urgently than any other novelist since James the cost that too rigid adherence to the codes of a ruling society exacts from its believers—"the undeveloped heart," that malady of the English middle and upper classes—and envisions at least the possibility of something better.

Howards End, which he published in 1910, the greatest of the four early novels, and to my mind the best he would ever write, catches with uncanny and prophetic exactitude the growing conflict between the world of "telegrams and anger" and the idealism and vulnerability of the liberal tradition at the end of its tether. Quite apart from its literary merits, that mix of the prose and the passion that has had so pervasive an effect upon English fiction that latter-day novelists tend to underestimate it, *Howards End* remains a prime document of Edwardian England, the more poignant as a novel for what it leaves unstated.

It was published when Forster was 31; it was widely admired, and it made him famous. By then there was an audience of Forsterians, and no doubt they were eager for more. But no more would be forthcoming for almost fifteen years. Why? We learn from Furbank that, after the success of *Howards End*, Forster began to fear "sterility as a writer, and this fear would dog him for the rest of his career." Such fear is not uncommon; the most productive writers have been known to complain of it. But Forster also suffered from sexual anxiety of a seemingly irresolvable nature, and the two together, I suggest, had a profoundly inhibiting effect upon him. He had had his vision of the way of art, and it had brought him a fair measure of fame and satisfaction. But he had no corresponding vision of the way of love that would bring him the Ideal Friend for whom he so passionately yearned.

Early at Cambridge he had recognized his homosexual nature; in the decade since it had expressed itself chiefly in those masturbatory fantasies of a great love with a young man of the lower class that would find literary expression in *Maurice*. In 1910, he had a brief first, experimental moment with an old Cambridge friend, Hugh Meredith, who one night took the lead and "made love to him, kissing and embracing him passionately on the sitting-room sofa." But this wistful little tryout went no further and was never repeated. Prior to that, and for several years after, he was in love with an aristocratic, handsome, and irredeemably heterosexual Indian, Syed Ross Massood, whom Forster had tutored for a while in 1906, before Masood went up to Oxford. Although Forster declared his love for him quite explicitly, and Masood declared himself honored but unavailable, the friendship went on in London and in Paris, and even in India, arriving at an artistic conclusion that more than justified it for Forster the artist. Out of this seriocomic romance that was never consummated grew the very moving relationship between Aziz and Fielding in *A Passage to India*.

It was not until 1916, when he was in Alexandria doing war work for the Red Cross, that he had his first fulfilled physical encounter, and soon afterward, he embarked upon an extended affair with an attractive Egyptian tram conductor. The fantasies of *Maurice* were at last—in his late thirties—being acted out. In theory, then, the way of art and the way of love had joined at last, and one might have looked for not only a renewal but an enrichment of his career. But in art, as in life, things are never as simple as they seem, and there remains, for his admirers and detractors alike, the Forsterian mystery to puzzle over, and perhaps to solve.

He was a prolific writer all his life, despite the impression of laziness he gave to some. Toward the end of his life the creative impulse returned again in several short stories. He published two volumes of collected essays, two biographies, he wrote pageants, the libretto (with Eric Crozier) for Benjamin Britten's opera *Billy Budd*, other books of nonfiction, numerous uncollected pieces and reviews. But after *Howards End*, for the next sixty years he wrote only one further novel, *A Passage to India*.

Published in 1924, it was recognized immediately as a major novel, and most critics would place it first among his achievements. Once again, the social and the visionary impulse are magically joined. Seldom has there been a more convincing portrait of decent men and women trapped in the impossibilities of the imperial situation. Or at another, no less persuasive level, a more haunting evocation of the irrationalism that underlies so much of human behavior. Flawed though it is by elements of caricature of its Anglo-Indian characters, it remains an unforgettable performance—at the very least, one of the indisputably great English novels of imperial India (the other is *Kim*)—and as it turned out, an extraordinary farewell to the novel.

Furbank records Forster's own theory that he stopped writing novels because he felt frustrated in not being able to deal with homosexual love. On the evidence of *Maurice*, however, one feels some discomfort in attaching too much weight to the theory: Forster may well have been one of those authors who gain by sublimating and transforming their material. In any event, it is difficult to believe, given the age in which he lived and the slightly old-maidish aspects of his character, that he would have produced a novel as penetrating and unembarrassed as Christopher Isherwood's *A Single Man*, that classic of the genre.

I find myself much more persuaded by Furbank's own view, tactfully given, that Forster was running out of material. That moment near Ravello had released his ability to draw upon the Edwardian world of his early manhood—his essential, quintessential subject—and he did not seem able to assimilate anything beyond 1914 for artistic purposes. Even *A Passage to India*—vague in terms of dates—was recognized by those who knew the country at firsthand as being laid in prewar India, when the novel was begun, though Forster spent another six months there in 1921, listening and watching, coming up in odd places and unexpected circles.

Or perhaps, simplest of all, the visionary moment had gone, and he was too honest to pretend otherwise. During the next forty-six years of his life he changed from a creator to a sage, and, almost against his will, came to embody those virtues we admire and think of as peculiarly English: a firm belief in liberty, in fairness, in standing up for individual values, in refusing to be pompous, hieratical, mythomaniacal, self-adulating, iconic, and self-professedly great.

One need not claim too much for him. He is an author we can value as much for his faults as for his virtues—a man who would be rare at any time, but especially so now when the messianic impulse is at large among us. On his eightieth birthday, W. H. Auden cabled to him that he was "old famous loved yet not a sacred cow." In an intensely personal way he was not so distant from his Thornton forebears: he improved the world, and helped the causes of public and private liberation. P. N. Furbank presents the full person, with his defects and crotchets, but a man ultimately to be admired. One is very grateful to author and subject. The reputation is justly enhanced.

19

John Maynard Keynes

John Maynard Keynes, probably the most distinguished economist of this century, died comparatively young in 1946. In 1951 Roy Harrod wrote an official biography, a useful and, if not surprisingly, an overly discreet study of the man. Robert Skidelsky, who previously has written about an economic planner of the far right, Oswald Mosley, is a little too defensive in putting Harrod's effort down. Skidelsky needs no justification for doing another biography. The first volume of his work, *John Maynard Keynes: Hopes Betrayed, 1883-1920*, easily takes its place as the most important Keynes biography so far. It is an already indispensable book for anyone interested in the history of this century, and of a man whose impact upon it continues to be felt even to this day. But in terms of Keynes's importance, it is the further volumes that will be far more significant. There will be discussed his greatest single contribution, *The General Theory of Employment, Interest, and Money* (1936), and his period of massive influence in the 1930s and 40s as a savior of capitalism and the chief financial officer of the British Empire. Not that he was without power and fame in his early years: after serving as the principal adviser to the British delegation at the Versailles conference, he had written his brilliant *The Economic Consequences of the Peace* (1919).

Surely one's most serious interest in Keynes is as an economist, about which Skidelsky writes fully and carefully. But it is only human to be intrigued by his sex life, to which Skidelsky also pays very close attention. In this he is less the explorer than the collector of minutest details. It is now years since Michael Holroyd's biography of Lytton Strachey, when the closet doors, slightly ajar before, swung wide open and revealed Keynes as a dedicated homosexual. It was said, characteristically of England, that Harrod's biography had allowed those already in the know to discover more: to them all was confirmed in the soulful photograph of Keynes and Duncan Grant staring at one another. Certainly before Holroyd's book, one was not aware of Keynes's intense commitment to homosexuality as a way of life, the importance of his affairs to him, most notably that with Duncan Grant, whom he took away from Lytton Strachey. Keynes in his turn was to lose him to Adrian Stephen, the brother of Virginia Woolf and Vanessa Bell.

Does Skidelsky make too much of this side of his life—would the same amount of detail be given if Keynes were a heterosexual? Will there be a change when he marries the ballerina of the Ballets Russes, Lydia Lopokova, in 1925? Skidelsky, in my opinion, stops just short of going too far. Questions of sex were extremely important to Keynes. Appearance as well as brains counted when he and Strachey were recruiting "embryos" for the great Cambridge discussion society, "The Apostles." But Skidelsky raises the question to what degree does Keynes's "sexual orientation"—to use the phrase of our days—influence his greatest contribution, his economics? He quotes Schumpeter's remarks that Keynes preached a "childless economics," as in Keynes's famous comment that "in the long run" we are all dead. But was his way of thinking any different from that of a childless heterosexual? Does sexual orthodoxy bring with it a different kind of economics?

The sexual question is one great strand in this study. Another is an excellent overview of English intellectual life at the turn of the century. Keynes was born into the high purple of Cambridge academic life, the "little mortal" in his parents' term, and, though deeply loved by them, he was trained like a racehorse, and won all the prizes at Eton and Cambridge. Skidelsky quite fascinatingly and legitimately views Keynes as much more than an economist. He attempted to deal with the problems that Britain faced intellectually and practically as both its power and its values were being challenged in the new century. More than he might have admitted, Keynes not only tried to compensate for the abandonment of Christianity but to work out a way of thought that would incorporate the public values of the Cambridge philosopher Henry Sidgwick and the economist Alfred Marshall, and the private emphasis on beauty and personal relations to be found in the guru of the Apostles, the philosopher G. E. Moore.

Skidelsky is excellent in making clear Keynes's relation to

Bloomsbury. He wished to straddle the public world, of little interest to most of his Bloomsbury friends, and the private world, of little interest to the world of finance and the civil service. It was amazing how well he did this. Perhaps his homosexuality, known to intimates but hidden from the outside world, was a clue to his attitude toward society—neither rebellious nor submissive, but privately going his own way. At the same time he managed to acquire more than his due from the riches of his world. Although in the early part of his life he was not much interested in politics, he took a middle road in his political values, being a lifelong Liberal. He disliked the values of the aristocracy and the proletariat, and was proud to demonstrate that being middle class was not the same as being philistine. Eventually he would play a crucial role in saving capitalism by means that some considered socialistic.

He seemed to be equally at home in the academic and the outside worlds, the theoretical and the practical. Although there is little discussion of E. M. Forster here, Keynes did seem able to combine "the prose and the passion" that Forster advocated in *Howards End*. Keynes adored his work: writing to Duncan Grant about the statistical confirmation to be found in his article on "Recent Economic Events in India," he remarked that "nothing except copulation is so enthralling." He cultivated the values of the middle class to their highest levels, with considerable emphasis on the world of the arts. He had no illusions, and was famously rude to those—in his view, most other people—whose minds were unimpressive. Yet at the same time, he ultimately dedicated himself to improving the quality of life for all. Can these values be labeled homosexual? Skidelsky has not yet resolved the question.

For Keynes the conflict between the public and private worlds reached a climax in the First World War. He entered into the fray, returning to the civil service, in almost a lighthearted way, challenged, as he was in all the administrative tasks he undertook, by the need to work out ways to pay for the war. His approach was the age-old one, similar to Pitt's at the time of the French Revolutionary Wars—Britain as paymaster while foreigners fought and died. But as the war ceased to be a short one—as Keynes and others had expected it to be—the toll in resources was matched by the growing toll in lives, and Keynes found himself weeping for the dead, even for those whom he knew and had ceased to like, such as Rupert Brooke. By 1916, he had come to the conclusion, reached by his Bloomsbury friends before him, that he was working "for a government I despise for ends I think criminal." The only accomplishment of the war was that it might change the social order.

Yet he remained with the government and was a leading adviser for the peace treaty at Versailles. Perhaps he erred in concluding that economics was more important than politics, but his fury about the misguided economics of the treaty resulted in one of the most powerful indictments ever written, *The Economic Consequences of the Peace*, in which he foretold the financial downfall of Europe. Keynes, at quite a young age, became one of the most influential figures of his time. The experience of the war was crucial in turning him into a Keynesian, holding the belief that economics could be manipulated for political ends, and might eventually help to create a better world. No doubt his vision had its limitations, but its practicality has considerable attractions. As Keynes attempted to balance values in his life—even sexually, apparently, for approximately half of his maturity was spent as a homosexual and the other half as a heterosexual—so too Skidelsky has cleverly balanced both the personal and the public in this highly intelligent, critical yet understanding, first volume of his life of Keynes.

The first volume of Robert Skidelsky's magisterial life of Keynes covered the years from Keynes's birth in 1883 to 1920. We were then promised a second volume for the rest of the life. The story has proved so rich that it will now be a life in three volumes—more than Victorian in length but modern in perception.

The first volume, with the subtitle *Hopes Betrayed, 1883-1920*, ended with Keynes's disillusionment, famously recorded in *The Economic Consequences of the Peace* (1919), with what the powers that be had made of the high hopes of Edwardian England: their betrayal of so many of the young in the slaughter of the war. It tracked Keynes's growing importance, and the interplay of his private and public lives, the private revolving to some extent around his interest in the "higher sodomy," fulfilling itself in a happy love affair with the painter Duncan Grant; and it dealt with Keynes's public, civil service, and academic careers. Although his Bloomsbury friends tended to regard him as too worldly, he was very much a member of their circle.

The second volume, *John Maynard Keynes: The Economist as Saviour, 1920-1937*, is more important. Here Keynes has become a figure on the world's stage. That being true, it must be confessed that it is a less compelling though significant story. No matter that ideas about economics may have more effect on our lives than does sex (perhaps not), it is certainly less interesting, at least for most of us, to read about. Life on a high plateau generally has less drama than the tale of how one got there. There is, however, a wonderful love story told in these pages: Keynes's affair and then marriage in 1925 with the Diaghilev ballerina, Lydia Lopokova. The marriage gives every indication of having been supremely happy. Keynes adored her, found her endlessly amusing and perceptive, received great pleasure from her fractured English, devoted a great deal of his considerable energies to her career, first as a dancer and then as an actress, particularly in Ibsen roles. They apparently had a rich and satisfying sex life and were quite disappointed that they failed to have children.

Bloomsbury behaved quite badly to Keynes and Lydia, finding her too much and too tedious—seeing less of her than one might expect considering that they lived so close to one another both in London and in the country. Skidelsky may exaggerate their dislike. The members of Bloomsbury knew one another so well that they were not only aware of each other's faults but enjoyed pointing them out, which did not prevent them from maintaining the connections formed in those early golden years. Keynes certainly did not disown his previous sexual life—Duncan Grant was a witness at Keynes's wedding, even though he mentioned that he had lost his inheritance—and Keynes continued to see Sebastian Sprott, a later lover. But there doesn't seem to be any indication that Keynes was ever unfaithful to Lydia.

What is rather surprising—in contrast to the almost excessive sexual concerns of the first volume—is that Skidelsky barely discusses what influence, if any, Keynes's sexual modification had upon his life and thought. He does claim, however, that Lydia brought him more into the world and made him more of an economic statesman than might have happened if he had remained in the Bloomsbury world, although he was hardly cloistered pre-Lydia. As his thinking became more adventuresome, his private life became more conventional.

Although during these years he lost quite a bit on currency speculations, he nonetheless made a lot of money for himself, for friends, and for his college, King's, at Cambridge. He spent his money on books, manuscripts, and paintings (and not very good furniture). He was Bloomsbury's ambassador to the outside world and was very active in it, deeply involved with his country's financial policies even though he did not yet have the dominating influence that he had achieved by the time of his death and retained for quite a while thereafter.

This necessary tension between the public and private worlds shaped Keynes's life and achievements. Skidelsky is superb in presenting Keynes's growing effect in the world of power and economics, and his evolving thoughts on how economic policy can make a better society.

Keynes was a lifelong Liberal, rejecting what he regarded as the class determination to be found in both the Labour and Tory parties. He had little use for Marx. "How can I accept a doctrine which sets up as its bible, above and beyond criticism, an obsolete economic textbook which I know to be not only scientifically erroneous but without interest or application to the modern world?" Unlike so many of his young friends in the 1930s, he felt that Washington, not Moscow, was the significant economic laboratory of the day. (Certainly he was more influential there.) By serving as the main "idea" person for the Lloyd George Liberals in the late 1920s, he put his stamp on much of the thought that has since shaped Britain in particular and the modern Western world in general. Theory was of interest to him as it helped him be a better applied economist, and he was happy to make his views known through journalism, most notably in the English weekly, *The Nation*.

Even as the Liberal party declined to insignificance in numbers, its ideas became dominant. The problems of Britain (and elsewhere) had become so complex that the state needed to play a growing role in solving them. But this had to be done in such a way that individual freedom would be increased, not diminished. Throughout the years covered in this volume, Keynes in his work moved toward the making of the Keynesian revolution, dedicated to restoring "the expectation of stability and progress in a world cut adrift from its nineteenth-century moorings."

Skidelsky discusses thoroughly Keynes's *A Treatise on Probability* (1921), which drew upon his prewar thought. After that theoretical study, he became increasingly involved with practical, contemporary problems: the importance of public works to cope with depression and unemployment; the need to spend not to hoard, and to make money work for the good of society through the effect of the multiplier. *A Treatise on Money* (1930) summed up his ideas of the 1920s. In 1936 he published his masterpiece, *The General Theory of Employment, Interest, and Money*. Skidelsky discusses it exhaustively, giving full rein to the criticisms made of it at the time. Yet he also makes clear how effective it was as a "tool for policy," how government should cope with the overwhelming economic problems of British (and world) society in the 1930s and beyond: "In its refusal to stale, the book reflects its author. Keynes was a magical figure, and it is fitting that he should have left a magical work. There has never been an economist like him; someone who combined so many qualities at such a high level, and allowed them all to fertilise his thought. He was an economist with an insatiably curious mind; a mathematician who could dazzle people with the most unmathematical of fancies; a logician who accepted the logic of art. . . . Even his sexual ambivalence played its part in sharpening his vision. He was, above all, a buoyant and generous spirit who refused to despair of his country and its traditions, and offered the world a new partnership between government and people to bring the good life within reach of all."

In the same year that *The General Theory* was published, Keynes's other major creation of the period, the Arts Theatre, opened in Cambridge, a monument to the private life of the arts. On a grander scale than had been true previously in his life, the 1920s and 30s marked a time that Keynes could devote himself to improving both the public and private worlds. His economic views had not yet become dominant but they were already extremely influential. This volume ends with him ill with what he described as a "pseudo angina"—he would live only nine more years—and writing from his nursing home a letter of condolence to Vanessa Bell on the death of her son Julian in the Spanish Civil War. Through that death, Bloomsbury had reluctantly paid the highest possible price in the public sphere. Keynes was, in effect, in his thought and activities trying to make sure that that sacrifice and those that were to come in the Second World War were not in vain.

20

LYTTON STRACHEY

It must be an unusual situation when the biography of a biographer, and its history, vies in interest with the subject himself. But such is the case with Michael Holroyd's biography of Lytton Strachey, *Lytton Strachey: The New Biography*, now reissued in a third version twenty-seven years after the publication in Britain of the first part of the first version.

Looking back to an earlier landmark in biography, we are interested in both Boswell and Johnson, but Johnson is still regarded as the more important. Yet Johnson is more significant than his own biographical subject, Richard Savage; and the seventeenth-century writer of brief lives, John Aubrey, is more intriguing than many of his subjects. So it is not unprecedented that Lytton Strachey has become, comparatively, increasingly less well known than his biographer, who has also written definitive lives of Augustus John and George Bernard Shaw, and thanks to them has become increasingly better known.

With the publication of Strachey's masterpiece of biography, *Eminent Victorians*, in May 1918, shortly before the end of the First World War, he became the most famous member of the Bloomsbury group. At that time Virginia Woolf had published only one novel, *The Voyage Out*, in 1915; John Maynard Keynes had not yet published *The Economic Consequences of the Peace*; E. M. Forster was an established author but had not yet written *A Passage to India*. Now, the situation is reversed, and Strachey's standing, as a writer, which was most important to him, may well be the lowest on the list. And although Holroyd has preserved Strachey's reputation as a most memorable person, he has de-emphasized his role as a writer and innovator of post-Victorian attitudes. He has done so in an intriguing and ironic way that his subject might have appreciated, but perhaps not exactly as he might have wished.

Eminent Victorians, which Strachey had been working on before the war as "Victorian Silhouettes," was given an increased and embittered power by the First World War. Its sketches of Cardinal Manning, Florence Nightingale, Thomas Arnold, and General Gordon were meant as antidotes to the huge, hagiographic biographies that were characteristic of the Victorian age. Strachey's studies also became in effect indictments of the public world, the emphasis on appearances, that had helped cause the Armageddon of the war itself.

The book was a first salvo of the skepticism that would mark the 1920s. That was the public Strachey for all the world to see. Bloomsbury in its private guise always believed in honesty in personal relations, which in practice frequently meant homosexual relations. But its members were not public crusaders in the sexual sphere; they did not agitate against the Labouchere amendment, which had made homosexual activities between males illegal. Forster anticipated a "better world" when his homosexual novel, *Maurice*, might eventually be published, and Strachey wrote some racy material for private circulation.

Thanks to Michael Holroyd's fine craftsmanship and indefatigable researches, his life of Lytton Strachey has become a major force in establishing the tradition of telling the full story, not only about Strachey but about others as well, be they homo-, bi-, or heterosexual. As Holroyd states, his was the first major post-Wolfenden biography. In Britain the Wolfenden Report on homosexuality and prostitution was released in 1957, but not until 1967 was homosexuality decriminalized. It was unlikely but possible that if that had not happened, Duncan Grant and Roger Senhouse, then still alive, could have been prosecuted (unless a statute of limitations intervened) for having been Strachey's lovers. Even so they had some ambivalent feelings over being "outed," though they had never pretended to be other than what they were. Keynes's homosexuality, as detailed in the book, was news to many. In a review, Nigel Nicolson was unenthusiastic about the book's frankness, then a few years later he revealed all in his *Portrait of a Marriage* about his parents: Harold Nicolson and Vita Sackville-West. Strachey's implicit belief that the private life was more important than the public was about to become "old-fashioned," even Victorian.

I suspect that Strachey would not have been displeased. He had enjoyed acting somewhat outrageously during his own lifetime. But he might have had mixed feelings about Holroyd doing so at such length and now in three versions. The original life was published in the United States in 1968 at 1,229 pages, in two volumes. In 1971 the life was revised, this time divided into a biography and a literary study. The present volume has excised the 250,000 words of the literary study, although some attention is paid to the written work. Holroyd has rewritten his original text, cutting 100,000 words but adding the same number to this newest version. The author describes this procedure, and the story of the book, particularly his relation to Strachey's brother, James, the translator of Freud, in a fascinating preface. In good part because of the trailblazing nature of the first version (an openness that was on its way, given the nature of the 1960s) and the greater detail and incorporation of the cascade of writing by and about Bloomsbury over the last quarter of the century, the latest version is much less startling. And the comparative disappearance of literary criticism in the text means that what to my mind is the chief purpose of a biography of a writer—an illumination of the writings, in Strachey's case, except for *Eminent Victorians*, now largely neglected—is hardly present. We are told a compelling life story, but it is not immediately obvious that we need to be told it at such great length and in a third version, useful though it is to have at hand.

There also seems to be a certain sadness in the tale, not only because of Strachey's comparatively early death in 1932 at the age of fifty-one. The premise of Bloomsbury's belief about private life was that honesty about one's feelings would certainly make for a better and perhaps even a happier life. Strachey enjoyed his fame and his fortune but as with other Bloomsbury figures he seemed to have a propensity to find himself in difficult ménages à trois. From 1915 until his death in 1932, he was in what was in effect a sexless marriage with the painter and bisexual Dora Carrington (whose life is depicted in a "major motion picture" with Emma Thompson as Carrington and Jonathan Pryce as Strachey), despite her having given him her virginity in a rare heterosexual act on his part. Strachey lived with her and her husband, Ralph Partridge, whom he adored but who was relentlessly heterosexual. (Almost immediately after Strachey's death, Carrington killed herself.) In my view, too much of the later part of this study is devoted to the sexual minuet, but in a minor key, involving Carrington, Partridge, Frances Marshall, Gerald Brenan, and Mark Gertler, most of whom have had their own biographies and who in this context are attendant lords and ladies who threaten to take over the court.

Strachey's great achievement was to demonstrate that biography need not be fawning or indeed respectable, although he had a certain odd affection for his subjects, even more apparent in his later works, his studies of Victoria herself and of Elizabeth and Essex. I don't think that he would have approved of what Joyce Carol Oates has happily called "pathographies," even though he led the way in that direction. Holroyd many years ago made a quantum leap forward, with great skill, to the new frankness. Now, which I guess is cause for rejoicing, there is nothing that cannot be told. One can but admire Holroyd for having rewritten his study for the second time and brought it up to date, although he might have made it easier to track down quotations. This considerable volume, if not quite as "new" as the subtitle would have it, is an extraordinary accomplishment.

PART FOUR

THE 1930S AND AFTER

21

ISHERWOOD, AUDEN, AND SPENDER

Christopher Isherwood, or Christopher William Bradshaw Isherwood as he then was, was born in 1904 into the gentry of Cheshire, including in his ancestry a leading regicide of Charles I. There was money and land—the house where he was born, Wyberslegh Hall, still exists; Marple Hall, where his grandparents lived, has been torn down. He received the education of his class—boarding schools, then university.

Like his mentor, E. M. Forster, he was deeply saturated in the culture of the English upper middle class; and though he would turn on it as the "Enemy," the particular power and authority one associates with that class in that time and that place endured in Isherwood. It explains, for example, why he should write of his homosexuality with an unapologetic frankness and poise that seems to elude American writers altogether.

His father, Frank Bradshaw Isherwood, had a professional career in the army, and was killed in the First World War. The idea of the "Test"—that a young man must prove himself—played an important part in Isherwood's literary career, as it did for many who were too young to be in the war yet old enough to remember it vividly—whether or not they lost a father or brother. Coming to terms with his inheritance—in both a literal and psychological sense—was a crucial element in Isherwood's life. When he did receive the family fortune on the death of his uncle (also a homosexual although a briefly married one) in July 1940, he handed it over to his mother and younger brother and noted in his diary "I often used to wonder just when this would happen—and I always half-knew that when it did, when Marple and all the money became mine, it would be too late. It is too late now—not merely because of the War but because the absurd boyhood dream of riches is over forever. It is too late to invite my friends to a banquet, to burn the Flemish tapestry and the Elizabethan beds, to turn the house into a brothel. I no longer want to be revenged on the Past." Not that the money wouldn't have been useful, as he has not been particularly prosperous as a writer, except from the various transformations of *Sally Bowles*, which started with the John van Druten play in 1951, the only version for which he has anything good to say.

An exhibition at the National Portrait Gallery in London celebrated Isherwood, along with Auden, Spender and others, as a writer of the 1930s. The legend of that decade is so powerful that, despite his considerable accomplishments since, I suspect he will be irrevocably bound to it. (He has done his best to free himself from the legend in *Christopher and His Kind*.) In a quite remarkable way the public and the personal came together in his work then. He was able to maintain a private voice while dealing with a violent public world. The personal life played out against the agony of Germany in the years before the triumph of National Socialism in 1933 made for writing of the most memorable kind. Perhaps because *The Berlin Stories* are so "personal," the politics in their background have an inevitability absent from all those aggressively political antifascist novels of the period that have long since been forgotten.

After coming to America he produced a sizable body of work that in itself would have assured another writer a major reputation. But his achievement of the 1930s—and the vast success of *I Am a Camera* and *Cabaret*—have tended to cast a shadow over everything else. Isherwood of the 1930s was a legendary figure, in his own right as the author of *The Last of Mr Norris* and *Goodbye to Berlin*, and as one of those gifted, leftward-leaning young English writers of the decade who became famous early, influenced a generation as much by their politics as by their poetry, and entered history collectively as "Auden & Co.," a Marxified successor group to Bloomsbury.

In 1940, George Orwell was merely restating the accepted version of how it was when he summarized the contemporary English literary scene in his essay "Inside the Whale": "For the middle and late thirties, Auden, Spender & Co. *are* the movement, just as Joyce, Eliot & Co. were for the twenties. And the movement is in the direction of some rather ill-defined thing called Communism." Orwell was hardly prejudiced in their favor—he had once described Auden as "a sort of gutless Kipling," and more than once he referred disparagingly to "the nancy poets"—which makes this neat little summary of his all the more revealing: that he should so far have yielded to the potency of the legend that he would balance Auden and Spender against Joyce and Eliot.

That was in 1939, and the accepted version has not appreciably changed since: a study by Samuel Hynes bears the inevitable title, *The Age of Auden*, and as its subtitle, *Art and Politics in the 1930s*—a linkage that is also inevitable. As the accepted version has it, Auden, Spender, and Isherwood experienced a part of their political education in Berlin in the early 30s. It was there they came to see in Communism the only viable alternative, in Germany to the rise of Nazism, and in the European democracies to a terrible inertia and spiritual decay. ("Or England falls, She has had her hour / And now must decline to a second class power." Thus, not unprophetically, Auden and Isherwood in their verse play *The Ascent of F6*.)

The effect of what they wrote in the early years of the decade—Orwell misdates the time of their greatest influence—was to convey an atmosphere of political excitement (Auden: "But today's the struggle") and messianic exhortation (Spender: "Oh young men oh young comrades"). Though at the end of the decade they were drastically to break with the past (Isherwood to Auden on board the ship bringing them to America: "You know, it just doesn't mean anything to me any more—the popular front, the party line, the anti-Fascist struggle"), their novels and poems, whether read as literary accomplishments or historical documents, are irretrievably there: survivals from what Auden was presently to call "a low, dishonest decade."

At the same time a fascinating exercise in "revisionism" has been unobtrusively in progress. Auden either suppressed or rewrote many of his poems of the period ("Spain" which Orwell thought "one of the few decent things that have been written about the Spanish War," Auden himself dismissed as "trash"), while Isherwood became involved in an intriguing multilayering of his past: the "I," incorporated into the novels he was writing in the later 30s, and that Isherwood annotated for accuracy in *Christopher and His Kind*. The result enriches the past, in the sense that we have more of the private life than we have had before, along with some illuminating and highly entertaining literary vignettes: When he and Auden are writing *The Ascent of F6*, Christopher notes in his diary, apropos of Auden's "Christian leanings," "I have to keep a sharp eye on him, or down slop the characters on their knees; another constant danger is that of choral interruptions by angel voices."

A further, less happy result of the later version of Isherwood's life is that, at times, it trivializes Christopher's 30s; they turn out to be a good deal less dedicated to political passions than the legend has had it. His remark that the "original" of Sally Bowles "wasn't a victim, wasn't proletarian, was a mere self-indulgent upper middle class foreign tourist who could escape from Berlin when she chose," comes perilously close to describing his own situation. (As he is too intelligent not to recognize and acknowledge when he titled his last fictional sortie into the decade, *Down There on a Visit*.)

Isherwood adopts a less ruthless attitude toward his work and his character than Auden, who banished poems from the canon and ordered his letters to be destroyed. Auden's biographer will have difficulties at every turn; Isherwood's will find his subject a model of helpfulness. It does not seem to me that there is now, in spite of the revisionism of *Christopher and His Kind*, one version of his life that Isherwood insists we accept; all continue to coexist for our delight and interest. In a way, the least important, though highly accomplished, versions are those done by others: the John van Druten play and movie *I Am a Camera*, and their glittering descendants, the musical and movie *Cabaret*. It is they who have given Christopher and his creation Sally Bowles, not to mention the naughty decadent pre-Hitler Berlin in which he and Sally lived and did or did not make love, an international, nostalgic chic.

Their very success in obliterating or softening the realities upon which they were based has made *Christopher and His Kind* necessary; once more Isherwood returns to the scene of his youth, and a new version is superimposed upon and sometimes corrects the original. *Christopher and His Kind* covers the decade almost exactly, opening on March 14, 1929, when he goes to Berlin for the first time—in search, not of a new politics, but of boys—and closing in January 1939, when he and Auden arrive in America, where Isherwood lived for the rest of his life, and Auden continued to live until a few years before his death, when he returned to Oxford.

"The book I am now going to write will be as frank and factual as I can make it, especially as far as I myself am concerned." The result is fascinating, and more than a little subversive, for Isherwood has set out to do in his legend, and indispensable for admirers of this truly masterly writer. But it has to be said that it is very often a commentary on a replica of an experience, and I can't help wondering what the reader who comes to it fresh will make of it all. A reading of the relevant works of the master—*The Last of Mr. Norris, Goodbye to Berlin, Prater Violet,* and *Down There on a Visit*—

would be a stimulating preparation, as well as a sensible precaution.

In some ways *Christopher and His Kind* is a revenge on the "camera" image, the author as no more than photographer, so irrevocably identified with the earlier versions. In *Goodbye to Berlin* Herr Issyvoo is the observer, although he plays a more active role than one might think—he is, after all, the connecting and at times a participating character in the action. But in *Christopher and His Kind* he is down front. The importance of the observer, and in particular his sexual tastes and matings, so neutralized in the novels as to be invisible, have come increasingly into prominence. We are told of his one experience with a woman—not Sally Bowles—and a very agreeable one it was too. But though, on the strength of that, Auden accused him of being a latent heterosexual, he never afterwards varied from his chosen path or regretted it; and a controlling theme of this book is the extent to which he is boy-driven, starting with Bubi, whom he meets on his first night in Berlin, in the Cozy Corner, a boy bar. Afterwards, a high-spirited, puppyish affair with Otto which leads him into the setting of his future fiction: working-class Berlin.

Then, five years with Heinz, with whom he is in love, and for whom he feels a continuing responsibility: their story is the potential novel he neglected to write. Innumerable brief flings. A long, casual, now-and-then, 10-year, in-and-out-of-bed-ship with Auden, of much less consequence to them than their very close, creative, extraordinary friendship—and indeed if this book has a hero (not a specialty of Isherwood's) it is certainly Auden, the driving and driven genius, already in his mid-twenties taking on the lineaments of the "sacred monster" he was ultimately to become: "His clothes are still out at the elbows, his stubby nail-bitten fingers still dirty and sticky with nicotine; he still drinks a dozen cups of tea a day, has to have a hot bath every night, piles his bed with blankets, overcoats, carpets, and rugs."

It would seem that Isherwood is asking us to believe, contrary to the accepted version, that politics had little to do with his attitude toward his world. There was the need to write; beyond that, it was mostly sex and love. He went to Berlin for boys, and much of his movements and actions in the ensuing years were taken up with trying to find a place where Heinz could live outside Germany, presumably with Christopher. Those efforts conclude with the expenditure of a thousand pounds—lent by Christopher's mother Kathleen, who emerges much more attractively than perhaps the author intends—for lawyers and the intervention of Gerald ("Mr. Norris")

Hamilton in a doomed attempt to get Heinz a Mexican passport. Rather oddly, it is decided that Heinz must first go back to Germany. No difficulty is anticipated, but he is arrested there all the same—the prelude, one is relieved to discover, not to tragedy but to a petit-bourgeois happy ending. Christopher survives the end of the affair (as he knew he would) and Heinz survives imprisonment, survives his years of service in the Wehrmacht during the war, and survives to be a happily married man in Germany today.

Homosexuality is Isherwood's nature, but it is also for him a form of social protest, his true politics. It is his major way of fighting the "Nearly Everybody" who are the heterosexual, successful, or unprotesting members of the upper middle class into which he was born. "But I'll admit this—even if my nature were like theirs, I should still have to fight them, in one way or another. If boys didn't exist, I should have to invent them." There is a famous passage in *The Last of Mr. Norris*—one of the emblematic passages of 30s left-wing fiction, and one of the underpinnings of the accepted versions—in which the "I" figure, there called William Bradshaw, describes his first visit to a Communist meeting. He is deeply moved by the response of the audience to the speaker, who "made their thoughts articulate. They were listening to their own collective voice. At intervals they applauded it, with sudden, spontaneous violence. Their passion, their strength of purpose elated me." And then, significantly, he adds: "I stood outside it. One day, perhaps, I should be with it, but never of it." *With it, but not of it*—a quizzical, tentative, self-deprecating commitment—and it is the clue to the subsequent history of Auden & Co. in the post-legendary years as its members sought for something they could be with and of.

That this shrewd and candid book, *Christopher and His Kind*—which is in no way prurient—can be published now (1976) without fuss or even a lifted eyebrow is one indication of how much the world has changed since the 1930s. Much more can be talked about, and much more openly, but it is as if "Nearly Everybody" is still in control, and the world does not seem notably improved these years later, only different.

Like George Orwell, W. H. Auden stipulated that there should be no biography written of him, but in both cases it did not appear to be a very firmly held belief. Orwell meant it in two senses: that he had used so much of his own life in his writings he saw little purpose in further investigation, and more seriously that he believed no biography could succeed in fully revealing the real person—which indeed is true, but as is also true of any other form of revelation—should there be a "real" person known to anyone, including the person himself. Auden appeared to hold his belief against biography for the rather traditional and important reason that an artist should be known by his work. There is no doubt that the work is by far the most important aspect. But that does not mean that biography cannot perform two functions—to illuminate the work, and to tell the tale of an individual—interesting in and of itself—who happens in this case to be one of the greatest poets of the century.

Auden himself had rather mixed feelings about biographies—despite his injunction. At times in some of his splendid essays he wrote approvingly of them; certainly he had a rich appreciation for the varieties of human nature. On the other hand, he did ask that all holders of correspondence destroy his letters to them—an injunction which fortunately quite a few people disobeyed—and he himself was of very little assistance. He lived in a general state of disorder and chaos, and probably in a vain attempt to reduce the confusion of his life somewhat, he didn't keep letters himself, but threw them out as soon as he had no further use for them. He tended at times deliberately to remove himself from a history; in one version of his *Collected Poems* having them printed in alphabetical order, although in later editions he was willing to present them chronologically. He believed in Valéry's dictum that a poem is never finished, only abandoned, but he followed that rule not by simply abandoning the poem, but by returning to it, revising and rewriting, too often without really noticeably improving it. Along the way he provided plenty of fascinating material for the critic of his work.

Auden's injunction against biography has, rather paradoxically, called forth quite a lot of activity: a collection of essays edited by Stephen Spender, an unsatisfactory life by Charles Osborne, and Humphrey Carpenter's *W. H. Auden: A Biography* (1981), an unauthorized life but one written with the permission of the estate, and with access to much previously unavailable material. It is unlikely that another biography will be needed, at least for a time. Carpenter's work will provide anyone interested in Auden's work with a careful, sympathetic, and apparently complete life. If anything, it is almost too dispassionate, too determined to be fair. Toward the end one almost feels that the author is a little impatient with his subject. He presents views favorable to the personality of the older Auden, but the dominant theme is of a man disoriented, dissatisfied, perhaps still writing well, devoted to his art, but ready to come to an end of his life at the comparatively early age of sixty-six—seeming much older, particularly with that extraordinary creviced face.

Here is essential background for the poetry. But considering the biography one need not come to issue with the poetry—which is perhaps one reason Auden had some doubts about the form. His being an important poet makes Auden's life significant. Here is a fascinating portrait of a member of the English upper middle class, the third son of a doctor, born in 1907, educated in a proper upper-middle-class way, at prep school, public school, and at Christ Church, Oxford, who in fact was so English that it was necessary for him to escape to America to free himself from his roots, bringing down obloquy upon himself as it was wartime, becoming an American citizen, while clearly remaining an English poet, with many characteristics of his nation and his class. His life was full of doubts and travails; at the same time he was full of that extraordinary sense of authority of the upper-class Englishman, and he became increasingly dogmatic in his pronouncements, "your old mother says," although presumably there was just a touch of irony, as when he said to Christopher Isherwood about his conversion to Vedanta "My dear, it's simply *not* a gentleman's religion." He had an extraordinary range of knowledge and technical ability—he was a splendid machine for making poetry, and he adored writing in as many forms as possible. He taught by providing his students with a full awareness of the styles of poetry—he knew he couldn't teach inspiration. He was a custodian and enricher of the language.

Auden as an undergraduate at Oxford seemed to plan a takeover of English letters, and to a large extent he and his friends—Isherwood, Spender, Warner, Day-Lewis, Lehmann, and others—succeeded in becoming the new and talked-about in the 1930s. Despite the fact that Auden's political period was comparatively brief—he came to believe that a poet could do nothing to change society—his depiction of a depression landscape in his poetry, his sense of the need to search for a solution, be it some form of psychology, or politics, made him deeply representative of the poetry of the period. But his poetry was so good that it transcends its time. Still, for a sense of and feel for the political thirties we must turn to Auden, and his picture of England, a country in which no one was well. That representative role is less interesting in Auden's later life, no matter what one thinks about the quality of his early as compared to his later poetry.

Two great themes of the book, Christianity and homosexuality, almost overshadow the poetry. Carpenter has previously written on Jesus, C. S. Lewis, Charles Williams, and Tolkien. (I'm pleased to learn that Tolkien apparently didn't care for Auden's characteristically dogmatic remark that he would consider no person literate who did not like Tolkien's writing.) The shape of the biography is largely determined, I believe, by Carpenter's interest in Auden's return to Christianity. He puts a fair amount of emphasis on Auden's early mystical experience while sitting on the lawn at the school at which he was teaching in June 1933, and he also is particularly interested in Auden's distress at the churches being closed—frequently destroyed—in Loyalist Spain during the Spanish Civil War and at the treatment of the nuns and priests there. The return to Christianity was not a spectacular reconversion, but rather a quiet going to church while he was living in an extraordinary ménage in Brooklyn Heights, which at one time included Gypsy Rose Lee. But some of the life goes out of this biography once Auden has reconverted. Much of the rest of his years, in Carpenter's version, lacks biographical shape. The book then becomes primarily an insightful, deeply interesting quotidian chronicle.

Auden's love life reached its crisis shortly after his conversion. In fact, Auden happened to return to religion—perhaps by chance—when he found his true love, but the dashing of his hopes of that happiness did not destroy his religious beliefs. Auden had a combination of guilt and joy in his homosexuality: he was quite unabashed in talking about it, although he was also a great believer in privacy—except in his last years when he was surprisingly open in several interviews. Carpenter is far from prudish and is specific about Auden's preferences in bed and his use of call boys. All is coolly told, in a detached fashion—inevitably fascinating, but with an attempt not to feed the reader's prurience. Perhaps there is a subtle denigration—would a biographer be so specific regarding sexual acts in the life story of a heterosexual? In his love life—as in other aspects—Auden is a fascinating combination. He is a liberator who was quite unabashed in seeking sexual satisfaction—frequently at teatime—and in his cool indulgence perhaps made others feel freer to follow their instincts. At the same time he yearned for a stable married relationship and he felt that he had found that with the American Chester Kallman. He was devastated, almost murderous, when he discovered that Kallman was unfaithful.

The relationship remained the central personal experience for the

whole of the second half of his life—after a while Auden sought sexual pleasure elsewhere, but Kallman, though no longer his bed partner, was continually the adored and central figure—however unworthy some of their mutual friends thought him to be. Auden was undoubtedly a difficult person to live with. He existed in seeming
chaos, but believed passionately in order, and in imposing it upon
others. Kallman described him "the most disheveled child of all dis-
ciplinarians. He demanded obedience even in his stance of seditious-
ness towards society—as when he wrote in the student paper while
teaching at Swarthmore, "'Fellow Irresponsibles, follow me.'"

Famous, comparatively well-off (although worried about money),
continuing to serve his art, he was yet so lonely, even though Kallman spent part of the year with him. After the war he became less
and less of an American resident, living first in Ischia and then in
Austria for a good part of the year. He believed in the necessity of
the artist to disassociate from his roots, and yet in his last years he
came back to live at Christ Church, Oxford. The ultimate sadness
was that it didn't work: his search for a community, with its religious overtones—returning to the place where his career had really
started—turned to dust. He may have enjoyed himself, with his endlessly repeated aphorisms, his holding forth, his drinking, the severe
organization of his life, but as depicted here, his life was increasingly
sad.

Fascinating as the story is, perhaps there was sense in which
Auden was right in his wish not to have a biography. The writings—
poetry and prose—are what count, and we are helped here to understand their making. But the writings have a life of their own. Apart
from them, as it were, is the life as it was lived. It has been well told,
with much material available to document it, and very skillfully
used. Granting that the relationship to the poetry is the major justification of the life, we have here too the story of an English Christian
Homosexual Eccentric, and that story is well worth reading, whether
or not it happens to be about W. H. Auden.

The Thirties and After: Poetry, Politics, People, 1933-1970 (1978),
by Stephen Spender, is an odd and fascinating mix made up for the
most part of previously published but hitherto uncollected essays, reviews, and reminiscences, along with a new connecting commentary.
It achieves coherence through the force of its author's remarkable
personality. It is best read as a kind of pendant to his classic self portrait *World Within World*, published almost thirty years earlier.

Since then a good deal has happened to Spender in the worlds of poetry, politics, and people, and one might have hoped for another full-scale volume of autobiography. In lieu of that the present work will do, and as one might expect, the best writing here is that which is the most immediate, the most personal, the most autobiographical.

There is an unnecessary but not untypical note of self-deprecation in his postscript: "I myself am, it is only too clear, an autobiographer. Autobiography provides the line of continuity in my work. I am not someone who can shed or disclaim his past." And yet he has an almost irresistible tendency to take off from his personal experience, so often touchingly and perceptively described, and to discuss in abstract terms what it may mean—to impersonalize it—to expect it to bear more significance than it deserves, in some senses to make it less interesting in attempting to make it more significant. So that a few lines further on in the Postscript he offers the sweeping and almost meaningless generalization, whose purpose would seem to be to blow himself up into a universal principle: "Politics without ideology and with a strong tendency towards autobiography equals liberalism."

It is W. H. Auden who, not surprisingly, discovers the telltale clue in a seriocomic, ever-so-Spenderian wartime anecdote, and it is characteristic of Spender's disarming personality that he would tell the story on himself. In 1941 he and his wife Natasha were living in Hampstead. A bomb fell on the house across the road, destroying it completely, but although the ceiling of the Spenders' sitting room collapsed and they were "rained on by rubble," the poet and his wife emerged unscathed. Spender comments: "Natasha, who seems without fear, was scarcely affected by this. I felt pulsingly alive and ran downstairs and out into the road and walked for miles and miles through London. The town seemed untouched, as though ours were the only bomb that had fallen then, and yet when it rushed out of the tunnel of darkness I had what I suppose to be my last thought: 'This is something I have all my life been waiting for,' and it seemed the end of the world." Then comes the telling parenthesis: "Later I told Auden this and he remarked: 'What an old solipsist you are!'" The world, whether it be that of poetry, politics, or people, is validated when seen from his own perspective, and illuminated by his response to it. Its main point would seem to be its relation to Stephen Spender, poet, and political and social being. This ought to be infuriating, yet there is a candor in the writing, waffly though it may be at times, and an authenticity and intelligence that make this book not only fascinating to read but also a crucial document for the 1930s in certain of their literary and political aspects.

The scheme of the book, its mix of old and new, leads to a fair amount of confusion: too often it is not clear at what point in time one is seeing the author or he is seeing himself. But through the essays, journals, reminiscences, and commentary, the intent of the autobiographical line emerges. Where, Spender seems to be asking, does he fit in the world of literature and politics of this century? By extension he is asking the same question about the group—W. H. Auden, Cecil Day Lewis, Christopher Isherwood, Louis MacNeice—with whom he has been so closely associated. He writes about them with great freshness, and, in the final section, hauntingly, as one by one the dead are recalled: MacNeice, Cyril Connolly (each in a poem published here for the first time), and then Auden, in the talk Spender gave about him at Christ Church, Oxford, a month after his death. (It was at Christ Church, of course, that so much of the Thirties movement began, orchestrated by Auden sitting in his darkened room and assigning the parts they were to play to the participants.) In that talk, and again a few pages further on, Spender quotes the famous lines with which Auden dedicated *The Orators* to him in 1932: "Private faces in public places / Are wiser and nicer / Than public faces in private places." One feels, perhaps unfairly, that the dedicatee may have some nagging uncertainty as to the continuing relevance of the dedication, preoccupied as he is with the public significance of his private concerns.

And yet, taken at their public-face value, the pieces of the book add up to an intriguing argument. Quite a few of its pages are devoted to a consideration of three of the masters of modernism—W. B. Yeats, D. H. Lawrence, and most particularly T. S. Eliot. Spender acknowledges how deeply he and his friends were influenced by them, and shared with them, an unshakable commitment to the importance of art and literature, even though they couldn't have been at a farther remove from their right-wing politics. The antithetical tradition—politics first, then art—he evokes in a younger, activist generation, represented by the poets John Cornford and Julian Bell, the first a Communist and the second a discontented and radical liberal, who lost their lives on the Government side during the Spanish Civil War. In effect, Spender sees himself partaking—although he doesn't say this so bluntly—of the virtues of both traditions: the commitment to literature of the one, and the political commitment of the other. This may indeed be the "liberal" position or solution that

Spender himself arrived at by the end of the Thirties. But how attenuated its effectiveness, how honorable, measured against the achievements of the great writers of the modern movement, or the inadvertent and inevitable nobility of Cornford and Bell, sacrificing their lives for a political cause!

The Thirties were a shaping time for Spender, casting a long shadow over all that came after, and in that sense the title of the book has a precise, ironic aptness. It would seem that the rest of his life, more even than he may himself realize, has been a matter of coming to terms with the Thirties, and the conflicting claims of literature and politics as he knew them in that decade of achievement, fame, and disillusion. "Spain was a death to us, Munich a mourning," Day Lewis wrote in his "Dedicatory Stanzas to Stephen Spender." After the traumas of Spain and Munich one might have expected that Spender would follow the example of Auden, who abandoned politics (and England) at the end of the decade to devote himself single-mindedly to poetry in America, and in the future would revise or disown those poems of his—no matter how famous—that reflected a politics in which he no longer believed.

But Spender, lacking Auden's single-mindedness, attempted to reconcile the seemingly irreconcilable, and in the exhilarating, stepped-up tempo of the war years he was able to put off a recognition of the difficulties inherent in the attempt. This was a rewarding period for him when he did seem able to be everything he wanted to be: poet, co-editor of *Horizon*, fire-watcher, husband, and father. No longer a rebel, he was at the very heart of the English cultural establishment. The latter-day Shelley had been tamed.

It was only after the war that he was forced to accept that the balance was tilting. He wanted to be an "anti-Communist liberal" but not a "cold warrior." This was a distinction that the history of his time and the particulars of his public career made it more and more difficult to recognize. He was frequently in attendance at congresses and conferences as a cultural/political spokesman from "our side" of the Iron Curtain. He became co-editor of *Encounter* with Melvin Lasky, not knowing of the CIA connection. Being useful, he was used. But one does not have to argue from a revisionist position to ask what all this ferment of political activity amounted to in any case. Where was the place, let alone the time, for art? The Fifties, as he acknowledges, were not his best decade. It is significant that his most enduring achievement (literary or otherwise) from that time should have been a return to his past in *World Within World*.

That masterpiece of autobiography, and the best of the poems, continue to remind us how much we owe to the private Spender. As a public figure he is no doubt the more "representative," but the glimpses of his "other self" in *The Thirties and After* make one hope again that he will yet write a sequel to his volume of autobiography. Let the somewhat indirect autobiographer pictured here return to his art directly. In the meantime, it is useful and gratifying to have this memorable collection.

22

CHRISTOPHER SYKES ON NANCY ASTOR AND EVELYN WAUGH

The subject of Christopher Sykes's excellent biography *Nancy: The Life of Lady Astor* (1972) might serve to illustrate the difference between prominence and performance. Posterity almost certainly will be bewildered by her immense contemporary reputation: whatever was all the fuss about? Even now, one is bemused by the phenomenon. Whoever is interested in British life in the first half of the twentieth century must have been made aware of Nancy Astor and will have caught flattering, but more frequently unfavorable, glimpses of her in one or another memoir, diary, biography, or political account of the period. At the very least she was someone to whom attention was paid.

Of course, on both sides of the Atlantic the Astors have always been paid a good deal of attention, but Nancy, an Astor by marriage (to Waldorf Astor) was exceptional in the amount of it she attracted and enjoyed throughout her life. Her dossier might have inspired a novelist, and has supplied her biographer with a formidable amount of material. Item: one of the beautiful Langhorne sisters from Virginia, the elder of whom married the illustrator Charles Dana Gibson and became the original Gibson girl (Nancy herself was depicted in a dashing if slightly empty portrait by John Singer Sargent in 1908, two years after her marriage to Astor). Item: mistress of Cliveden, that famous country house overlooking the Thames near Maidenhead. Item: the first woman to take a seat in the House of Commons. Item: a humorist, more a clown than a wit, who exchanged badinage with everybody who mattered in English political life, and who, despite her somewhat Philistine nature, was a friend of such literary figures as Belloc, Shaw, and T. E. Lawrence. But how do these items add up?

One is grateful to Sykes for his authoritative and entertaining biography. Yet the sad truth which appears to emerge is that Lady Astor, however audible, visible, and risible, was not a figure to be taken very seriously in the political world in which she performed for three decades. With the light of the personality extinguished, little else survives.

The impression made upon me by this careful record of her life has only confirmed my own personal, if very indirect experience of the lady. I first saw Cliveden in 1967, three years after her death in her eighty-fifth year, on a day before an auction sale to dispose of the private contents of the house. This had followed upon the comparatively early death in the previous year of the third Lord Astor, Nancy's son, and the family decision to move out of the house, which had belonged to the National Trust since 1942. (Cliveden was the principal Astor residence; but they owned several other houses, most notably 4 St. James Square in London.) By a coincidence wholly unanticipated in 1967, I found myself a little more than three years later living in Nancy Astor's rooms in Cliveden, as a faculty member at Stanford's English campus.

American undergraduates were crowded into its many rooms, enjoying its swimming pool and tennis courts, and in the Great Hall, under the very eye of the Sargent portrait of Nancy, they chatted at ease upon a huge upholstered object, covered in red damask, they referred to as the Christine Keeler memorial couch. The house—the third on the site since the earliest Cliveden—has a certain interest as the work of Sir Charles Barry, the architect of the Houses of Parliament, and the grounds are splendid, brought to their finest cultivation during the long residence of the Astors. And yet, such historical feelings as the house and grounds still have seem to be chiefly associated with its original builder, the second Duke of Buckingham, or its famous eighteenth-century tenant, Frederick Prince of Wales, or its owners in the nineteenth century, the Duke and Duchess of Sutherland, friends to Victoria and to Garibaldi. While one still hears anecdotes about the Astors in general, and Nancy in particular, she is far less prominent in spirit than I had expected and hoped—after being a commanding presence there for so many years, it is almost as though she hadn't existed—and her ghost did not disturb my slumbers.

I think, on the whole, I'm just as glad that she didn't. Apparently Nancy could, in her chaffing way, get on with almost everyone, but I suspect she would have scared me, and I doubt that she would have liked the idea of an American academic in her bedroom. But I certainly know much more about her from this biography than I knew when I was in residence, and much more than was supplied in the pleasant but relentlessly anecdotal life of her by Maurice Collis, published in 1960, or even from the fascinating account, *Tribal Feeling*, written by her son Michael Astor in 1963.

Christopher Sykes is an accomplished biographer, and once he gets over the hurdle of the American years, where he does not seem really comfortable, all goes smoothly. He handles the tale of Nancy's first marriage to the Bostonian Robert Shaw well, and he deals compassionately and truthfully with the wasted life of the son of that unhappy marriage. But he is much more at ease from the moment (1903) when Nancy came over to England to hunt in order to distract herself after her divorce and fell in love with Lord Revelstoke, an aristocratic member of the Baring family. Revelstoke wanted to marry her, but she felt, despite all his protestations to the contrary, that he was patronizing her, and the courtship ended.

Perhaps the chaffing manner that became so characteristic of her was a strategy she adopted as a way of dealing with the English, with whom she didn't feel entirely secure. As she wrote in another context, "the trouble with so many English people is they cannot, however hard they try, be quite natural with other people. It is difficult for them not to be just a little patronizing." Waldorf Astor was an ideal solution—an American who had become an Englishman, and would use the vast Astor American wealth to live a worthy life of service in his father's adopted country. He was a minor figure in the political landscape, a Tory with social concerns, ultimately the owner of the *Observer*, one of the " posh" Sunday papers which "everyone" reads, while his brother, John Jacob, to whom he wasn't particularly close, came to control *The Times*. It was a marriage that ensured that Nancy, beautiful, willful, and with an irrepressible sense of comedy, would be at the least a memorable political hostess.

But in 1916 her father-in-law was made a peer, just after it became possible for naturalized subjects to achieve that honor. Three years later, at his death, her husband became the second Lord Astor, and was forced to give up his seat in the House of Commons and enter the House of Lords. Meanwhile, in February 1918 women in England had been given the vote, and in November of that year a law had been passed making it possible for them to sit in the House of Commons. Seventeen women stood in the General Election in December 1918, but only the Countess Markievicz was successful. At that moment, however, she was in prison, and as a loyal member of Sinn Fein, she would not take the oath of loyalty to the King, and her election was invalidated. Some months later, Nancy Astor ran for her husband's seat in Plymouth, in the special election caused by his elevation to the House of Lords. She won, was introduced into Parliament by Lloyd George and Arthur Balfour, and hence secured a place for herself in history as the first woman to sit in the House of Commons. (It is a characteristic English touch that the first woman member should be a Tory.)

All through her life she remained loyal to women's causes, demanding equal pay for equal work, and equal job opportunities. She was always a colorful figure—good copy—and though she fell into the shouting habits of the House of Commons, she managed not to be called out of order too often. She piloted a private bill through the House—no mean feat—that brought about a stiffening of the drinking regulations. Yet beyond her symbolic role as the first woman in Parliament, it is hard to see that she had any really important political significance.

During the Second World War, when Lord Astor was Lord Mayor of Plymouth, she did a splendid job, helping to keep up the morale of that battered navy town. In parliament, however, her superficiality, her inability to grasp the point, increasingly curtailed her effectiveness. As Harold Nicolson said of her in 1943, when in a debate she was arguing indirectly that the Catholic influence in the Foreign Office was too strong: "She has one of those minds that work from association to association and therefore spreads sideways with extreme rapidity." Answering her, Nicolson felt, was "like playing squash with a dish of scrambled eggs." She was an M.P. from 1919 to 1945; then her family forced her to retire, and she never really forgave them.

Sykes devotes a fascinating chapter to the Cliveden Set. Legend has it that Nancy was a leading figure of a cabal of powerful people in the 1930s who met at Cliveden and were determined that England should give in to Hitler's every whim. Sykes crushingly demonstrates how little basis in fact there was to the legend, that the Astors and their friends were (as one might guess) not very different in their thinking from most fearful, peace-loving unimaginative Englishmen, for whom Neville Chamberlain was so earnest a spokesman. One might have hoped that such powerful and highly placed people would have had a better sense of the realities of England's situation, but certainly there was no "conspiracy," nothing so "sinister" as the legend would have it. All this makes for an admirable corrective. But in an odd way, one feels a little sad that even this sort of negative glory has been taken away from Nancy—she is not even an important villainess. Unsurprisingly, she was an ardent supporter of Chamberlain's position at Munich. But changeable and whimsical as she was, it was not surprising that she should be one of the forty Tories who voted against Chamberlain at the time of the Norway debate, and helped bring about his fall, although she was no friend of Churchill's.

Prominence, her great friendship with Shaw, knowing "everybody"—all that has now been reduced to the simple chapel at Cliveden, where the three Lord Astors are buried, and Nancy's ashes are mingled, as she wished, with those of her husband. Writing of her with tact and discrimination, Christopher Sykes is aware of her faults and virtues, her impulsiveness and flightiness, the power of her friendships and dislikes, her sense of comedy, her possessiveness, her generosity. His biography makes a fitting memorial.

Christopher Sykes has written the life of his friend Evelyn Waugh (1975) at the request of Laura Waugh, the novelist's widow, and his eldest son Auberon, himself a novelist. In spite of its auspices, this is anything but a work of piety: it is very funny, and sometimes very sad, and richly informative; and I do not see how anyone interested in English letters and society of this century, and one of its most remarkable writers, can afford not to read it. At the same time, I feel constrained to add that, judged by the highest standard, it is something of a disappointment. Sykes has fallen into a trap of his own devising: he has attempted to write a memoir as well as a biography, and the two forms, despite their kinship, make very different demands upon him, knocking the proportions of the book askew. It does meander, to allow room for the author's own recollections (which are delightful): it is also, at certain crucial biographical moments, irritatingly thin or secretive, as though the author knows more than he is prepared to tell, or else has not done his homework, particularly for the period before 1930, the year he himself enters the picture, and can therefore write of Evelyn as he knew him.

Let me illustrate with two contrasting examples. First, what I will call the "faun" motif. Sykes, the biographer, writing of Waugh in the period 1922-24, quotes from Harold Acton's *Memoirs of an Aesthete*: "An almost inseparable boon companion at Oxford was a little faun called Evelyn Waugh. Though others assure me that he has changed past recognition, I still see him as a prancing faun, thinly disguised by conventional apparel." And so on for a dozen lines of quotation. Thereupon Sykes tells us, "Acton gave another and fuller account nearly twenty years after the appearance in 1948 of these memoirs." And again we have a rich extract, from which I single out the relevant sentence: "Short, slim, alert, with wavy hair and wide-apart eyes that often sparkled with mischief, he seemed a faun . . . alternately wild and shy." So much for the faun—biographically speaking—but now, Sykes, the memoirist, has an anecdote of his own to insert in the narrative, which he does with a fine disregard for chronology:

> "In his book," said Evelyn to me one day when we were walking together in Gloucestershire, "Harold Acton described me as a faun. What did he describe you as?"
> "He didn't mention me in the book."
> "Oh?" said Evelyn on that high note which he could suddenly use. "Why not? Didn't he think you were important enough?"
> "Maybe. But you see the time at Oxford which Harold describes was before I went up. I could only have appeared as a digression."
> Evelyn looked grave. "That's your alibi, is it?" he said.
> "I regard it as unbreakable," I answered.
> We walked on in silence till Evelyn turned to me and said in a deep, grating voice: "You're jealous of me because Harold Acton said I was like a faun, and no one has ever said that you are like a faun."
> The last remark was quite true.

That the "faun" motif—thereafter dropped from the book—has been given generous treatment seems undeniable. How scanty, by contrast, is Sykes's treatment—one brief paragraph—of what would seem a matter of much greater biographical significance: Evelyn's attempted suicide by drowning when he was a schoolmaster, after leaving Oxford, at a boys' school in North Wales. Waugh had made of this botched semi-comic episode the conclusion of his autobiographical volume *A Little Learning*, which Sykes depends on as a source here and elsewhere. He writes: "In the autobiography he gave details of the dignified pathos with which he contrived to surround the tragedy, and of how he was surprised out of his plan by a jellyfish." And he concludes dryly, "The reader of the diaries may be surprised to find no mention of this episode." But the reader of the biography may be equally surprised to find no further mention of the episode here, as though it were an occurrence of the most commonplace sort.

Again, it seems odd that Sykes should barely mention Waugh's brief but "extreme homosexual phase" as a very young man, conceding to it no more than minimal biographical, literary, or psychological significance. Odder still is the conclusion he draws, when writing of Evelyn's first marriage—in June 1928, to Evelyn Gardner (to their friends of that time they became known as He-Evelyn and She-Evelyn)—which ended in August 1929, when She-Evelyn ran off with John Heygate, "a friend to them both." Readers familiar with *A Handful of Dust* will not be surprised to learn from Sykes that "the effect on Evelyn was not light. He felt lost again in a world where he believed that, at last, after a painful struggle, he had found safety. He fell into a state of absolute despair. . . . Some of his friends saw, or believed they saw, a change in his character after August 1929: they saw a new hardness and bitterness and an utter disillusion." These are strong words, but not unjustified; certainly they go a long way to explain much that is otherwise inexplicable in the man and the writer. Sykes, however, is at pains to detach himself from the question implicit in the evidence he has given. "In so far as I allow myself an opinion, I believe that Evelyn, for all the anguish he endured, was not radically changed. But again I must insist that I have no memory of him earlier than 1930." Which is a scrupulous admission from a memoirist with a store of memories of his own to draw upon, but rather beside the point, one would think, for a biographer who must achieve a coherent portrait out of the material assembled about his subject.

Sykes, of course, has had full access to the diaries, which Waugh kept intermittently, and in which he gave free rein to his sense of farce and fantasy. When extracts from them were published in England their extraordinary nastiness caused something of a sensation. Their revelations of Evelyn Waugh as monster made some wonder why the family had consented to let them be published. Very likely the decision was not unrelated to Waugh's own lack of hypocrisy about money and its necessity in an age when he regarded the state's taxes as confiscatory. He adored libel actions, successfully initiating two, as the proceeds were tax-free; and he once wrote to Nancy Mitford, on the point of his setting out for a trip to Rhodesia, "I have insured my life for £50,000 for the two days of the journey (only costs a tenner). I couldn't possibly earn that sum however hard I worked in the few years of activity left to me (not with taxes) so it will be much the best thing for my poor children if the aeroplane blows up. In fact the only chance they have of a liberal education.

But I suppose I ought not pray for it on account of the other passengers who may not have been so foresighted."

The diaries—edited by Michael Davie, whose work will be cut out for him, sorting fact from fantasy—will be unfair to Waugh if they are not read in conjunction with this biography, so that the man can be seen in his very considerable round. Indeed, the diaries—always assuming they can be trusted—will reveal more to us, for better or worse, than we are given here. Which is not to say that Sykes has produced an adulatory work. He knew, not only having heard it from others but from his own experience, that Waugh could be totally impossible. It is not surprising that during the war his commanding officer, at one point, felt that he must place a guard over Captain Waugh so that he would not be murdered by his own men, and that he was rather shuttled about from post to post as an officer who with his anarchistic tendencies was not really meant to serve in any army. As Sykes remarks, "it never seemed to occur to him in those days that his own temperament, his difficulty in establishing tolerable relations with his colleagues and subordinates, his delight in causing offense, his childish and ostentatious indiscipline, had anything to do with it at all." And yet it was from this experience, so essentially uncongenial to him, that he fashioned his magnificent trilogy of war novels, *Sword of Honour*. However incompetent and willful in the service of his country, he was never less than masterful and disciplined in the service of his art.

And that, as Sykes well knows, is the justification for this book, and of Evelyn Waugh's life. On the way to monsterdom he became one of the great writers of his generation: perhaps the two things are (in his case) inseparable. George Orwell, in the last year of his life, intended to write an article on Waugh, with whom he had a very slight acquaintance and whose work he greatly admired. The article remained unwritten, but in a manuscript notebook some jottings for it survive, of which the most pertinent observation is that "Waugh's loyalty is to a form of society no longer viable, of which he must be aware." That he was aware of this is, I think, beyond question. When he wrote of himself in the guise of Gilbert Pinfold, he admitted that "He abhorred plastics, Picasso, sunbathing, and jazz—everything in fact that had happened in his own lifetime." The paradox of his life as an artist—or as he would have preferred to say, as a craftsman—is that for the best of his writings he drew upon his own time. Out of the 1920s came *Vile Bodies*, out of the 1930s *A Handful of Dust*. The great novel of the phony war, *Put Out More Flags*, is his; and as I have already suggested, *Sword of Honour* is one of the major achievements in the literature of the Second World War.

Yet the cost to him was great. In spite of the comparative security of literary success, a profound faith as a Catholic (having converted in 1930), and an extremely happy second marriage blessed by many children, he could not conquer his deepening melancholy. His books are hilariously funny and painfully sad, and accurate descriptions of his life. In his youth he had been a faun; in his middle age he had made himself into a monster. His rudeness was appalling. It became a weapon, used sometimes as a rapier (as when, having elicited from Edmund Wilson that *Memoirs of Hecate County* would not be published in England for fear it might be banned as pornography, he remarked, "Mr. Wilson, in cases like yours I always advise publication in Cairo") and sometimes as a bludgeon of a peculiarly nasty sort. To the latter category, surely, one must assign his reply to a hapless American lady at a dinner party who ventured to praise *Brideshead Revisited*: "I thought it was good myself, but now that I know a vulgar, common American woman like yourself admires it, I am not so sure." Once when Nancy Mitford reprimanded him for behaving badly and in an un-Christian way, he remarked that she had no idea how much worse he would have behaved if he weren't a Catholic.

Sykes can show us how, but does not explain why, this happened. He is fully aware that much of it was a game, a farce, that Waugh for mysterious reasons chose to play—that he overacted the part of the country squire, that no man other than a racetrack tout would have had suits made of the wide-checked material that Waugh insisted upon. But we are not told why he created this impossible persona that held him in its grip. He loved to make trouble—sometimes with hilarious results, as when, on a mission in Yugoslavia, he persisted in announcing his belief that Tito was a woman until Tito himself was presented to Waugh, turned to his commanding officer, Fitzroy Maclean, and said "Ask Captain Waugh why he thinks I am a woman." It was the only occasion, Maclean reported to Sykes, "when Evelyn was at a loss for a reply." But the line between the hilarious and the hateful is a fine one, and Waugh too often couldn't or had no wish to distinguish between them.

Clearly his art was achieved at a terrible personal price—his vendettas, his ungovernable rages, his need to needle people, his absurdly reactionary political position. Why this was necessary is perhaps beyond the capacity of any biographer to explain who is reluctant to theorize or speculate. If Christopher Sykes has not made a very serious attempt to do so, he has nonetheless provided invaluable glimpses into the life of the writer and into those aspects of English society in the first half of this century that engaged Waugh's imagination, awakened his nostalgia, and invited his satire.

Was the creation of an angry man, his eyes popping over his garden gate, forbidding to strangers, and frequently to friends, necessary to preserve the private man who wrote? Evelyn Waugh almost seemed to will himself hateful, to give his love to a very few friends, to his family, to his faith, and to his writing. His life is easily criticized; his art is not—and in the long view, surely, it is art, not the eccentricity and ill temper of the artist, that matters.

23

OSWALD MOSLEY AND UNITY MITFORD

British respectability is frequently derided, but at times it has its advantages. One suspects that the lack of success of Sir Oswald Mosley's British Union of Fascists owes at least something to this unexciting but sensible trait. The British are fully capable of brutality and nastiness—as much as any other group—but they do not appear to like private military units, or violence getting out of hand at political meetings, or overt anti-Semitism. Despite his disclaimers, Mosley fostered all three in his attempt to make Britain fascist. Respectability joined with common sense and would not have it: Sir Oswald failed.

The writing of self-justifying memoirs is an occupation for failed politicians, and garrulousness is the prevailing vice of political memoirs generally. It is not surprising, then, that Mosley should have written at great, even tedious, length what amounts to several books in one, *My Life* (1972), about his career, or that the text should be marred by continual self-justifications and pieties. The preaching is almost unremitting in the second half of the book, from the time of his founding of the British Union of Fascists in 1932—when he withdrew from the orthodox political system and closed off his future—and this half of the memoir will be of interest chiefly to those who wish to study a cosmetic version of British fascism.

The flow of minute particulars that enliven the earlier pages and make them worth reading, gives way here to abstractions and ruminations. The eyewitness testimony, when it comes to historic figures Sir Oswald knew from a special vantage point, is less penetrating than one might hope. Doubtless Hitler and Mussolini have been misrepresented by those who find it somewhat hard to look at them as objectively as perhaps one should; even so, it is a little trying to hear of Mussolini's "peculiar sense of fun"—when he tells Mosley about the coincidental death from a heart attack of the Chief Rabbi of Rome the day after he had, allegedly, insulted Il Duce in a personal interview; or to be assured of the truly humorous and music-loving nature of Hitler and Goebbels. The focus is very soft, and Mosley's activities in the 1930s, and after the war, are presented in a bland, self-serving way, designed to demonstrate how reasonable a man he was, but in fact revealing his failure to grasp the galling illogic and brutality of his theories.

The earlier part of the book, however, is an interesting memoir, a first cousin to the many chronicles of politics and privilege which have appeared over the years—self-indulgently written, wandering, but with a charming and intriguing picture of life among the grandees of the British political scene after the First World War.

Centuries before, the Mosleys made money from trade, but as quickly as possible they became wealthy landed gentry, and baronets. Elizabeth I gave them the family motto of *Mos legem regit,* "which was understood to mean 'Our custom is above the law.'" In fact, the motto has a certain irony in light of the sixth baronet's career, and his imprisonment without trial for three and a half years during the Second World War, when he claimed that he was doing no more than urging a negotiated peace.

Sir Oswald rejects the theory that his broken home, his alcoholic father, and his colorful grandfather, who engaged in a serious boxing match with his son, marked him off from others of his class. (And of course he is right that many an eccentricity flourished unnoticed or unimpeded in the English countryside in those affluent days before 1914.) Nor was it unusual that he should have had a fairly unhappy schooling, in his case at Winchester, where he took up athletics (fencing and boxing), but not what he saw as the other prime activities of an English public school: learning and homosexuality.

Like many of his generation, he was an officer in the First World War, fought bravely, grew disillusioned, and came back to England with a determination that war must be avoided at all cost thereafter. This he claims to be his central political conviction, and his motive for entering the world of politics. But his version of the experience itself, measured against the descriptions of the war in the countless memoirs that have preceded his, seems oddly muffled; and it is not always easy to sort out sincerity from high-flown rhetoric.

He is more successful in reviving his childhood, and his early political and social career, giving us amusing, sharp glimpses of high life in the 1920s (those meetings with Princess Jane di San Faustino,

Elsie de Wolfe, Lady Cunard), and vivid pictures of politicians he knew, most notably Lloyd George, Balfour, his father-in-law Curzon, and Churchill, who advises him "Bartlett's Familiar Quotations, my boy, never be without them." There are some memorable vignettes of Margot Asquith, who might have qualified for Bartlett's with her advice to the young Mosley, "Your speech reminded me in some ways of my old friend Lord Randolph Churchill, but, dear boy, do not share his vices, never live with six women at once, it is so weakening."

But these are filigrees on the essential story of Mosley the politician, who entered Parliament in 1918 at the age of 22, the youngest man in the House of Commons, and had an extremely successful career through the decade, helped by his social position ("The old boy or old girl network"), by what he himself calls the "youth racket," and by his undoubted gifts. He was then a Tory, but perhaps the noblest moment in his career came when he grew disgusted with the Government support of atrocities by the Black and Tans in Ireland in the early 1920s, and broke with his party. He moved to the left, came to the notice of Beatrice Webb, who wrote on first meeting him in 1923 that " so much perfection argues rottenness somewhere."

He joined the Labour Party and rapidly rose in its ranks. As early as 1925, and again in 1930 in his famous proposals—the Mosley Memorandum—he sensibly advocated drastic action for coping with economic distress. Yet even in those documents there are signs of authoritarianism, his ever-growing belief—covered with a certain gentlemanly mock-modesty—that he knows best. A fine line separates self-righteousness from megalomania, and presently he was to cross it: he became the leader of the British Union of Fascists. Self-righteousness sustains him through the many pages of his memoir, a sad story if it were not so complacent a one.

The descriptive portion of the title of David Pryce-Jones's biography of Unity Mitford suffered a sea change when it crossed the Atlantic. In England, where the book was first published, it was titled *Unity Mitford: A Quest* (1977); in America, the subtitle has become *An Inquiry into Her Life and the Frivolity of Evil*. The English version sums up efficiently the form of the biography that Pryce-Jones set out to write: a quest for Unity Mitford as she was, based upon as many facts and quasi-facts about her as could be gathered from as many surviving people who knew her, no matter how slightly, and were willing to talk about her, no matter how inconsequentially.

(Perhaps it would have been better if he had not been so generous with his more than two hundred interviews, disgorging in such profuse and repetitive detail what he was told over the teacups in this or that Schloss; nor so generous and unskeptical with his interviewees, only seldom subjecting what they told him to unkind scrutiny, or wondering what they might have left untold.)

"Quest" has the further advantage of a second level of meaning. It describes the trajectory of Unity Mitford's life, for this peer's daughter who strikes one as being more than a little dotty, this sister-in-law of Sir Oswald ("Ozzie-Mozzie") Mosley, the British fascist leader, herself embarked upon a quest that would have seemed unattainable to anyone less obsessed than she: to meet, to know, to worship Adolf Hitler. Ultimately her quest was successful, for Unity got Hitler, though rather less of him than she would have liked; and Pryce-Jones has succeeded in his quest, for he has got Unity, though rather more of her than he actually needed.

Perhaps it was to endow Unity with a significance she doesn't intrinsically possess that the American subtitle was called into being. The simple quest becomes something more complex: an inquiry into "the frivolity of evil." No doubt the echo of Hannah Arendt is intended; but what is one to make of the phrase? The more one thinks about it, the more enigmatic it becomes. In what sense can evil be frivolous? Is there a distinction to be made between a serious and a frivolous evil? When the evil is anti-Semitism—and I would like to think that no civilized, no humane man or woman would deny that anti-Semitism is evil—is it a matter of degree? Is anti-Semitism frivolous up to a point, and after that point is reached, does it then become serious?

Unity was, it seems clear from reading Pryce-Jones, "frivolous" in her style—"The darling Führer's coming past, let's go and waggle a flag"—and superficial in her thinking, but she was noxiously serious in her anti-Semitism. If it was merely a question or style, then it was already, as early as 1935, a style gone rotten, when she would write a letter to Streicher's paper, beginning, "Dear *Stürmer*! As an English Fascist I would like to express my admiration for you. For a year I have been living in Munich and each week have read the *Stürmer*. If only we had such papers in England. Ordinary people in England have no idea of the Jewish danger. . . . We look forward to the day on which we shall declare with full power and might 'England for the English!' Jews out! With German greetings! Heil Hitler. Unity Mitford. P.S. If you should happen to find room in your paper for this letter, please print my name in full. I do not want my letter initialled U.M., for everyone should know that I am a Jew hater."

Later still, the possibility of this behavior being written off as merely questionable style, doesn't even arise. In a grim, climactic passage that is already famous, and deservedly so, Pryce-Jones tells how, in the spring of 1939, "on Hitler's orders" she was offered "a short list of four apartments in Munich requisitioned from Jews . . . and that May she made her choice. She inspected the four apartments. Some of the Jewish owners, on the eve of their forcible dispossession, were still in their homes, actually looking at her and listening to her in the very rooms which Unity was absorbed in measuring up, imagining colour schemes and decorations and improvements. She was oblivious to the cruelty of the scene. . . . Not even victims suffering in front of her could count on simple pity and understanding. And she was the instrument of their victimization. It was cold-blooded, self-seeking, as deliberate as anything the bullies were up to outside. The abstract *Stürmer* hatred culminated here, when she was brought finally to the real meaning of the slogans and swastikas and did not even notice. This was what Nazism had done for her. Debasement could be carried no further. Anti-Semitism at the last meant that Jews had no faces, no children, no anguish, nothing but a suitable flat, and here is the kernel of the horror which was the holocaust."

This is horrifying, and it is understandable that certain readers should recoil from its implications. Much more reassuring to assign Unity to a niche in a chamber of grotesques: someone freakish and unique. But I think it closer to fact—discomfiting though it may be to admit it—that hers was an extreme case of a not uncommon disease, especially before 1939, among members of her class, and even among members of her family. Her maternal grandfather, Thomas Gibson Bowles, was a naval commander who was also the author of a book of travels, *The Log of the 'Nereid.'* Describing a visit to the Wailing Wall in Jerusalem, he writes with ham-fisted humor—the humor of the wardroom or the gentlemen's club, so to speak—"I don't see what the Jews have got to wail about. If they have been expelled from Jerusalem, they are the rulers of London, Paris, and Berlin." This is standard fare, of the sort to induce an approving chuckle over port. But the Commander could also reach a depth of expression that might have graced the *Stürmer*: "There is, I suppose, no human animal more utterly devoid of all dignity and nobility, none that bears an aspect at once so abject and so dangerous as the lower class of Russian Jews who have recently overrun the Holy City. Their pale, womanly faces, rendered loathesome by a long, greasy curled lock in front of each ear; their narrow shoulders, bent carriage, filthy gaberdines, and furtive glances, mark in every point a race that has been oppressed for centuries, and that has so deserved oppression as to make it hard not to oppress it." Whether or not his granddaughter read this passage, one can't say; one feels reasonably certain, however, that she would have applauded it.

Pryce-Jones seems to wish to depict Unity as some sort of rebel, which is to endow her with a kind of historical significance she doesn't deserve: the "mirror image" of the young men and women on the Left in the 1930s. I'm afraid the explanation is simpler and more awful, that she took the anti-Semitism of her family to its extreme, and failed to allow for the paradoxes of English character which frequently combined total beastliness of expression with decency of action. It is hard to believe that the anti-Semitism of her parents and grandparents would have led them, as it did Unity, not only to endorse the murder of Jews in theory, but also to roam about in their apartments in Munich, wondering which would suit her best. The concluding lines of a famous poem of the 1930s, William Empson's "Missing Dates," make a tragic and apt summation: "Slowly the poison the whole blood stream fills. / The waste remains, the waste remains and kills."

24

ISAIAH BERLIN

Only the title of Isaiah Berlin's *Personal Impressions* (1980) is bland. The contents of this fourth volume, edited by Henry Hardy, of Isaiah Berlin's "Selected Writings" bear the distinctive stamp of one of the great thinkers and writers of our age. The general reader, unfamiliar with his work, or put off by the formidable subject matter of the earlier volumes—*Concepts and Categories: Philosophical Essays, Against the Current: Essays in the History of Ideas, Russian Thinkers*—will find *Personal Impressions* altogether welcoming and rewarding.

Berlin is something of a mythic figure, not least in the dazzling flow of his conversation. His writing reflects the diversionary excursions, unexpected self-interruptions, and recommencements of a great talker—at home equally with Russian history and literature, political philosophy, Marx, Herder, and Vico, or subtle ruminations on the world as he has known it. We are assured in his company of a supremely intelligent, highly civilized approach to whatever he touches upon. In the present book, he is at his most conversational. And yet, for all the brilliance of these pieces, they are, with a few quite extraordinary exceptions, perhaps a little muted—at least I am tempted to think so, comparing their relative restraint with the exhilarating experience of listening to him discourse impromptu. I can still remember an occasion, many years ago, when, in an hour of subdued fireworks, talking nonstop to William Abrahams and myself, he provided us with arresting views of the young writers of the 1930s. Enlightening though his recollections were of those writers he knew—Auden, for example, and Stephen Spender—he was, if possible, even more incandescent on those he hadn't actually known, about whom his hypotheses, speculations, and interpretations proved astonishingly on the mark—a reminder that biography is more a matter of intelligence, intuition, and understanding than a mere collection of external facts.

Noel Annan, in his Introduction, resorts to the French word éloge—eulogy, encomium, praise—to characterize these essays. Two of them indeed were originally delivered as eulogies at memorial services for colleagues at Oxford (where Berlin has spent a good part of his life as a Fellow of All Souls, and the first president of Wolfson College), while several others were written for memorial volumes and symposia. Despite this, they are all, even the slightest of them, free of pieties and the glossings-over such occasions tend to encourage. Sir Isaiah—he was knighted in 1957—knows that to speak less than truthfully of his friends is to do them a disservice. He can distinguish astutely between a virtue and a flaw, and appreciate what a less subtle intelligence might fail to recognize: how a flaw may contribute as much to greatness as a virtue.

Greatness, in all its variety and peculiarity, shows itself in the men and women about whom he is writing, whether dominating figures in the world at large (Churchill, Roosevelt, Chaim Weizmann), or in the more special, sometimes recondite worlds of literature, science, history, classics, and linguistic philosophy. How wide his acquaintance has been! Except for Einstein and Roosevelt, he has known all his subjects—whether Boris Pasternak or Anna Akhmatova, Lewis Namier or Aldous Huxley—which adds a particular authority to what he would modestly have us read as no more than personal impressions.

So much of the book was written to order, as it were, that one might assume it to be no more than a gathering of occasional pieces. But as one progresses from the earliest (on Churchill) to the most recent (his meetings with Russian poets), one becomes aware of certain recurrent concerns that provide a unity of tone and conviction and emphasize the contrast between the world into which he was born—and from which he was uprooted at the age of ten—and the world in which he has lived ever since. This is a contrast that Berlin himself may not have consciously set out to create, but to this reader at least it is impressively and movingly there.

In his opening essays, on Churchill and Roosevelt, he pays tribute to the former as "the saviour of his country" and to the latter as "the greatest leader of democracy, the greatest champion of social progress in the twentieth century." The world the Prime Minister and the President came to symbolize and did their best to serve and preserve was the world that welcomed Berlin, a Latvian Jew, as well as such figures as Chaim Weizmann, a Russian Jew, Lewis Namier, a Polish Jew, and Felix Frankfurter, an Austrian Jew. Each was entranced by a vision of England, more ideal perhaps than real, that offered a future far richer in possibilities of self-fulfillment (and even survival, as things turned out) than the future accessible to them in Eastern Europe. Writing about Frankfurter—but the passage applies with equal relevance to the others—Berlin recalled his "touching and enjoyable Anglomania—the childlike passion for England, English institutions, Englishmen—for all that was sane, refined, not shoddy, civilised, moderate, peaceful, the opposite of brutal, decent—for the liberal and constitutional traditions that before 1914 were so dear to the hearts and imaginations especially of those brought up in eastern or central Europe, more particularly to members of the oppressed minorities, who felt the lack of it to an agonizing degree, and looked to England and sometimes to America—those great citadels of the opposite qualities—for all that ensured the dignity and liberty of human beings."

As emigrants to the democracies of the West, they would make their mark in their new countries: Namier as historian, Berlin as philosopher, Weizmann as scientist, Frankfurter as jurist. Namier and Berlin would both be knighted; Weizmann, the greatest of Zionists, won the friendship of Balfour and through him the support of England for the establishment of a Jewish homeland in Palestine; while Frankfurter, in America, became professor at the Harvard Law School, a friend and adviser of Franklin Roosevelt, and in due course a Justice of the Supreme Court. Honors heaped upon honors! For Jews, prepared by temperament and ancestral memories to expect the worst, it was an ironic, marvelous fate. Marvelous, too, in that it seems to have reinforced in them a sense of their own Jewishness—there was no arriviste pretension to being other than what they were, and it was not really inconsistent that they should have been both Anglomaniacs and Zionists. Thus Weizmann, with his "passion for England," as Berlin notes, "wanted the new Jewish society—the new state—to be a political child of English—almost exclusively English—experience."

I suspect that they learned quite early to temper "Anglomania" with irony. Berlin himself, writing from the center of the English establishment, has preserved a measure of distance from it even as he cooperates with it—he has done useful service to the state and made notable contributions to English education and philosophy. Yet his

Jewishness is as essential a part of his character as his Englishness. It fortifies the detachment—not an intellectual coldness but a simple recognition and appreciation of difference—that enables him to see things around him (and about himself) with exceptional clarity.

This proved of inestimable value when he returned to Russia in the summer of 1945 for the first time since his family left in 1919—a visit that "affected me profoundly and permanently changed my outlook," and that, some 35 years later, found enduring expression in "Meetings With Russian Writers in 1945," the last, most impressive, and most recent of the essays in *Personal Impressions*.

That summer Berlin, who had been working as a temporary official in the British Embassy in Washington, was told that he was being sent to the embassy in Moscow to fill "a gap until the New Year, when someone less amateur would be free to come." His assignment was to read, summarize, and comment on the content of the Soviet press. The task was not arduous, in part because the periodicals he read were so predictable, the facts and propaganda virtually identical in them all. This meant that he had ample time for the usual sightseeing, but in addition, "unlike many foreigners, at any rate non-Communist visitors from the west," he writes, "I had the extraordinary good fortune to meet a number of Russian writers, at least two among them persons of outstanding genius." Those two were the poets Boris Pasternak and Anna Akhmatova. In his powerfully evocative and moving accounts of them both, Berlin proves himself a master of memoir.

Here is his meeting with Pasternak (in the writers' village of Peredelkino, outside Moscow): "It was a warm, sunlit afternoon in early autumn. Pasternak, his wife, and his son Leonid were seated around a rough wooden table in the tiny garden at the back of the dacha. The poet greeted us warmly. He was once described . . . as looking like an Arab and his horse: he had a dark, melancholy, expressive . . . face . . .; he spoke slowly, in a low tenor monotone, with a continuous, even sound, something between a humming and a drone, which those who met him always remarked; each vowel was elongated as if in some plaintive, lyrical aria in an opera by Tchaikovsky, but with more concentrated force and tension."

Here is Akhmatova (in Leningrad in a sometime palace converted to a kind of tenement): "We climbed up one of the steep dark staircases to an upper floor, and were admitted to Akhmatova's room. It was very barely furnished—virtually everything in it had, I gathered, been taken away—looted or sold—during the siege; there was a small table, three or four chairs, a wooden chest, a sofa and, above the unlit stove, a drawing by Modigliani. A stately, gray-haired lady, a white shawl draped about her shoulders, slowly rose to greet us. Anna Andreevna Akhmatova was immensely dignified, with unhurried gestures, a noble head, beautiful, somewhat severe features, and an expression of immense sadness. I bowed—it seemed appropriate, as she looked and moved like a tragic queen—thanked her for receiving me, and said that people in the west would be glad to know that she was in good health, for nothing had been heard of her for so many years."

In an earlier essay, Berlin remarks, "Although I am far from taciturn myself, I was, for once, perfectly content to listen." This was obviously true in his Russian encounters. He listened, and, as a corollary, answered the multitude of curious, often touching questions that were put to him. There is a memorable vignette of one of Pasternak's guests at lunch, "a woman with an indescribably innocent and sweet expression . . . a teacher who had recently returned after 15 years in a labour camp, to which she had been condemned solely for teaching English." She asked Berlin if Virginia Woolf "was still writing—she had never seen a book by her, but from an account in an old French newspaper, which in some mysterious fashion had found its way into her camp, she thought she might like her work." "I told her (and the other guests) all I could of English, American, French writing: it was like speaking to victims of shipwreck on a desert island cut off from decades from civilization—all they heard, they received as new, exciting and delightful."

The richness of this essay, the wealth of particularities that illuminate each page and make it so fascinating—yes, and troubling—to read, by the same token make it extremely difficult to summarize. Doing so, one is conscious of the injustice being done to it: in a masterpiece of 70 pages, Berlin encompasses a society that still remains painfully remote, for all that we have been told of it.

Perhaps the single most haunting, truly terrible passage in this extraordinary memoir comes in the course of Berlin's visit with Akhmatova. "She broke off and spoke of the years 1937-8, when both her husband and her son had been arrested and were sent to prison camps (this was to happen again), of the queues of women who waited days and nights, week after week, month after month, for news of their husbands, brothers, fathers, sons, for permission to send food or letters to them—but no news ever came, no messages ever reached them—when a pall of death in life hung over the cities of the Soviet Union while the torture and slaughter of millions of innocents were going on. She spoke in a dry matter-of-fact voice, occasionally interrupting herself with 'No, I cannot, it is no good, you come from a society of human beings, whereas here we are divided into human beings and . . .' Then a long silence. 'And even now.'"

The contrast is inevitable between a world exemplified by two poets of genius, Russians passionately attached to the country that was preparing to silence them, and a world of "constitutional traditions that . . . ensured the dignity and liberty of human beings," to which their visitor would be returning. It is a contrast heartbreaking to contemplate, though Berlin himself is too modest and too much the artist even to allude to it. At the end he writes, "I remember vividly the expression on their faces, their gestures and their words. When I read their writings I can, to this day, hear the sound of their voices." These "Meetings With Russian Writers in 1945"—like so much of this splendid book—bring the past to life. It lives for Berlin, and thanks to him, it lives for us.

PART FIVE

GEORGE ORWELL

25

UTOPIA AND ANTI-UTOPIA: WILLIAM MORRIS AND GEORGE ORWELL

It seems certain that as long as the world is an imperfect place to live, we shall have Utopians, envisioning a world in the future in which all imperfections have been cleansed away. And it is equally certain also that, as long as the world is imperfect, we shall also have anti-Utopians, envisioning a world of the future in which the imperfections of the present have dramatically worsened and reached a kind of appalling fulfillment.

The two attitudes are exemplified in William Morris and George Orwell, and nowhere more so than in the two texts of theirs I intend to emphasize: Morris's *News from Nowhere*, published in 1890, and Orwell's *Nineteen Eighty-Four*, published in 1949. (On Orwell's part the choice of 1984 was largely a matter of coincidence. He had written the book in 1947 and 1948, and simply reversed the last two digits of the second year to achieve his title. Doing so, he provided a catchword for futurologists, editorial writers, and literal-minded pundits determined to measure the historical 1984 against the Orwellian *Nineteen Eighty-Four*, or vice versa.)

In any event, we have from one hand, Morris's, a clear instance of a Utopia, and from the other, Orwell's, an equally unmistakable anti-Utopia. Since I believe that these two texts and their respective authors are as striking in their similarities as they are in their differences, I trust that the juxtaposition will not seem merely a point-making device. Both Morris and Orwell were socialists with a hatred of state socialism; both nourished an affection for smallness, which would encourage the individual life, and a mistrust of largeness, fearing it would swallow up the individual in the mass. Each wrote out of a deep dissatisfaction with the world in which he found himself. Less than a decade separates the death of Morris and the birth of Orwell, but how different were the worlds in which each came to maturity.

It was perfectly logical that Morris, at the end of the Victorian age, should write as a late work an optimistic Utopian novel, intended to show that the ideals to which he had dedicated his life, might indeed be fulfilled. It was equally logical that Orwell, at the end of a half century of unparalleled bestiality—from the slaughter in the trenches of World War I to the Holocaust of World War II— should produce as his final work an unyieldingly bleak and anti-Utopian novel that may be taken as writing off the fulfillments of all ideals—everything he believed in most deeply—as an impossibility.

In his early, pre-socialist days, Orwell tended to be rather snotty about Morris, or rather, about the watered-down version of one of the side effects of Morris's teaching and preaching—let us call it the artsy-craftsy, or, more rudely, the artsy-fartsy side—a daft eccentricity that was certainly an aspect of the early socialist movement in England and probably elsewhere (in short, the crank fringe). Orwell, not free of crankiness himself, always had a sharp eye and tongue for such things. But the fact is, fringe groups need a home, and before the Labour Party came into existence, many of them had gravitated to the respectable Liberal Party, thereby, according to some historians, dealing it a mortal blow. Possibly. And it is rather ironic, then, that the formation of a party to the left of the Liberals should have indeed attracted to itself the same eccentric fringes; and in spite of them, triumphed.

I do not know enough about developments in other countries to say to what degree nineteenth-century criticisms of society were based on aesthetic ideas—perhaps it is unique to England. It is certainly true that Ruskin moved from aesthetic to social criticism, or rather, combined them in his special way, claiming that art and labor were intimately related. Morris followed him devotedly in this, but perhaps it may have been something of an error in terms of achieving a new sort of society. That the New Jerusalem to be built, in England's green and pleasant land, should be taken as a literal program as well as a utopian promise, brought what Morris regarded as an essential aesthetic dimension to the new society to be created. And it almost certainly brought to the movement those whose primary interests were aesthetic rather than political, and created a fringe that was perhaps a little too dirndl-skirty, too homespun tweedy, and surely too upper-middle-class, to fire up the downtrodden masses.

But, as Orwell observed, and later his friend Cyril Connolly, in every fat man there is a thin man crying to get free. Similarly, even in the most philistine Englishman there lurks an aesthete. Orwell was famously unconcerned about his looks and his surroundings, yet one of the characteristics of *Nineteen Eighty-Four* is the physical repulsiveness of the society it depicts, the inhumane, monstrous townscape that it evokes. For Orwell, as for Morris, good things—particularly love and sex—happen in the country. In that respect, both writers are in the long-standing English tradition—frequently a conservative tradition—of pointing out the virtues of the country over the city. In varying degrees, both Orwell and Morris have their place also in the great, seemingly eternal, English tradition of Tory Radicalism, and hence provide the opportunity for doubts and debates as to whether in fact they may be "hidden"—in Orwell's case, not so "hidden"—"enemies of the working class." Engels despaired of what he regarded as Morris's sentimentality and utopian Socialism; and Orwell is so frequently, as in the notorious second part of *The Road to Wigan Pier*, the "devil's advocate," discovering with such zeal the flaws of socialism and his fellow socialists, that one wonders whether he has not turned into the devil himself.

Be that as it may, both men were professed socialists, both were critics of their society, both were visionaries—though what they envisioned drastically differed. It thus seems inevitable that they would ultimately have written novels as alike and as different as *News from Nowhere* and *Nineteen Eighty-Four*.

Both Morris and Orwell wrote their books—arguably their most important—at moments of comparative disillusionment. In 1890, the year that *News from Nowhere* appeared as a serial in *Commonweal*, the paper of the Socialist League, the League was on the verge of splitting apart, with Morris, until then its leading figure, losing out in a dispute with the anarchist faction. The struggle further disillusioned him, for as early as November 13, 1887—"Bloody Sunday," when an illegal but peaceful outdoor gathering of workers and militant radicals was dispersed by the police with a good deal of brutality—he had come to accept that the social revolution he believed to be essential was unlikely to take place in his lifetime.

Utopian fiction has a way of compensating for the disappointments of everyday life. Thus in the *Commonweal* version of *News from Nowhere*, Morris pinpoints the revolution, a sort of spontaneous uprising of the working class, and a victory for them, as taking place in the early years of the twentieth century. But in 1891, he had become still more pessimistic, and in the book version published that year, he moved the date of the revolution forward half a century, to 1952.

Actually, by that date, a demi-semi revolution had occurred in England: a welfare state was firmly in place, dedicated to a demi-semi Socialism that Morris would have hated, and that Orwell excoriated as he projected it forward into 1984. It is almost as if the two versions of a postrevolutionary world—Morris's and Orwell's—intersected, with Orwell depicting in a reverse-of-the-coin way the dangers latent in the paternalistic, state semi-socialism that the Labour government had achieved.

News from Nowhere was Morris's most important writing in his late period and, it might be argued, his most important literary work. Opinions vary about the value of his poetry after his remarkable first collection, *The Defense of Guenevere*, but most critics accord a high place to *News from Nowhere*. One of the great Utopian novels, it is probably now the most read of all of Morris's works, although of course its audience can't begin to approach in size all those millions who are thrilled and chilled by *Nineteen Eighty-Four*. In many ways, *News from Nowhere* is a summation of Morris's thought; its vision represents his hope for England, and for the rest of the world.

Set in the future—that is, some years after 1952—the pattern of the book was suggested to Morris by his excursions on the Thames, the first in August 1880, and then again the following summer, sailing upstream from Kelmscott House, in Hammersmith in London, to his country house, Kelmscott Manor, in Oxfordshire. That journey, from urban to rural England, from discontent to content, is paralleled in the final third of the book that Morris would write at the end of the decade. But the immediate impulse for him to begin writing it was the publication in 1884 of Edward Bellamy's *Looking Backward*, presenting a utopian version of Boston in the year 2000 that Morris found horribly mechanistic—in his words, a "cockney paradise." He was distressed also by the *Fabian Essays*, published in 1889 and advocating a state where the numerous vices of want, the evils of a capitalistic society, might be eradicated, and the material needs of the people be gratified, but where—and this was a crucial point for Morris—there would be none of the spiritual values that a new society ought to provide.

News from Nowhere—Nowhere, of course, is the English for Utopia—uses a common narrative convention: the "I" of the book, who is called the Guest and tells the story, wakes up in the future, in a house—in fact, it is on the site of his own—but it has now become a hostel on the banks of the River Thames that is no longer polluted and is full of salmon. (Salmon, I note in passing, have only recently begun to return to the Thames—in the 1980s—which suggests that some environmental progress has been made and that, just possibly, some other of Morris's improvements of life may yet be realized.) The narrator finds a society in which, to borrow a phrase from the aging young, "small is beautiful," based on decentralization, and small units of production. Until fairly recently, such an approach to modern Western society would have seemed hopelessly romantic. But now, a few at least think that it is what must happen if our top-heavy society is not to topple over and do us all in. The move toward communes in the 1960s and early 1970s suggests this—even that rather pre-Raphaelite, semi-medieval dress of so-called hippies or flower children is similar to the dress of Morris's utopians.

Unhappily, the possible lack of realism in this Nowhere is not so much in the sort of society depicted, but rather in Morris's other basic premise: that humans need not be aggressive. And yet, that has been the very reason that most communes have not been able to survive—human beings are not sufficiently able to maintain peaceful relations with one another. For Morris the perversion of human character brought about by capitalism meant that humans are alienated from themselves, from others, from their work, and from their environment. He may well be right, but unfortunately there has not been a society yet, no matter what it may call itself—capitalist, communist, or even our own democracy—that has been able to solve the problems of the aggressive manifestations of human nature.

But once one gets past this tiny stumbling block of reality, what a delightful utopia he has imagined for us. For here in Nowhere, there is no central government; law courts and prisons had been abolished; there is a series of self-governing communes in some sort of communication with one another. Once the revolution had ended—the violence, whatever it was, is all out of sight—society fairly rapidly became peaceful and people live in beautiful rural places—the dream of the English and others of a quiet pastoral existence, where sordidness has been eliminated, as well as wealth and poverty. Equality has been achieved. The world is very much as if Morris & Co. had designed everything, and the inhabitants have learned Morris's lesson that pleasure in work results in more beautiful objects.

No doubt there is a price that has to be paid for this idyll, and it would seem to be an absence of a sense of the past. The atmosphere of this new society is nonintellectual, perhaps even anti-intellectual; nobody seems to read, or has much interest in doing so; they are leading a healthy, outdoor life, yet as children they learned how to read early—as Morris did—and picked up Latin and Greek. It is a society which appeals to the somewhat philistine side of the Englishman's nature—but also reveals the frequent temptation of the intellectual to be excessively attracted to the more mindless life, under the impression that it is more prone to happiness. There is no formal education in this society; living in the country, being close to nature, are the guarantees of a happy life. So the trip from the city Kelmscott to the country Kelmscott puts the cap on the idea of the rural utopia, ending in the feast to celebrate the haymaking at the small Kelmscott church, which has become a banqueting hall. It is at that point that the narrator begins to fade away from Nowhere—perhaps because he had never learned how to wield a scythe—and finds himself returned to "dingy Hammersmith."

Dingy indeed, but dinginess is relative, and even Hammersmith on the Thames is a very different and preferable landscape from that of *Nineteen Eighty-Four*, where Orwell is attempting to serve, I believe, the same values that inspired Morris—the belief in a humane and fully realized life for the individual—but by means of an anti-Utopia.

Orwell came from a similar tradition and class as Morris: both belonged to the middle class. If anything, Orwell was more in a grand class tradition, being of distant aristocratic descent, a religious and civil servant family. Morris's father was a stockbroker, less socially "suitable," but far wealthier than Orwell's. And Orwell himself was less secure, materially and psychologically, than Morris. Part of his genius was his ability to notice the specifics of class, a factor which made him a founder of literary sociology. Orwell helped to bring into heightened consciousness the nuances of the English class system. He was far more of a naysayer than Morris. The one chose a positive presentation of the future, the other, a negative—and this was a matter not only of temperament, but of history. When Orwell sat down in his farm on the island of Jura in 1947 to write *Nineteen Eighty-Four*, he was animated, as he was in so much of his writing, by a nostalgia for the sense of community he felt had existed in the past—up to, say, the outbreak of World War I—and that he thought could exist in the future, under a true and fruitful socialism. Whatever community is depicted in *Nineteen Eighty-Four* couldn't be less attractive: the togetherness of the two-minute hate, and the demonstrations in public squares (most likely Trafalgar Square, so associated with radical protests in Morris's time, and both before and since). Orwell was writing from a far more disillusioned position than Morris. Yet Morris, for all his surging optimism, knew that the revolution would not turn out as one wished. As he put it in *The Dream of John Ball* (1888): "How men fight and lose the battle, and the thing they fought for comes about in spite of their defeat and, when it comes, turns out not to be what they meant, and other men have to fight for what they meant under another name."

In Orwell's case there had been further years of disillusion. And unlike Morris he was temperamentally attuned to look on the grim side of things, really from the beginning—can there be a grimmer account than he furnished of his schooling in "Such, Such Were the Joys," where, had he wished, he might have recalled the joys of exploring the Downs, much as Morris had enjoyed himself in Epping Forest and in Wiltshire when he was at Marlborough?

If Orwell's temperament predisposed him to see the worst, history provided the material. His experience in the Spanish Civil War—Morris had had no experience of a comparable nature—had allowed Orwell to see at first hand how a revolution could be betrayed. This "tragic view" was intensified by the "Betrayal of the Left," the Soviet-Nazi pact; and then the war itself. Orwell had never lived well, and so the wartime deprivations were not particularly painful for him, though they hardly helped his always doubtful health, and they hastened his wife's death in 1945. But the war, and then the even greater deprivations when the war was won, ushering in the age of austerity, provided Orwell with direct experiences of what an anti-Utopia might be like. Even more vividly than Morris—in his dislike of the mechanistic simplemindedness of Bellamy—Orwell knew the ways in which advanced technology, with its telescreens and listening devices, could make modern life a nightmare.

Both Morris and Orwell, in the tradition of British Radicalism, were backward looking. This is not as evident in *Nineteen Eighty-Four* as it is in other of Orwell's writings, most notably his last traditional novel, *Coming Up for Air*, in which he was almost as romantic about early twenthieth-century England as Morris is about the fourteenth century. In *News from Nowhere*, the journey is westwards, and the consummation of the story is near the source of the Thames. So too, in *Nineteen Eighty-Four*, although less specifically, Winston and Julia travel from Paddington, the station for the West Country, and consummate their love in the countryside toward the West. The attitude toward sex and love is in fact rather similar in

both books, although of course in Morris's case it was more unusual
for the time—a celebration and belief in animal nature. The countryside is the location for good, in the great English tradition.

But in one particular, among others, Orwell is very different from
Morris: his attitude toward the past. In *News from Nowhere*, an elderly character, described as the grumbler, the grandfather of the
heroine, finds utopia boring and longs for a world in which books
are more important. Morris presents the grumbler not unsympatheti-
cally—perhaps books *are* a solace for the imperfections of the
world—yet he seems to feel that anti-intellectuality is bound to be
present in a utopia. Although a good deal of the book is devoted to
telling how the revolution came about, the past is primarily there as
something that is gotten away from. Knowledge of the past, though
important for the tale, is not important for the society. In Nowhere
there would not be much employment for historians.

But in Orwell's society they are fully employed, in a way that is
shameless, disastrous, and a total betrayal of history. As *Nineteen
Eighty-Four* is an anti-Utopia, so Winston Smith is assigned to work
as an anti-historian. His job is the rewriting of the past in the Ministry of Truth, so that it conforms to the latest changes in the party's
line. The idea was derived from Orwell's experience during the
Spanish Civil War, where he saw the newspapers of the rival parties
alter facts to suit policy with no regard for truth whatever. Such distortions were not unknown before, but they seemed particularly
ruthless in the Communists' attack on the POUM, with whom Orwell served, and the ease with which switches were made, the total
transformation of the Communist line at the time of the Nazi-Soviet
pact, and yet again a switch, after the Russians entered the war. Innocence was lost in the First World War; cynicism was enthroned at
the time of the Second. Winston's job of transforming the newspapers of the past to conform to the newest party line, through technological devices, might have seemed fairly far-fetched at the time
Orwell was writing—"utopian," even—but in our age of computers
and word processors, it is all too plausible for tapes or microfilms to
be transformed on demand, if the right program is written and the
right commands given.

For Orwell a society that has lost its history is beyond decency:
"The past is whatever the records and the memories agree upon. And
since the Party is in full control of all records, and in equally full
command of the minds of its members, it follows that the past is
whatever the Party chooses to make it." Memories are controlled

through doublethink. "Ultimately, it is by means of doublethink that the Party has been able—and may, for all we know, continue to be able for thousands of years—to arrest the course of history." In the ironic, optimistic political scene where O'Brien passes himself off as an enemy of the party, he, Julia, and Winston drink a toast. O'Brien asks what it should be: "'To the confusion of the Thought Police? To the death of Big Brother? To humanity? To the future?' 'To the past,' said Winston. 'The past is more important,' agreed O'Brien gravely."

Morris, writing in an earlier and (as Orwell would insist) a better age, was more inclined to look on the positive side, to believe more firmly in pleasure, in the joy that ought to be associated with labor. Orwell's vision was bleaker. He was aware of the association of the term "earthly paradise" with Morris. In an essay on Arthur Koestler, he takes him to task for moving into a position of political hedonism which leads him to think of the earthly paradise as desirable. "Perhaps, however, whether desirable or not, it isn't possible. Perhaps some degree of suffering is ineradicable from human life, perhaps the choice before man is always a choice of evils, perhaps even the aim of Socialism is not to make the world perfect but to make it better. All revolutions are failures, but they are not all the same failure."

Here Orwell is using "earthly paradise" in a pejorative sense— this was written in 1944. But two years later, reviewing a group of books on socialism, he used the term in a more positive way. "The 'earthly paradise' has never been realized, but as an idea it never seems to perish, despite the ease with which it can be debunked by practical politicians of all colours. Underneath it lies the belief that human nature is fairly decent to start with and is capable of infinite development. This belief has been the main driving force of the Socialist tradition. . . . It could be claimed that the Utopians, at present a scattered minority, are the true upholders of the Socialist tradition." And as he wrote in 1948 about *News from Nowhere* and other similar works, "they do at least look beyond the era of food queues and party squabbles, and remind the Socialist movement of its original, half-forgotten objective of human brotherhood."

It is clear that that indeed is an objective of *News from Nowhere.* Given the grimness of *Nineteen Eighty-Four*, however, it is more difficult to see human brotherhood as its objective. When the book was published and taken up by cold warriors, Orwell had to issue a succession of statements, especially for anti-communist America, reaffirming his belief in socialism and the Labour party. As *The Road to*

Wigan Pier has shown, he could be too brilliant as a devil's advocate. But both men, I believe, were passionately devoted to fellowship, perhaps because both of them lacked it to a degree in their own
lives. There is the shattered fellowship in *Nineteen Eighty-Four* of
Julia, Winston, and O'Brien, not sufficiently worked out and, within
the context of the book's design, doomed to end badly. Yet even in
those despairing pages, a source of vitality and possible change and
redemption is to be found in the proles. In part this was because
Orwell, like Morris, held a rather English distrust of intellectuals.
More positively, both men had faith that ordinary English humanity
would eventually triumph and create a socialist society. It is, in the
quite literal sense of the word, an act of faith—consistent, however,
with abiding English characteristics.

The form that faith takes gives, I believe, insight into the nature of
England, as well as some suggestion of what may be the more enduring appeal of Morris's and Orwell's writings. The most persistent
and attractive quality in Orwell, I would argue, is his regard for the
ordinary and unique individual: the Spanish militiaman glimpsed
briefly in a barracks but not forgotten; the friendly tramp; the family
around the fireside; and all those others who formed in his mind an
ideal of English society—one that would enjoy the positive qualities
of the English tradition, yet be freed from exploitation. So too did
Morris believe. His book was a utopian dream, Orwell's, a nightmare—but both had unexpectedly similar visions of something better
for England, and for the world.

26

SAHIB AS VICTIM

George Woodcock's *The Crystal Spirit* (1966) is an interesting and intelligent study of George Orwell, but it too falls into some of the traps that Orwell seems to have laid for his critics. Woodcock properly uses the brief essay "Why I Write" (1947) as a crucial document. The title of his concluding section, "Prose like a Windowpane," is drawn from the passage in the essay where Orwell declares, "It is also true that one can write nothing readable unless one constantly struggles to efface one's personality. Good prose is like a windowpane." Orwell wrote good and readable prose, but not for the reasons he suggests, and indeed the whole passage is almost characteristically misleading. Orwell's contradictory personality—his forthright, complex, modest, assertive, open and secretive personality—is all over his prose. In this respect, of course, he is no different from Shaw or Lawrence or Forster, and his windowpane is not the crystal clear colorless glass it appears to be, but a glass tinted with Orwellian colors. It is the proof of his skill as a writer of prose that when we look through the pane we think we are seeing the truth as it actually is, rather than the truth as he believed it to be. Often in his essays he will begin with an experience of his own and advance from it to a generalization, sometimes inaccurate or unfair, but which we do not pause to question because it has been based on particulars so honestly and fairly given. Thus the prose secures its effect: it would be downright ungracious not to agree with Orwell, especially when he credits us with far more generous thoughts and feelings than we deserve. "I never went into a jail," he wrote, "without feeling (most visitors to jails feel the same) that my place was on the other side of the bars." Now, while this tells us a good deal about Orwell himself, it tells a good deal less about most visitors to jails who, it might reasonably be claimed, feel that the right people are on the appropriate side of the bars. But it is the sort of seductive point where Orwell scores: the apparent transparency of the writing leads the reader to imagine that it is himself rather than the moralist instructing his readers who has identified with those prisoners on the other side of the bars.

This would account, I think, for the various Orwells who emerge from the critical studies: a case of every critic creating an Orwell with whom he feels in sympathy. Among others we have had a Socialist Orwell, a Christian Orwell, and an exemplary quietist Orwell, the secular man of virtue detached from active political commitment, ideally suited to the needs of the 1950s. The present study is written by an eminent Anarchist scholar, and so, not surprisingly, it is the anarchist, libertarian aspects of Orwell, hitherto somewhat neglected, that are given their due, while others, less congenial or interesting to Woodcock, tend to be minimized. It is a critic's privilege to emphasize those aspects of the man and his work of particular importance to himself, and in this instance Woodcock has a valuable contribution to make. The danger for the critic, however, which Woodcock and others have not avoided, is a kind of wish fulfillment: the temptation to correct this bit, and that point, to make the reflection more accurate, the casual utterance more emphatic, and thus to bring the work more firmly into line with the position the critic himself holds and believes Orwell to have held, sometimes without his having been more than half aware that this was the case. In so many of the books and articles on Orwell, there are private little discussions between author and subject about various failures of logic and lapses of judgment, none of them of much interest to the reader, who may well have an Orwell-figure with whom to argue fondly, and is not prepared to let go.

More than most writers Orwell was capable of deceiving his readers and friends about himself, perhaps the more easily because he rarely gave the appearance of doing so. Woodcock was a friend of Orwell's in the later years of his life—they met in 1942—and he includes a fascinating account of their friendship. His memoir, which opens the book, makes clear how self-revealing, but also how reticent Orwell could be. For all his candor, he was determined to disclose only as much of himself as he wished. Friends who were in close relation to him in his political and literary life knew next to nothing of his personal life. To each, it might be said, he would show one snapshot of his life, and very honest and revealing it might be, but never a series—hence the curious differences in the recollections that have been published by his friends and acquaintances.

Of course the most obvious example of Eric Blair's determination to reveal only so much of himself and no further is that he should be known to us as George Orwell, the nom de plume he adopted at the time of the publication of *Down and Out in Paris and London* (1933). When Woodcock met him for the first time a decade later, he was firmly established as George Orwell, with nine books published under that name, and it was as Orwell, not Blair, that he knew him. Writing of him now, he is finely aware of the significance of Eric Arthur Blair's having transformed himself into George Orwell; he knows that a good deal more was at stake than the mere taking of a pseudonym.

Woodcock begins this book by stating, "Many people have argued that the man they know as George Orwell was more important as a personality than as a writer, for what he was than for what he said. I suspect that time will reveal this opinion to be a fallacy." This seems to me a sensible defensible statement, yet the very fact that it has to be made at all is odd. It is not the sort of thing one would feel compelled to say about Shaw or Lawrence or Forster, for example, and it points to the dilemma confronting anyone who wants to write about Orwell. Woodcock himself seems tacitly to acknowledge this, for only a few pages later he writes, "One has difficulty in envisaging a future in which critics will ever be able to think of Orwell's writing separately from his life." The problem, simply, is that so much of what he wrote, whether fiction or nonfiction, is a kind of edited autobiography, and it is almost impossible as one reads to separate the man from his work. The defects of the novels of the 1930s, their inconsistencies and improbabilities, represent a failure to assimilate the elements of autobiography into the fiction. But Orwell's personality is immediately compelling and it is the presence of the writer himself in whatever guise he may choose to assume—even as a clergyman's daughter—that gives these novels their undeniable vitality. It should not be surprising, then, that much the most vivid part of Woodcock's book is the personal memoir. The subsequent portion, for all the intelligence, sensitivity, and thoroughness with which it has been written, runs somewhat downhill, seemingly demonstrating that it is impossible to construct a taut, unified study of the works without keeping the personality of their author to the forefront.

What cannot be emphasized sufficiently is the use that "the man they knew as George Orwell" made of the experience of Eric Blair, in his work, and in his life. There was always in Orwell the residue of Eric Blair; he remained Eric to those who knew him before 1936; he never changed his name legally. George Orwell, as Woodcock says, was a persona, and it was the persona that most of those who have written about him knew. (There are exceptions, most notably his fellow Etonians, Cyril Connolly, Richard Rees, and Christopher Hollis, who have written about the man they knew as Eric Blair. Connolly met him first at prep school; Hollis, at Eton. Rees, in his study *Fugitive from the Camp of Victory*, tells us that he did not actually meet him until 1930, when, as editor of *The Adelphi*, he accepted some of Blair's earliest writings, which had been submitted and were published under that name.) The creation of George Orwell was an act of will by Eric Blair, and it was carried on at almost every level of his existence, affecting not only his prose style— Woodcock is excellent on this point—but also the style of his daily life. Becoming George Orwell was Eric Blair's way of making himself into a writer, at which he brilliantly succeeded, and of unmaking himself as a gentleman, of opting out of the genteel lower-upper-middle class into which he was born and going down a class, at which, as one would expect, he had only an equivocal success. An endearing, if slightly comic, part of the creation was Orwell's attempt to ape proletarian manners, cooling his tea in a saucer, being more aggressively indifferent to the quality of his food than any working-man. But this was not a constant affectation: he celebrated the selection of *Animal Farm* by the Book-of-the-Month Club with a banquet for Woodcock and himself at one of the better restaurants in Soho, although he insisted upon eating in his shirtsleeves. (Woodcock, not to be outdone, followed suit.) He got on perfectly well with tramps, who took him as an Etonian down on his luck, which he was, and with his comrades in Spain, who were impressed with his air of authority and recognized him as a leader, but he did not appear to have a circle of friends among the workers, even at his local pub in Islington.

The more enduring and significant result of the creation was that it allowed Eric Blair to come to terms with his world. Eric Blair was the man to whom things happened, George Orwell the man who wrote about them. The autobiographical raw material and the esthetic "distancing" were both essential to the artist. In his discussion of "Shooting an Elephant," Woodcock suggests the function of the persona generally when he remarks that "the killing of the elephant, which for Eric Blair the police officer was an unpleasant necessity, becomes in the hands of Orwell the artist a symbolic event."

Much of his life, especially before 1936, was an attempt to escape from the system into which he had been born, and which inexorably provided him with an education, an accent, and a standard of judgment that might be turned against himself. The system, he felt, had almost crushed him in his prep school days, and toward the end of his life he left a grim record of them in "Such, Such Were the Joys." This essay, which continues to be a source of unease to his admirers and of ammunition to his detractors, is an arranged, disciplined, intensely conscious piece of writing. Its importance lies not in its truth or exaggeration as a report of living conditions in an English boys' prep school, but in the clear evidence it gives of what Orwell thought his childhood meant. It was then that he was presented with the system with which he had to come to terms. To his school-fellow, Cyril Connolly, he might appear a "true rebel," but in his own mind he thought himself doomed: "I had no money, I was weak, I was ugly, I was unpopular, I had a chronic cough, I was cowardly, I smelt." That he felt was the judgment of St. Cyprian's, and by inference of the system. Even after he went to Eton, and from there to the Imperial Police in Burma, he continued to believe that it was an unalterable judgment, and that your place in the world did not depend on your own efforts but on "what you were." This mood continued to afflict him until his return from Burma in 1927; and his novels, including *Animal Farm* and *Nineteen Eighty-Four*, accept the omnipotence of the system, while his heroes are its victims.

Yet Orwell made himself a happier man than he had ever dreamed of being, and a powerful writer also. It was here that he was best served by his creation. Much as Orwell in conversation with friends would pick and choose what he would reveal of himself, so Blair, through Orwell, could pick and choose among the elements of his past. Ironically, many of the qualities that contribute to the Orwell personality and style as we are familiar with them in his work, are precisely the qualities Blair had thought despicable in his schooldays. Eric Blair saw himself as a smelly, impoverished member of the lower-upper-middle class who because of his being bright enough for a scholarship and coming from a suitable Anglo-Indian background had received an inappropriate gentleman's education. But George Orwell was an idiosyncratic socialist, who, no matter how badly he dressed or austerely he lived, would never lose the air of authority in his prose which marks a public school "old boy." Orwell could transform the upper-class values that Blair resented and infuse them with the egalitarianism he envied among the miners in Wigan and learned at firsthand as a soldier among soldiers in Spain. Eric Blair looked back unforgivingly on the world before 1914—it was that world that had sent him to his prep school—while George Orwell could believe it was superior to what came after it, and recorded the period nostalgically in *Coming Up for Air*. And if Eric Blair was enraged by the hypocrisies endemic to a boys' school in England of the First World War, George Orwell was moved to a simple and intense patriotism during the Second World War when England was endangered.

There were moments when Blair and Orwell were at one: in the comradeship of the Spanish Civil War, and in the inspiriting early years of the blitz when it was possible to believe in a brave new England to come. They were moments of honor and decency, in which Blair and Orwell could participate and feel at ease. But such moments could not last: they would be undone by the Stalinists, as in Spain, or by the thought police, as in 1984. Then the struggle would be resumed, between the patriot and the radical, the idealist and the skeptic, the sahib and the victim. Out of the tension came the masterpieces, *Homage to Catalonia*, *Animal Farm*, and the essays.

27

ORWELL AND THE PAST

I would like to discuss George Orwell's relationship to the past and the novel *Nineteen Eighty-Four*. Throughout the actual year 1984, a dominant theme appeared to be to what degree did reality correspond to what Orwell wrote about in his novel of the same name? In Walter Cronkite's introduction to the 70th printing of the mass-market paperback (the book has sold more than 10 million copies in English and has been translated into 60 languages), Cronkite points out that even if Orwell's world has not come about exactly on schedule, there is always 1985. (Anthony Burgess had already tried to cope with that in his not very good novel published in 1978: *1985*.)

But the present and future, although I will discuss them to a degree, are not my principal concern. It is the past I wish to write about, in three ways, raising and attempting to answer three questions. What was it in Orwell's own past that went into the shaping of the book? What past literature influenced the book? And most important, what is the attitude toward the past in the book? Thus, I wish to think about *Nineteen Eighty-Four* in a different way, and contrary to what I take to be the dominant note in much that has been written about it. One might argue that in the book the past is as important, perhaps even more important, than the future.

But as a kind of prologue, let me say something about what happened in 1984 where Orwell and *Nineteen Eighty-Four* are concerned—all the events that were being devoted to the man and his book. There was a fantastic amount of activity even before the arrival of the fateful year itself, and the pace quickened month by month, accompanied by an outpouring of editorial comment. Much of the writing and talking took place in the United States, although

the most serious literary project originated in Britain: a newly prepared edition of all Orwell's novels and book-length reportage, and
volumes of essays, letters, and journalism, finally published in 1998.
In Britain there were also three separate television productions on
Orwell, the novel, and the year. Orwell appeared on the cover of the
New Republic, Harpers, and *Time.* The *New Republic* offered a
piece by Irving Howe excerpted from the book of essays he had edited, *1984 Revisited: Totalitarianism in Our Century;* in *Harpers*
Norman Podhoretz claimed Orwell for neoconservatism; and in
Time the man and the book were surveyed in the knowing style we
associate with that publication. *On Nineteen Eighty-Four,* for which
I served as editor, a collection of essays by Stanford scholars, was
published by W. H. Freeman. E. L. Doctorow wrote about him in
Playboy! In December, one month before Orwell's year, the Smith-
sonian Institution sponsored a conference in Washington entitled
"The Road after 1984: High Technology and Human Freedom, a
Tribute to George Orwell," and there was an associated art exhibition nearby at the Hirshhorn Museum, "Dreams and Nightmares:
Utopian Visions in Modern Art." And that was just the beginning of
the flood tide. Not surprisingly, *Nineteen Eighty-Four* turned up as
the #1 bestseller in paperback. In Europe there was comparatively
less activity: still, a large science fiction conference was held in Ant-
werp, and a considerable gathering was sponsored by the Council of
Europe in Strasbourg ("1984: Myths and Realities: Man, the State
and Society in Question").

With all these words written and spoken, triggered by a book
whose title happens to be the same as the year, there is some danger
that the book in its own right (and Orwell, the man who actually
wrote it) will be somewhat forgotten, if we think only about the present and the future.

On one television show in the United States devoted to the book,
the claim was made that there were 130 predictions in it, and 120
had become true. (I've also seen the figures 100 out of 137.) I have
no idea how that calculation was made or how accurate it is. If one
looks specifically at some of the depictions of the future in the book
it seems to me that they have not turned out to be true—although
the general tendency of government to have an increasing capacity to
interfere in our lives is certainly accurate. In Orwell's picture of the
world just descended upon us, according to the calendar, the details
are wrong.

To mention some of the most famous creations of the book:

Thought control. "The party is not interested in the overt act: the thought is all we care about. We do not merely destroy our enemies; we change them." Perhaps this is the most important individual issue in the book, and indeed it is fundamentally an alteration of an individual's past—the destruction of the previous pattern, the shape of memory and its documents—the history of an individual and in a wider form the history of a society. To put it another way, emphasizing the personal or rather the anti-personal: "With the development of television, and the technical advance which made it possible to receive and transmit simultaneously on the same instrument, private life came to an end." There is no doubt that Orwell was prescient in realizing what might happen technically. There is no reason to think that he was alone in grasping the mechanical capacities for the future, although perhaps he was unusual in seeing to what use they might be put. What is frequently forgotten, however, is that all this supervision, the two-way television sets, the total bugging (surely possible, if government wished to do it, and to devote the financial resources and number of employees such a system would require) are largely restricted in the book to supervising the members of the inner and outer Parties. The vast majority of the population, although organized to participate in rallies, has been so deprived that it is considered harmless. Winston Smith hopes that the proles might revolt. "But the proles, if only they could somehow become conscious of their own strength . . . needed only to rise up and shake themselves like a horse shaking off flies. If they chose they could blow the Party to pieces tomorrow morning." In the book, it is clear that such a revolution is not going to happen, and presumably that is also true in the world today.

The Leader, Big Brother, may not even exist; he is a mixture of Hitler and Stalin. Certainly in their time both leaders were subjected to adulation, but the number of such worshiped leaders probably is fewer today. Are functionaries, such as Winston Smith, tortured in order to achieve the climax of the last line of the novel proper—"He loved Big Brother"? As the work of Amnesty International makes painfully clear, there are many around the world who are violently mistreated for their beliefs, but how often can regimes achieve the *inner* conformity aimed at in *Nineteen Eighty-Four*, although there are of course cases of brain-washing? Such conformity was what Orwell feared most. In that sense the book is extremely powerful as a warning; we can only be grateful that it does not appear to be a prophecy fulfilled.

Again, Orwell's brilliance in the defense of language—his devastating analyses of what he termed "Newspeak"—seems more a warning than a prophecy—although it may be somewhat closer to the truth than one might like. When Orwell was living in Paris in the 1920s—a grubbier existence than that of more famous literary expatriates—he saw a great deal of his aunt, Nellie Limouzin and her lover, Eugene Adam, both of whom were workers on behalf of Esperanto. That might be seen as a benign version of Newspeak, an attempt to reduce the language to a minimum, even if the objective of Esperanto is to achieve an international language for wider understanding. But its effect is to rob language of its richness. "It's a beautiful thing, the destruction of words," as Syme, one of the compilers of the Newspeak Dictionary, says.

It is a commonplace to bemoan the attacks upon language—which by its nature is in a state of continual decay and renewal. Clichés and jargon are offensive, sometimes sinister when used as a substitute for thought: Orwell, in *Nineteen Eighty-Four* and in his essays, most importantly "Politics and the English Language," has made us acutely aware of this. Ironically and inadvertently, he has, however, contributed jargon to the language—as almost all of us, whether we have read the book or not, have an instant unreflective reaction to the mention of *Nineteen Eighty-Four*, to the term "Orwellian," and to the more famous phrases in the novel itself. Through the media, "psychobabble" and other catch phrases of the moment can be more rapidly disseminated than ever before. But by the same token, new cant phrases easily replace the old. It is a common human trait to believe that the present is a state of decline; in terms of language it is certainly not proven that we are worse off than before. One primary reason that this has not happened is, in part at least, the result of Orwell's warning us that it might, a welcome instance of a deflating rather than a self-fulfilling prophecy.

Orwell has, also, fortunately been proved wrong if he was predicting a decline of sexuality. "All this marching up and down and cheering and waving flags is simply sex gone sour. . . . There was a direct, intimate connection between chastity and political orthodoxy." He may well be right that personal and political freedom can be indicated by the degree of sexual freedom available, and the more repressive a regime the more likely it is to try to control the sexuality of its subjects. But though we may have retreated somewhat from the permissive atmosphere of the late 1960s and early 1970s, perhaps the most permanent legacy of those days is a greater degree of sexual freedom and less hypocrisy. In the novel the heroine Julia is forced to belong to the Anti-Sex League, even though it goes directly against her personality.

Perhaps Orwell came closest to prophecy rather than warning when he was writing about the state of international affairs. It did not require a large amount of unusual insight in 1948 to see that Russia and the United States were likely to be enemies, and that China might be the third superpower. Orwell was wrong that the European Continent would be part of Eurasia, but he was right that Britain—Airstrip One—would be a somewhat uneasy outpost of Oceania. Nothing is shown in the novel other than London and a brief excursion into the countryside so that Winston and Julia can make love. Yet Orwell captures the feeling of the present situation, in an impressively accurate way. "War, however, is no longer the desperate, annihilating struggle that it was in the early decades of the twentieth century. It is a warfare of limited aims between combatants who are unable to destroy one another, have no material cause for fighting, and are not divided by any genuine ideological difference. . . . In a physical sense war involves very small numbers of people, mostly highly trained specialists, and causes comparatively few casualties."

In the novel warfare primarily takes place in Africa, the Middle East, and the Far East. At the same time, Orwell—at least through the mouthpiece of his Trotsky figure (perhaps invented by the Government), Emmanuel Goldstein in his *The Theory and Practice of Oligarchical Collectivism*—has a frightening picture of the world of today, when the arms control talks have broken down and both Russia and the United States are deploying missiles. "Atomic bombs first appeared as early as the nineteen-forties, and were first used on a large scale about ten years later. At that time some hundreds of bombs were dropped on industrial centers, chiefly in European Russia, Eastern Europe, and North America. The effect was to convince the ruling groups of all countries that a few more atomic bombs would mean the end of organized society, and hence of their own power. Thereafter, although no formal agreement was ever made or hinted at, no more bombs were dropped. All three powers merely continue to produce atomic bombs and store them up against the decisive opportunity which they all believe will come sooner or later." This is certainly a frightening prospect to contemplate, and one reason why the book, apart from the immediate appropriateness of its title, has been able to sear itself into the consciousness of its millions of readers. We can only hope that it is not a prophecy but a warning. That is certainly what Orwell meant it to be.

So much for looking at the present and the future. What elements were there in Orwell's own life that contributed to the making of the book? I do not wish to go into too much biographical detail. In many ways, although he was able to live, write, and love as he wished, Orwell had similarities to Winston Smith. His background was somewhat more elevated, but his family tradition was of those who served the state as minor civil servants, much as Winston Smith did. His family asserted the role of power in the state, and perhaps one might even suggest that at times it might have been power for its own sake. In the eighteenth century, his ancestors had intermarried with the aristocracy, but as younger sons his grandfather, a country clergyman, and his father, a civil servant, were less well-off. His father had an appointment in the Indian Civil Service, in the Opium Department, in which his role was to supervise the growth of opium that the Chinese were forced to buy from the British. Orwell, who was born—as Eric Arthur Blair—in 1903, spent his first four years in India, a country ruled by the British. (Are there similarities between the role of the Viceroy and Big Brother?) The British Empire existed for many reasons, but surely power was one of them. As Alex Zwerdling has pointed out, Orwell's fictions are generally about individuals attempting to escape from a total system—John Flory in *Burmese Days*, Dorothy Hare in *A Clergyman's Daughter*, Gordon Comstock in *Keep the Aspidistra Flying*, George Bowling in *Coming Up for Air*, and certainly Winston Smith in *Nineteen Eighty-Four*. In its way, the Empire was a total system as well, and Orwell spent the first twenty-four years of his life in authoritarian, if not totalitarian systems: family, school, police—one need not strain to detect a considerable autobiographical component in *Nineteen Eighty-Four*. On the other hand, one must be careful not to be psychologically reductionist.

Orwell described himself as being a member of the "lower-upper-middle class," and as such he spent much of his early life moving from one extremely powerful institution to another—at a particularly high level of strength in Edwardian England. At the age of eight he left his family—that notorious institution—for boarding school, standard practice for a member of his class. Orwell was clearly very bright and he was accepted on a scholarship at St. Cyprian's by Mr. and Mrs. Vaughan Wilkes, the proprietors of the school, on the assumption that he would go on to win a scholarship at an eminent public school and hence cast credit on St. Cyprian's. His years there, recalled long afterwards, produced one of his minor masterpieces, "Such, Such Were the Joys," an ironic use of a line from a poem of William Blake's on the joys of childhood. Despite his hatred for the school, he acknowledged it was doing its job in ramming facts into him and preparing him for the examination which would take him to the next stage in the training to be a proper member of the English ruling classes. And he acquired, quite rightly, a profound reverence for facts and their importance—the right to believe in "true" facts is an extremely important part of *Nineteen Eighty-Four*. Also, the English schools as well as the boarding schools such boys go to until the age of eighteen or nineteen are famous for their emphasis on how to write, and on the importance of the word. He wrote, however, surprisingly badly for a King's Scholar at Eton—and had little of that easy maturity of the precocious English schoolboy—his style would not reach its now familiar strength until the 1930s. Yet his early training was profoundly important for Orwell. His last three years at the school were during the First World War, when an unquestioning admiration for England was at its height. His first two publications were in the *Henley and South Oxfordshire Standard*, first "Awake! Young Men of England!" which urged enlistment in the army, and the second an elegy on the death of Lord Kitchener, the famous general and Secretary of State for War, drowned at sea. (His face was that on the most famous poster of the First World War with its demand: "Your King and Country Need You." This is clearly an early version of the Big Brother poster, and Kitchener very much occupied a parallel position in the mentality of the British during the First World War.) Growing up during the First World War left an indelible mark on him, as suggested in the title of his essay of 1940, "My Country, Right or Left," and helped shape him as the patriotic socialist that he became, one with a rich sense of his country's traditions.

Although he did win scholarships at Wellington and Eton, and appeared to be a success, he also imbibed from Mrs. Vaughan Wilkes a belief that he was doomed to be a smelly little clerk, doomed to failure. (Rebellion is to be found in the seemingly totally conformist individual—Winston Smith.) What might be called Orwell's "double life" continued, in his being a conventional schoolboy at the most intellectual part of one of the most famous schools in the world—being in College at Eton—but then he took a step downwards by entering the "family" business: becoming a police officer in Burma. Although it was not until later, most notably in *The Road to Wigan Pier*, that he saw himself as a rebel against the system, his shaping of that experience definitely dwells on the main theme of *Nineteen Eighty-Four*: inner nonconformity. That is what John Flory hoped to achieve in *Burmese Days*, and his failure is marked by his suicide. The theme of the two great essays that arose from Burma, "A Hanging" and "Shooting an Elephant," is the necessity for the state to kill a man, kill an elephant, not because of need but in order to assert its authority, to play the role of power, whether reluctantly or not, for its own sake. And Orwell, particularly in the second essay, plays a vital part in the action. Lately there has been some dispute about whether the incidents actually took place or not, but their greater significance is as psychological rather than actual truths. (The same can be said about the actuality or not of Orwell's experiences at St. Cyprian's. It is a comparative waste of time to worry whether or not Mr. Vaughan Wilkes broke his riding crop while beating Orwell—the importance is the significance of the memory in the making of the author.)

In *The Road to Wigan Pier*, Orwell writes of spending a night in a train with another official denouncing the empire, and then parting the next morning as if they were an adulterous couple. Orwell felt compelled to take his own steps of rebellion, to freedom—first artistic in making himself a writer, and then political in the latter part of the 1930s. But what is striking about Orwell is that unlike so many slightly younger rebels of the 1930s he did not feel any need to embrace another total system—such as Communism. At the same time that in his ultimate commitment to democratic socialism he came to work for a radical transformation of his own society while keeping it a recognizable England—his description of his country in his superb pamphlet of 1941, *The Lion and the Unicorn*, as a family with the wrong members in control.

These early institutions in his life were, I believe, the most important in the making of *Nineteen Eighty-Four*. His experience in the British Broadcasting Corporation in the early years of the war also provided much of the atmosphere in the Ministry of Truth, and the quality—or rather lack of quality in food and housing—during the war and the years immediately afterwards suggested the grimy quality of Victory Mansions, of the streets of London, and of life in general.

I think I have said enough about what elements in Orwell's life contributed to the book. Let me very briefly mention literary influences. Much of the book is derivative; yet Orwell was able to bring the elements together in such a way that the book sears itself into our consciousness. He conceived the book as one about zones of influence, based on his observation of the big power conferences toward the end of the war. The book is intensely political. Yet it is Orwell's power—despite the lack of depth in his characters—to convey the personal—this is really what it might be like for you and me—to his readers, upon whom it has an extraordinary effect. He took quite a few of the elements from Y. I. Zamyatin's *We*, an anti-utopia which he reviewed in 1946, the year he started to work seriously on *Nineteen Eighty-Four*, although he had thought of it as early as 1943. *We* was written in 1920, and has the same sort of total control of the world as *Nineteen Eighty-Four*, with thought police, torture, elimination of love, and so forth. H. G. Wells was an obvious influence (Orwell's early reading beneath the bedclothes with a flashlight while at school—which makes particularly ironic the attack upon the book by Wells's son, Anthony West, as being a fable designed to send the whole world to Orwell's prep school.) He was also influenced by Jack London, and of course the other most famous anti-utopia of the twentieth century, *Brave New World*.

It is Newspeak that leads to the third aspect of *Nineteen Eighty-Four* that I wish to discuss, one that I find of great interest being a historian myself, and one perhaps that has not received as much comment as it should. With the really extraordinary international attention paid to the book, although with rare exceptions limited to the West—series in many newspapers, editorials, conferences, calendars, etc.—it is not surprising that there has been such an emphasis on the question of to what degree the fictional year resembles the real one and the years to come. To what degree is the book predictive? As he wrote in a statement denying that his book was an attack on socialism, "I do not believe that the kind of society I describe necessarily will arrive, but I believe (allowing of course for the fact that the book is a satire) that something resembling it could arrive. . . . The scene of the book is laid in Britain in order to emphasize that the English-speaking races are not innately better than anyone else and that totalitarianism, *if not fought against*, could triumph anywhere."

For Orwell, the word was the way to maintain independence, and it is highly significant that Winston Smith begins his rebellion by writing an unauthorized diary. Language for Orwell was a richly historical vehicle. Newspeak is dedicated to cutting down language to its minimum meaning, so that it will have no past. To create a changing past that has as its main object the service of the state is a prime object of the regime. If I might venture a personal and biased observation, the decline in the study of history is one way in which the predictions of Orwell are coming true. In order truly to exist, we must know who we were. Orwell felt that the political history of a society needed to be known and preserved in order for that society to have a full sense of itself and in order truly to be free.

What, after all, is Winston Smith's role in the novel? He is an employee of the Ministry of Truth, which is dedicated to falsehood. His particular task is the rewriting of the past in order to make it conform to the latest twist in the party's line. Orwell had observed the ruthless willingness of the Communists at the time of the Spanish Civil War to transform the story of the past and the present—to call particular fighters against Franco traitors—as it suited the needs of the party. History is a game of documents, and such contentions can be disproved by documents. They of course can also lie but presumably by consultation with all documents available the historian can achieve the best possible reconstruction of the past.

But the historical sin against the Holy Ghost is the actual tampering with or willful destruction of a document in order to change the record of the past. The sanctity of history is a comparatively modern attitude perhaps at its height in the early years of the twentieth century when history became fully established as a field of study. The Victorians and their predecessors did not hesitate to destroy documents which they felt reflected badly on their authors, to mutilate them, or at the least to quote them as they wished. But they did not have the mechanical devices that Orwell envisions in the book— and in this sense his work has an element of prophecy rather than warning. Not only can the past be destroyed but it can be rewritten so that the researcher—hard to imagine in any case in the world of the novel—will read a document that is false and will have no way to discover that fact.

Smith has vague memories which go against what has become the record of the past—and once holds such a document in his hand— but even if an individual believed something contradictory—based on memory—to the party line it could only extend back one lifetime. Even the oral tradition is gone, as demonstrated in the scene where Smith tries to discover something about the past from a prole in a pub. Winston offers him the party version of the past, and its depiction of itself as overturning oppression. Winston quizzes the poor old man in a most academic fashion, and receives in return reminiscences of being drunk on the day of the Oxford-Cambridge boat race. Winston gives up, and then meditates on the importance of history, giving a justification for the pursuit. "Within twenty years 'Was life better before the Revolution than it is now?' would have ceased once and for all to be answerable. But in effect it was unanswerable even now, since the few scattered survivors from the ancient world were incapable of comparing one age with another. They remembered a million useless things, a quarrel with a workmate, a hunt for a lost bicycle pump, the expression on a long-dead sister's face, the swirls of dust on a windy morning seventy years ago; but all the relevant facts were outside the range of their vision. [But they do not sound like such a bad set of memories.] They were like the ant, which can see small objects but not large ones. And when memory failed and written records were falsified—when that happened, the claim of the Party to have improved the conditions of human life had got to be accepted, because there did not exist, and never could exist, any standard against which it could be tested."

It is after this vain attempt to recapture the past that Smith takes a further daring act to teach himself about the past that he has lost, by considering renting a room from kindly old Mr. Charrington, from whom he had bought the old book of fine quality blank pages that he used for his diary. The antique dealer is depicted in a Dickensian way, and the whole scene has the echoes of the England Orwell elsewhere so devotedly believed in. Here is the description of the room Winston eventually rents as his love nest: "The room had awakened in him a sort of nostalgia, a sort of ancestral memory. It seemed to him that he knew exactly what it felt like to sit in a room like this, in an armchair beside an open fire with your feet in the fender and a kettle on the hob, utterly alone, utterly secure, with nobody watching you, no voice pursuing you, no sound except the singing of the kettle and the friendly ticking of the clock."

In *Nineteen Eighty-Four* there is the importance of the past of a society. Orwell also knows the significance of a personal past, both for his characters and for himself. The romance in the novel takes place in the West of England—where Orwell's family came from and where he grew up. That is where Winston and Julia go to make love. Orwell loved to fish and that is reflected in the scene. "'There are fish in [the stream], great big ones. You can watch them lying in the pools under the willow trees, waving their tails.' 'It's the Golden Country— almost,' he murmured. 'The Golden Country?' 'It's nothing, really. A landscape I've seen sometimes in a dream.'" And then the next paragraph is devoted to the song of a thrush, but even so they wonder if the field is bugged. "Perhaps at the other end of the instrument some small, beetle-like man was listening intently—listening to *that.*"

The room, and Winston's relationship to Julia, and the song about St. Clement's, these are tokens of the good world of the past, and Winston attempts to persuade Julia of its importance. (Orwell is not very enlightened in his view of women. Julia accepts without demur Winston's description of her as a rebel only from the waist downwards.) Winston tells her of the instant that he had a fragment of paper in his hand that proved that the party's version of the past was wrong. "Do you realize that the past, starting from yesterday, has been actually abolished? If it survives anywhere, it's in a few solid objects with no words attached to them. . . . Already we know almost literally nothing about the Revolution. Every record has been destroyed or falsified, every book has been rewritten, every picture has been repainted, every statue and street and building has been re-named, every date has been altered. And that process is continuing day by day and minute by minute. History has stopped. Nothing exists except an endless present in which the Party is always right. I *know*, of course, that the past is falsified, but it would never be possible for me to prove it, even when I did the falsification myself. After the thing is done, no evidence ever remains." Winston is determined to fight this, to believe in a real past. The great tragedy of the novel is that he is forced to renounce this, through torture, in the melodramatic last third of the novel.

When Winston is fighting the Party, and thinks that O'Brien is a leader of that fight, he and Julia go to O'Brien's flat, and there they drink a toast. O'Brien asks what the toast shall be. "'To the confusion of the Thought Police? To the death of Big Brother? To humanity? To the future?' 'To the past,' said Winston. 'The past is more important,' agreed O'Brien gravely." O'Brien appears to demonstrate his rich credentials for being a revolutionary through knowing about the past, most specifically the last line of the old song about the churches of London that Winston has been desperate to find out.

The book which O'Brien smuggles to the new recruits, *The Theory and Practice of Oligarchical Collectivism*, by Emmanuel Goldstein, the Trotsky figure, also emphasizes the importance of the past, although the reading of the text bores Julia so much that she falls asleep after she and Winston have made love. The past must be suppressed by the Party, according to Goldstein, first because members of present-day society must not know that life was better before, but also as a continual justification for the Party, in its predictions, and also that the present "line" and present state of warfare has always been true. The changing nature of the past is a key to the stability of the regime. "The mutability of the past is the central tenet of Ingsoc. Past events, it is argued, have no objective existence, but survive only in written records and in human memories. The past is whatever the records and the memories agree upon. And since the Party is in full control of all records, and in equally full control of the minds of its members, it follows that the past is whatever the Party chooses to make it." Doublethink provides the way in which this is done "to deny the existence of objective reality and all the while to take account of the reality which one denies."

Orwell may be said to have a somewhat naive attitude towards the task of historians. For in some senses the past is mutable in a perfectly respectable way. We see it through contemporary eyes, and shaped by our own present concerns. All history is selective; even a mindless chronicle is not a complete or accurate picture. At present, we are particularly aware of this dilemma. This is one reason for the popularity of the approach of the French Annales school with its emphasis on *mentalité* and its attempt to get inside a society through an intense study of aspects of it that may have been previously neglected. But Orwell is certainly right that no history of any kind can exist if the records of the past can be continually changed.

Orwell tended to be a rather gloomy chap, something of a "naysayer," but in the service of a vision—even if expressed in a negative form—of a future that would preserve the past. *Nineteen Eighty-Four* is a satire and a warning—if it were a prophecy the despair would be total. But in the context of the book, the past, and then the individual's most private thoughts, are totally destroyed. This is made abundantly clear in the scene in which Julia and Winston are arrested. Winston has his intense hope that the proles might rebel. But the old picture falls away revealing the telescreen, and the glass paperweight from the past that had meant so much to Winston also breaks—and it turns out that kindly old Mr. Charrington is in fact a thirty-five-year-old member of the Thought Police. All is not what it appears, and O'Brien is the chief torturer.

I hope I've made it clear how important the past was to Orwell, not only in the conventional sense that his own history shaped him as an author, and that he was influenced by what he read, but most importantly that in the book itself he recognized how important a rich and uncensored knowledge of the past is to preserve civilization.

28

THE ENGLISHNESS OF GEORGE ORWELL

The year 1984 was Orwell's year, and the Western world celebrated the occasion, if that is the right word. Actuality, at least in the sense of the calendar, had caught up with fiction. A question in my mind during that year was whether in 1985 and thereafter a novel about the future that has as its title a date in the past will affect the book's readership. Up to 1984, the book had an astounding number of readers, in the tens of millions, which has effectively removed the text from consideration of ordinary literature into almost a special genre of its own. The spurt of interest starting with the fall of 1983 was intense.

Surveys of the book and of the life of the man were available, perhaps overly available, during this year. What I should like to discuss, however, is a somewhat more general consideration, or theme, in Orwell's life which is of special interest to a historian, particularly to a historian of modern Britain such as myself: Orwell's Englishness. It is essential to an understanding of the man, and his intention in writing *Nineteen Eighty-Four*. And it is not an aspect of his life that will concern those who are likely to use the book as a jumping-off point, or pretext, for an assessment of today's world and the world of the future.

My intention is to examine the background for Orwell's achievement, which in a literal and sad sense climaxed in *Nineteen Eighty-Four*. (It was the last book he published, in June 1949, seven months before his death of tuberculosis in January 1950 at the tragically early age of forty-six.) I hope that such a discussion may be helpful not only for a better understanding of Orwell himself, but also that it may illuminate some aspects of the English character, and the nature of political and social change in England.

It is a cliché about English society, emphasized by those photographs of dark-suited, bowler-hatted English gentlemen walking along with their tightly furled umbrellas in a street in the City of London, that it is made up of conformists. It is another cliché that the education in boarding schools, the so-called public schools, provides a sort of privileged experience dedicated to furthering conformity. Yet the society that created the public schools at the same time produces brilliant mavericks who are out to use existing institutions for aims of their own. Up through the eighteenth century the English had a reputation for being unruly, and a vast historical literature exists on the transformation of their society—how it was made more orderly as it sustained those traumatic shocks at the end of the eighteenth century that transformed England into the first modern nation. I've always felt that under the veneer of good manners and restraint, English society is prone to disorder. Hence, strong institutions are needed to tame it. For most Englishmen and women, such institutions work as they are intended to do. But the brilliant exceptions, the mavericks, both violate and use those institutions, perhaps at a considerable psychic price to themselves.

One only has to think of the two greatest prime ministers of the nineteenth century—William Gladstone and Benjamin Disraeli—and the two greatest prime ministers of the twentieth century—Lloyd George and Winston Churchill—to realize that those who have succeeded politically in the most overwhelming way in Britain have tended to be mavericks—and were intensely hated and distrusted by the more tradition-bound and conventional elements in the land. The fulminations against those four men that took place at the dinner tables of the great and the good would have convinced any eavesdropper that they were considered mad. All four violated the traditions of their society in order to preserve it. William Gladstone became increasingly radical as he grew older, and busily upset the old ways of the universities, the civil service, the army, the electorate, the church, all to create a society which to his mind would be closer to one that was serving God. Disraeli, Jew, dandy, novelist, Tory democrat, supporter of the Chartists, became the representative of the "gentleman of England" and the great inspiration of that tradition of modern Toryism, now apparently abandoned. Lloyd George and Churchill helped preserve their country during the two devastating wars of this century. Each of them was deeply distrusted by almost all their fellow-politicians. Both began as social radicals out to transform society, although they were much less radical than they were thought to be. Only the fact that the country was in a terrible state in the middle of the First World War, and on the verge of defeat in the first year of the Second World War, forced the more traditional politicians to turn to these "wild men," seeing them as unfortunate necessities at a time of extreme peril.

And yet—with the possible exception of Lloyd George—each of the four great prime ministers was deeply wedded to the nation's institutions and determined to strengthen them as best he could, but—a most significant but—according to his own conceptions, which were very reluctantly accepted by others. As a "character type," Orwell belongs among the mavericks. A writer and artist who brilliantly succeeded in his chosen career, he was never a highly active political figure, and he had no wish to be. Yet he was a relentless political commentator and in his life, and in his writing he had, I believe, quite a few resemblances to the four great men of politics.

Of the four, Lloyd George, as an outsider and a Welshman, had the least respect for English institutions. Gladstone, the son of an extremely successful Liverpool merchant, was perfectly happy to fulfill his father's wishes that he become a member of the English Establishment through education (Eton and Christ Church, Oxford) and through marriage—to Catherine Glynn, the member of an old and rich Whig family. Although eventually he would be regarded by many as a man out to destroy traditional English society, Gladstone always saw himself as its defender. Benjamin Disraeli couldn't have been more of an outsider, but his aim was to penetrate into the heart of the English world, while not sacrificing any element of his colorful personality. Winston Churchill, a grandson of the Duke of Marlborough, certainly an "insider," was determined to use his connections for all they were worth, to establish a position and a point of view that was strongly his own.

Orwell was of course somewhat different from all these gentlemen, but not so much as one might think. Like Churchill, he too was descended from the aristocracy, as the great-great-great-grandson of the Earl of Westmorland. But apart from a family Bible and a few mementos, the noble connection was quite faint by the time Orwell was born in 1903, while it was very much present in Churchill's life from the moment of his birth in Blenheim Palace. But in their differing ways both men were born to families that had a strong tradition of serving, and profiting from, the state. In Churchill's case, the tradition began in a grand way with his illustrious ancestor, the first Duke of Marlborough, the great general and victor at Blenheim in

1704. In Orwell's case, *his* ancestors, the earls of Westmorland, had been serving the state since 1624; the Westmorland grandfather of Lady Mary Fane, who married the wealthy Charles Blair, Orwell's great-grandfather, had been an officer under Marlborough, and built the family's Palladian villa, Mereworth, in Kent, near where Orwell—or to use his real name, Eric Arthur Blair—would pick hops as part of his apprenticeship as a writer. (He made use of the experience in his novel *A Clergyman's Daughter.*) The Blair family did not serve England in so high-level or lucrative a way as the Westmorlands, but Thomas Blair, Orwell's grandfather, followed the more modest pursuit of a country clergyman, after having served God in the Empire. His parish was Milbourne St. Andrew in Dorset, and the position was given to him by a cousin, Mary's niece's son, General Sir John Michel. Although the Blairs may have originally been Scottish, it was in this area in a beautiful part of southern England that the family resided, perfectly respectably but not increasing the family fortune.

The tradition of service to the state continued in the next generation. Richard Walmesley Blair, a younger son of the Reverend Thomas Blair, spent his working life in the Opium Service in India, seeing to it that enough opium was grown to supply the highly profitable sale of the drug to China, a right that had been assured through the Opium Wars between Britain and China. Richard Blair made a late marriage to Ida Mabel Limouzin, half-French and half-English. They had three children, their son Eric surrounded by an older and a younger sister, Marjorie and Avril. It was for the son that the better education was reserved, but rather than sending the children home alone to attend school, Mrs. Blair returned with Marjorie and Eric (Avril was not yet born) from India in 1907, five years before Mr. Blair retired and came back to England permanently himself. Young Eric received a proper upbringing in the Thameside town of Henley, where his mother made sure that he played with the right children, and did not pick up a wrong accent.

The crucial development, in terms of Orwell's relation to authority, was his being sent away to prep school in 1911, at the age of eight. The school was St. Cyprian's, on the South Coast at Eastbourne. Eric Blair was clearly a very bright boy, and he was accepted on a scholarship by Mr. and Mrs. Vaughan Wilkes, the proprietors of the school, on the assumption that he would go on to win a scholarship at an eminent public school—which he did, at Eton—and thus reflect credit upon St Cyprian's. He was following the standard educational course of the English "lower-upper-middle class"

(Orwell's own designation) and a course earlier followed by Gladstone and Churchill. Like Orwell at St. Cyprian's, Churchill was intensely unhappy at *his* prep school, St. George's, where beatings were administered by the sadistic headmaster, and his parents completely neglected him. Churchill, also like Orwell, had a better time at his public school, Eton's great rival, Harrow, but like Orwell, he decided (or had it decided for him) not to continue his education at one of the ancient universities. Instead, after training at Sandhurst, he went out to serve the Empire in the Army in India. Churchill was less reflective and introspective than Orwell; in any case he was more indubitably and securely in the upper classes. There is little evidence that he ever basically questioned, even in his reforming days, the social system of the country and its education in particular, no matter how unhappy he was at his boarding school from his eighth to his twelfth year.

Yet despite his hatred of his school, Orwell acknowledged it was only doing its job in ramming facts into him and preparing him for the examinations which would take him to the next stage in the training of a proper member of the English ruling classes. He was at St. Cyprian's from 1911 to 1917; and of course, during his last three years there, Britain was at war. Patriotism, especially in the first years of the war, was at its height. On the surface at least, and perhaps more profoundly, Orwell participated in the feeling of patriotic excitement. His first two publications, written while he was still at St. Cyprian's, appeared in his "hometown" newspaper *The Henley and South Oxfordshire Standard*. In the second month of the war that paper printed a short poem of his, "Awake! Young Men of England!" Its concluding lines, rather awful as verse even perhaps from an eleven-year-old, were strong in sentiment, exhorting young men who were old enought to enlist. "For if, when your Country's in need, / You do not enlist by the thousand, / You truly are cowards indeed." Two years later, on July 21, 1916, another one of his poems was published by the *Standard*: an elegy mourning Field Marshall Lord Kitchener, who had been drowned at sea. In his literary efforts, on the surface at least, he was certainly a conformist child.

But, like many clever children, there was also present in him a young cynic, a state of mind confirmed by his contemporary at St. Cyprian's and Eton, the man of letters Cyril Connolly. Orwell imbibed an irreconcilable double message at the heart of his education. "The essential conflict [at the school] was between the tradition of nineteenth-century asceticism and the actually existing luxury and snobbery of the pre-1914 age. On the one side were low-Church Bible Christianity, sex puritanism, insistence on hard work, respect for academic distinction, disapproval of self-indulgence: on the other, contempt for 'braininess' and worship of games, contempt for foreigners and the working class, an almost neurotic dread of poverty, and, above all, the assumption not only that money and privilege are things that matter, but that it is better to inherit them than to have to work for them. Broadly, you were bidden to be at once a Christian and a social success, which is impossible." Whatever the truth of the matter, his own feeling at the school was that he was despised there, most notably by the headmistress, and many of his fellow little boys, as one who was comparatively poor. (The power of Mrs. Vaughan Wilkes and the capriciousness of her putting the little boys in and out of favor at her "court" are confirmed by a whole series of memoirs by others who attended or knew this hotbed of a prep school: among them Cyril Connolly, Cecil Beaton, and Gavin Maxwell.) Connolly, in his *Enemies of Promise* (1948), writes about the school: "It was worldly and worshipped success, political and social; though spartan, the death-rate was low, for it was well run and based on that stoicism which characterized the English governing class and which has since been under-estimated. 'Character, character, character.'" Connolly described Orwell either at the end of this period at prep school, or at the beginning of his time at Eton, as a "true rebel," in contrast to himself; he knew he was a "stage" one. The school nurtured in Orwell a belief in his personal worthlessness. "The conviction that it was *not possible* for me to be a success went deep enough to influence my actions till far into adult life. Until I was about thirty I always planned my life on the assumption not only that any major undertaking was bound to fail, but that I could only expect to live a few years longer."

Designed to produce conformists, these exclusive private schools, certainly in the case of Orwell, Gladstone, and Churchill, produced gifted young men ready to question their society. The paradox of Orwell—a very English paradox—was that although he was highly skeptical and prone to question the status quo, his background—as the son of a family that served the state—his education, and his class position indoctrinated him with a certain reverence for England, an engrained patriotism. Both attitudes were paralleled in the four prime ministers. Such attitudes came naturally to Orwell, but were not shared by many other prominent intellectual figures on the Left in the 1930s—most famously, the writers that clustered around W.

H. Auden. They were much more likely to be children of the professional middle class with traditions less tied to serving the state. Their
rebellious feelings reached an apogee at the time of the Second
World War. Orwell himself had gone through a period of some confusion as the war drew nearer. For a while he was tempted by paci-
fism; then, vehemently and rather intolerantly, he rejected it. His attitude toward his country was nicely summed up in his short essay of
the autumn 1940 with its brilliant title "My Country, Right or Left."
It concludes: "I grew up in an atmosphere tinged with militarism,
and afterwards I spent five boring years within the sound of bugles.
To this day it gives me a faint feeling of sacrilege not to stand to attention during 'God Save the King.' That is childish, of course, but I
would sooner have had that kind of upbringing than be like the left-
wing intellectuals who are so 'enlightened' that they cannot understand the most ordinary emotions. It is exactly the people whose
hearts have *never* leapt at the sight of a Union Jack who will flinch
from revolution when the moment comes. . . . [There is] the possibility of building a Socialist on the bones of a [Colonel] Blimp, the
power of one kind of loyalty to transmute itself into another, the
spiritual need for patriotism and the military virtues, for which,
however little the boiled rabbits of the Left may like them, no substitute has yet been found." This, of course, is Orwell at his most dogmatic and abrasive, but his feelings are clear.

A belief in an essential patriotism, along with a belief in an essential revolution, emerged also in *The Lion and the Unicorn*, the little
book he wrote in 1941 during the worst of the blitz. He had come to
believe in a need for revolutionary transformations in the social, political and economic structure of Britain so that the war was to be
won. But he was wrong, thanks in part to Churchill's dynamic leadership. Far fewer changes were necessary in the fabric of society than
Orwell had predicted, although Britain did emerge from the war as a
country ready for the transformations of the welfare state under the
Labour government of 1945-50. But this was not the sort of total
revolution that Orwell had hoped for. "This war," he had written in
The Lion and the Unicorn, "unless we are defeated, will wipe out
most of the existing class privileges. There are every day fewer people who wish them to continue. Nor need we fear that as the pattern
changes life in England will lose its peculiar flavour. The new red
cities of Greater London are crude enough, but these things are only
the rash that accompanies a change. . . . The intellectuals who hope
to see [England] Russianized or Germanized will be disappointed.

The gentleness, the hypocrisy, the thoughtlessness, the reverence of law and the hatred of uniforms will remain, along with the suet puddings and the misty skies. It needs some very great disaster, such as prolonged subjugation by a foreign enemy, to destroy a national culture. The Stock Exchange will be pulled down, the horse plough will give way to the tractor, the country houses will be turned into children's holiday camps, the Eton and Harrow match will be forgotten, but England will still be England, an everlasting animal stretching into the future and the past, and, like all living things, having the power to change out of recognition and yet remain the same."

But that was in 1941. Although now a Socialist, Orwell came to be positively Burkean in his belief in the conservative nature of change. He was supportive of what he saw as the eternal verities of English life even as he wished for radical and immediate change at the surface. After the war, in his two masterpieces *Animal Farm* and *Nineteen Eighty-Four*, he was anxious to point out how socialism might become perverted and destroy what he valued most in the central aspects of English society: a respect for truth and the past, the virtue of common sense, the importance of privacy, and personal independence.

How did Orwell come to this position which reconciled him with the idea of authority in his own country, but an authority he wanted totally transformed? He was a rebel who believed, as did the four prime ministers, that they could now work with the established powers because it was they—the established powers—that had changed. (Of course a crucial difference is that Orwell was a critic who never had power and hence was not identified, as the prime ministers were, with the state itself. Yet in the last five years of his life, he was closer to the "powers that be" than he had been at any other time previously.) All five men were rebels of sorts who saw themselves as being dedicated to the most lasting and important values of their society, its eternal verities which had been forgotten by their conformist fellow members of the ruling class, but that might be found in more "ordinary" people.

The politicians were able to make an extraordinary appeal to the multitude and convey a great generosity of spirit. They were able to suggest that they were talking for and to those who were neglected by other politicians. One only has to remember the intense popularity of Gladstone, the "People's William"; or Disraeli's posthumous role as the inspirer of the Tory popular organization, the Primrose League; or Lloyd George's vehement public speeches. As Churchill

remarked about his own role during the war, he had been privileged
to give the "roar" of the lion for his fellow countrymen. Orwell too
saw himself as speaking for England, as far more in touch and respectful of the point of view of ordinary English men and women
than other intellectuals. In *The Road to Wigan Pier*, his 1937 report
on the depressed state of the north of England, he emphasized the
need to identify with the ordinary person, as he himself was able to
do in his unforgettable glimpse of a poverty-stricken woman seen
from a train, cleaning a drainpipe. He could identify with coal miners and with the working class, as in the almost Dickensian family
picture he presents at the end of the first section of the book. "On
winter evenings after tea, when the fire glows in the open range and
dances mirrored in the steel fender, when Father, in shirt-sleeves, sits
in the rocking chair at one side of the fire reading the racing finals,
and Mother sits on the other with her sewing, and the children are
happy with a pennorth of mint humbugs, and the dog lolls roasting
himself on the rag mat—it is a good place to be in, provided that you
can be not only in it but sufficiently *of* it to be taken for granted."

How had he reached this position of reconciliation with society
and with authority, so far from the downtrodden and bitter little
schoolboy who left St. Cyprian's at the age of thirteen in 1917? At
Eton from 1917 to 1922 he had mixed with the future leaders of his
country, and most particularly, as he was a King's Scholar, with
those who were the more intellectual among the students. Right after
the First World War, Eton went through a somewhat "bolshevik"
period with doubts about militarism and the sacrifice of so many old
Etonians on the battlefields of France. So Orwell would have been
both dubious about his country's values, and at the same time imbued with them, while at Eton. The same rather schizophrenic experience awaited him, certainly in retrospect, when, after Eton, he
went, in a manner of speaking, into the family business, and became
a police officer in Burma, in the Indian Imperial Police. He came to
hate his work, keeping the Burmese in order; and yet, unlike so many
others who moved to the left, he did not idealize those who were oppressed; in fact he rather hated them. But he came to believe that the
British had no right to rule other countries, and he asserted India's
right to independence, should she wish it, at the time of the Second
World War. The relationship with authority was most famously
summed up in his brilliant essay "Shooting an Elephant" of 1936.
The four prime ministers had spoken and written thousands, perhaps
millions, of words on imperialism, its triumphs and tragedies, but its

nature has probably never been so succinctly evoked as in Orwell's essay, which tells of his having to shoot a rogue elephant, once dangerous, now harmless, simply to keep face among the Burmese. That was the way a representative of empire was expected to act. Orwell could achieve the rare balance of both being an anti-imperialist without being sentimental about those under British rule. As he wrote, "The sole thought in my mind was that if anything went wrong those two thousand Burmans would see me pursued [by the elephant], caught, trampled on and reduced to a grinning corpse. . . . And if that happened it was quite probable that some of them would laugh. That would never do. There was only one alternative. I shoved the cartridges into the magazine and lay down on the road to get a better aim."

In 1927 Orwell returned to England in order to become a writer, but also because, at least so it seemed to him when he wrote about the period fifteen years later, he could not bear to stay on and take part in an oppressive colonial system. The prime ministers never had quite such a squeamish attitude toward power, although Gladstone at the very beginning of his career, resigned from the Government over an issue of conscience. But however different, all these figures, with their complex relationship to authority, were anxious to transform it into something of which they could approve. The experience of being a police officer was so embittering for Orwell that he went "down and out" in Paris and London in order to purge himself of his guilt, the shame of having been a figure of authority in Burma. His novels of the 1930s, *Burmese Days, A Clergyman's Daughter, Keep the Aspidistra Flying*, are all about figures caught in the dilemma of coming to terms with the society in which they live, and which they don't approve of. John Flory in *Burmese Days* hates the role-playing imposed upon him as an English businessman in Burma and is driven to suicide; Dorothy Hare in *A Clergyman's Daughter* flees into amnesia in order to escape the role of a dutiful daughter that society expects her to play. She eventually returns to it when she recovers her memory, but with her faith destroyed, and her belief in what she is doing gone. Gordon Comstock, in *Keep the Aspidistra Flying*, tries to abandon the worship of the money god, but accepts the obligations of ordinary existence when he gets his girlfriend pregnant and agrees to marry her: having a "stake" in society forces him to conform, even to placing an aspidistra in their living room, the ultimate symbol of lower-middle-class respectability.

Homage to Catalonia, Orwell's masterful account of serving on the side of the Loyalists in the Spanish Civil War, charts the disillusionment and danger that befell him as a member of the militia of a political party, the Party of Marxist Unification. His political education came to a crisis, when he discovered in Spain that to achieve their aims the Communists would both murder their enemies (seeming to hate those on the left more than those on the right) and murder the past, in their willingness to rewrite it for political purposes.

Like the politicians I've been using as a counterpoint in this discussion, Orwell recognized the need for authority, but also that it must be treated with some reserve, looked at carefully, as it was far too prone to take over the society that it was meant to protect, to transform itself into Big Brother. One should not be swallowed up by the Establishment, but preserve an independent critical stance; that was Orwell's determination. He had been trained to be a "responsible leader," but like the politicians, he would not fit easily into that role; rather, he would redefine the role so that it would serve his own values of independence and imagination. Out of that experience came *Animal Farm* and *Nineteen Eighty-Four*, wherein he depicts the perversion of authority. After Spain he knew what he wanted: to turn society around, and to preserve what he saw as the abiding values of the England that he loved.

Much the same feeling imbues some famous lines in the *Lion and the Unicorn* that he is writing while "highly civilized human beings are flying overhead, trying to kill me." And he goes on: "England is not the jewelled isle of Shakespeare's much-quoted passage, nor is it the inferno depicted by Dr. Goebbels. More than either it resembles a family, a rather stuffy Victorian family, with not many black sheep in it but all its cupboards bursting with skeletons. It has rich relations who have to be kow-towed to and poor relations who are horribly sat upon, and there is a deep conspiracy of silence about the source of the family income. It is a family in which the young are generally thwarted and most of the power is in the hands of irresponsible uncles and bedridden aunts. Still, it is a family. It has its private language and its common memories, and at the approach of an enemy it closes its ranks. A family with the wrong members in control—that, perhaps, is as near as one can come to describing England in a phrase."

Orwell undoubtedly would not have shared all the goals of the four political leaders I have mentioned. But he shared with them a feeling of strong support for their society, combined with a critical stance, a feeling of rebelliousness and a conviction of a need for both a transformation of England as he knew it, and the need to preserve its standing values. The relationship of these maverick figures to their society was a complex one. They were using it—indeed almost exploiting it—for their own personal fulfillment. But their ultimate purpose was both to protect and enrich—despite Orwell's disclaimer—"this jeweled isle."

I think it useful to provide some context for the book, in particular the context of the author himself. *Nineteen Eighty-Four* quite rightly is taken to have general significance, but, as Orwell himself stated, it is a blending of the traditional realist English novel with elements of fantasy. His original title for the book—"The Last Man in Europe"—is in fact much more accurate than the quirkily chosen date. But then if that first title had been retained, the phenomenon of so much attention being paid to the book would not have occurred—it would have been just a novel—and the power of its message would not have been as fully experienced.

Orwell was defending English values in classic, negative, and perhaps overstated ways in *Nineteen Eighty-Four*; doing so, he was expressing his Englishness. The novel is concerned with three great competing powers in a vast world system. Yet it takes place mostly in London with a very brief visit to the countryside of Airstrip One for a love scene. Orwell believed in privacy—the privacy of personal life and the privacy of one's own thoughts. He believed in the great importance of the word and the protection of language for our intellectual freedom. He believed in the preservation of the past in its records and artifacts, such as an antique paperweight, or folksongs handed on through generations, the memories of ordinary people. He was a social historian before his time. He demonstrated the dangers of totalitarianisms of the left—and by implication, of the right—to these freedoms. He wished to achieve a state of democratic socialism that would preserve the values of his country, right or left. *Nineteen Eighty-Four* is not a great monument of literature, but in its depiction of a dehumanized world, it is a warning of what the future might bring if we allow Englishness—or Americanness, or any sort of individualness—to wither away. Better a last living man in Europe then a horde of live-seeming robots, crying out, "We love Big Brother."

29

NINETEEN EIGHTY-FOUR TEN YEARS LATER

In the last years of his life, George Orwell, who had written so much of the past he knew, chose to write of the future he would never know. Doing so, he became in the eyes of some a kind of prophet; others have seen him, in my view more correctly, less as a prophet than as a critic of certain tendencies of his own time and what they might lead to. Either way, it is hard to believe he could have anticipated what the future held in store for his own work, how much attention would be paid to it, so that almost fifty years after his death he would still be the centerpiece of concentrated study by students, and continues to enthrall millions of readers around the world. (The American paperback of *Nineteen Eighty-Four* was in its 96th edition in 1994.)

Animal Farm, his brilliant fable about the perversion of Socialism in Stalin's Russia, was published in 1945. Its nonstop popular success then and ever since transformed Orwell from a moderately recognized English literary figure into one of the best-known writers in the world. His next book was *Nineteen Eighty-Four*, which he wrote in 1948. Its publication in June 1949 added to his fame and his fortune. Unhappily he did not have long to enjoy his phenomenal success; he died in January 1950, of tuberculosis, at the age of 46.

The story of his early life is fairly well known, but I would like to indicate some elements in it that played crucial roles in shaping *Nineteen Eighty-Four*. There is a sense of a betrayed society, an English world that had once been secure, a "Golden Land" that is glimpsed in the countryside where Winston and Julia make love.

Unusual in Orwell, certainly for someone who came to political maturity in the 1930s, was his combination of socialism and patriotism, a deep love of England. But it was always a rather paradoxical love, as suggested in the famous last paragraph of *Homage to Catalonia*, describing his return to peaceful England after he had fought on the side of the Loyalists in the Spanish Civil War. "And then England—southern England, probably the sleekest landscape in the world. Down here it was still the England I had known in my childhood: the railway-cutting smothered in wild flowers, the deep meadows where the great shining horses browse and meditate, the slow-moving streams bordered by willows, the green bosoms of the elms, the larkspurs in the cottage gardens; and then the huge peaceful wilderness of outer London, the barges on the miry river, the familiar streets, the posters telling of cricket matches and Royal weddings, the men in bowler hats, the pigeons in Trafalgar Square, the red buses, the blue policemen—all sleeping the deep, deep sleep of England, from which I sometimes fear that we shall never wake till we are jerked out of it by the roar of bombs."

That sense of a lost paradise, even keener in *Animal Farm* than in *Nineteen Eighty-Four*, owes a great deal, I think, to the fact that the first eleven years of Orwell's life belong to the period before the First World War. As we all know, there were plenty of indications in that prewar decade that the world was changing for the worse, that the securities of Britain, the greatest power in the world, were already being challenged, but such indications were not necessarily apparent to a child born in 1903 into the English establishment.

Allow me to digress for a moment about names. Orwell was born Eric Arthur Blair. He never changed his name legally—he told his friend Anthony Powell that if he did so he would have to find a new writing name. Although he was Eric Blair in private life, even after he had published his first works, he became known as George Orwell to friends that he made in the late 1930s and beyond, and signed letters to them as such. But his legal name remained Eric Arthur Blair, and he is buried under that name in the churchyard of the Oxfordshire village, Sutton Courtenay, near where he grew up in Henley. His declared reason for taking a pseudonym was that he was afraid that *Down and Out in Paris and London* might offend his family, and he offered three possibilities to his publisher: H. Lewis Allways, Kenneth Miles, or George Orwell. He admitted that he preferred Orwell and the publisher Victor Gollancz agreed with him. Later commentators have made much of the significance of the name—George, unlike Eric, the quintessence of an ordinary English name—and Orwell, the river in East Anglia near Southwold, where his family moved after several years in Henley. Both names are English through and through. So too, Winston Smith, in *Nineteen Eighty-Four*, can be seen as the epitome of an English name, Winston taken from Winston Churchill, the lion who had done so much to win the Second World War, at the time that Winston was born, and Smith standing for everyone. Is it too speculative to see O'Brien as deliberately not an English name for the betrayer in the novels, the authority figure that Blair himself had been trained to be and became in his early years? Ironically, it is Winston Smith, the minor functionary, whose position most resembled that held by Richard Blair, Orwell's father. In their different ways both were servants of empire and part of its ruling class, Blair in relation to the Bengali, Winston in relation to the proles.

Orwell's nostalgic ideal was to combine the security of his very first years—raised in India, where the lowliest British civil servant could lead an elegant life—with the decencies of an egalitarian society. His mother and sisters lived with him in England some years before his father retired to one of the idyllic spots of the Home Country, Henley, site of the annual regatta. In his childhood years, if it is not too psychoanalytical a point, Eric had the reassuring experience of being the one male in a household of women. That of course was in those unreconstructed days when it was accepted without question that males were the most important members of the household (despite the fact that his mother was quite a strong-minded lady).

The paradise was not to last. His father came home from India, and Eric, aged 8, was sent away to boarding school—the English style for such families. As Orwell would later set out the paradox: he was part of the ruling class; at the same time, in that exact English way, in terms of family income, he would characterize himself as a member of the "lower-upper-middle class." At heart, it was a matter of status rather than of income, though lack of income would make status even more difficult to maintain. England is a land of accepted hierarchies. While the vast part of the population of the country was beneath him, to Orwell the significant difficulty came from those who were above. Such hierarchies were certainly to have a place in *Nineteen Eighty-Four*, transposed from prewar England.

The boarding school to which he was sent in 1911 was one of the best in the country, St. Cyprian's, on the South Coast on the Sussex Downs near the sea. The Blairs could not afford the fees but the proprietors of the school—the Vaughan Wilkses—and such private prep schools were and are profit-making institutions—took on some bright boys on reduced fees in the belief that they would win scholarships to grand public schools such as Eton and Wellington and enhance the reputation of the school. And so Orwell did.

Insecurity within security. He knew from his own experience the deeply insecure individual—Winston—who nevertheless tries to take a stand for the truth—within a totalitarian system that is committed to arbitrary power, power apparently for its own sake. Mrs. Vaughan Wilkes was an O'Brien / Big Brother figure. The experience of the school was, at least to some degree, one of the formative influences in the making of *Nineteen Eighty-Four*. This was also true of the reading that he did at St. Cyprian's. Like most "advanced" schoolboys, he was a devotee of H. G. Wells and would stay up late at night reading his books with a flashlight under the bedclothes. Wells, as a leading science fiction writer and inventor of utopias, proved a counterinfluence in the shaping of Orwell's own great antiutopia.

Orwell's memoir of the school—"Such, Such Were the Joys"— was written in the late 1940s in the same half-decade as his two bitter fables. In that essay, he does present St. Cyprian's as a totalitarian system in which rewards and punishments were likely to depend on the whims of the headmaster, and particularly of his wife. To a degree, this was a personal view; others have testified to the good education they received at the school. Its emphasis was upon facts, particularly historical facts, and their immutability. Orwell learned that lesson: that there was a firm past that should not be changed for the benefit of the ruling class. But he was aware, probably at the time and certainly in retrospect, that he was learning a set of facts designed to glorify the "island story" of Britain and the "world story" of the British empire. It may seem minor, but this early experience in dealing with a capricious "total" system is an important factor in shaping the nightmare vision of *Nineteen Eighty-Four*. Orwell also tells us that at this school he became convinced of his worthlessness—the sense of emptiness that Winston Smith was to experience.

On the other hand, it does not do to exaggerate. During these years Orwell was also well educated, and imbued with a love of England that never left him, the Golden Land, through his reading, and wandering over the downs of Sussex, experiencing the beauty of the south of England, that complacent, powerful land. These roots of patriotism were extremely important for their contribution to that sense of the betrayed state at the heart of the two anti-utopias. In each, the individual is intrinsically good, but is betrayed by the leaders of a state who are only interested in power. Although eventually Orwell became a Socialist, he never lost this love of country. His love of England—and his fear that it might someday become a totalitarian system—was a driving force in the writing of his final novel.

What other elements in his life shaped the two books and their vision? His education accomplished a primary purpose: infusing him with a love of language and reinforcing that sense of authority imbued in the English upper classes. The elite form of English education appears committed to creating at one and the same time outward conformists and inward rebels, and it would be hard, I believe, to find better definitions of Winston, O'Brien, and Julia, even though O'Brien is playing the role, in order to ensnare—and as a result, Winston's and Julia's rebellions sadly crumble.

The education that the young Orwell received was also singularly committed to the "word," how to write it in order to secure good examination results, how to understand it through the exercise of translating it into Latin and Greek, how to revere it as the greatest English art form. It is particularly significant that Winston Smith's job is to rewrite the once canonical paper of England, *The Times*, so that it conforms to the party line of the moment. Orwell took an intense pleasure in language. Some of his more famous essays, most notably "Politics and the English Language," insist on the need to protect language from jargon, and the political power of language intentionally misused.

That concern culminates in the role of "Newspeak" in *Nineteen Eighty-Four*. Orwell would have understood the "linguistic turn" in present-day literary studies and history, although he probably would not have agreed with it. Syme, in the book, hopes by reducing language, by destroying words, to eliminate "thought-crime." One can sense Orwell's fascination with words and their power in the rather diabolical pleasure—parallel to Syme's—that he must have taken in writing the appendix, "The Principles of Newspeak," and its discussion of the definitive dictionary of the language, the Eleventh. This was no doubt a deliberate echo of the much revered edition of the *Encyclopaedia Britannica*, the Eleventh, published in 1910, the summation of knowledge before the Western World moved toward great changes.

There is a certain compulsive literary quality in Winston Smith's work, as he uses language to pervert the truth. Orwell knew, and it is one of his most important contributions, that language was sacred to the preservation of truth and culture; that those who control the word can control the past, the present, and the future. In his novel he succeeded better than he might have wished. Even those who have not actually read *Nineteen Eighty-Four* are familiar with the terms Orwell has given the language—"Big Brother, Newspeak, doublethink, Thought Police," among others—and are affected by them. There is an irony here, for these phrases—such brilliant examples of Orwell's fecundity and imagination—have almost become the sort of jargon terms which he, as a critic of language, so detested: they call up images in an automatic and easy way, and are shortcuts to thinking.

Orwell was different from many writers in that he had a more direct experience of the role of power in this world. The wielding of power by those who had previously been denied it frequently begins with an attempt to help those who are in need, and downtrodden. Presumably that was originally the message of Ingsoc, and might have been true in Russia at the time of the Revolution. It was also, with a radically different ideology, one of the major ways the British Empire thought of itself. Many of those who are in a powerful position in relation to others see themselves as benign improvers of the world, and end up, or certainly their successors do, having as their chief purpose the preservation of their power. Lord Acton's dictum is a cliché, but one that should frequently be repeated: "power corrupts and absolute power corrupts absolutely."

Orwell was wonderfully perceptive in realizing, as has happened in so many political situations in the world, in the past, in the present, and in the future, that it is not a question of there being "goodies" and "baddies." Rather, those with power run the danger of being "baddies" and those without power have goodness thrust upon them. It was a lesson that Orwell learned in the unusual step, for a member of his class, that he took after completing his secondary education at Eton.

He became a policeman, or rather a police officer, in Burma, the "Cinderella" province in the command of the Indian Imperial Police. He was turning back to the modest attainments of his father, rather than the possibilities of university education and further advancement that his time at St. Cyprian's and Eton prepared him for. He was following the minor functionary style of a Winston Smith. But in the Empire, as a police officer, he was powerful, and he experienced the irrationality of power, the need to perform the ruling role. His imperial experience taught him the need of the state for outward conformity—as in *Nineteen Eighty-Four*—both on the part of the state's servants, as he had been in Burma, and on the part of those who are ruled. The rulers themselves, the O'Briens, are caught in the same complicity.

Orwell's political experiences in the 1930s were to teach him the dangers of inner conformity. Desperate world events conspired to bring him—perhaps reluctantly—to politics, and he became one of the most truthful political writers of the century. His earlier writings may be seen as political by implication; they depicted the classic novelistic situation of the individual against society, Flory in *Burmese Days*, Dorothy Hare in *A Clergyman's Daughter*, Gordon Comstock in *Keep the Aspidistra Flying*, George Bowling in *Coming Up for Air*.

But in the last four years of the decade of the 1930s the events and the man were well matched. (In a way his first book, *Down and Out in Paris and London*, dealing with those at the very bottom of society, in effect the homeless, was a reaction to the Depression, but there was little sense in it that politics or economics had much to do with the situation.) He became increasingly aware that the grimness of his literary vision was being matched by outside events: the Depression and the rise of Fascism. Poverty was certainly a major factor in his writings (and it remains in the sordidness of the world of *Nineteen Eighty-Four*, reflecting the experience of the war itself, and then, postwar austerity in Britain). But his first four novels had been rather solipsistic, seen from the point of view of the particular figure, a version of the author. His political experiences lifted him out of himself so that he could create, in the character of Winston Smith (who is hardly a charm boat but is nevertheless someone who can stand for every person), someone who is trying to fight for the truth that 2 and 2 equals 4, that one has the right to love, apart from the state, that one should be able to think for oneself.

But in 1936, almost by chance, Orwell was exposed not to the poverty of tramps but of those who would have worked if they could, in his investigation of what the Depression meant for the North of England. His publisher, Victor Gollancz, had formed the Left Book Club, a highly successful and proselytizing publishing operation that needed a constant flow of new books. He asked Orwell, a professed socialist, to look into conditions in the North brought about by the Depression. The result was one of Orwell's most powerful books—*The Road to Wigan Pier*—an account of his journey, depicting both the desperate situation of the unemployed and the solid virtues of the English working class. (The proles in *Nineteen Eighty-Four* are a debased version, but even they still have some of the qualities that Orwell admired, as did Boxer in *Animal Farm*.) In the second part of the book, Orwell acted as the devil's advocate; he presented a fairly strong case against the English version of socialism while asserting his belief in it. Here too one sees a prefigurement of *Nineteen Eighty-Four*—the case for Socialism put in a negative way—by showing how it can go wrong, which has meant that the novel has frequently been taken, against Orwell's intention, as an anti-socialist tract.

But it was the events in Spain that made him truly a Socialist and committed him to a vision of life that is then betrayed. The Spanish Civil War had broken out on July 18, 1936, while Orwell was in the midst of writing up his experiences in the North of England. When he was free, in December, he went to Spain and discovered in Barcelona what he regarded as a Socialist paradise, a state for which he was happy to fight. This was a brief moment when he saw what an ideal world could be like. It unleashed his genius. Much of his best writings came after the Spanish experience: the great flowering of his essays, and their defense of democratic Socialism "as I understand it"—and the two anti-utopias by which he is chiefly remembered. But in Spain he found that his vision of the ideal Socialist society was being betrayed, by those elements on the Left who were primarily interested in power, and in serving a foreign policy, Russia's, that had little to do with the socialist aspirations of the Spaniards on the side of the Republic. This was done through the manipulation of the past, the truth, the press, by the Communists. He was appalled by their claim that the group with which he himself was fighting—the semi-Trotskyist Worker's Party of Marxist Unification, the POUM— were traitors rather than fighters for the cause. Orwell was dedicated—and it is a great English virtue and a theme in *Nineteen Eighty-Four*—to the importance of the individual: the man risking his life on the front line who, because he was a member of the POUM, might well be arrested and imprisoned as a Fascist in Barcelona. This is all discussed in his wonderful book of reportage, *Homage to Catalonia*. It is the vision there, of a Socialist state and its betrayal, that provides the compelling force behind *Nineteen Eighty-Four*.

In the remaining years of his life were further experiences that he drew upon for the novel. Life in the British Broadcasting Corporation where he worked in the early years of the war provided much of the atmosphere and the language of the Ministry of Truth. The austerity made necessary by the war (and even its pleasures, so-called, such as Victory Gin), combined with the Puritanism of Orwell and his wife, was drawn upon for the grimy atmosphere of the book. The war would reinforce the experience of Spain—he saw the honor and decency of ordinary people in their fight against Hitler. As in Spain he felt much more at one with them under wartime conditions. Too old to fight, and not particularly well, he mucked in with ordinary men in the Home Guard, and he wrote down his thoughts in his column, "As I Please," for the Labour weekly, *Tribune*, celebrating his commitment to an individual vision. He also started to compose those magnificent essays of his own special kind of sociological/anthropological observation that have been so influential on such topics as smutty comic postcards and boys' school stories. Although not paid much attention to nowadays in this context, he is a crucial figure in shaping our sense of the importance of non-canonical works of imagination.

In a lesser extent than had been true in Spain, he also saw during the Second World War itself that power could be maintained by its traditional leaders with little more than lip service to changes in society, that ideology could be mere window dressing for the maintenance of power, and that power in and of itself was the point. He had felt, in the early years, that a Socialist revolution would be necessary to win the war, as argued in his splendid pamphlet with its characteristic patriotic title, *The Lion and the Unicorn*. But as the war progressed he recognized that the traditional power in England—which he was part of by birth and training—in fact could win the war without the revolutionary changes that he had thought essential and wanted.

As Orwell had been a premature anti-Fascist in his involvement with the Spanish Civil War, so too he was a premature anti-Communist in his involvement with the Cold War. There were, of course, many anti-Communists (but many of them, led by Churchill, had abandoned that position for the duration of the war) and some socialist anti-Communists. But, with the Soviet Union as an ally, their numbers dwindled. Orwell wrote *Animal Farm* from November 1943 to February 1944. He knew that it was "politically incorrect," and of course it was a great irony that it was turned down for that reason by the conservative T. S. Eliot, an editor at Faber & Faber, and by many other publishers. Orwell described *Animal Farm* as the first book in which he attempted "to fuse political purpose and artistic purpose into one whole." Shortly thereafter he was also thinking about *Nineteen Eighty-Four*. Both books attest to the power of ideas and of myths but also demonstrate how they can be perverted. In that sense they continue to be extremely relevant. Both did play off the Soviet Union, and then became Cold War documents; now that the Cold War has ended, they have a new layer of history laid upon them.

Nineteen Eighty-Four was, in many ways, a variant of *Animal Farm*, although its style was very different and it lacks, even if the Farm story is grim, that fabulist charm as well as an intense sense of sadness. The novel takes to extreme lengths real possibilities, as is implied by the dust jacket of the first English edition which had its spelled-out title superimposed on the year in numerals. In 1949, 1984 seemed a long way away. Through the literary title he was suggesting that he was writing a satire or fantasy or a warning of how existing tendencies might eventuate, not necessarily a prediction of what was likely to happen by 1984. His appreciation for technological discoveries in the future shaped part of what he put into the book; and at another level, so much of the political structure of the world as he imagined it—endless rivalry of superpowers justifying the state's actions—turned out to be correct up to the "fall" of the Soviet Union and the Communist regimes in Eastern Europe. Even so, it can be argued that this accuracy is almost coincidental to the main purposes of the book. By spelling out the title, Orwell was, in effect, telling us that we were not to take the novel too literally as a document; that we were to remember the ways in which it was a work of imagination. There is an unmistakable power (and violence) in the work that removes it from the literary genre to which it belongs—a novel of fantasy—and gives it an intensity that sears it into the minds of its readers.

Both *Animal Farm* and *Nineteen Eighty-Four* deal with the corruption of power, and how the corruption of ideas can support that. I think that the significance of *Nineteen Eighty-Four* itself, and how Orwell's life went into its making, was well summed up in a front-page review in *The New York Times* on June 12, 1949, by the eminent critic Mark Schorer. He did make one statement that has proven wrong: "[The book's] greatness [may be] only immediate, its power for us alone, now, in this generation, this decade, this year." But Schorer followed that sentence with another that is absolutely correct: "Nevertheless it is probable that no other work of this generation has made us desire freedom more earnestly or loathe tyranny with such fullness." All of the *events* of Orwell's life, most importantly those during the Spanish Civil War, went into the making of

Nineteen Eighty-Four. Ultimately, in the most literal way, the life of the man himself went into the writing of the book.

My title has been perhaps a little misleading. Of course, at this moment, it is correct: I am considering *Nineteen Eighty-Four* in 1994, ten years beyond its title. There can be little question that the existence of the Cold War during the first forty years since the book's publication was a cold fact about *Nineteen Eighty-Four*, and it has influenced our reading of it. Indeed the Cold War was a major reason why in 1984, the year itself, there would be so much fighting for possession of the text between right and left, most vehemently between such neo-cons as Norman Podhoretz and radicals such as Christopher Hitchens. It is testimony to a great text that it can provide material for many differing and contradictory points of view. But has the end of the Cold War changed our reading of this particular text?

Orwell thought of himself as a democratic Socialist. The adjective "democratic" represented, I believe, his commitment to the individual, his heritage from his English background, and his hatred of elitists such as the Fabians, prone to fall for dictators, who believed that ordinary persons needed things done to them for their own good. Socialist, as he used the word, stood for his commitment to egalitarianism, and his belief that a means must be found for redistributing the goods of the world. Individualism, with its commitment to privacy, was destroyed in Winston's world by the two-way tele-screen. (The technical aspects of the book are quite fascinating and seem far more believable now than they may have been when it was first published.) In Orwell's view, elitism led to a worship of power for its own sake, combined with—and this intensifies the nightmare quality of the book—the need to make others suffer as evidence of that power. Orwell did not believe in the possibility of an enlightened despotism. The crucial battle is between the rulers and "thought-crime," the attempts of Winston and Julia to rebel through private thoughts and through that most private of activities, the sexual. It is obviously significant that the Thought Police come crashing into their secret bedroom hideaway, chanting as Winston and Julia have just said themselves: "You are the dead." Those outside the system, the proles, might have some freedom as they are apolitical. For those within the system, the everlasting threat is of a boot crashing into one's face, one's worst horror being realized in Room 101: the reflective individual is destroyed.

Ten years ago the Western world went Orwell mad, with conferences, books, articles, Peanuts, Walter Cronkite, the Today Show, art shows, an extraordinary demonstration of how the coincidence of choosing a title can have an effect. Perhaps many of the celebrants were simply grateful for having survived up to that point. But we should hardly be complacent, even though the Orwellian vision seems more firmly a warning now, rather than a prophecy, than it might have done in 1984. As Walter Cronkite, a benign Big Brother figure perhaps, wrote in his preface in the so-called "commemorative" edition, "It has been said . . . that Orwell's terrible vision has been averted. Well, that kind of self-congratulation is, to say the least, premature. 1984 may not arrive on time, but there is always 1985. Still, the warning has been effective; and every time we use one of those catch phrases, . . . recognize Big Brother in someone, see a 1984 in the future, . . . note something Orwellian [which is now a word in the dictionary], . . . we are listening to that warning again."

Orwell was writing about what *might* happen, not what would happen. It is not, to my mind, a correct question that many asked, most notably at a grand conference I attended that year at Strasbourg, in the chamber of the European Parliament: "Was Orwell mistaken or had he correctly interpreted the history of his time?" To the degree that his book has proven to be "wrong," to that extent it has served one of its major purposes. What Orwell attempted to do was take to a logical conclusion the destructive elements inherent in Nazism and Stalinism, the two great totalitarian systems. Sometimes he was correct in crucial guesses, sometimes not. Was Orwell unusual in foreseeing two central developments of the postwar world? First, the extraordinary growth of technology that would permit a degree of mechanical manipulation of our lives and potential supervision of them not known in the 1940s. Though Orwell put more emphasis on television as a two-way system and less on computers, one has the impression that Winston must have done his work of rewriting the past with some sort of primitive computer. Second, a world divided into armed camps. Will the latter return or have we now achieved a permanent abandonment of that configuration?

To my mind, one crucial question implicit in the book a half century after it was written is whether or not we have internalized a set of conformities to the needs of the state. Presumably it might be argued that if this *has* happened, we would not be aware of it. I suspect nonetheless this has *not* happened: Orwell's direst warning of what the future might hold has not yet taken place. Most individuals are still free to think what they wish, although in many places there are severe restrictions on what they may say or do.

But what about the state? What has taken place in parts of the world where there are mini-totalitarian governments? Dictatorships of today do not appear to be threats to world peace. But obviously there is considerable death and destruction in the so-to-speak *small* wars that are still going on in the world. Perhaps, as with Oceania, wars are used as the way in which the state defines and justifies itself. But the situation is not the continual worldwide war envisioned in Orwell's book. It was the threatened universality of Orwell's picture that made it so terrifying; such a possibility now seems so much more unlikely than it might have been ten years ago.

It would be an intriguing but difficult study to discover the degree and in what ways Orwell played a part in the changes in Eastern Europe. I suspect he should be given a decent amount of credit. The considerable number of readers of *Nineteen Eighty-Four* in the Soviet Union and Eastern Europe were helped by that book to see that, whatever their leaders might claim, they were not driven by a desire to create a better world but rather to maintain power for its own sake.

Despite the extraordinary developments in the computer world, the developments in cyberspace, and the information highway, and its quite scary potential for "Big Brother" and pretty much anyone who wants to know all about us, our present situation still hasn't reached the continual spying and the total ability to destroy the past that is present in the novel. On the other hand, even though its methods were more primitive, the range of activity of the Stasi in Eastern Germany would seem to justify the novel's assumption that the state could run away with itself, and wish to supervise, know about, and control every aspect of an individual's existence. On a far less sweeping scale the FBI and the CIA have been guilty of invasions of our privacy and intrusion into legitimate activities. Through computer developments, the potential for such invasions has increased to an Orwellian degree.

Orwell had transformed his own nightmares and our half-conscious apprehensions into fiction; he asks us how we live and what are our primary political concerns. Are we free? Individual liberty and equality are, he believes, the cornerstones of our values, and his aim is to make untrue that powerful phrase in *Animal Farm*: "some are more equal than others." Orwell wrote *Animal Farm* before, and *Nineteen Eighty-Four* three years after, the Second World War ended, the war in which the Soviet Union was an ally of Britain and the United States. He built his vision of the particular dangers of totalitarianism on his experiences in the Spanish Civil War where he observed how the Communists were perfectly capable of rewriting the past to conform to their present needs and of executing those on the Left with whom they disagreed. (Of course historians are always rewriting the past, and so they should, as they see it with different eyes. Presumably they try not to do it in such a way that they are consciously forcing it to fit a particular agenda as was poor Winston's job. In an intriguing and perhaps disconcerting way the new ideas about the social construction of reality, increasingly important at the moment, not only in literary theory but also in historical thought, are connected with the idea of making us aware of how the present, and the past, may be constructed to conform to certain agendas. But these ideas run the danger of a postmodern nihilism that Orwell would not have shared.)

The significance of the past, its shaping of the ideologies that are tearing some societies apart, has never been more critical than now when we no longer have a world divided into two armed camps. Stalin and his successors, and the lesser dictators, presumably for the sake of power (but also to insure a certain degree of stability), suppressed the forces of nationalism and religion. They controlled the past in order to control the future. Although Orwell was deeply concerned with ideology, he might not have appreciated how explosive those feelings of nationalism and religion would prove to be in bringing about change.

Nineteen Eighty-Four is a very rich text and it is a testimony to its strength that it provides material, as should all great texts, for multiple interpretations from varying points of view. Is it demonstrating that socialism can never work, or is it demonstrating the dangers of the perversions of socialism? Now that we are in a different world than that of the Cold War for which it was in many ways a crucial document, it still talks to us of the dangers of the drive to power and the efforts made to crush individual thought and, indeed, love.

Nineteen Eighty-Four is about power, about words, about the past, about love, about the individual and the state. It is also a work of art and literature that is read for its ideas, for its skill as a novel, for the light that it sheds on the time it was written and on the time since. Will the text have different meanings in 2004 and beyond?

Part Six

The Other: The Jew

30

ANGLO-JEW OR ENGLISH/BRITISH

It is blatantly true, as Todd Endelman pointed out quite eloquently in a 1991 essay, that, contra a statement made in the *London Review of Books* by David Cannadine, the history of the Jews in England has become one of the liveliest areas of historical investigation over the past several years, as indeed has Jewish Studies in general.[1]

The reasons are not far to seek, and indeed the new series of the journal *Jewish Social Studies*, where this piece was originally published, is one not insignificant piece of evidence. It is edited by two members of my own history department at Stanford: Steven Zipperstein and Aron Rodrigue, both of whom have new appointments in the department. Professor Zipperstein holds the Koshland Professorship, which was previously occupied briefly by Amos Funkenstein. I happened to chair the search committee that recommended Professor Funkenstein, and I vividly remember receiving at the time a characteristic letter from Irving Howe pointing out that now it had become fashionable among Jews to support chairs in Jewish Studies at American universities. Indeed there has been a vast increase in such positions, one of the few "growth" areas in the academy.

In a way, the development has paralleled the pattern in research interests. Over the years Jews have frequently been very generous in their donations to educational institutions, but in their gifts to colleges and universities that were not particularly associated already with Jewish studies, such gifts tended to be to non-Jewish areas. Indeed Jewish Studies itself probably did not exist until fairly recently at many leading universities and colleges as an entity for Jews to give to. Now the situation has changed quite dramatically. On the aca-

---

[1] Todd M. Endelman, "English Jewish History," *Modern Judaism* 11 (1991): 91.

demic level there is much more willingness to be self-aware, to be much less intent on assimilation and acculturation. Jews have, on the whole, become as integrated with their society, as, in the American case, such groups as Italian-Americans, German-Americans, and the other vast immigrant groups of the late nineteenth and early twentieth centuries. At the same time it is my impression, based on my own angle of vision, that they are more self-conscious and concerned about their position than the older immigrant groups. On the other hand, they are similar yet quite different from other new areas of ethnic study: African-American, Asian-American, and Hispanic-American. But they share with them, in recent years, a willingness to assert the importance of studying themselves and being studied not only at "historically" Jewish places of learning, but at major universities and colleges, those, at least until after the Second World War, that were marked by their "lily-white" tone.

The story of the increase of the number of Jewish academics, certainly in the United States, and presumably elsewhere, has been notable since the end of the Second World War. But until quite recently, that increase has not been paralleled by an equivalent growth in the number of Jews and others studying Jewish subjects. To turn to the subject at hand, although I have never done any systematic investigation of this question, it has been my impression that, at least in the United States, there has been a fairly high percentage of Jews among those who have become professionally concerned with British history, perhaps more than the general percentage of Jews in the academic world. But within that field very few wrote on Jewish topics.

To give the most prominent example in Britain from the between the wars period, Sir Lewis Namier was extremely active in the Zionist movement, but his great scholarly work on Britain in the eighteenth century had nothing to do with Jews. Nevertheless, his concern with the period connected with his Zionist activities through his conviction of how important land was to those in control then and how important acquiring land was for the future of the Jewish people.

It has been over the last decade or so that this situation has changed. The shift in approach transcends, I believe, whatever might be the origins of the author. For many years, at least in the Anglo-Jewish field when much of the history was written by non-professionals, the aim tended to be rather celebratory, to mark how well the Jews were getting along and at peace with the general society. Britain has never had the pretense of the "melting pot" ideology of the United States, and there is a much deeper tradition of groups keeping their distinctive identities. But as Gladstone said in a somewhat different but analogous situation, the political story in Britain has been from at least 1688 on, if not before, of various groups coming within "the pale of the constitution," that is, becoming functioning members of the political world, most clearly marked by the right to vote. Voting, in the British view, was an accolade and mark of a full membership of the society, of which the final accreditation was the right to be a member of that great club, the House of Commons, and possibly even being glorified by becoming a member of the House of Lords. The goal of acceptance on the terms of the society held sway, I should guess, until the 1960s and 1970s. The alienations of those decades, combined with the surprisingly gradual seeping into historical consciousness of the Holocaust for *all* minority groups—there is no absolute guarantee of the right to exist—made it apparent that assimilation, maybe even acculturation, were not necessarily the goals devoutly to be wished.

For European Jews the Holocaust had meant destruction. For those communities fortunate enough to survive, the awareness of the Holocaust has gradually created a different sense of what might be the Jewish connection with the larger society, combined with a new feeling that there might be some similarity to others who were also not part of the dominant group. In the United States the situation is marginally different: we are all immigrants, except for the American Indians. But in Britain, until fairly recently, the Jews were one of the comparatively few immigrant groups. They acquired political rights in ways parallel to the Nonconformists—the Protestant non-Anglicans—and to the Catholics, although unlike those groups they had been exiled from the country in 1290 and not readmitted until 1656.

The ambiguities of being a Jew in Britain are captured in an anecdote told in a recent biography of the late Stanley Olson, the biographer of another expatriate, John Singer Sargent. Olson was an American who lived in England and followed the not unknown pattern of becoming more English than the English. He made no secret of being American, but he felt that that was a sufficient degree of "otherness." He did not wish to burden himself with having it being also known that he was Jewish. I apologize for giving this story at some length but I find it emblematic for the special nature of the situation for Jews in Britain.

Phyllis Hartfield writes in *Pencil Me In*, her recent biography of Olson:

It may be difficult (especially if one is a Jew and viscerally aware of how many of one's people involuntarily disappeared) to excuse Stanley's willed attempt to pass as a gentile, yet one must acknowledge the brilliance of his strategy given his overall aim: to achieve a perfect fit in English society, where to be a Jew is to be somehow un-English. An American acquaintance illustrates the point with an anecdote set at about the time Stanley arrived in London and began to forge his English character: 'I was having dinner with a certain noble lord twenty years ago, a real old Tory Lord Salisbury type, who said: "We really don't have a Jewish problem in England. Jews in England are thoroughly accepted. That embarrassing business back in the time of Edward, the expulsion of the Jews"—and he of course meant not Edward VII—"they're thoroughly accepted now. They're not really Jewish here in England, the Jews." And then there was a long pause and he looked up and said: "Of course they're not really English either."'[2]

Another example of the growth of interest in Jewish studies at "main line" universities is the expansion of library resources. At my own university, Stanford, that has meant the purchase of the extraordinary Salo Baron library, and the acquisition of further items to support the study of the Jews. By great good fortune, the Library acquired recently Sir Isadore Spielman's own extra-illustrated copy of the *Catalogue of the Anglo-Jewish Historical Exhibition*, held in 1887. Spielman served as the Honorary (that is, unpaid, as befits an English gentleman) Secretary of the Exhibition, and holding the exhibition may well have been his idea.

The exhibition was English Jewry's considerable contribution to the celebration that year of Queen Victoria's Jubilee. It can also be seen as the "coronation" of the "Cousinhood," that interlocking and interrelated group, discussed perhaps most notably in Chaim Bermant's *The Cousinhood* (1971) with its descriptive notation on its dust jacket: "A vivid account of the English-Jewish aristocracy: Cohens, Rothschilds, Goldsmids, Montefiores, Samuels, Sassoons." This was the romantic popular notion of Anglo-Jewry that, despite the significance of the vast Eastern European influx, dominated Anglo-Jewish history even in a scholarly sense until the publication of Lloyd Gartner's *The Jewish Immigrant in England, 1870-1914* in 1960.

With a keen sense of the new scholarship, that world is vividly recaptured in its less romantic guise in Eugene C. Black's *The Social*

---

[2] Phyllis Hartfield, *Pencil Me In* (1994), p. 95.

Politics of Anglo-Jewry, 1880-1920, in which the author discusses the operations of the "Grand Dukes," and the lower ranks of that particular "aristocracy," not as businessmen but rather as those who were in "charge" of the community that, starting in the 1880s, was dramatically enlarging with the emigration from Eastern Europe. It grew from a population of 65,000 in 1880 to one of 260,000 in 1914. These grand figures took their responsibilities very seriously. Their aim was to "socialize" the new immigrants and try to make sure that they behaved well, were at the least part of the "respectable" poor and might be inspired to be upwardly mobile. Black concludes, and one fears that he may be right, although I suspect (hope?) that there may have been somewhat more division than he suggests: "The vast majority of British Jews accepted, with token qualifications, the philosophy and values Anglo-Jewry sought to impart— pride in being Jewish, anglicization, self-help, and upward mobility. They became, in fact, what Anglo-Jewry wished them to be: English people of the Jewish persuasion."[3] More intensely than other groups that had come within "the pale of the constitution," and perhaps mistakenly, quite a few Jewish leaders appeared to have a sense of a "contract," that in return for "emancipation" (marked by a Rothschild becoming a member of the House of Commons in 1858) they had an obligation, more onerous than that placed on other communities, to behave themselves.

That perhaps innocent, certainly powerful, vision of "English people of the Jewish persuasion" we patronize at our peril. It was, I am sure, the conception that the exhibition was designed to convey. It was a whiggish view, appropriate to the nineteenth century, when "emancipation" had been achieved, when Jews could vote and could even sit in both Houses of Parliament. In the English way, it was a path that was open to all in a very restricted sense. As with the English class system itself, being a member of the right family could give one innumerable advantages, in many ways deeply unfair. But at the same time it was possible for a young person, most commonly male, who had great talents, to move upwards and make a great success of himself, most particularly in the professions. And so too Jewish grandees could achieve the apotheosis of the English gentleman, being men of leisure, even on a comparatively modest income. Such a person would spend his time pursuing worthy occupations that

---

[3] Eugene C. Black, *The Social Politics of Anglo-Jewry, 1880-1920* (1988), p. 391.

would benefit one's society. As *The Times* wrote of Spielman in its obituary of him in 1925: "A man of means, he was able to devote himself to [the furthering of British Art]."[4]

The Spielman family had come to London from Schocken in Poland in the 1820s, and Isadore's father, Adam, had been a successful banker and bullion merchant. Chaim Bermant regards Sir Mayer Spielman, Isadore's brother, as the most distinguished member of the family. A stockbroker until he was fifty-five, he devoted the rest of his life to the cause of helping juvenile delinquents, for which he was knighted. (His daughter, Eva Hubback, was a prominent feminist.) Isadore, born in 1854, trained as an engineer. He made a dynastic marriage, apparently not a love-match, according to his granddaughter, in 1879 to Emily, the daughter of Sir Joseph Sebag-Montefiore, the nephew and heir of Sir Moses Montefiore.[5]

In 1887 he found his true vocation as an entrepreneur of art. The cultural and social implications are manifest. He began with Jewish art in the exhibition we are considering here, but he made his career, as an exhibition organizer and civil servant (he held the position as the Director of Art for the Board of Trade, Exhibitions Branch). He presented British art at the international exhibitions held at Brussels in 1897, Paris in 1900 (where he emphasized William Morris and Edward Burne-Jones), Bruges in 1902, St. Louis in 1904, the famous Franco-British exhibition in 1908 (for which White City was built in London by the Anglo-Hungarian-Jewish entrepreneur Imre Kiralfy), Turin in 1910, as well as the Empire Exhibition of 1924. His dislike of the Russians because of their persecution of the Jews led him to refuse to participate in the Russian Fine Art Exhibition of 1904. He was active in the formation of the Jewish Historical Society in 1893 and served as its President from 1902 to 1904. In many ways the Society, which did pioneering work in British Jewish history, was largely dedicated to putting forward a melioristic version of that story that is now under attack and undergoing revision.

Spielman became part of the army of the "great and the good" and in 1903 was one of the founders of the National Art Collections Fund, which was dedicated to acquiring masterpieces for British museums and also helping to prevent some of the great works of art in

---

[4] *The Times*, 11 May 1928, p. 8.
[5] Up until a certain point the family seems to have spelled its name Spielmann, but more recent generations seem to have dropped the second *n*, which is the form I shall follow. Chaim Bermant, for instance, in his *The Cousinhood* (1971), uses one *n* in the index and two in the text.

private hands in Britain from moving into the collections of wealthy Americans. He was particularly instrumental in acquiring for the nation Holbein's *Christina of Denmark, Duchess of Milan*. He was knighted in 1905. In some of these activities, he worked with his brother Marion who was one of the leading art critics of the period.

The history of modern international exhibitions started with the Great Exhibition at the Crystal Palace in London in 1851, and from then on they became a standard way for the self-presentation of a society. The planning for this exhibition started in May 1886, and four rooms were hired at the Royal Albert Hall for display purposes. Spielman was assisted in the organization of this by two contemporaries—all were in their thirties—the compilers of the catalogue. One, Joseph Jacobs, was born in Sydney in the same year as Spielman, 1854, and had a career as a journalist. The other, Lucien Wolf, only thirty at the time (he had begun his career at the age of seventeen at *The Jewish World*), had a very distinguished career as both a Jewish historian and a journalist, who rapidly expanded his activities to the non-Jewish press, particularly in *The Times* and the *Fortnightly Review*. He was a diplomatic activist (particularly as an opponent to Russia). He would be the first president of the Jewish Historical Society. As always with such enterprises, there were distinguished figures who served as its officers, with one of the greatest Jewish philanthropists of the time, and a figure who was very active in coping with the considerable influx of East European Jews, F. D. Mocatta, serving as chairman. He had retired at the age of forty-seven to devote himself to philanthropy, and he paid for a reception for 3,000 to mark the opening of the exhibition. He was intensely proud both of being Jewish and of being English. As he said: "It is not necessary to profess the religion of the majority to be a patriot."[6] This was an issue of some concern to the Jews of the time. Their traditional association with the Liberals had been troubled in the previous decade, when many Jews were more likely to side with their former co-religionist, Disraeli, on the Eastern Question (by supporting Turkey), rather than with Gladstone.

Creating a sense of Jewish history in Britain was a way to identify with the country and to be a part of it, and this was what the exhibition determined to do. There were formidable obstacles as illustrated by the comment Austen Chamberlain made some years later about

---

[6] See Ruth Sebag-Montefiore, *A Family Patchwork* (1987), p. 52. Her narrative contains the rather touching and revealing sentence: "In opting for the advantages of assimilation, we lost the security of faith" (p. 48).

Edwin Montagu, who was desperate to be as English as possible, and was passionately anti-Zionist. He was the third Jew to attain Cabinet rank, after Herbert Samuel and Rufus Isaacs. But one despairs of the project of the exhibition to assert the right to be both English and Jewish if Chamberlain could remark about Montagu: "A Jew may be a loyal Englishman and passionately patriotic but he is intellectually apart from us and will never be purely and simply English."[7] If the situation were such for the most assimilated of Jews, how much more disturbing for the established Jewish community, as well as for the non-Jewish community, were the recent immigrants. As the journalist Arnold White, a leading agitator for restricted immigration, wrote in *The Destitute Alien in Great Britain*, the book he edited in 1892: "As they come, so they remain—aliens, children of another race, amongst us, yet not of us. And the East End produces no type of man or woman so unfit, so un-English and morally and personally so alien, as the pauper immigrant when he becomes a settler in the . . . East End."[8]

To emphasize the ecumenical nature of the enterprise of the exhibition, a Christian, John Evans, served as vice-chairman and he also served to authenticate the seriousness of the historical dimension as he was the president of the Society of Antiquaries. On the committee were leaders of the Jewish community such as Lord Rothschild, who had become the first Jewish peer three years before, as well as Samuel Montagu, two Sassoons and Christians such as Robert Browning and the Reverend Samuel Barnett, the founder of Toynbee Hall in the East End. Included in the Stanford catalogue is a letter from Browning to Spielman telling him how much he enjoyed the display.

The exhibition was open to the public from April to June 1887 as part of the Queen's Jubilee celebrations. In the catalogue its aims were announced as "to promote a knowledge of Anglo-Jewish History; to create a deeper interest in its records and relics, and to aid in their preservation" and "to determine the extent of the materials which exist for the compilation for a History of the Jews in England." There were 2,945 items on exhibit not only at the Royal Albert Hall, but also in supplementary displays at the Public Record Office, the British Museum, and the South Kensington Museum (now the V & A). The opening day was April 4, with a private view

---

[7] Bermant, p. 173.
[8] In Judy Glassman, "Assimilation by Design: London Synagogues in the Nineteenth Century," in Tony Kushner, ed., *The Jewish Heritge in British History: Englishness and Jewishness* (1992), p. 190.

the previous Saturday which 1,250 attended, apparently with no difficulty about being in conflict with the Sabbath. Indeed, the organizers took a progressive position on the question of "sabbath" opening, in this case being Saturday, as that day during the month of June it was open without charge, as the one time that it was "accessible to those Jewish visitors who were only disengaged on their Sabbath."[9] There was a total of 12,000 visitors.[10] There was also a series of nine public lectures, including ones by the compilers of the catalogue: Jacobs on London Jewry in the year of the expulsion, 1290, and Wolf on those Jews who were in England in the years between the expulsion and the readmission in 1656. There was also a concert of Jewish music.

The exhibition was part of the general increase in interest in the past that was notable in Britain in the last part of the nineteenth century, made manifest in the formalization of the study of history at Oxford and Cambridge, the founding of the *English Historical Review* in 1886, and in that same year the successful campaign, against the wishes of the leaders of the congregation itself, to save the Sephardic synagogue, Bevis Marks, built in 1701, from being torn down. The exhibition was celebratory of the past and the present in terms of the grandees. It ignored the London East End, where from the beginning of the decade poor East European Jews were flocking, although it had only been a comparatively few years that such had been the case.

The introduction to the catalogue noted the steady progress the Jews had made in Britain, and the degree to which they had been incorporated in the state. Included was a silver salver presented to Cromwell by Menasseh ben Israel, the major figure in arranging the readmission. The building of synagogues not only in Britain but in British possessions around the world marked further progress—in particular, the synagogue built in Bombay in 1880 by the Sassoon family in memory of E. D. Sassoon.

In the nineteenth century, improvement had been marked when Jews had acquired the right to hold municipal offices. Most importantly, in 1858, after being denied following his election and reelections ever since 1847, Rothschild was allowed to take his seat in Parliament. (A petition to the House of Commons to abolish the phrase—"on one's oath as a Christian" which was the sticking

---

[9] Joseph Jacobs and Lucien Wolf, comps., *Catalogue of the Anglo-Jewish Historical Exhibition* (1888), p. 211.
[10] Ibid., p. 210.

point—was on display.) A portrait of Rothschild's son, taking his oath on a Jewish Bible in 1885 as the first Jewish peer, was also included. (Considering that the exhibition came about to honor Queen Victoria's Jubilee, it is perhaps worth mentioning that Victoria had protested vehemently at the idea of a Rothschild becoming a member of Parliament, but she did not make a murmur when his son was made a peer by Gladstone, an indication of the slow but significant change of atmosphere.) Documents displayed celebrated the fact that a Jew, George Jessel, was Solicitor-General from 1871 to 1873 and Master of the Rolls from 1873 to 1883. (A Jew would not be a member of the Cabinet until Herbert Samuel became Chancellor of the Duchy of Lancaster in 1909.) In the first part of the exhibition the great names were honored, most notably in a section called "Montefioriana." Sir Francis Goldsmid was recorded as the first Jew to be called to the Bar, in 1833. Some attention was paid to Disraeli, even though he had "seceded from the Synagogue."[11] The Anglo-Jewish tradition of prize fighting was present through portraits of Aby Belasco, the "leary Israelite," and Daniel Mendoza. The seedier side of Jewish life was not totally neglected, as there was a caricature of 1777 depicting Jews receiving stolen goods. There was some depiction of the ordinary life of Jews in Britain in earlier days. There was even a less solemn presentation of the notables through twenty caricatures from *Vanity Fair*, including Disraeli, four Rothschilds, and Sir Albert Sassoon.

The second section in the Albert Hall was devoted to Jewish Ecclesiastical Art, a pioneer effort and an important part of the exhibition, which was clearly a further example of the increase of historical consciousness of the time. There were almost a thousand items on display. Included was the Strauss collection from France, a little more than a hundred items, which some years before had been the first public display of Jewish art in the West (and is now in the Musée de Cluny in Paris) and thirty items from the important collection of Reuben Sassoon, which he had purchased from the estate of Philip Salomon. These were considered the most significant collections of Jewish ecclesiastical art at the time. The inclusion of ritual art in an exhibition that was otherwise devoted to a social and political history of the Jews in Britain was a critical moment, indicating that such art would be taken seriously. From then on this happened to an increasing extent on the Continent, but less in Britain itself,

---

[11] Ibid., p. 63.

with the founding of societies and museums dedicated to Jewish art.[12]

The next section reflected an area where Jewish and Christian interests converged: antiquities from the Holy Land, and perhaps it was noteworthy that items were loaned not only by Sir Julian Goldsmid, Bart., M.P., and Victor Sassoon, but also from the Earl of Crawford and Balcarres, a family much associated with the collection of art. There were items lent by the Palestine Exploration Fund, an enterprise near to Mocatta's heart. As the catalogue stated: "The relation of Jews with the Holy Land is so close that no lapse of time can dissever their connection."[13] There was a certain irony here as it was not too far in the future that the issue of Zionism and the future of the "Holy Land" would deeply divide the British Jewish community as well as complicate the relationships between British Jews and the British state. Further items of ecclesiastical art were displayed at the South Kensington Museum and printed material at the King's Library at the British Museum. The latter included cartoons from the debate on the Jew Bill of 1753, which was passed and then rescinded because of popular pressure. The Bill would have granted naturalization to those Jews not born in Britain. Its rejection revealed British anti-Semitism, and yet, when satisfied, how fleeting it might be. One cartoon had as its caption "No Jews, no wooden shoes" (as the bill would have particularly helped Jews born in Holland), and another, referring to the earlier vote on the Bill, "The Circumcised Gentiles: Jews 96, Christians 55."

The next section listed in the catalogue were the documents at the Public Record Office. They told of the history of the Jews in Britain from the time before the expulsion as well as some material on converted Jews between the expulsion and readmission. That event was celebrated through the display of Menasseh ben Israel's petition to Cromwell of 1655 as well as the pension Cromwell gave him and a portrait of him, a drawing based on an etching by Rembrandt.

There was a quite self-conscious determination in the catalogue and the exhibition to make British Jews aware of themselves. The aim had been "to revive, we might almost say to create, interest in

---

[12] See Michael E. Keen, *Jewish Ritual Art in the Victoria and Albert Museum* (1991). Interestingly enough, the catalogue is dedicated: "In memory of Joseph Jacobs (1854-1916) and Lucien Wolf (1857-1930), authors of the catalogue of the 1887 Anglo-Jewish Exhibition, in acknowledgement of the part they played in establishing awareness of Jewish art."

[13] Jacobs and Wolf, p. 133.

the history of the Jewish race in England."[14] The catalogue provided a defining moment in the history of the Jews in Britain, and this extra-illustrated copy, No. 2 of the deluxe edition, combined with 21 letters touching on the exhibition, mostly addressed to Spielman, make for a rich resource for the study of Anglo-Jewish history.

Although the exhibition did not only deal with triumphs, the feeling it conveyed was that Jews, without losing their own sense of identity, were not only able to but should assimilate to British society. At the time of the exhibition, marriage "out" to non-Jews was comparatively rare, but it would become increasingly common among the grandees of the community. Nevertheless, the emphasis upon them in the success story of the Jews in Britain continued to dominate the story until after the Second World War, climaxing perhaps in the exhibition and publications of 1956 designed to celebrate the tercentenary of readmission.

The beginning of the second wave of studies of the Jews in Britain was marked by Lloyd Gartner's study of 1960 on Eastern European Jewish immigration. The turn toward social history meant a much greater emphasis on "ordinary life," and it was appropriate that in June 1987, a hundred years after the nabobs had granted free admission to the earlier display for the working class on Saturdays in June, the Tower Hamlets Environment Trust had a display celebrating the life of the East European Jews in the East End, the 120,000 to 150,000 immigrants who had come between 1880 and 1915, in contrast to the 2 million who came to the United States. The emphasis upon Israel, and what has been called identity politics, seemed to suggest to some that Jews in Britain had to choose between being Jewish and being British, or at the least that one identity was more important than the other. The postmodernist, and one must say quite attractive "take" on this question, appears to be that one needn't choose but one can celebrate being both, but in a much more self-conscious way than might have been true in the earlier period. (There seems to be an appealing parallel on American campuses where quite a few students of Asian American/Caucasian, African-American/Caucasian or other mixed backgrounds see no reason that they shouldn't identify with both groups.) In much recent scholarship there has been a rejection of assimilation and indeed even of acculturation of the sort suggested by the exhibition of 1887. But now

---

[14] Ibid., p. 207.

there seems to be a growing and powerful idea that national identity can well be a plural or indeed a multicultural identity.

The collection edited by Tony Kushner in 1992, *The Jewish Heritage in British History*, has the significant subtitle *Englishness and Jewishness*. As with most such collections, the essays are rather disparate, but on the whole they attempt to move on from the defensiveness of being Jewish that might be seen to characterize the activity of British Jews who had shaped the events of 1887. The English heritage industry has an air of emphasizing the grand dominant note rather than ethnic groups; it is the Rothschilds' Waddesdon Manor, now belonging to the National Trust, that is open to the public. The ambiguities of the situation are perceptively explored in David Cesarani's essay "Dual Heritage or Duel of Heritages? Englishness and Jewishness in the Heritage Industry." The thrust of the exhibition in 1887 was "let us in," but it must be remembered that the terms were, so to speak, a compromise, and the establishment Jews believed that they could be both Englishmen and Jews, as the title of David Feldman's book has it, perhaps ironically.[15] But in theory at least heritage should encompass all levels. In the 1887 exhibition there were some efforts to do so, though it was generally the grand that dominated. Now there is an increased consciousness of ethnic groups, but there is also present, on the part of some of a Thatcherite persuasion (despite the comparatively high number of Jews who were present in her Cabinet), a desire to return to a more old-fashioned conception of the British state, as a Christian country made up of English, Welsh, and Scots. As Kushner points out, at least one, but not the majority, of the creators of the National History Curriculum in Britain would like the Jews more or less to disappear from the history of their country as it existed before 1950.

Kushner's own essay in the collection, "The End of the 'Anglo-Jewish Progress': Representation of the Jewish East End, 1887-1987," charts the coming to terms with East End Jewish life. The 1887 exhibition took place in the early years of the great immigration, but that event set the style that continued for many years afterwards. It also created an emphasis, by concentrating on the period from the last part of the nineteenth century to the Second World War, on the so-called "contract school" of analysis: that in return for "emancipation," the Jewish community should behave and police

---

[15] David Feldman, *Englishmen and Jews: Social Relations and Political Culture, 1840-1914* (1994).

itself, or rather its grandees would do the policing. Much recent scholarship has attempted to fight free of this syndrome through different means of analysis, by investigating new areas and by facing up, contrary to the wishes of many of the leaders of the community, to those aspects of Jewish life which might be less "attractive."

A greater willingness on the part of the community to do what it thought was right, no matter what others might think, is suggested in the fascinating recent controversy over the issue of erecting an "eruv" in Northwest London, creating an area in which Sabbath restrictions needn't be followed. It did raise the issue of whether the state need help a religious group cope with the restrictions that its own practices impose upon it. The ultimately successful application made the point that the state is obligated not only to favor the Established Church but also to concern itself with the needs of other religions.[16] The agitation marks a moving away from the earlier concept of an "Anglican" Jew through the organization of his religion and even through architecture so that it parallels the Established Church, as Judy Glassman argues quite fascinatingly in her essay "Assimilation by Design: London Synagogues in the Nineteenth Century."

There can be little question that the "contract" idea was in the minds of quite a few Jewish leaders. As Bill Williams, the non-Jewish and superb historian of Manchester Jewry, writes in his essay: "During the struggle for political emancipation in the mid-nineteenth century, the leaders of Anglo-Jewry came to believe (or perhaps they were persuaded by liberal England to believe) that full acceptance of Jews by English society depended upon their good (and very English) behaviour. . . . The leaders of Manchester Jewry took on this mission. Their community had to be seen to be anglicized, integrated, respectable, civic-minded and patriotic. They sought to promote these virtues through a myriad [of] institutions. They became the agents of social conformity and Englishness."[17]

This argument is made relentlessly and one suspects excessively and over-schematically in Richard Bolchover's study of British Jewry and the Holocaust. He acknowledges that as the knowledge of the full horror of the Nazis' murder of the Jews became known to the British Jewish community, there was still a division between know-

---

[16] See Calvin Trillin, "Drawing the Line," *New Yorker* (12 December 1994), 50-62.
[17] Bill Williams, "Heritage and Community: Manchester's English Past," in Kushner, ed., p. 137.

ing and believing. He argues that the "contract" idea prevented the Jewish community from making enough of a fuss that might have led the British government to have done more to save Jews, through more immigration to Britain and to Palestine, and through bombing of the camps and/or the rail lines leading to them. There is little question that the British government should have done more. But it is unclear whether they would have done so if the various parts of the Jewish community had acted differently. In theory, winning the war transcended other goals, an argument that was hard to contradict. But in the course of his discussion, Bolchover presents a rich mosaic of the make-up of the Jewish community, and its conflicts, during the Second World War. There was the ever-present irony during the war that the influx of Jewish refugees ran the risk of increasing British anti-Semitism, and indeed there was a degree of anti-refugee feeling among the more acculturated British Jews.

As he states, it is hard to imagine among the 385,000 Jews in Britain at the time of the Second World War, that there was absolute agreement of thought. Yet he does go on to argue that "British Jews took civic loyalty to mean conformity. . . . Jews sought respectability."[18] He contends that the Jewish community was too deferential; it feared that the state would abrogate its "contract." He may well be right that the Jewish community should have done more, but one suspects that it was more the wartime situation and the tendency to accept the status quo rather than a sense of some sort of contractual relation with the state that prevented more dramatic steps. And of course there were some who tried to take more action, such as Chimen Abramsky, who accused the heads of the Jewish community of "appeasement."[19]

There is valuable material in this study, but it becomes increasingly judgmental and intolerant. It seems highly unlikely that British Jews failed to do more because they had "neither collective self-esteem nor a sense of being in control of their own lives."[20] The more imaginative work in Jewish history would appear to be done by those who do not necessarily treat, whether for good or ill, Jews as a unique group—interesting as they may be—but rather as one who have similarities (as well as some special characteristics) to other "outsider" groups that may have a problematic relationship to the British state and society.

---

[18] Richard Bolchover, *British Jewry and the Holocaust* (1993), p. 78.
[19] Ibid., p. 110.
[20] Ibid., p. 156.

Much of the newer scholarship, frequently using the techniques of social history, is based on the dynamics of the interrelationships between Jews and the broader society. In a series of very effective chapters, although they tend to be somewhat separate studies, David Katz provides a rich sense of Jewish life in Britain over a long sweep of time in his *The Jews in the History of England, 1485-1850* (1994). He includes the period when there were still not officially any Jews in Britain, discussing the small Sephardic community.

Katz has a splendid and much-needed concern with the question of how Jews affected the wider community, or indeed were used for political purposes. One reason that the agitation against the Jew Bill of 1753 did not have much lasting effect was that it was in truth more a stick for the Tories to use to fight the Whigs than an issue of genuine religious concern, although it may have raised some primitive fears of circumcision. He also discusses the rather attractive philo-Semitism of the royal dukes, the sons of George III, most particularly the visit of the Duke of Sussex to the Great Synagogue in 1809. As Katz points out, Jews did not move forward politically at the same pace as non-Anglican Christians, and it was not until 1845 that municipal offices were open to them. Britain could more easily think of itself as a nation consisting of Welsh, Scots, and English than of Christians and non-Christians. It is only recently that "Christian name" has ceased to be common usage in Britain for an individual's first name.

One can understand how the "contract" theory came into being, as powerful Jews appear to have a closer "flirtation" with the state, a willingness to be of some use to it, than may be characteristic of other minority groups. Katz's excellent essays are, in a sense, a compromise between the older view of leading up to the "emancipation" of 1858, with which the epilogue of the book concludes, and a highly commendable aim to present a history that is illuminating for both Jewish and more general British historical concerns. As Katz reminds us, this "emancipation" was for a comparatively small community of 35,000 then mostly in London, one-tenth of its present size. Even that, of course, is only approximately a half of a percent of the present British population.

In varying ways recent scholarship demonstrates the new vitality in Jewish studies. Geoffrey Alderman, in his *Modern British Jewry* (1992), sympathetically tells the more exclusively Jewish story, dominated by the needs of those Jews in residence and in many ways doing quite well, having to cope with the influx from Eastern Europe.

There is a certain irony in a remark Balfour made about the Jews in 1905. He was at the time Tory Prime Minister but he later gave his name to the Declaration pledging Britain to support a Jewish national home. (As Bevin was memorably and nastily to point out after the Second World War, support for Israel and keeping out Jews were not irreconcilable positions.) Balfour was supporting the immigration bill of that year: "A state of things could easily be imagined in which it would not be to the advantage of the civilisation of the country that there should be an immense body of persons who, however patriotic, able and industrious, however much they threw themselves into the national life, remained a people apart, and not merely held a religion differing from the vast majority of their fellow-countrymen, but only intermarried among themselves."[21]

The sort of dilemma I've been attempting to consider here could hardly be stated more concisely. The historic alliance with Liberalism was further weakened through the failure of the Liberals to repeal the Alien Act when they came to power at the end of 1905. The community was buffeted in the late nineteenth century and beyond by what was seen as Jewish support for socialism and its questioning of the status quo, and also, perhaps to a greater degree, by the dilemmas presented by Zionism to the position of a diasporist Jew. Lucien Wolf, who had done so much for the exhibition of 1887, was during the period of the First World War, a chief representative of the view emphasizing the Englishness of the English Jew. As Alderman writes of this dispute, quoting Moses Gaster: "The claim to be 'Englishmen of the Jewish persuasion' was condemned as 'an absolute self-delusion.' Thus began a literary and pamphlet war which carried on through to 1917: at its heart was the clash between two view of Jewish identity and two views of what Emancipation (more especially in Britain) actually meant."[22] Some Jewish leaders even believed that Emancipation might be repealed if Palestine became a reality as a Jewish state.[23] Alderman concludes his highly useful study by stating that there is no longer an Anglo-Jewish community. Yet he feels that there needs to be a new institutional arrangement that will reflect the present diversity among British Jews. One suspects that most British Jews, no matter how uninvolved, still consider themselves Jewish, and that it remains a potentially disturbing factor in their relations with the other inhabitants of their islands.

---

[21] Geoffrey Alderman, *Modern British Jewry* (1992), p. 133.
[22] Ibid., p. 246.
[23] Ibid., p. 251.

Perhaps the most ambitious recent work is David Feldman's *Englishmen and Jews: Social Relations and Political Culture, 1840-1914* (1994), which nobly attempts to write English Jewish history as part of the general story from 1840 to 1914, while providing a rich picture of many aspects of Jewish life during that period. As a firmly grounded political and social nineteenth-century historian, he is more sympathetic than many historians of the Jews have been to the concerns of those who opposed their "emancipation," not on the basis of some primitive anti-Semitism, but on the foundation of a reasonable position—that Britain was a Christian state and should remain so. After all, political rights were not guaranteed, and it would be very rare for any of these opponents to believe that the Jews should be persecuted.

By discussing the state as a different concept than the nation, a community of shared interests, Feldman sharpens our understanding of the difficulties of Jewish relations to the state and to the nation. Our current concern, as the essays in the Kushner volume make clear, with "Englishness" highlights the question of how "Jewishness" connects with that concept. The very implication of Feldman's title is that there is quite a profound difference. The title with its suggestion that it is individuals who make up groups quite splendidly conveys the special paradox of English society: group thinking combined with the idea that individuals can transcend their particular group. The question is whether transcending means leaving one group for the other. Jews themselves have no agreement to what extent their identity goes beyond a religious one, or perhaps even to a greater degree of complexity, to what degree and in what ways does the identity remain when the religion diminishes. What does it mean in the United States or in Great Britain to be a secular Jew? Feldman projects a less benign picture of English Liberalism, previously seen as more welcoming to Jews who are willing to accept its terms. Perhaps the English Liberals were too demanding? Male Jews were already circumcised—were they to be emasculated? They were the genital other. Were Jews to be made into Englishmen, or even better, Christians? As Feldman reminds us, there were powerful conversion organizations in operation during this period.

In discussing immigrant Jews in the second part of his study, Feldman steers a convincing middle path between the older conceptions that saw Jewish immigrants as either upwardly mobile individuals or proletarian socialists. Feldman sensibly depicts English Jews as part of the history of the development of capitalism that, as recent studies have shown, had a greater persistence of small work-places than one might have expected. He interestingly weakens the English immigrant Jews' claim to be special. One is grateful to him for bringing Jewish history in from the margins: "The workshop trades of the Jewish East End were an integral part of industrial expansion in the late nineteenth century."[24] So too the Jewish labor movement, as in the three strikes that Feldman examines, was part of the general growth of activity and militancy that marked labor history from the latter part of the nineteenth century on. But it also had special characteristics because it was Jewish, particularly in the involvement of Russian Jewish revolutionaries.

In the last section of his work, Feldman examines the relation of Jews to the state. He points out the paradox that even though the Jews were undoubtedly far more persecuted in Eastern Europe, they had more control there over the mores of their own community than in the liberal West. In the East, they were to a greater degree self-governing, even though in a very circumscribed way. The oppressive state left little room for the ambiguities that were present in Britain. The situation became even more complex after the passing of the Alien Act in 1905. It became harder to be naturalized: being a good citizen in terms of taxes was no longer sufficient. Potential new subjects were expected to possess a degree of Englishness, as manifested in the ability to read the language. As the government became more activist in looking after its charges, it became more restrictive in defining those for whom it would be concerned. (Sound familiar?) Feldman perceptively points out that in the area of worker rights (and in very different ways over the question of Zionism), many Jews became political participants not as they had in the earlier period, in order to emphasize the degree they were moving away from traditional Jewish concerns, but rather to serve them.

The three sections of this study may not be integrated as well as one might hope (much like Jews and the English?), but there is no question that this book examines significant questions in imaginative ways, and is part of the new wave in history that merges Jewish and British history.

The same can be said of Bernard Wasserstein's *Herbert Samuel: A Political Life* (1992). Is Wasserstein an Anglo-Jewish historian, or a British historian who uses Jewish topics, or both? Over the years he has written a series of books, most particularly *Britain and the Jews*

---

[24] Feldman, p. 190.

of Europe 1939-1945 and *The Secret Lives of Trebitsch Lincoln*, marked by their brilliance and sophistication. Now with the biography of Herbert Samuel, a member of the Cousinhood, the first Jewish member of the British Cabinet, he has made a significant contribution to both areas. Samuel was an important politician at the secondary level, if that is not a contradiction. Indeed, Samuel would have been a less interesting figure if he hadn't been Jewish. To a degree, he was a victim of anti-Semitism when it appeared to some that he was involved in the Marconi scandal. In fact, he was an individual of overwhelming propriety; he conformed perhaps excessively to being a proper Englishman. Although he had little interest in Judaism, and abandoned his faith while at Balliol College, Oxford, he compromised with his family and "returned, if not to the faith, at any rate to the fold."[25] He was elected to Parliament in 1902 and became a proponent of the new Liberalism. Ironically, as undersecretary at the Home Office in the Liberal government of 1905 he had to enforce the Alien Act, although perhaps not as stridently as the Tories who passed it might have wished. Samuel was not particularly well liked and he seemed rather a stick. And yet, much to Chaim Weizmann's surprise, he turned out to be very interested, knowledgeable, and sympathetic to the cause of Zionism (unlike his cousin Edwin Montagu). And he would be, after the war, the first British High Commissioner in Palestine (although some felt he may have leaned over backwards to be fair to the Arabs). He would have remained in the country if it had not been considered awkward for his successor. "Zionism helped him reconcile the conflict between belief and action that had troubled him so deeply. . . . Zionism was the one political passion of a singularly passionless career."[26]

It was not an exciting life, exemplary as it was in many ways. He became something of a popular figure from 1942 to 1949 as a member of the very successful broadcast program, the Brains Trust. His career can be taken to stand for both the triumph and the limitations of the world vision that was put forward in 1887. It was an outlook with limitations as well as high aspirations. It led perhaps to the idea of the Jew in Britain as someone who needed too much to compromise with the needs of the state, and also in Feldman's terms, with the needs of the nation. It was a vision which allowed for triumphs for the Jewish community in Britain and for its leaders. But it is no

---

[25] Wasserstein, *Herbert Samuel*, p. 21.
[26] Ibid., pp. 201-4.

longer a vision that can illuminate how we should think now about Britons who happen to be Jews, and to what degree they are, and are not, Anglo-Jewish or English/British. All the evidence suggests that the study of British Jewish history is demonstrating an extraordinary vitality.

31

Two Views of Chaim Weizmann

Norman Rose's *Chaim Weizmann* (1986) is an extremely satisfactory biography, encompassing within comparatively few pages the grand sweep of the life of one of the most important personages of the twentieth century: Chaim Weizmann, first president of the State of Israel, one of its founding fathers, and, one might argue, the most important. It was he who painfully and slowly brought the dream to fruition. That the present state is different from what he might have hoped and that his particular conception, like everyone else's, was not perfect, can be accepted as inevitable, and do not diminish his stature. There is room for many further and ongoing investigations into his life and influence, most notably the multivolume biography by Jehuda Reinharz, the first volume of which was published too late to be used by Rose. But in its own right the present book is a very welcome achievement.

I am not a historian of Zionism or of Israel, or of British foreign policy, such a central concern in the creation of Israel and in Weizmann's life. What I have attempted to do in my work is to understand the nature of British society, how it functions, how it comes to decisions, what are its values, what are its strengths and weaknesses. It might be said that Weizmann, in a far more important way—as a matter of life and death and the creation of a state—was engaged in something of the same endeavor. Much of his life was a love/hate relationship with Britain and that is admirably documented and discussed in Rose's book. It is no doubt an advantage that Rose himself was British before he was Israeli and has written previously on the "Gentile Zionists," as well as the diplomat Vansittart, and Sir Lewis Namier.

Born in Motol in Russia, and then moving to Pinsk, Weizmann

traveled steadily westward, to Switzerland, and then as far as Manchester and London. His Zionist work meant that he spent much time in the United States, where he had dramatic and extremely important encounters with Roosevelt and Truman, and struggled with Louis Brandeis and Abba Hillel Silver. But America was too far west for him: his fund-raising trips across the country were hard tasks rather than pleasures. Like many others before and since, he did not savor the broad welcome of America (however mitigated by restrictive practices). Rather, he was profoundly attracted to the far more selective, indeed snobbish and complicated response that Britain gives to distinguished foreigners. Ultimately he would turn—in many ways, but never completely—in bitterness and in disgust from his hosts.

Historians are frequently too influenced by the present state of world powers, so it is relevant to remind oneself of the overwhelming position that Britain occupied in the early twentieth century, and to recall that the future possibility of a Jewish state was to such a degree in her gift. Weizmann certainly realized this when he wrote about his first visit to London in 1903: "I have never in my life felt so well as here. . . . This is the hub of the world and, really, you sense the breathing of a giant, the city of cities" (p. 76). The English Jews had been his early heroes—Sir Moses Montefiore and the Rothschilds—but he would become a dedicated adversary of those generally very well placed and wealthy English Jews who were staunch enemies of Zionism. Elegant, multilingual (but it is striking that he was most effective as an orator in Yiddish), a cosmopolitan, in due course a wealthy and highly distinguished scientist, seen by his detractors as being corrupted by his admiration for the English and their way of life, he was nevertheless fully aware of the dangers of assimilation and the considerable degree to which it impeded the development of Zionism. Weizmann was firmly dedicated to the return to Palestine: it was the determining principle of his life however diplomatically he might seem to consider alternatives.

This study is primarily a political one. But Rose has a keen sense of Weizmann's personality, and does not hesitate, while fundamentally deeply admiring him, to point out his defects. There is in the middle of the book a splendid character sketch, "The Chief," that focuses on that personality, so crucial to an understanding of his career. Rose writes about Weizmann: "If Weizmann had one political idée fixe, it was his faith in the connection between the Zionist movement and Britain. This runs through his career from the un-

formed, intellectual gropings of the boy of eleven to the mature re-
flections of the elder statesman" (p.269).

A major irony of Weizmann's life was that, despite his awareness
of the dangers of assimilation, so much of his own drive was in that
direction. In many ways, of course, it was extremely valuable for the
Jewish cause that he would learn how to deal with the British in order to secure his aims. As he made more and more money from his
scientific patents, he increasingly adopted the style of the English
nouveau riche anxious to join the higher ranks of English society: the
grand house in London (a fifteen room mansion), the love of English
gardens, the Rolls Royce, the assumption that the grandest way of
living was the proper one. In this he was strongly supported by his
stylish and snobbish Russian Jewish wife Vera to whom apparently
he was not particularly faithful. With his busy life he paid the almost
inevitable price of having his two sons Benji and Michael become
somewhat estranged and uninterested in Zionism. Their governess,
Miss Usher, whom Benji would ultimately describe as a Rasputin in
the household, dedicated herself "as a Christian" to giving the boys
a "normal" upbringing. They were educated in the very proper way
of public schools—Westminster and Rugby—and Cambridge: Michael refused Abba Eban's invitation to join the University Zionist
organization, saying that he had more than enough of that at home.

Weizmann's distance from his own immediate family was in contrast to his closeness to his mother and siblings in Israel. It is also revealing that two of his most valued advisers were Baffy Dugdale,
Balfour's niece, at the heart of the British Establishment, and the
great historian of eighteenth-century England, Sir Lewis Namier.
Namier, of Polish-Jewish descent, but raised as a Roman Catholic,
ultimately becoming an Anglican, firmly identified with the idea of a
National Home because of his belief that only land, as in the England that he was concerned with as a historian, would provide his
people, the Jews, with stability. (And Weizmann remarked about
Mrs. Dugdale in 1937, "She is what is left of the Balfour Declaration" [p. 331].)

In Rose's recounting of the story, the high point of Weizmann's
career is reached, not with the bittersweet achievement of the presi-
dency, but with the Balfour Declaration of November 1917, which
pledged British commitment to a National Home in Palestine. Weizmann's adroit diplomatic skills had been crucial in bringing about
the Declaration. Although the next three decades would be tragically
marked by the disowning of this original document, it was central in

the creation of the State of Israel. By 1936 Weizmann realized that the cause of Zionism could no longer be dependent on Britain, yet he never abandoned his emphasis—stated to numerous Commissions—on the significance of the British interest in doing something for Jews, particularly marked in three centuries by Cromwell, Palmerston, and Balfour. In the British tradition, Weizmann, though moved by strong ideals, was a firm empiricist. In the late 1930s he was quietly willing to adopt the idea of partition as the way to achieve statehood.

Weizmann first worked his wiles in Manchester, securing the assistance and advice of the great editor of the *Manchester Guardian*, C. P. Scott. Lloyd George no doubt exaggerated the degree to which the Declaration was made in return for Weizmann's contribution to the war effort—his scientific work on acetone used in the production of explosives. But that work, in addition to giving him the financial security that is so frequently a mark of the "chief players" in the British political game, also opened the way for him into the corridors of power where he could advance the Zionist cause. It is deeply impressive how throughout his life he was able to maintain his career of scientist and Zionist leader.

While the "Englishing" of Weizmann was central to his achievements, it provided the reasons for his enemies later to attack him, when the British in the postwar years backtracked on their pledge, and the pro-Arab sentiments of officials, mostly in the Foreign Office, came to influence policy. The tragic consequence—as Hitler's persecution of the Jews grew more violent and more evident in the 1930s and during World War II—was that these officials undermined even the attempts to save mere segments of European Jewry. Weizmann, who had predicted the destruction of the six million, increasingly turned on the British.

Rose has framed his study with vignettes of Weizmann in Israel. He begins with a prologue of his arrival there in 1948 as its president; he ends with Weizmann as the "Prisoner of Rehovot." By then, Israel had triumphed over Britain, with the Weizmann Institute encompassing the Sieff Institute, named in memory of a member of the Marks & Spencer families, and Weizmann himself living in a country house—designed by the great modern architect, Erich Mendelsohn—not of the sort that one would have found in England.

It was in New York, not London, that the great rallies at the time of the creation of Israel were held. But it was Weizmann's commitment to Britain that made so much of what he accomplished possible. Looking at both Weizmann and Britain realistically, Rose has made that relationship, with all its defects and tragedies, abundantly clear. He has written, to my mind, a compelling biography.

Jehuda Reinharz's *Chaim Weizmann: The Making of a Statesman* (1993) is the second volume of a multivolume biography of its subject. *The Making of a Statesman* covers a mere eight years, from 1914 to 1922, but those years contained decisive events for the country that became Israel: the Balfour Declaration of 1917, committing Britain to support of the idea of a Jewish national home in Palestine ("a," not "the," to avoid the implication that this was where all Jews should be); the founding of Hebrew University in Jerusalem; and the declaration of the British mandate in Palestine, a crucial step along the road to the building of the state.

The strength and paradoxically also the weakness of Jehuda Reinharz's detailed, indeed overly detailed, study is summarized in the very first line of the book: "This multivolume biography of Chaim Weizmann is in many ways a history of the Zionist movement from the last quarter of the 19th century to the creation of the state of Israel in the mid-20th." Reinharz does provide the reader, in his conclusion, with a brilliant character sketch of Weizmann. But whether by choice or inadvertence he does not penetrate as deeply as he might into his subject. The research is immense; the reader learns of the endless to-and-fro, the many individuals, agencies, actions, and reactions that necessarily are a part of the life of negotiation— particularly intense at the time of the First World War, when much of normal politics was suspended. In all this Weizmann was a major player. Yet we are not told enough, as the story goes forward, of how his personality shaped the events in which he was so crucially involved.

That story, of course, is fascinating. Weizmann was born in 1874 in Motol in western Russia. Since the age of 11 he had been a committed Zionist, and even then, in a letter to a teacher, he recognized that Britain needed to play a crucial role. From the beginning he pursued intensely his double career as a scientist and as a Zionist. In 1904 he came to Britain to be a chemist, and Reinharz provides a helpfully detailed chapter on Weizmann's scientific work on acetone and its importance for explosives. With the outbreak of war, this work became a factor of very great practical significance. While Reinharz dismisses the myth that the Balfour Declaration was a thank-you for Weizmann's scientific work, there is no question that it was his achievement as a scientist, and his contribution to the war effort, that moved him into the highest levels of British life.

Weizmann and high British politics are the nub of this volume, but it is not until the character sketch at the conclusion that the earlier pages cohere and acquire biographical depth. It is a pity we are not told more, earlier in the book, of the interplay between Weizmann's personality and the style of the British who were essential to his grand design. He had the ability, rare in a foreigner, to understand the nuanced complications of British life and its special hierarchical style.

Unlike many of the most distinguished and rich members of the Anglo-Jewish community at that time, Weizmann was stirred from his earliest days by the vision of a Jewish national home, largely secular, as a necessity for world Jewry. As he observed, the Jew "is felt by the outside world to be still something different, still an alien, and the measure of his success and prominence in the various walks of life which are thrown open to him is, broadly speaking, the measure of the dislike and distrust which he earns."

Weizmann's genius was that he was able to take advantage of the social situation he was in; he could charm and persuade such leaders as Lloyd George and Balfour, as well as the powerful editor of *The Manchester Guardian*, C. P. Scott. He did so without demeaning himself; he remained his own man, and was respected for it.

Weizmann was not asking Britain to support the idea of a Jewish homeland without receiving a great deal in return. With the war on, Germany and Austria were aware that they could use Zionism to encourage the Jewish communities in their countries to give even more help to their war effort. For Britain there was, too, the glittering prize of the Jews of the United States: Weizmann worked to persuade the most influential of them that Britain was likely to do more for the Zionist cause than Germany.

For Weizmann, however, this American game was far less attractive than the British one. At the time—although he would later turn from Britain in despair—he relished what he considered the complicated and sophisticated responses of the British mandarins. Weizmann, the Russian Jew, was determined to conduct himself so that the most powerful nation in the world would fulfill his wishes.

Palestine was part of the Turkish empire. If the Allies won the war, that empire was ripe to be dismembered. For Weizmann, Reinharz explains, Palestine might be both British and Jewish. (Indeed, after the war it did come under the authority of the British state, in cooperation with the Zionist organizations, through the mandate system.)

Of course, nothing is as simple as that. We are spared few of the endless controversies that Weizmann was involved in with his colleagues, and his rather excessive use of the threat of resignation to get his way. He was fully aware of the Arab problem, for instance. Were there possibilities that the Jews and the Arabs might have achieved some sort of compromise? Weizmann worked with Lawrence of Arabia and others in the years after the end of the war, attempting to reach such a compromise. It was not to be.

Israel itself would have been unlikely to come into existence if Weizmann had not brilliantly played the British game. His triumph was the letter that Balfour, at that point Foreign Secretary, sent to Lord Rothschild, the most eminent English Jew in 1917, a declaration that "His Majesty's Government view with favor the establishment in Palestine of a national home for the Jewish people." At the same time, the brief statement pointed out that such a step should not "prejudice the civil and religious rights of existing non-Jewish communities in Palestine, or the rights and political status enjoyed by Jews in any other country."

Weizmann went home and, joined by friends, celebrated with a Hasidic dance. It was his greatest moment.

32

NINETEENTH-CENTURY JEWS

Michael Ragussis's *Figures of Conversion: 'The Jewish Question' and English National Identity* (1995) is a literary study with quite interesting broader implications for England in the nineteenth century, and both before and since. At first, one thinks its claims are excessive—can the Jewish question really be that important for English society as a whole? But by the conclusion of the study the reader is at least convinced that the position of Jews in the English world sheds considerable light on wider questions.

It has been a tragedy over the centuries that non-Jews have obsessively concerned themselves to such a negative extent about the Jews, culminating in this century in the horror of the Holocaust. A majority in most societies does not seem capable of living comfortably with minorities in its midst; English society, with far less tragic consequences, has been no exception. As Linda Colley has reminded us, in the eighteenth century (and earlier), Britons frequently defined themselves in contradistinction to the other as Catholic. The Jews, having been expelled from Britain in the thirteenth century, were readmitted in the seventeenth. The evangelical tradition in Britain had a special relationship to the people of the book, the coreligionists of Jesus (also seen as his murderers). But for many this resulted in a determination to convert Jews to Christianity. The English tradition is somewhat paradoxical and possibly unique. Although conversion may be the goal, those who do not convert are still tolerated and not persecuted; in fact, in the course of the nineteenth century Jews were granted wider political privileges. At the same time, English society is hierarchical: the Jews, as was true for other outsider groups, were hardly regarded as being at the same level as English Anglicans.

Michael Ragussis somewhat raises one's historical expectations as it would almost appear at first that he is going to give us an analysis of the societies dedicated to the purpose of conversion: the London Society for Promoting Christianity amongst the Jews, and the British Society for the Propagation of the Gospel among the Jews. Such is not the case, although the role of conversion is central to his discussion. In many ways, his is a traditional literary study in the modern mode, with a careful and insightful treatment of a group of nineteenth-century novels. Although attention is paid to a wide range of writings, the major texts (some comparatively neglected, others much discussed) are Maria Edgeworth's *Harrington* (1817), Sir Walter Scott's *Ivanhoe* (1819), Grace Aguilar's *The Vale of Cedars* (1850), Benjamin Disraeli's trilogy, *Coningsby* (1844), *Sybil* (1845), and *Tancred* (1847), some of Anthony Trollope's novels, and then concluding with George Eliot's *Daniel Deronda* (1876). There are also twenty illustrations, mostly anti-Semitic political cartoons.

Does Ragussis exaggerate in his claim for the significance of the conversion story? Perhaps a bit. The Jews were a minute proportion of the English population, although they were no doubt more important than their numbers might suggest. Ragussis is convincing that the issue of conversion has a significant place in the preoccupations of nineteenth-century England, but I am not sure that after the publication of *Ivanhoe*, Scott "rewrites English history as Anglo-Jewish history—a history of persecution and subsequent guilt. . . . The representation of Jewish persecution, including the history of Christian efforts at proselytizing the Jews, became a critical tool in constructing English identity in relation to other European identities." That "'the Jewish question' [was] at the center of England's national agenda, . . . at the heart of English national identity" is perhaps possible but certainly not provable.

Ragussis presents fascinating points and insights. There is a frequent playing off against the metaphor of the Spanish Inquisition and the expulsion of the Jews from Spain in 1492. One aim in England was to convert the Jews, to make them properly English. But mightn't they, as was claimed in Spain, frequently continue to be secretly Jewish? It was an extraordinary coincidence that the most important Conservative politician of the second half of the nineteenth century was a converted Jew: Benjamin Disraeli. Unlike Trollope's characters, the Rev. Emilius and Ferdinand Lopez, Disraeli, as his name revealed, had no desire to hide his origins. Thanks to the legalism of English society, political doors were open to Disraeli that were closed to his former coreligionists. He reveled in the financial power of the Jews, as depicted in fiction in his character Sidonia in *Coningsby*, and in fact from the help he received from the Rothschilds in purchasing the Suez Canal. He adored the traditions of the Jews, and claimed that he saw their culmination in Christianity. One would have thought that he had done what English society wished: he had converted. Yet like the Marranos of Spain, he aroused profound suspicion: how genuine was his conversion? In his support of Turkey against Russia over the issue of the Balkan atrocities, and his apparent indifference to those deaths, wasn't he subjecting English policy to Jewish desires to support a possibly sympathetic power in the Middle East, rather than helping the Christians by supporting Russia, the enemy of the Jews? Disraeli's case raised the fundamental question, which has fueled much of recent work in Anglo-Jewish history: can a Jew be completely English? There is no question about the importance of that question. One is less sure that it needs to be resolved in order for the English to have a firm sense of their own identity.

This study concludes with a fine discussion of *Daniel Deronda*. Earlier Matthew Arnold plays a prominent part, particularly in his famous depiction of the role of Hellenism and Hebraism in *Culture and Anarchy* (1869) and elsewhere. He was more sympathic to the Jews than his father Thomas, who saw them as "voluntary strangers" in the land. Although Arnold recognized the importance of both traditions, he favored Hellenism. George Eliot favored Hebraism, and in her novel challenges the conversion strategy. Deronda has been raised as an English gentleman. Not knowing that he was Jewish, he cannot secretly be one. With trepidations and hesitations, he confronts his true identity as a Jew, culminating in an interview with his mother, a prominent singer, in Genoa, a way station in the past for the Jews fleeing Spain. She had converted from Judaism years before and had given away her son to be raised as a Christian. He marries the Jewish Mirah and leaves for Palestine to work toward a Jewish national home. The resolution of the novel would appear to answer the question raised in this study in a negative way: indeed, it is not possible to be both an English gentleman and a Jew. In the course of the work, however, Ragussis has told us much about English society and the role the Jew—and the idea of the Jew—played in it.

PART SEVEN

SERGEANT PEPPER

33

SERGEANT PEPPER'S LONELY HEARTS CLUB BAND

The Beatles have been looked at in many ways, and I would like to look at one album of theirs, *Sergeant Pepper's Lonely Hearts Club Band* (1967), as a social document of England.

The Beatles' attitude to politics seems somewhat unconcerned and unattached. In that, as in so much else, they reflect their city of origin, Liverpool, in the county of Lancashire. They moved to plush, if at times somewhat psychedelic houses outside of London, not quite the Englishman's dream of the countryside, but perhaps more a lower middle-class dream on a grand scale of suburbia gone riot. In short, the dream of the poor boys of Liverpool of what money could buy. The Beatles are refreshingly beyond the attitudes of earlier decades—not for them any of the disillusion with the world of the 1920s, or the guilt about money of the 1930s, or the sense of anger yielding to a sense of making it of the 1950s. Not that they are complacent, and there is a certain simpleminded religiosity in their former interest in the Maharishi. They did not pretend to be more than they are—entertainers. But at the same time, like all the greatest entertainers, they are also artists, and probably of their many albums, *Sergeant Pepper* is the most sustained, the most thought-out of all—a single work of art.

That album, like their others, reflects their background and environment. And the fact that they are from Liverpool can tell us something about provincial life in England. England tends to be rather London-oriented. Ironically, Liverpool is now probably better known to Americans, at least those of the Beatles' generation, than London. Allen Ginsberg has characteristically somewhat exaggerated in his remark that "Liverpool is at the present moment the center of the consciousness of the human universe." At the same time the city can be taken to stand for signs of liberation in English culture and society. Perhaps a new pattern, a certain freedom from the conventions, from the Establishment, is finally happening in England. Undeniably there is a selfishness—a sort of hell-with-you spirit—"I'm all right, Jack." But the Beatles themselves are extraordinarily free—in their kookiness and directness. As they saw with startling candor, they were more popular than Jesus. Of course they are so rich they needn't worry about what they do or say—and they have used their money to help others to achieve a great sense of liberation. The North had come into its own, and the North tends to be much freer of self-consciousness, that besetting sin and virtue of so many Englishmen, particularly the literary members of the middle class. The North—the unposh part of England above a line that can be drawn from Bristol to the Wash of Norfolk—is much more direct, much more humorous, sometimes crude, sometimes sly, and very clever, but not sophisticated, and it is that sense of directness, of immediacy, to which the Beatles owe a lot of their appeal. They are artful and wildly imaginative, without getting lost in convolutions, and in the sophistications which one might expect in the many rooms, nuances, and social relationships of a country house in the South. In the past, provincial young men were doing their best to "make it" in London. London was the beloved object, and although the Beatles lived there, they still seem to be more of Liverpool than of the metropolis. As Roger McGough, a Liverpool poet has said: "I think of [the Beatles, the Liverpool movement in art, poetry, and music] as a Liverpool thing as opposed to a London thing, or a capital thing, or a public school thing." Or as Adrian Henri, another Liverpool poet and artist has remarked, "The Beatles were the first cultural phenomenon of any kind who made it outside London first."

Liverpool has a long and distinguished history, and although in so many ways it is a dreary nineteenth-century industrial city of the North, it has at the same time the excitement, the sort of freshness of the sea air, of a port, with its sense of being able to get out, cut loose, to see new worlds, and easily come back home. By its very location, where the Mersey meets the Irish Sea, it acts as a mixing place of cultures, where Englishmen and Welsh would naturally congregate, and where there is a mammoth Irish population. It is here that the cheapest passage from Ireland lands one—wasn't it in Liverpool that Brendan Behan learned to be a rebel? At the same time, as a port, the second-greatest port to London, the world headquarters for Cunard, it was from here that so many immigrants from England, and the rest of Europe came to America, while Chinese, Africans, and West Indians congregate in Liverpool in considerable number. It is a much freer community than much of the rest of England—less a man's town than London or Manchester, where women are as saucy or free in their Northern respectable way as anywhere else in England, and less reluctant to go about than in other places—perhaps suggested by that famous Amazonian Labour M.P. for the Exchange district of Liverpool, the late Bessie Braddock. In their way, the politics of Liverpool also conspire to make it the ideal place for the launching of a sense of freedom, a certain ambiguity and excitement of political positions. It is the sort of city one would expect to be on the Left. In fact, it has alternated over the years between being controlled by Tory and Liberal, and later Labour, and the greatest political figures to come from Liverpool, Canning and Gladstone, were both extremely flexible: Canning a Tory of the most imaginative and adventuresome leanings, and Gladstone, beginning as a Tory, then an increasingly radical Liberal. (Before we think only in terms of rosy glow, let's not forget that much of Liverpool's early prosperity was based on the slave trade.) The third but lesser great political figure associated with Liverpool, whose statue which like the other public statues in Liverpool, is subjected to the Beatles-like game of continually being mucked about with—that is, moved from place to place as it suits the whims of the inhabitants—was Huskisson. He was that extremely imaginative statesman and economist who was killed so foolishly at the opening of the Liverpool and Manchester Railway in 1830. (His death almost had the feeling of a Beatle happening. He was, I believe, an albino, and had difficulty seeing—and as he was stepping up to his carriage at some point in the ceremonies, he was run down by the famous locomotive *Rocket*, and became the first railway casualty.)

The city was a great commercial center. But not until the Beatles has it had any particularly creative, cultural significance, although it has had that sort of heavy but impressive cultural seriousness that one associates with the North. The South disdained it, from the eighteenth century on, if not before, as caught by one eighteenth-century traveler: "Their buildings and places of amusement may please the natives, but they have neither novelty nor a superior elegance to attract the notice of the judicious itinerant, and are consequently deficient in essentials to embellish the historic page." It is a city with much of its population living close to the margin, but that does not prevent so many of its inhabitants from having a largeness of spirit and a fierce sense of local independence and pride, particularly in its two famous local football teams. Culture was important throughout the nineteenth century. While no famous writers or artists came from Liverpool, even to begin there and go on to London, the city fathers approved of art. Though they tended to be rather conservative, they were willing to support such endeavors as the Walker Art Gallery, founded by a great local brewing family. Leyland, Whistler's patron with whom he quarreled so bitterly, was a Liverpool figure. Augustus John had an important Liverpool period, in which he painted a famous portrait of the Lord Mayor, making him and his footman, in their costumes, look rather like Don Quixote and Sancho Panza, much to the horror of the city fathers. In any case the Lord Mayor kept the portrait, and with a sensible regard for "brass," he sold it to a man from Sussex for £1,000, refusing to acquire the offered immortality in the Tate Gallery for a far lesser price.

The grandness of Liverpool, and its eclecticism, are summed up in its cathedrals. As Quentin Hughes has written: "Where else are to be found two giant cathedrals facing each other at opposite ends of a street called Hope Street?" These are the Anglican and Catholic cathedrals—the plans for their very creation suggest the sureties of the end of the nineteenth century in Liverpool. The Anglican one was designed in the Gothic Style, as stipulated in the set competition, by Giles Gilbert Scott, at the age of 23, still slowly completing itself years later with many modifications. The Catholic one was designed by the great Edwardian architect of mammoth buildings, Edwin Lutyens. But only the crypt was built, and the rest, revolutionary in design, has been completed later by a young architect, Frederick Gibberd. The new building is monumental and exciting, and aiming at modernity and freedom, and away from tradition, although at the same time committed to the sense of life at the heart of religion.

And so too are the Beatles. They are certainly tied to the visual and popular artist tradition of their city—the thriving port city of so many diverse groups. And it helps make them receptive to so many ideas and currents within and without their society. In that city, they participated in both the visual and pop life, the noise of the Cavern Club and the Mersey Sound, that came to the fore at the end of the 1950s. John Lennon, perhaps the greatest member of the group, whose father was associated with the music halls—the old Edwardian strain that runs through the songs of Sergeant Pepper—was himself a student at the Liverpool College of Art. And so was the fifth

Beatle, Stuart Sutcliffe, a painter and bass guitarist, depicted on the cover of *Sergeant Pepper*, who died in Hamburg at the age of 21 of a brain tumor. As John Willett has written of him, "Probably no recent Liverpool painter has worked with anything resembling this intensity; and the range, variety and colour of his last few months' works made a very strong impression when they were shown at the Walker Gallery in May 1964."

The historian's job is to find roots and explanations if possible. Without stretching the point, I do think that in Liverpool itself, home of the sound, one has an example of the working of particular traditions within England. But there are other traditions, English and otherwise, that influenced them, and they are suggested by the famous cover, or sleeve, of the record.

Let's look at it with a little care: that pop version of the countless Victorian group photographs, or the group photographs of school classes that fill the halls of any school but seem particularly prevalent in English schools, or those photographs of Edwardian house parties in which the men and women look so well fed and civilized that it is hard to imagine them doing anything so rural as sitting on the grass. The Edwardian note is further struck not only on the cover, but on the accompanying sheet of cutouts in which Sgt. Pepper appears in all his grand if somewhat stiff Edwardian splendor, and the button suggesting the art nouveau character of the Philharmonic Hotel in Liverpool, and the letters of the name of the band are brimming over with Edwardian beauties. The Beatles themselves of course are in satins and silks, with only George having a rather Indian magic square on his chest. They are dressed in a triumph of gear, the furthest development of the exaggerated dress of the teddy boys of their early youth. They have come all dressed up to their own funeral, a fantasy that most of us have indulged in, and of course they are attending their own funeral themselves, as corpses, as waxworks. The grave is nicely but not vulgarly decorated and some marijuana is growing demurely about it. What friends of the Beatles have turned up (on?) for the occasion?

The Victorian world is only slightly represented, but in an interesting way. There, of all people, is Sir Robert Peel, the great Conservative of the first half of the nineteenth century whose considerable family fortune originated outside Manchester, also in Lancashire, but who had no particular connection with Liverpool, as does, say, Albert Stubbins, the Liverpool footballer, also on the cover. One would have thought that Peel's creation, the beginning of a national police force, in the form of peelers or bobbies would not have been particularly attractive to the Beatles. He did represent a certain flexibility and imaginative thought in politics, a non-aristocrat in the Tory party, but perhaps in his case they simply liked his face. The others of the older generation are more obvious: Lewis Carroll, the great fantasist whose world the Beatles have entered in their own idiosyncratic way. In our own mores, frequently quite similar to late Victorian and Edwardian ones, we are concerned with full expression of ourselves in rather rich, erotic, exaggerated ways. There may be the healthiness of release, but there is the potential sickness of lack of control, and of the horror of our fantasies. Some sort of discovery of a true identity, paradoxically through the means of role-playing, is also suggested by the presence of Oscar Wilde on the cover—the whole idea of Dorian Gray, the double life, appearance and reality—suggested by the very conceit of the record itself—we know that it is the Beatles pretending to bury themselves and be someone else. Similar feelings of fantasy and potential evil are suggested by other earlier figures, such as Edgar Allan Poe, and Aleister Crowley, the black magician who flourished in the 1920s. And of course there are also present potential philosophical solutions to the problems of the world—there is not a scorning of the intellectual life here. I believe the cover is also particularly important because it represents such a cross section of influences, intellectual and otherwise, upon England in this century. Of course there is Marx, but not with Freud, his usual companion in terms of great influences, but rather Jung, This is not surprising, considering the potential religiosity of the Beatles. This free-floating religiosity is further represented on the cover by various gurus who may also be simply those figures who cannot be identified. Then the cover makes a bow to those two great liberating figures of the early part of the century, read by every advanced schoolboy: George Bernard Shaw and H. G. Wells.

One considerable group reflects the immense American influence, the movie stars. The American world, particularly the world of the movies, was a way of liberation—another society, perhaps with vulgar values, but not caught in class paralysis, with its stifling effect. If these movie heroes and heroines were not great artists themselves, they had the value of being "camp," of inviting an amused and amusing response to the foolishnesses of the contemporary world. The heroes, presumably, would be such figures as Marlon Brando, Charlie Chaplin, W. C. Fields, Laurel and Hardy.

The great ladies, suggesting the world of elegance and sex, perhaps more sex than elegance, the grand musicals of Hollywood, captured and used to an extent in the Magical Mystery Tour, are Marlene Dietrich, Mae West, Marilyn Monroe. Other dominant Hollywood figures are present: Shirley Temple, Fred Astaire, Tyrone Power, and the epigoni such as Tony Curtis and camp figures such as Johnny Weissmuller and Tom Mix—the masters of fantasy on the great silver screen, the world of escape for the poor of Liverpool and others like them. Another means of escape, the drug route, is suggested by the presence of Aldous Huxley and William Burroughs, although Huxley also conjures up the novels of the 1920s. There are hero figures, English and American, such as Lenny Bruce, Dylan Thomas, Richard Burton, Bob Dylan, T. E. Lawrence, and such comparatively obscure figures as Tommy Handley, a wartime comedian harking back to the Beatles' childhood. Also present are important intellectual influences such as several painters, and most notably the avant-garde composer Stockhausen. Obviously the figures on the cover are an idiosyncratic choice as the backers of the band, and the mourners of the Beatles, but it is not a bad anthology of the shapers of modern English culture, in both the broad and narrow senses of that term.

What about the record itself? Certainly at the least, its cover is, starting from its very title, with its suggestion of a small organization in a country town, for those who are unhappy, perhaps led by the most popular and the least intellectual of the Beatles, Ringo Starr as the Sergeant—note the stripes—three. I would not dare to comment upon the Beatles musically, but they have come to be taken very seriously by serious musicians, and in this sense at least are far superior to almost all other such groups. What an extraordinary achievement really to have been such a huge popular mass success, and at the same time to have analytical articles about them in the *Partisan Review* and the *New York Review of Books*. One fears that they may be having all us ponderous academics on. But would even the Beatles dare to take *The Times* on (of London, of course), and it was their music critic, William Mann, who helped start the serious musical criticism of the Beatles in 1963 when he discussed their pandiatonic clusters, and their flat-submedian key-switches, and their melismatic tone. And Ned Rorem in an article has remarked that "She's Leaving Home" is a "mazurka equal in melancholy and melodic distinction to those of Chopin."

The very beginning of the record suggests a concert, a set performance, the creation of illusion with the presentation of the group, with the noise of the stirring of the audience, and some sense of tuning up, if it was all taking place in some vast music hall of the North, of the sort where Gracie Fields held forth. Then the compere introduces the act, and there is some sense of generational succession, in the English way, as if perhaps it was when the Beatles themselves were very young "twenty years ago today," when Sergeant Pepper taught them to play. The whole feeling of their introduction is that they are old-fashioned, at times unfashionable, and at times taken up, and the music of their past has a certain oom-pah, and even a large organ sound. It's an old popular act, which the audience loves with the sort of screams which they generally reserve for the Beatles. Their own song is the sort of flattering of audiences which one would expect in a music hall—telling the audience how good they are, and the audience responds with pleased roars. The Band wants to take the audience away, it wants to take them home, but this is meant with just the general sentimentality, the excess of pseudo-love of most performers. The next act is the singer Billy Shears and the band itself—and they are greeted with wild cheers. But it is illusion upon illusion, and the framework of a music-hall performance evaporates, for a more private and quiet, and somewhat pathetic song, with its sentimental, but somehow rather moving title "A Little Help from My Friends." In fact the glorification of friendship in the song is somewhat ironic in its contrast between love and friendship. Friendship is primarily important for its "little help" for the periods when one is not in love, but the love too seems to be a need—someone, somebody, perhaps the first person one sees, and there is a certain sad emphasis on perfection, as if Billy's previous love had left him because he sang out of tune. There is a sense in the song of the somewhat broken down entertainer, alone in a bed-sitter, who manages by seeing a few friends, who give him enough support so that he can just survive, who help him with drink or pot, and give him some, but not much reason to go on. His friends' questioning about love seems to be somewhat gently mocking, as if sentimental love can't last in the North Country. One feels that Billy just needs a love object to possess at the end of the day, a simple if somehow rather sad picture of friends in a pub and a wife. Yet the voices are young, and although English pop singers have now realized that something closer to their own accents are preferable to the imitation American they used to use, the voices are still somewhat anonymous, so that the particular English sense of the song is submerged.

It might be said that this is even more true of the next song, with its obvious LSD title "Lucy in the Sky with Diamonds"—and it seems unlikely that the Beatles mean pounds, shillings, and pence, for which LSD are the symbols. According to Paul McCartney the title was invented by Lennon's son, and "We did the whole thing like an Alice in Wonderland idea, being in a boat on the river, slowly drifting downstream and those great cellophane flowers towering over your head. Ever so often it broke off and you saw Lucy in the sky with diamonds all over the sky. This Lucy was God, the Big Figure, the White Rabbit." It really is the fantasy world of the nineteenth century, a sort of Edward Lear or Lewis Carroll creation coming together with twentieth-century preoccupations.

Richard Poirier has pointed out that the whole Sgt. Pepper record is a collection of "fragmented patterns" and "evocative fragments," in the same way as *The Waste Land*, and that it has a similar literary power and merit. I'm not sure that I would go quite that far, but I think that the lyrics do unquestionably evoke an English past and an English present.

"Getting Better" could be seen by a pedant as a song about education, and how it stifles the young, but it is true that in England, as in any other country, school is a way of teaching children about the social world in which they find themselves, and for adapting themselves to the status quo, the "rules." There is a subdued refrain in the song, which I make out as "can't complain," which has the double meaning that one is not allowed to complain about the system, but also that things are getting better, and so at least gently and not too enthusiastically, one says "can't complain." The protagonist of the song used to be an "angry young man," but unlike the earlier angry young man hiding his head in the sand, who simply emerged to beat his woman, he is now trying to reform.

"Fixing a Hole," which Ned Rorem considers one of the best musically, has been taken to be a song about a junky preparing a heroin fix on his arm. Paul McCartney has denied this, although, in that charming Beatle way of his, he is willing to accept any interpretation: "If you're a junky sitting in a room fixing a hole then that's what it will mean to you, but when I wrote it I meant if there's a crack or the room is uncolorful, then I'll paint it." McCartney has also said that the song is about fans and their attempt to impose themselves into the life of their idols, but for whom they have no genuine interest in terms of their own life and gift. In an important way, at least to me, the song is about the need for artists, perhaps more so in England where the conventions are particularly powerful, to go their own way, and to remain true to their own gift—the hole is the connection with the outside world which admits distractions, people, and ideas, everything that "stops my mind from wandering / Where it will go."

The next two songs, "She's Leaving Home" and "Being for the Benefit of Mr. Kite," have perhaps the firmest sense of any on the record of an English environment. Richard Poirier has suggested that "She's Leaving Home" harkens back to the songs of Bea Lillie and Noel Coward, but I would think that it was not quite that sophisticated. The setting is more a lower-middle-class home in Liverpool, not a Mayfair flat, one of those endless semidetached villas, where the parents have tried to be as respectable as possible, and have done everything, by scrimping and saving, to give their daughter a respectable life. In fact they have imprisoned and isolated their daughter, as middle-class life can: "She's leaving home after living alone." It is a song of the tragedy—although middle-class life can rarely produce this—of the respectable life, and in that sense comes closer to Orwell's *A Clergyman's Daughter*. The song begins with the quality of a harp; the whole song is one of the tearoom in that deadening English middle-class way, where self-expression is to be firmly controlled, so much so that one feels that even the daughter's rebellion will not be successful—her farewell note "she hoped would say more / She goes downstairs to the kitchen / clutching her handkerchief." Her parents operate within the context of the selfishness, the self-regarding nature, of self-sacrifice. The song claims, halfheartedly and perhaps even ironically, that the daughter is now having "fun" through her assignation with "a man from the motor trade," presumably something of a bounder and a cad. She has left home too late.

But after this sad ballad, more in tune with England of the 1920s or 1930s, perhaps, than the 1960s, the spirit of *Sergeant Pepper* returns in the splendid song for Mr. Kite, which was inspired by an old poster. It is the fantasy world of the circus and the imagination, conveyed in the lyrics, and the lilt of the music, which sounds as if it is an old calliope world of imagination, which always appears associated with a golden past, but which indeed through the genius of the Beatles can be summoned up for the present.

"Within You Without You," the first song on the second—should one say flip—side is perhaps an unfortunate example of one of the by-products of England's being connected with India. Probably the influence of the raga has been very important in terms of music, but the interest in Eastern philosophy does not appear so valuable. I admit, though, to being very non-comprehending in these matters. But with the next song, "When I'm Sixty-Four," the lower civil servant is back from the East—or rather, contemplating retirement, with summers spent on the Isle of Wight, home of Victoria and Tennyson, those combinations of the private and public voices, and also a very popular holiday resort, as in a famous Auden line: "August for the people and their islands." There is a certain sadness at the end of the song, with the picture postcard on which one precisely states one's point of view. But on the whole, the song seems to be sweetly sentimental, sung in a lilting music hall voice, with a picture of domestic bliss. If husband and wife are still together—there is an element of the Donald McGill comic postcard—why shouldn't the wife lock him out if he comes in at quarter to three?—at the same time there is the projected picture of the Orwellian dream from those who knew it much better than he: sitting by the fireside, going for a ride, doing the garden, the picture of the grandchildren "Vera, Chuck & Dave" coming for a holiday with the grandparents at their little cottage. But there is an ambiguity about the song, as if the sentimental relation of the old folks—when they are sixty-four, not such a great age after all—will be somehow "official," and perhaps reduced to feeding, and a rather low level of needing: the geriatric world of the welfare state.

"Lovely Rita" by contrast appears to be more of the contemporary scene—the girls who are in charge of parking meters all over England, whose manners can be taken to be severe and military. There is a slight sense of antagonism in the song, for a meter maid is sort of an enemy who attacks one's car—but in this case it is the protagonist's heart and not his car which is towed away. Yet nothing quite works out. Neither the gentility of tea nor the swingingness of pot seems to claim her. There is a sense of the "cash nexus" in the song, with Rita paying for dinner—but the failure of the affair is perhaps suggested by the fact that Rita's job is to collect cash, which seems to be continually jingling in the background, and the suggestive big beat of the song in the end may represent more a triumph of frustration than any satisfactory relationship.

Perhaps the frustrations of urban life are at issue—there is still that dream of the country persisting even for Liverpool boys, more evident in "Good Morning, Good Morning." The song appears to me to present the pity of empty aimless urban life in contrast to the cock-crow which begins the song, and is reflected in the refrain of "good morning." There is little more to do than standing around the downtown district where everything is closed. The only comparative pleasure is tea with the wife, or going to a show with a girl. Life in the city hasn't changed from its dreariness for years, symbolized by a walk by the old school, contrasted with the happy barnyard "natural" noises of the countryside that end the song. Even that may be overwhelmed by the rich, who have expropriated so much of the countryside, as caught by the baying of dogs and the galloping of the horses of the hunt. Yet the song ends with the twittering of birds.

Although perhaps the songs on the record are not as coherent in total as I suggest, and they do not pretend to be songs with a progressive plot, they are nevertheless certainly a song cycle, and a cycle which seems to me to be primarily devoted to a sort of review of English life, and also to suggest elements from the past in England, most notably in the concept of Sgt. Pepper and his Band. The Band now returns, and the listener is transported back to a music hall, or perhaps now an outdoor field or a stadium or parade ground—a meeting place in the great Methodist tradition, to hear a reprise of the Band's song, which also acts as an introduction to the most distinguished song of an extraordinary collection: "A Day in the Life."

This song is in three parts, and it deals with life and death, and in a contemporary English context. The first part deals with the emptiness of success, the man who made it, the property millionaire or what have you, cracking up, probably in his big Bentley. (He is probably not the Guinness heir as some have said, as the implication is that the money was made by the man himself.) At any rate, he appeared to be someone important, perhaps someone from the House of Lords, and the same sort of emptiness of achievement, the empty grandness of today's Britain, is suggested in the rest of the first longer section, where the protagonist has seen a film of the old Alexander Korda sort of some garrison out in the empire having won its war, and making those back home happier. This too had the emptiness of success, which would catch the momentary interest of the curious crowd. The first section is sung as if the singer were on a deserted beach—romantically alone after the crowds of the reprise of Sgt. Pepper, but then a crescendo, almost unbearable, moves the song to what would appear to be the beginning of a realistic English movie: with the sound of an alarm clock, the young man wakes up who is trying to make his way. Unaware of how empty success will be, he rushes to work; only once he gets there, there is nothing to do but have a smoke. Yet in this section there are the realities of workaday English life.

The conclusion of the song appears to deal with the universality of death, as suggested by English experience. This section is introduced rather symphonically, and the news of the single death of a man who was allegedly a success is transformed into another—one might almost say, villainy of our society—the death of children, in reference to, probably, the Moors murder trial of 1966, of the man and woman who tortured, sexually abused, and murdered three children. It was in the Beatles country, but inland, near Manchester: the children were buried in the moors. Sticks were used, making 4,000 holes, to search for the bodies. There is an echo of the concentration camp here—the senseless brutality of life, so that these 4,000 corpses could be transformed into an audience in the Albert Hall. But despite the horror of modern life, there is still some possibility of salvation through connections—"only connect"—through relationships, as the singer quietly and wistfully says "I'd love to turn you on," and the accelerating music is followed by a long chord of resolution. Like *A Passage to India*, the song, and indeed the whole cycle, seems to reveal for England both a desperate and very hopeful situation—that English good sense and character may be bulwarks against a world full of false values and horror.

In a strange way there would appear to be a new sort of alliance of the private and public voices in *Sergeant Pepper's Lonely Hearts Club Band*, or rather a quiet private coping with public problems, that in an age of decline, and possibly worldwide destruction, one must try, with wit, a particular sort of elegance, and a literary and musical genius, one must try to carry on, and also in a sense muddle through as in the jolly sound of the very last lines printed on the back of the original sleeve "A splendid time is guaranteed for all." The Beatles in their way can tell us about contemporary England, and its more recent past, particularly a sense of the importance of the Edwardian era of solidity, accomplishment, but often false values. But they also can tell us about the great strengths of English character, the English vitality and imaginativeness, their ability to lead better and better lives over the course of this century, both in a material way, but also in the ways of the imagination, so that they can play with their perceptions of the world. The Beatles look at the English world with humor and compassion, and what could be a finer hope than that the purpose of political arrangement is to serve personal relationships, the persistent English belief in individualism and self-consciousness, despite the great doubts of the 1930s, and persisting doubts before and since about the English system. Still, England would appear to be a society where the goals as expressed by the Beatles might be achieved, and there might be that change of heart, that triumph of personal relations suggested by "I'd love to turn you on."

Bibliography, 1954-1998

Entries followed by an asterisk appear in revised form in this volume.

Books

Ambitions and Strategies: The Struggle for the Leadership of the Liberal Party in the 1890s (1964)

England Since 1867: Continuity and Change (1973)

Gladstone: A Progress in Politics (1979)

William Morris (1983)

Redesigning the World: William Morris, the 1880s, and the Arts and Crafts (1985)

On or About December 1910: Early Bloomsbury and its Intimate World (1996)

Another Book that Never Was: William Morris, Charles Gere and the House of the Wolfings (1998)

(with William Abrahams) *Journey to the Frontier: Julian Bell and John Cornford, Their Lives and the 1930's* (1966)

(with William Abrahams) *The Unknown Orwell* (1972)

(with William Abrahams) *Orwell: The Transformation* (1979)

(with William Abrahams) *London's Burning* (1994)

Edited Books

The Left and War: The British Labour Party and the First World War (1969)

John Morley: Nineteenth Century Essays (1970)

Winston Churchill: A Profile (1973)

The Victorian Revolution: Government and Society in Victoria's Britain (1973)

On Nineteen Eighty-Four (1983)

(with Rodney Shewan) *The Aesthetic Movement and the Arts and Crafts Movement* 73 volumes (1976, 1979)

Conference on British Studies Biography series 6 volumes (1968-1974)
(with Leslie Hume) *Modern British History Series* 18 volumes (1982)
Modern European History Series 47 volumes (1987-1992)

ARTICLES, REVIEWS, AND PAMPHLETS

"Graves, Diaghilev, Orwell" *Litterair Paspoort* November 1954 18-19

"Stephen Spender" *Litterair Paspoort* May 1955 113

"Haldane of Cloan by Dudley Sommer" *Cambridge Review* October 8, 1960 13-15

(with William Abrahams) "Looking for a Laureate" *History Today* October 1961 683-692

"Lyttelton and Thring" *Victorian Studies* March 1962 205-223*

"The Wound in the Heart by Allan Guttmann" *Massachusetts Review* Winter 1963 420-423

"Approaches to History ed. by H.P.R. Finberg" *History and Theory* 1964 123-127

"Asquith by Roy Jenkins" *Canadian Historical Review* 1964 176-177

"The Liberals in Power by Colin Cross" *Victorian Studies* September 1964 86-87

"General Education in a Free Society" *Oxford Magazine* November 1964 125-126

"King Edward the Seventh by Philip Magnus" *Partisan Review* Winter 1965 141-147

"Edwardian England 1901-1914 ed. by Simon Nowell-Smith" *Canadian Historical Review* June 1965 176-177

"The Unbought Grace of Life" *Victorian Studies* March 1967 268-272

"English History 1914-1945 by A.J.P. Taylor" *Journal of Modern History* September 1967 329-331

"A Cab at the Door by V.S. Pritchett" *Baltimore Sun* May 26, 1968

"An Orwell Conspectus" *Atlantic Monthly* November 1968 122-124*

"The Headmaster: Roxburgh of Stowe by Noel Annan" *Journal of Modern History* December 1968 632-635

"An Expanding Society by G. Kitson Clark" *Canadian Historical Review* December 1968 435-437

"Diaries and Letters, 1930-1939, Volume I by Harold Nicolson" *Journal of Modern History* December 1968 632-635

"J.B.S. Haldane by Ronald W. Clark" *New York Times Book Review* January 12, 1969 1, 20

"Pax Britannica by James Morris" *Baltimore Sun* January 26, 1969

"Contemporary England by W.N. Medlicott" *Social Studies* February 1969 81

"The Chamberlains by D.H. Elleston" *American Historical Review* February 1969 998-999

"A Wreath to Clio by J.W. Wheeler-Bennett" *Journal of Modern History* June 1969 214-215

"John Morley by D.A. Hamer" *Victorian Studies* September 1969 105-107

"The First British Workmen's Compensation Act, 1897 by David G. Hanes" *Victorian Studies* December 1969 227-229

"The General Election of 1880 by Trevor Lloyd" *Journal of Modern History* December 1969 602-604

"Leonard Woolf's Journey" *Atlantic Monthly* May 1970 116-119*

"Land Fit for Heroes by P.B. Johnson" *Journal of Modern History* June 1970 277-280

"John Morley by Stephen Koss" *Journal of Modern History* December 1970 687-688

"Decade of Reform by G. Finlayson" *Journal of Economic History* 1971 476-477

"George Orwell" *Atlantic Brief Lives* 1971 566-568

"The System by Max Nicholson" *Social Studies* January 1971 39-40

"Lloyd George by Francis Stevenson" *New York Times Book Review* January 30, 1972 4, 36

"My Life by Sir Oswald Mosley" *New York Times Book Review* March 12, 1972 2*

"The Diminishing Post-Edwardians" *Journal of Interdisciplinary History* Summer 1972 153-166

"A Chapter of Accidents by Goronway Rees" *New York Times Book Review* June 18, 1972 5, 10-11

"Victoria's Heyday by J.B. Priestley" *Saturday Review* August 12, 1972 50-51

"Beaverbrook by A.J.P. Taylor" *New York Times Book Review* October 8, 1972 3, 20

"Queen Victoria by Cecil Woodham-Smith" *Saturday Review* November 18, 1972 84-86

"Nancy by Christopher Sykes" *New York Times Book Review* November 26, 1972 4, 26-27*

"The English Poor Law ed. by Michael E. Rose" *Social Studies* November 1972 295-296

"Liberal Politics by D.A. Hamer" *Victorian Studies* December 1972 252-254

"British Social Policy by Bentley B. Gilbert" *Canadian Historical Review* December 1972 465-467

"The Quest for National Efficiency by G.R. Searle" *Journal of Modern History* December 1972 627-628

"Royal Griffin by John Walters," "George III by Stanley Ayling," and "George III by John Brooke"*Saturday Review* January 21, 1973 65, 70-71

"Contemporary Britain by Barbara Wootton" *Social Studies* March 1973 137-138

"The Manchester Guardian by David Ayerst" *Journal of Modern History* March 1973 134-136

"Wellington by Elizabeth Longford" *Saturday Review* May 1973 82-83

"Sir Edward Walter Hamilton ed. by Dudley W.R. Bahlman" *Victorian Studies* June 1973 482-483

"In the Light of History by J.H. Plumb" *San Francisco Sunday Chronicle and Examiner* June 21, 1973

"Bethune by Roderick Stewart" *Canadian Historical Review* September 1973 340-341

"John Strachey by Hugh Thomas" *New York Times Book Review* September 30, 1973 2, 47

"The Diplomatic Diaries of Oliver Harvey ed. by John Harvey" *Social Studies* November 1973 295-296

"The British General Election of 1910 by Neal Blewett" and "The Last Liberal Governments by Peter Rowland" *Journal of Modern History* December 1973 699-701

"Social Welfare ed. by E.W. Martin" *Social Studies* December 1973 339-340

"The Liberal Imperialists by H.C.G. Mathews" and "Liberals, Radicals, and Social Politics by H.V. Emy" *Victorian Studies* March 1974 330-332

"George Gissing by Gillian Tindall" *New York Times Book Review* September 8, 1974 3

"R.H.Tawney and His Times by Ross Terrill" *American Historical Review* October 1974 1183-1184

"Churchill at 100" *New York Times Book Review* November 24, 1974 4-5

"Introduction" and with others "William Morris and his Work" *Morris & Co.* 1975 9-11, 47-68

"Governing Passion by A.B. Cooke and John Vincent" *Victorian Studies* March 1975 360-362

"Thinking About Biography" *New Republic* April 19, 1975 25-27*

"The Bloomsbury Group" *New York Times Book Review* June 1, 1975 7, 18-21*

"The Great War and Modern Memory by Paul Fussell" *New Republic* October 4, 1975 26-27*

"Evelyn Waugh by Christopher Sykes" *New York Times Book Review* November 30, 1975 2-3, 58-59*

"Gladstone and Radicalism by Micahel Barker" *Victorian Studies* December 1975 267-268

"George Orwell and the Origins of '1984' by William Steinhoff" *Modern Language Quarterly* March 1976 101-103

"Uncle of Europe by Gordon Brook-Shepherd" *New York Times Book Review* March 21, 1976 5, 18-21

"Art, Industry, and the Aspirations of William Martin Conway" *Victorian Studies* June 1976 465-484*

"The Formation of Fabian Socialist Doctrines, 1881-1889 by William Wolfe" *American Historical Review* June 1976 593-594

"The Damnable Question by George Dangerfield" *New York Times Book Review* July 25, 1976 1-2

"Christopher and His Kind by Christopher Isherwood" *New York Times Book Review* November 28, 1976 31-34

"Melbourne by Philip Ziegler" *New York Times Book Review* February 6, 1977 2, 22-23

"C.R. Ashbee Visits Stanford University" *Imprint* April 1977 1-23

"The Marble Foot by Peter Quennell" *New Republic* May 7, 1977 28-29

"William Morris by E.P. Thompson" *New York Times Book Review* May 15, 1977 7, 48-49*

"Hanoverian London by George Rudé" *University Publishing* Summer 1977

"Salisbury and Gladstone" *Historian* Summer 1977 332-334

"History & Biography" *New York Times Book Review* June 5, 1977 10-11, 41

"Unity Mitford by David Pryce-Jones" *New Republic* August 20 and 27, 1977 33-35*

"The Governance of Britain by Harold Wilson" *American Historical Review* December 1977 1260

"E.M. Forster by P.N. Furbank" and "E.M. Forster by Francis King" *New York Times Book Review* 1978 1, 68, 70*

"Brains and Numbers by Christopher Kent" *Journal for Interdisciplinary History* 1978 171-173

"The General Strike by G.A. Phillips" *Labor History* Winter 1978 143-145

"'1984' Revisited" *New York Times* February 18, 1978 23

"The Lights of Liberalism by Christopher Harvie" and "The Liberal Mind by Michael Bentley" *Historical Journal* March 1978 199-202

"The Spirit of Reform by Patrick Brantlinger" *Nineteenth Century Fiction* March 1978 473-476

"The English Working Class by Standish Meacham" and "Labour History ed. by Asa Briggs and John Saville" *ILLWCH* May 1978 43-46

"The Bloomsbury Flood" *Inquiry* June 12, 1978 24-27*

"The British Experience by Peter Calvocoressi" *New York Times Book Review* August 13, 1978 9, 23

"Poetry, Politics, People by Stephen Spender" *New Republic* September 23, 1978 27-29*

"Isherwood by Jonathan Fryer" *New Republic* October 14, 1978 33-35*

"The Past in Pictures" *Inquiry* December 11, 1978 24-27

"Toward 1984" *Is Britain Dying?* 1979 269-276

"Christopher Isherwood by Brian Finney" *Inquiry* May 14, 1979 23-25*

"The Early Community at Bedford Park by Margaret Jones Bolsterli" and "The Queen Anne Movement by Mark Girouard" *Victorian Studies* Autumn 1979 114-117

"Lewis Carroll Letters ed. by Morton N. Cohen" *Books and Arts* October 26, 1979 8-9

"The Visible College by Gary Wersky" *New Republic* October 27, 1979 32-33

"Royal Charles by Antonia Fraser" and "The Image of the King by Richard Ollard" *New York Times Book Review* December 9, 1979 1, 30-31

"Preface" *The Lily and the Lion* 1980 7

"The Fourth Man by Andrew Boyle" *New Republic* February 9, 1980 34-37

"Wilfrid Scawen Blunt by Elizabeth Longford" *Inquiry* February 18, 1980 27-28

"British Interparty Conferences by John D. Fair" *British Politics Group* Autumn 1980 15-17

"Abroad by Paul Fussell" *Book World* September 21, 1980 11

"Lyulph Stanley by Alan W. Jones" *Canadian Journal of History* December 1980 473-475

"The Nature of Biography by Robert Gittings" and "Studies in Biography ed. by Daniel Aaron" *Journal of Interdisciplinary History* Winter 1981 515-517

"W.H. Auden by Humphrey Carpenter" *Inquiry* December 7 and 21, 1981 28-29*

"John Ruskin by Joan Abse" *New Republic* December 9, 1981 28-31

"Class by Arthur Marwick" *Business History Review* 1982 446-448

"Elie Halévy by Myrna Chase" *History and Theory* 1982 143-149

"The Last Country Houses by Clive Aslet" *Art Book Review* 1982 4

"English Culture and the Decline of the Industrial Spirit by Martin Wiener" *Victorian Studies* Winter 1982 240-242

"Political Press in Britain by Stephen Koss" *Victorian Periodicals Newsletter* Summer 1982 74-78

"William Morris and George Orwell" *The Threepenny Review* Summer 1982 3-5. Reprinted *History Today* February 1983 33-38. Reprinted *Revista de Occidente* February/March 1984 79-93*

"1900 by Rebecca West" and "Rebecca West selected by Jane Marcus" *Inquiry* June 1982 48-50

"Churchill by Ted Morgan" *New York Times Book Reivew* June 13, 1982 12, 30-31

"Diana Cooper by Philip Ziegler" *San Francisco Chronicle* July 11, 1982

"What Dizzy Did" *The Dial* August 1982 44-45

"The Return to Camelot by Mark Girouard" *The Threepenny Review* Autumn 1982 10-11

"Religion and Public Doctrine in England by Maurice Cowling" *Journal of Modern History* September 1982 568-571

"The English Gentleman" *Raritan Review* Spring 1983 122-130

ed. *Virginia Woolf Miscellany* Spring 1983

"The Pastoral Impulse in Victorian England by Jan Marsh" *History Today* April 1983 48-49

"Modern British Politics by Martin Pugh" *American Historical Review* June 1983 678-679

"Disraeli by Sarah Bradford" *New York Times Book Review* July 10, 1983 1, 30

"Lord Randolph Churchill by R.F. Foster" *Historian* August 1983 564-565

"Disraeli Letters ed. by J.A.W. Gunn et al." *Albion* Autumn 1983 255-257

"Socialist Diary by William Morris ed. by Florence Boos *Victorian Studies* Autumn 1983 132-133

"Spanish Civil War by Peter Wyden" *Inquiry* October 1983 44

"The Herbert Horne Collection" *Imprint* October 1983 32-38

"Harold Nicolson by James Lees-Milne" *Journal of Modern History* December 1983 710-712

"The Orwell Year" *DLB Yearbook* 1984 52-62

"British History 1870-1914" *Recent Views on British History* 1984 299-326

Four Letters from William Morris 1984

William Morris, C.R. Ashbee and the Arts and Crafts 1984

"Good Times, Bad Times by Harold Evans" *San Francisco Chronicle* February 19, 1984

"Gladstone by Richard Shannon" *Victorian Studies* Spring 1984 377-378

"The Labour Movement by Kenneth Brown" *Industrial and Labor Relations Review* April 1984 451-452

"John Maynard Keynes by L.H. Hession" *New York Times Book Review* May 20, 1984 7

"Exploring Bloomsbury" *Charleston Newsletter* August 1984 22-27

"The Past and the Present by Lawrence Stone" *The Threepenny Review* Autumn 1984 9

"William Morris Letters ed. by Norman Kelvin" *Albion* Autumn 1984 325-327

"1984" *San Francisco Sunday Examiner and Chronicle* December 30, 1984 6-7

"The Rise and Fall of the Political Press by Stephen Koss" *Victorian Periodicals Review* Spring 1985 37-40

ed. *Virginia Woolf Miscellany* Spring 1985

"George Orwell" *Conference at the Library of Congress* April 30- May 1, 1984 1985 25-53

"The Diary of Beatrice Webb ed. by Norman and Jeanne MacKenzie" *International History Review* May 1985 286-290

"Gladstone by Peter J. Jagger" *British Politics Group Newsletter* Summer
    1985 25-26
"The Strange Death of Liberal England by George Dangerfield" *Times
    Higher Educational Supplement* July 1985
"Mountbatten by Philip Ziegler" *San Francisco Chronicle* July 21, 1985 3, 7
"The House of Mitford by Jonathan Guinness" *Boston Globe* July 14, 1985
"The Invention of Tradition ed. by Eric Hobsbawn and Terence Ranger"
    International History Review August 1985 506-509
"The Orwell Mystique by Daphne Patai" *American Historical Review* Oc-
    tober 1985 937-938
(with William Abrahams) "Double Image" *Peter Pears: 75th Birthday* 1985
    86-87
"Bloomsbury/Freud ed. by Perry Meisel and Walter Kendrick" *New York
    Times Book Review* December 29, 1985 14
"Henry Moore and the Blitz" *Political Culture of Modern Britain* 1986
    228-242
"Rural Life in England In the First World War by Pamela Horn" *Agricul-
    tural History* Winter 1986 99-100
"The Strange Death of Liberal England by George Dangerfield" *Albion*
    Winter 1986 401-403
"The Fringes of Power by John Colville" *San Francisco Chronicle Book Re-
    view* January 5, 1986 3-4
"British Politics by Greenleaf and Harrison" *Journal of Modern History*
    March 1986 307-312
"John Maynard Keynes by Robert Skidelsky" *Boston Globe* April 27, 1986
    96, 98*
"Gladstone's Boswell by Lionel A. Tollemache" *International History Re-
    view* May 1986 296-298
"The Collected Essays of Asa Briggs" *Victorian Studies* Summer 1986 616-617
"The Scaremongers by A.J.A. Morris" *Victorian Periodical Review* Summer
    1986 71-72
"Queen Elizabeth by Penelope Mortimer" and "The Royal Family by John
    Pearson" *San Jose Mercury* June 1, 1986 21
"The First Labour Party ed. by K.D. Brown" *American Historical Review*
    June 1986 670-671
"Treasure Houses" *History Today* August 1986 7-9
"The Gladstonian Turn of Mind ed. by Bruce L. Kinzer" *Victorian Studies*
    Autumn 1986 147-148
"C.R. Ashbee by Alan Crawford" *Albion* Autumn 1986 527-529
"Gladstone by Matthew," "Democracy by Parry," "Gladstone by Lough-
    lin" *Albion* Winter 1987 654-58
ed. *Virgina Woolf Miscellany* Spring 1987

"Chaim Weizmann by Norman Rose" *Studies in Zionism* Spring 1987 127-131*

"Aneurin Bevan by John Campbell" *Boston Sunday Globe* August 9, 1987 12-16

(with William Abrahams) "A Note on Julian Bell" *Charleston Newsletter* September 1987 37-38 Also in Julian Bell *Still Life and Other Poems* 1987 5-6

"The Diary of Beatrice Webb, Vol. 4" *Journal of Modern History* December 1987 846-848

Introduction to *A Day in Surrey with William Morris* 1988

"Rule of Darkness by Patrick Brantlinger" *English Literature in Transition* 1988 75-78

"The Neo Pagans by P. Delany" *English Literature in Transition* 1988 467-469

"Grimes, Popper, and Stanford" *Sandstone and Tile* Winter/Spring 1988 8-11

"Charleston Past and Present by Q. Bell" *Virginia Woolf Miscellany* Spring 1988 4

"William Morris Letters ed. by Norman Kelvin" *New York Times Book Review* April 17, 1988 14

"Victorian Bloomsbury by S.P. Rosenbaum" *Victorian Studies* Summer 1988 587-588*

"The Unsinkable Mrs. Thatcher" *Boston Globe* October 30, 1988

"The Rise of Respectable Society by F.M.L. Thompson" *Journal of Interdisciplinary History* 1989 293-294

"Christopher Caudwell by Robert Sullivan" *Journal of English and Germanic Philogy* 1989 553-554

"Parliamentary Politics by W.C. Lubenow" and "Forster's Irish Diaries ed. by T.W. Moody and Florence Arnold" *Albion* Spring 1989 152-155

Foreword *Rediscovering Herbert Horne* by Ian Fletcher 1990 ix-xiii

"Humphrey Jennings and *Fires Were Started*" *Cities, Class, and Communication* 1990 234-248

"Gladstone, Whiggery, and the Liberal Party by T.A. Jenkins" *Victorian Studies* Winter 1990 352-353

"Professional Society by Harold Perkin" *British Politics Group Newsletter* Winter 1990 23-25

"Harold Macmillan II by Alistair Horne" *San Francisco Chronicle Review* January 7, 1990 3-4

"The Crumbling Frontiers of History" *Pacific Historical Review* February 1990 1-14*

"Artisans and Architects by Mark Swenarton" *Victorian Studies* Spring 1990 518-520

ed. *Virginia Woolf Miscellany* Spring 1990

"The Eminent Strachey" *The Threepenny Review* Summer 1990 18-19*

"The Decline and Fall of the British Aristocracy by David Cannadine" *Boston Globe* October 28, 1990 20-21

"William Morris by Helen Dore" *Charleston Magazine* Autumn/Winter 1990 50-51

"William Morris by Frederick Kirchhoff" *English Literature in Transition* 1991 343-346

Introduction to *In Self-Respect & Decent Comfort* 1991 4-6

"Gladstone Diaries ed. by H.C.G. Matthew" *Albion* Winter 1991 786-788

"The Duel by John Lukacs" *New York Times Book Review* March 3, 1991 7-8

"The Passionate Apprentice by Virginia Woolf" *Virginia Woolf Miscellany* Spring 1991 3-4

"A War Imagined by Samuel Hynes" *Boston Globe* July 7, 1991

"Reconstructing the Criminal by Martin J. Wiener" *Journal of Economic History* December 1991 974-975

"The Scramble for Africa by Thomas Pakenham" *New York Times Book Review* December 8, 1991 1, 44-45

"Particulars in Huxley's Intellectual Climate" *Julian Huxley* 1992 45-48

"Great Britain: Historians" *Collier's Encyclopedia* Vol. 12 1992 150-151

"The Cambridge Social History of Britain ed. by F.M.L. Thompson" *Victorian Studies* Winter 1992 215-218*

ed. *Virginia Woolf Miscellany* Spring 1992

"Edmund Blunden by Barry Webb" *American Historical Review* June 1992 85

"William Morris by Charles Harvey and Jon Press" *English Literature in Transition* 1993 65-68*

"Chaim Weizmann by Jehuda Reinharz" *New York Times Book Review* April 25, 1993 27*

"A Moment of War by Laurie Lee" *Book World* August 1, 1993 7

"C.P. Snow by John de la Mothe" and "The Intellectuals and the Masses by John Carey" *Albion* Autumn 1993 548-551

"E.M. Forster" *After the Victorians* 1994 127-146

"British Politics Since 1900" *Guide to Historical Literature* 1994 792-793

"Whistler v. Ruskin by Linda Merrill" *Journal of Interdisciplinary History* Winter 1994 536-537

"The Economist as Savior by Robert Skidelsky" *Boston Globe* January 23, 1994*

"Churchill by John Charmley" *Dimensions* Spring 1994 30-32

ed. *Virginia Woolf Miscellany* Spring 1994

"Private Lives, Public Spirit by Jose Harris" *Victorian Studies* Spring 1994 473-475

"Clouds by Caroline Dakers" *Albion* Autumn 1994 552-553

"The British Way with Culture" *Journal of British Studies* October 1994 414-424*

"Franco by Paul Preston" *Book World* October 30, 1994 4

"Bloomsbury Group," "E.M. Forster," "Humphrey Jennings," and "George Orwell" *Twentieth-Century Britain: An Encyclopedia* 1995 89-91, 306-308, 410-411, 596-598

"Culture" *Oxford Companion to the Second World War* 1995 1157-1159

"Edwardian Bloomsbury by S.P. Rosenbaum" *English Literature in Transition* 1995 205-208*

Nineteen Eighty-Four Ten Years Later 1995*

"Myths of the English ed. by Roy Porter" *Journal of Interdisciplinary History* Spring 1995 687-688

"Virginia Woolf by James King" *Charleston Magazine* Spring/Summer 1995 47-50

"Lytton Strachey by Michael Holroyd" *Los Angeles Times* June 11, 1995 12-13*

"A Recent Acquisition in Jewish History" *Imprint* Autumn 1995 19-27

"Anglo-Jews or English/British" *Jewish Social Studies* Autumn 1995 159-177*

"Liberal Government in Victorian Britain by Jonathan Parry" and "Sir Edward Hamilton ed. by Dudley Bahlman" *Victorian Studies* Autumn 1995 465-468

William Morris and Bloomsbury 1996*

"Disraeli by Ian Machin" *Historian* Winter 1996 439-440

"Harold Laski by Isaac Kramnick and Barry Sheerman" *Journal of Modern History* March 1996 184-186

"Hellenism and Homosexuality by Linda Dowling" *Journal of Pre-Raphaelite Studies* Spring 1996 102-103

"London by Roy Porter" *Albion* Spring 1996 147-148

"Figures of Conversion by Michael Ragussis" *Victorian Studies* Spring 1996 407-409*

"William Morris by Fiona MacCarthy" *Victorian Studies* Summer 1996 549-551*

"Roger Fry" and "A Roger Fry Reader" *Virginia Woolf Miscellany* Autumn 1996 5-6

"Gladstone by H.C.G. Matthew" *Historian* Autumn 1996 912-913

"Architecture and Social Reform by Deborah E.B. Weiner" *Journal of Pre-Raphaelite Studies* New Series, 5 Autumn 1996 115-116

"A Morris Diary" *Quarterly News-Letter of the Book Club of California* Autumn 1996 106-112

"Letters of William Morris" *English Literature in Transition* September 1996 463-467*

"William Morris" *Dictionary of Art* Vol. 22 1997 141-147

Foreword to *The Strange Death of Liberal England* by George Dangerfield 1997 9-12

"Joseph Chamberlain by Peter Marsh" *British Politics Group Newsletter* Winter 1997 24-25

"William Morris Diary II" *Quarterly News-Letter of the Book Club of California* Spring 1997 79-83

"Anti-Semitic Stereotypes 1660-1830 by Frank Felsenstein" *American Historical Review* April 1997 452-453

"The Great War and the Shaping of the 20th Century" *American Historical Review* April 1997 593-594

"Aldous Huxley by David King Dunaway" *Public Historian* Summer 1997 68-69

"Sites of Memory by Jay Winter" *Social History* October 1997 362-364

"William Morris ed. by Linda Parry; Art, Enterprise by Charles Harvey and Jon Press" *Victorian Studies* Autumn 1997 156-160*

"British History and Its Discontents" *History Teacher* November 1997 104-107

"The New Police in Nineteenth-Century England by David Taylor" *Journal of the International Society for the Study of European Ideas* February 1998 157-158

"Capital Cities at War by Jay Winter" *International History Review* March 1998 214-216

"Victorian Girls: Lord Littleton's Daughters by Sheila Fletcher" *Victorian Studies* Spring 1998 5211-523

"Bloomsbury Pie by Regina Marler" *English Literature in Transition* September 1998 317-320

INDEX